# THE NEW MIDDLE AGES

BONNIE WHEELER, *Series Editor*

*The New Middle Ages* is a series dedicated to pluridisciplinary studies of medieval cultures, with particular emphasis on recuperating women's history and on feminist and gender analyses. This peer-reviewed series includes both scholarly monographs and essay collections.

PUBLISHED BY PALGRAVE:

*Women in the Medieval Islamic World: Power, Patronage, and Piety*
edited by Gavin R. G. Hambly

*The Ethics of Nature in the Middle Ages: On Boccaccio's* Poetaphysics
by Gregory B. Stone

*Presence and Presentation: Women in the Chinese Literati Tradition*
edited by Sherry J. Mou

*The Lost Love Letters of Heloise and Abelard: Perceptions of Dialogue in Twelfth-Century France*
by Constant J. Mews

*Understanding Scholastic Thought with Foucault*
by Philipp W. Rosemann

*For Her Good Estate: The Life of Elizabeth de Burgh*
by Frances A. Underhill

*Constructions of Widowhood and Virginity in the Middle Ages*
edited by Cindy L. Carlson and Angela Jane Weisl

*Motherhood and Mothering in Anglo-Saxon England*
by Mary Dockray-Miller

*Listening to Heloise: The Voice of a Twelfth-Century Woman*
edited by Bonnie Wheeler

*The Postcolonial Middle Ages*
edited by Jeffrey Jerome Cohen

*Chaucer's* Pardoner *and Gender Theory: Bodies of Discourse*
by Robert S. Sturges

*Crossing the Bridge: Comparative Essays on Medieval European and Heian Japanese Women Writers*
edited by Barbara Stevenson and Cynthia Ho

*Engaging Words: The Culture of Reading in the Later Middle Ages*
by Laurel Amtower

*Robes and Honor: The Medieval World of Investiture*
edited by Stewart Gordon

*Representing Rape in Medieval and Early Modern Literature*
edited by Elizabeth Robertson and Christine M. Rose

*Same Sex Love and Desire among Women in the Middle Ages*
edited by Francesca Canadé Sautman and Pamela Sheingorn

*Sight and Embodiment in the Middle Ages: Ocular Desires*
by Suzannah Biernoff

*Listen, Daughter: The* Speculum Virginum *and the Formation of Religious Women in the Middle Ages*
edited by Constant J. Mews

*Science, the Singular, and the Question of Theology*
by Richard A. Lee, Jr.

*Gender in Debate from the Early Middle Ages to the Renaissance*
edited by Thelma S. Fenster and Clare A. Lees

*Malory's* Morte D'Arthur: *Remaking Arthurian Tradition*
by Catherine Batt

*The Vernacular Spirit: Essays on Medieval Religious Literature*
edited by Renate Blumenfeld-Kosinski, Duncan Robertson, and Nancy Warren

*Popular Piety and Art in the Late Middle Ages: Image Worship and Idolatry in England 1350–1500*
by Kathleen Kamerick

*Absent Narratives, Manuscript Textuality, and Literary Structure in Late Medieval England*
by Elizabeth Scala

*Creating Community with Food and Drink in Merovingian Gaul*
by Bonnie Effros

*Representations of Early Byzantine Empresses: Image and Empire*
by Anne McClanan

*Encountering Medieval Textiles and Dress: Objects, Texts, Images*
edited by Désirée G. Koslin and Janet Snyder

*Eleanor of Aquitaine: Lord and Lady*
edited by Bonnie Wheeler and John Carmi Parsons

*Isabel La Católica, Queen of Castile: Critical Essays*
edited by David A. Boruchoff

*Homoeroticism and Chivalry: Discourses of Male Same-Sex Desire in the Fourteenth Century*
by Richard E. Zeikowitz

*Portraits of Medieval Women: Family, Marriage, and Politics in England 1225–1350*
by Linda E. Mitchell

*Eloquent Virgins: From Thecla to Joan of Arc*
by Maud Burnett McInerney

*The Persistence of Medievalism: Narrative Adventures in Contemporary Culture*
by Angela Jane Weisl

*Capetian Women*
edited by Kathleen D. Nolan

*Joan of Arc and Spirituality*
edited by Ann W. Astell and Bonnie Wheeler

*The Texture of Society: Medieval Women in the Southern Low Countries*
edited by Ellen E. Kittell and Mary A. Suydam

*Charlemagne's Mustache: And Other Cultural Clusters of a Dark Age*
by Paul Edward Dutton

*Troubled Vision: Gender, Sexuality, and Sight in Medieval Text and Image*
edited by Emma Campbell and Robert Mills

*Queering Medieval Genres*
by Tison Pugh

*Sacred Place in Early Medieval Neoplatonism*
by L. Michael Harrington

*The Middle Ages at Work*
edited by Kellie Robertson and Michael Uebel

*Chaucer's Jobs*
by David R. Carlson

*Medievalism and Orientalism: Three Essays on Literature, Architecture and Cultural Identity*
by John M. Ganim

*Queer Love in the Middle Ages*
by Anna Klosowska

*Performing Women in the Middle Ages: Sex, Gender, and the Iberian Lyric*
by Denise K. Filios

*Necessary Conjunctions: The Social Self in Medieval England*
by David Gary Shaw

*Visual Culture and the German Middle Ages*
edited by Kathryn Starkey and Horst Wenzel

*Medieval Paradigms: Essays in Honor of Jeremy duQuesnay Adams, Volumes 1 and 2*
edited by Stephanie Hayes-Healy

*False Fables and Exemplary Truth in Later Middle English Literature*
by Elizabeth Allen

*Ecstatic Transformation: On the Uses of Alterity in the Middle Ages*
by Michael Uebel

*Sacred and Secular in Medieval and Early Modern Cultures: New Essays*
edited by Lawrence Besserman

*Tolkien's Modern Middle Ages*
edited by Jane Chance and Alfred K. Siewers

*Representing Righteous Heathens in Late Medieval England*
by Frank Grady

*Byzantine Dress: Representations of Secular Dress in Eighth-to-Twelfth Century Painting*
by Jennifer L. Ball

*The Laborer's Two Bodies: Labor and the "Work" of the Text in Medieval Britain, 1350–1500*
by Kellie Robertson

*The Dogaressa of Venice, 1250–1500: Wife and Icon*
by Holly S. Hurlburt

*Logic, Theology, and Poetry in Boethius, Abelard, and Alan of Lille: Words in the Absence of Things*
by Eileen C. Sweeney

*The Theology of Work: Peter Damian and the Medieval Religious Renewal Movement*
by Patricia Ranft

*On the Purification of Women: Churching in Northern France, 1100–1500*
by Paula M. Rieder

*Writers of the Reign of Henry II: Twelve Essays*
edited by Ruth Kennedy and Simon Meecham-Jones

*Lonesome Words: The Vocal Poetics of the Old English Lament and the African-American Blues Song*
by M.G. McGeachy

*Performing Piety: Musical Culture in Medieval English Nunneries*
by Anne Bagnell Yardley

*The Flight from Desire: Augustine and Ovid to Chaucer*
by Robert R. Edwards

*Mindful Spirit in Late Medieval Literature: Essays in Honor of Elizabeth D. Kirk*
edited by Bonnie Wheeler

*Medieval Fabrications: Dress, Textiles, Clothwork, and Other Cultural Imaginings*
edited by E. Jane Burns

*Was the Bayeux Tapestry Made in France?: The Case for St. Florent of Saumur*
by George Beech

*Women, Power, and Religious Patronage in the Middle Ages*
by Erin L. Jordan

*Hybridity, Identity, and Monstrosity in Medieval Britain: On Difficult Middles*
by Jeffrey Jerome Cohen

*Medieval Go-Betweens and Chaucer's Pandarus*
by Gretchen Mieszkowski

*The Surgeon in Medieval English Literature*
by Jeremy J. Citrome

*Temporal Circumstances: Form and History in the Canterbury Tales*
by Lee Patterson

*Erotic Discourse and Early English Religious Writing*
by Lara Farina

*Odd Bodies and Visible Ends in Medieval Literature*
by Sachi Shimomura

*On Farting: Language and Laughter in the Middle Ages*
by Valerie Allen

*Women and Medieval Epic: Gender, Genre, and the Limits of Epic Masculinity*
edited by Sara S. Poor and Jana K. Schulman

*Race, Class, and Gender in "Medieval" Cinema*
edited by Lynn T. Ramey and Tison Pugh

*Allegory and Sexual Ethics in the High Middle Ages*
by Noah D. Guynn

*England and Iberia in the Middle Ages, 12th-15th Century: Cultural, Literary, and Political Exchanges*
edited by María Bullón-Fernández

*The Medieval Chastity Belt: A Myth-Making Process*
by Albrecht Classen

*Claustrophilia: The Erotics of Enclosure in Medieval Literature*
by Cary Howie

*Cannibalism in High Medieval English Literature*
by Heather Blurton

*The Drama of Masculinity and Medieval English Guild Culture*
by Christina M. Fitzgerald

*Chaucer's Visions of Manhood*
by Holly A. Crocker

*The Literary Subversions of Medieval Women*
by Jane Chance

*Manmade Marvels in Medieval Culture and Literature*
by Scott Lightsey

*American Chaucers*
by Candace Barrington

*Representing Others in Medieval Iberian Literature*
by Michelle M. Hamilton

*Paradigms and Methods in Early Medieval Studies*
edited by Celia Chazelle and Felice Lifshitz

*The King and the Whore: King Roderick and La Cava*
by Elizabeth Drayson

*Langland's Early Modern Identities*
by Sarah A. Kelen

*Cultural Studies of the Modern Middle Ages*
edited by Eileen A. Joy, Myra J. Seaman, Kimberly K. Bell, and Mary K. Ramsey

*Hildegard of Bingen's Unknown Language: An Edition, Translation, and Discussion*
by Sarah L. Higley

*Medieval Romance and the Construction of Heterosexuality*
by Louise M. Sylvester

*Communal Discord, Child Abduction, and Rape in the Later Middle Ages*
by Jeremy Goldberg

*Lydgate Matters: Poetry and Material Culture in the Fifteenth Century*
edited by Lisa H. Cooper and Andrea Denny-Brown

*Sexuality and Its Queer Discontents in Middle English Literature*
by Tison Pugh

*Sex, Scandal, and Sermon in Fourteenth-Century Spain: Juan Ruiz's* Libro de Buen Amor
by Louise M. Haywood

*The Erotics of Consolation: Desire and Distance in the Late Middle Ages*
edited by Catherine E. Léglu and Stephen J. Milner

*Battlefronts Real and Imagined: War, Border, and Identity in the Chinese Middle Period*
edited by Don J. Wyatt

*Wisdom and Her Lovers in Medieval and Early Modern Hispanic Literature*
by Emily C. Francomano

*Power, Piety, and Patronage in Late Medieval Queenship: Maria de Luna*
by Nuria Silleras-Fernandez

*In the Light of Medieval Spain: Islam, the West, and the Relevance of the Past*
edited by Simon R. Doubleday and David Coleman, foreword by Giles Tremlett

*Chaucerian Aesthetics*
by Peggy A. Knapp

*Memory, Images, and the English Corpus Christi Drama*
by Theodore K. Lerud

*Cultural Diversity in the British Middle Ages: Archipelago, Island, England*
edited by Jeffrey Jerome Cohen

*Excrement in the Late Middle Ages: Sacred Filth and Chaucer's Fecopoetics*
by Susan Signe Morrison

*Authority and Subjugation in Writing of Medieval Wales*
edited by Ruth Kennedy and Simon Meecham-Jones

*The Medieval Poetics of the Reliquary: Enshrinement, Inscription, Performance*
by Seeta Chaganti

*The Legend of Charlemagne in the Middle Ages: Power, Faith, and Crusade*
edited by Matthew Gabriele and Jace Stuckey

*The Poems of Oswald von Wolkenstein: An English Translation of the Complete Works (1376/77–1445)*
by Albrecht Classen

*Women and Experience in Later Medieval Writing: Reading the Book of Life*
edited by Anneke B. Mulder-Bakker and Liz Herbert McAvoy

*Ethics and Eventfulness in Middle English Literature: Singular Fortunes*
by J. Allan Mitchell

*Maintenance, Meed, and Marriage in Medieval English Literature*
by Kathleen E. Kennedy

*The Post-Historical Middle Ages*
edited by Elizabeth Scala and Sylvia Federico

*Constructing Chaucer: Author and Autofiction in the Critical Tradition*
by Geoffrey W. Gust

*Queens in Stone and Silver: The Creation of a Visual Imagery of Queenship in Capetian France*
by Kathleen Nolan

*Finding Saint Francis in Literature and Art*
edited by Cynthia Ho, Beth A. Mulvaney, and John K. Downey

*Strange Beauty: Ecocritical Approaches to Early Medieval Landscape*
by Alfred K. Siewers

*Berenguela of Castile (1180–1246) and Political Women in the High Middle Ages*
by Miriam Shadis

*Julian of Norwich's Legacy: Medieval Mysticism and Post-Medieval Reception*
edited by Sarah Salih and Denise N. Baker

*Medievalism, Multilingualism, and Chaucer*
by Mary Catherine Davidson

*The Letters of Heloise and Abelard: A Translation of Their Collected Correspondence and Related Writings*
translated and edited by Mary Martin McLaughlin with Bonnie Wheeler

*Women and Wealth in Late Medieval Europe*
edited by Theresa Earenfight

*Heloise and the Paraclete: A Twelfth-Century Quest* (forthcoming)
by Mary Martin McLaughlin with Bonnie Wheeler

# WOMEN AND WEALTH IN LATE MEDIEVAL EUROPE

*Edited by*
*Theresa Earenfight*

palgrave
macmillan

WOMEN AND WEALTH IN LATE MEDIEVAL EUROPE


First published in 2010 by
PALGRAVE MACMILLAN®
in the United States—a division of St. Martin's Press LLC,
175 Fifth Avenue, New York, NY 10010.

Where this book is distributed in the UK, Europe and the rest of the world, this is by Palgrave Macmillan, a division of Macmillan Publishers Limited, registered in England, company number 785998, of Houndmills, Basingstoke, Hampshire RG21 6XS.

Palgrave Macmillan is the global academic imprint of the above companies and has companies and representatives throughout the world.

Palgrave® and Macmillan® are registered trademarks in the United States, the United Kingdom, Europe and other countries.

ISBN: 978–1–4039–8432–6

Library of Congress Cataloging-in-Publication Data

Women and wealth in late Medieval Europe / edited by Theresa Earenfight.
p. cm. — (The new Middle Ages)
Includes bibliographical references and index.
ISBN 978–1–4039–8432–6 (alk. paper)
1. Women in politics—Europe—History. 2. Women in public life—Europe—History. 3. Wealth—Europe—History. I. Earenfight, Theresa, 1954–

HQ1236.5.E8W645 2010
305.48′96210940902—dc22 2009024120

A catalogue record of the book is available from the British Library.

Design by Newgen Imaging Systems (P) Ltd., Chennai, India.

First edition: March 2010

10 9 8 7 6 5 4 3 2 1

Printed in the United States of America.

# CONTENTS

# ACKNOWLEDGMENTS

The chapters in this volume were inspired initially by work presented at two conferences in 2004. The first was the International Medieval Congress at Western Michigan University in May, where the Society for Medieval Feminist Scholarship sponsored six sessions on women and money. The second was an interdisciplinary conference organized by János Bak, "Medieval and Early Modern Queens and Queenship: Questions of Income and Patronage" held at the Department of Medieval Studies, Central European University, Budapest, in October. These two conferences brought together scholars currently at work on royal finances seen from the queen's point of view. Since then, the project has grown significantly and has become far richer in thematic and theoretical depth and range. Bonnie Wheeler's suggestion that this wealth of research be collected into a single volume was the impetus for this edited collection, and I am grateful to the anonymous reviewers for their generous and insightful comments and to the editors at Palgrave Macmillan for their expertise in guiding these essays to publication.

Authors in this volume have received generous support from the National Endowment for the Humanities and the Program for Cultural Cooperation between Spain's Ministry of Education, Culture, and Sports and United States' Universities. I am grateful to my colleagues at Seattle University Women Studies Program, Medieval Studies Program, and Department of History for brainstorming, critiques, and for providing a deep well of intellectual and personal good will and an always welcome wry and wicked humor.

# INTRODUCTION

*Theresa Earenfight*

Money makes things happen, as Daniel Murtaugh cogently notes in his study of Old French *fabliau*. It is an important motive force for economic, political, and personal power. But money in its concrete quantifiable form—pennies, pounds, florins, *reials*, *maravedís*, and *livres*—is just the starting point for a study of gender and the sociology of economics in Europe in the Middle Ages. The authors whose essays are collected in this book emphasize that in the complex and subtle intersection of women and money, the question was not a simple calculus of how women got money and spent it, but also what money meant in terms of human values and morals. Their questions revolve on the nexus of work, commerce, and power but they use money to illuminate the operations of gender in the power structures, social conflicts, and cultural traditions, how wealth was experienced by women, and the subtle shifts in meaning of abstract notions of wealth.[1]

The authors demonstrate that for people in the later Middle Ages, money was a heap of coins used to pay the tax collector, the fishmonger, or the draper, but wealth signified something more capacious and rich. It not only signified the abundant possession of things that constitute riches in the popular sense—rich and costly possessions, luxuries, worldly goods, affluence—but it was much more than that. Medieval ideas on the common or public welfare, the commonwealth, and the collective riches of a people or realm are often lost in the narrow modern definitions of wealth that calculate indices of wealth in terms of profit and loss, wages and prices, inflation and stagnation. Money mattered greatly to women of all social ranks, but not necessarily in ways immediately recognizable to a modern reader who equates wealth with material prosperity. In a definition that seems archaic to the modern sensibility, both Murtaugh and M. C. Bodden demonstrate, wealth in the Middle Ages meant a sense of well-being and of felicity and thus serves as a marker for the richness or poverty of married life. Wealth, as Lara Farina notes in her chapter on English anchoresses, was also spiritual, intimately connected to theology, so that even the poorest nun living a solitary life of spiritual devotion in an anchorhold was blessed with wealth beyond measure.

Economists and anthropologists have long noted that money is a powerful semiotic emblem and a telling marker in the history of mentalités and emotions in the transition from economies where gift exchange is common to one where money circulates and becomes a key unit of measurement of value.[2] One such moment and place in this history is Europe in the later Middle Ages, from roughly 1100 to 1500 CE, a pivotal period that marks an upswing in the velocity of the circulation of coinage, the emergence of a market economy, and the growth of a fluid, flourishing commercial economy.[3] An unease with money, especially with credit and the generation of interest on money, as contrary to Christian precepts was giving way to a general sense of the possession of money as a necessary condition for a good life.[4] This commercialization of the European economy fundamentally changed attitudes toward the relationship of women, work, wealth, and power, leaving persistent traces of misogyny that still remain.[5]

The chapters in this volume significantly deepen and expand on the classic work of economic historians.[6] To earlier generations of medieval economic historians, most of whom did not specifically address women, economic history most often meant getting and spending money, managing finances, fiscal policy, and wages and prices.[7] Historians of women shifted the masculinist focus from economic institutions and studied women and work (structures of production, gilds, and labor organization),[8] finance, and moneylending,[9] and consumption as a display of social and cultural capital that bestows power on the spender.[10] Feminist economists ground their work with the household based on the a priori presumption that all women, even if unmarried, are part of a household that privileges the man's contribution but is predicated on women as key elements in the organization.[11] The extent to which women were part of this household economy varied temporally, geographically, and according to rank and status, but it is striking to consider the extent to which women, even a countess or a queen, always bumped into a glass ceiling that limited their potential to exercise their talents.

But the authors do much more than simply document the activities of women in commerce, landholding, patronage, production, and consumption. Their work provides vital evidence in the shifting interplay of gender and money in a burgeoning cash economy. Generally, they track important changes in not only how women acquired or made money (work, commerce, dowry, inheritance, as queen) and how they used their money to make things happen, but also attitudes toward women's social and economic value. The chapters are eloquent witnesses to the complex, contradictory, and fluid attitudes toward women and wealth, and the power that wealth bestows.

In this regard, these chapters provide important evidence that reinforces new studies that argue that between 1200 and 1700 "a new cultural narrative about gender and newly gendered social practices" emerged in Europe.[12] This new narrative developed in the context of a growing cash economy and industrialization that exacerbated the separation of the spheres of home and production. As production shifted from the household or pragmatic "all hands on deck" ethos of the family workshop to the more strictly gendered factory, attitudes toward work and money changed correspondingly. Privileging men as producers relegated women to the role of consumers and most "good" women were gradually excluded from production in the wage economy where the poor engaged in physical labor.[13] This new discourse reshaped ideas on the relationship between gender and work, particularly as it pertained to the growing middle class, and this, in turn, molded modern ideas on what it meant to be male and female.

The authors in this book approach the changing economics of the later Middle Ages from a variety of perspectives—history, literary studies, art, and architectural history—but their work is thematically bridged by the centrality of the family economy. Bodden and Murtaugh use medieval literature to explore money as semiotic marker of how a cash economy became a metaphor for the value of women and the worth of marriage. Sally Livingston and Núria Silleras-Fernández complement these literary marriages and actual ones, that of Abelard and Heloise and an Aragonese concubine who became queen. Sharon Farmer and Shelley Roff examine women and work, but from opposite sides of the spectrum—women as producers of luxury goods and women working in the construction trades. Helen Gaudette studies a particular queen as a patron of civic building projects, not as a worker. The theme of patronage is picked up by Erin Jordan who looks at Flemish aristocratic women who formed a key part of the spiritual economy, a theme discussed in detail by Farina in her chapter on the economics of anchorite women. As Anna Dronzek shows, women's relationship to land was part and parcel of their family identities. Aristocratic women were more than patrons, they were landholders who could and often did exercise lordship. Silleras-Fernández, Gaudette, Ana Maria S. A. Rodrigues, and Manuela Santos Silva and I work on queens as a fundamental part of the marital-monarchical economy.

The multifaceted word "economy" can signify an economy of violence,[14] a political economy,[15] social economy and social capital,[16] and sexual economics.[17] More familiar to us are the economics of commerce—money and material wealth, with its spectrum of meaning, from the lavish spending of the wealthy to the frugality and thrift of the less well-off. But to the people living in the Middle Ages, it meant more broadly the management of resources and retained its close association to the Greek meaning in which a society or other structure was ordered after the manner of a family. It was, at its essence, household management, which implied the careful management of resources. More broadly, it meant the management or administration of the material resources of a community, which to medieval political theorists meant the method of divine government of the world, or of a specific aspect or part of that government; to theologians, it meant the judicious management of doctrine. The authors in this book detect the shift in attitudes in the subtle linguistic differences that are analyzed carefully to describe the gender dynamics of the medieval economy. The language of money is nuanced, not just numerical or arithmetic. Thus, words such as "profit," "bargain," "debt," "commerce," "purchase," and "price," are loaded words and the subtleties are never lost on the medieval men and women in these pages. The authors take up these definitions while not neglecting the more familiar modern usage: the organization or condition of a community or nation with respect to economic factors, especially the production and consumption of goods and services and the supply of money.

Sensitive to the subtle shadings of meaning, the authors were prompted by the monetary and commercial terms—coins, wages, and prices—but drawing on methods and theories from both anthropology that concern nonmonetary exchange and gift economies and from feminist and gender studies, they situate their work in a medieval text or context while extending the analysis further and define the term more broadly. For example, Farina notes that "the financing of anchoritism was bound up with the larger thirteenth-century discourse on commerce in the practice of intercession." Devotional literature, especially written by voluntarily poor anchoresses, might seem an unlikely source for the study of women and money, but as Farina shows, it is a rich semiotic field that has much to say about the value, worth, and exchange of women and "knowing a bargain." Intercession was spiritual service work and the financing of anchoritism "was bound up with the larger thirteenth-century discourse on commerce in the practice of intercession. This is valuable labor that could be provided charitably or in exchange for remuneration of various kinds."[18] This attention to the cultural meaning of money to women, rather than to the strictly empirical analysis of broad economic trends of wages and prices, monetary circulation, trade and commerce, means that this collection lacks charts and graphs. Wages, prices, and the relative value of pennies, *livres*, florins, *maravedís*, and *reais* are clearly part of the discussion, such as Farmer's chapter that traces women in prominent Parisian families who were well-known retailers in their own right. But all the authors engage in a broader conversation on what money meant to women, how it affected their ability to act with agency or autonomy, and how we can use evidence from economics to understand the cultural and social value and wealth of women.

The theme of knowledge is a common thread throughout the chapters. Queens, likely to be educated at home, learned early in their lives how to navigate the fiscal realm and its attendant political and religious implications. Abelard and Heloise, highly intelligent lovers, debate the fine points of the worth of marriage. Farina's well-read anchoresses and Jordan's Flemish noblewomen know full well the spiritual value of patronage. But not all knowledge comes from books. Murtaugh's peasant wife with keen math skills and Bodden's shrewdly savvy wives all possess a clear understanding of their spiritual and market value. Ysabel, the protagonist-wife is very clever in her management of money; she is literate and has a head for numbers, two skills that serve her very well in her dealings with her husband and her neighbors. She operates in an economy of wit, where "wit" signifies both humor and intelligence. A woman—peasant, noblewoman, merchant, construction worker, or anchorite—may be subordinate to the men around them—fathers, husbands, lovers, sons—and they may not always get what they want, need, or deserve, but their intelligence makes it clear that they are not to be taken for granted. All of them are shrewd sharp operators, even as subordinate members in the hierarchy of gender and wealth. Their leverage is a crucial aspect of a wider economy in which they, like women today who take advantage of microcredit, are empowered coin by coin. That they—the women, and the men who often write about them—are aware of the changes taking place is evident in the language used to tell the story.

Money is a powerful symbol of the economics of marriage that recurs throughout all the chapters.[19] These tensions are evident among all the nonliterary women, from Farina's anchorites to Silleras-Fernández's queen, from Farmer's merchants of luxury goods to Roff's construction workers, and from Dronzek's landholding women to the ill-fated Abelard and Heloise. But the purchase of women through marriage is most vividly seen in the literary characters where money is itself merely a sign and its relation to what it stands for is both arbitrary and symbolic. In the case of the three women at the center of Bodden's chapter (Margery Kempe and two fictional creations, Dorigen and the Wife of Bath from Chaucer's *The Canterbury Tales*) the transaction involves their physical freedom and their identity. The agency they secure from possessing money allows them to disrupt masculine notions of femininity and rewrite themselves in a more meaningful and dignified way. Murtaugh examines how these semiotic emblems change as society adjusts to changes wrought by the expansion of commerce and wage labor and the decline of forms of labor predicated on a personal servile relationship: in the old French fabliau where "the role of money in the story is symptomatic of a new order controlled by negotiation and wit that replaces an old order based on coercion." In the fabliau of *Constant du Hamel*, money signifies prestige, with three suitors seeking the favors of Ysabel, the beautiful wife of a rich peasant. The economy of relationships here is in Ysabel's favor because she is smart and clever; she converts her wits and beauty into wealth. She is in tune with the times, unlike the men who do not think in terms of power other than the older feudal forms of power derived from a fixed position in an estate fixed in a hierarchy.

The strongest and most durable hierarchy was, however, the family regardless of social rank or status. Women's place in the management of household resources forms the framework for understanding economics in broader sense, meaning the way in which something is managed. Livingston explores the "economics of relationship" as a way of managing intimate relations between a man and a woman, which spanned a range from whore to concubine (*concubina* or *scortum*) to wife (*uxor*). Debt (*debitum*) would have implied marriage debt, obligation, owing something, ownership. In her letters that set out the economics of relationship, Heloise accuses Abelard of holding her "cheap" (*vilitatem*), implying a sales transaction, making her an object of exchange. As Livingston reminds us, commerce (*commercium*) could mean trade, traffic, commercial intercourse, a mercantile right, but that *carnale commercium* was widely understood to mean sexual intercourse and, by extension, illicit commerce.

Livingston's study of the epistolary exchange between Abelard and Heloise and Jordan's study of the countess of Flanders and Hainault are valuable reminders that as useful as literary sources and chronicles are, they filter the period through a personal and often politicized frame. Silleras-Fernández explores the theme of *carnale commercium* as part of the royal economy of marriage and the tension between concubine and wife in the case of Sibil·la de Fortià, Queen of Aragon (1377–87). To a king, a marriage represented a threat to his royal patrimony. "The rise and fall of Sibil·la de Fortià demonstrates that while a queen's power and authority was based almost entirely on the wealth and influence she derived from the publicly-expressed esteem and confidence of the king, and her own coronation, this alone was not enough to ensure a successful and secure reign, particularly one that would outlive that of her husband." The economy of a royal relationship extended beyond the intimacy of concubinage or marriage: "If a queen did not have the support of the upper nobility, or a significant portion of that elite, she could not hope to effectively exercise power. Queenly power depended also on the recognition of her subjects." Lineage was a form of currency that enabled a woman to supersede disadvantages of concubinage or widowhood; without the enormous symbolic value of a bloodline and the very real influence attached to family, money meant very little.

Jordan, Dronzek, Farmer, and Roff work with sources most familiar to economic historians—charters, household accounts, property records, business transactions, wills and bequests, city ordinances, tax assessments, legal records, and wage records, but they do so fully attentive to the methodological concerns particular to the study of women. Jordan focuses on the expenditure records, while Rodrigues, Santos Silva, Silleras-Fernández, and I work with the wealthiest and most powerful women, queens, using sources that range from chronicles, fiscal accounts, treasury records, letters, and administrative records. The elite Parisian women that Farmer studies have tremendous opportunities from their husbands' businesses, but they were still constrained by powerful social norms, so that no matter how successful in business, even a luxury trade that catered to the wealthiest sector of society, these wealthy women in the later Middle Ages encountered a "glass ceiling" that prevented them from taking part in the highest echelons of city governance. It is not that these women were entirely absent from view—all were taxpayers, some were situated at the pinnacle of the economic hierarchy as official purveyors of goods and services to the royal household, and some served the royal household directly as concierges. But wealth, social prominence, and proximity to the royal person were not necessarily passports to political power. No matter how rich they were, the women Farmer studies always occupied a secondary status relative to the men in the household. Her chapter provides an illuminating glimpse into the lives and work of women as merchants and producers at the crucial moment in the later Middle Ages when women shifted from producers to consumers.

On the opposite end of the social and economic spectrum are poor women working in the demanding physical and artisanal labor in building construction rather than in the commerce of luxury items. Roff provides a valuable temporally and geographically comparative overview of women in late medieval and early modern Europe that dovetails with Farmer's wealthy Parisian merchants. Roff's core group are single women and widows who lacked the capital, education, or privilege of elite birth that would keep them out of poverty. These are the women who worked on the building projects sponsored by patrons like Queen Melisende in

Jerusalem, elite women in Paris, or the queens of Portugal. Despite some variation across time and space, the employment of women in the building trades was fairly commonplace until the sixteenth century, when economic crises and a concomitant hardening of attitudes toward women in the trades made their engagement more difficult. For day laborers on the construction site, the stigma of women employed in manual labor left them poor and disempowered. However, their unskilled work meant that they did not face legal barriers or bans against their work as seen with women in the building crafts, and there were no corporate organizations overseeing or protecting male employment. And as Roff notes, the same key shift in access to cash and credit in the thirteenth century that enriched the Parisian merchants studied by Farmer, also benefited the poor.

Aristocratic women are a case apart from all other women. They were more likely to be literate, wealthy, and not engaged in commerce. The family economy still determined their status and delineated their economic actions, but did so not just in terms of marriage. Jordan's study of the spending habits of Jeanne, the hereditary countess of Flanders and Hainaut, while her husband was imprisoned after the battle of Bouvines in 1214 shows that after Ferrand's release, Jeanne was not forced into retirement, but shared governance of her inheritance with him. Her inheritance and status as countess trumped her marital status so that after her husband's death, Jeanne's religious patronage increased gradually, in proportion to her age, experience, and the security of her position. Dronzek contends that among aristocratic women in fifteenth-century England, family mattered at least as much if not more than age or experience. The stronger a woman's family identity was—as mother, wife, sister, daughter, widow—the less often she would face legal challenges to land held by right of that family identity. For these women, wealth and family were intertwined and family identities and claims to property empowered women legally and granted them a measure of economic agency. Land and family, with its attachment to lordship and political power, also forms the basis of the work of Rodrigues and Santos Silva, but the subject in this case is Portuguese queens who received land as part of their reginal accounts, but these lands were part of the royal patrimony and thus could not be alienated or bequeathed. But the income generated by these properties granted the queens considerable wealth that they could use to support their households and bestow patronage, which granted them a prestige and power that extended beyond the royal household.

The work of queens was unique but vital, and differed greatly from realm to realm and among individual queens. Gaudette shows in her study of the resource investment and spending policy of king and queen that Melisende's spending and patronage was a strategy for good governance. But Melisende was a strategic spender who embodied the virtue of *largitas* or generosity, the female personification of which is prominently featured on the beautifully carved ivory front cover of the *Melisende Psalter.*[20] She had to "woo" not only the city of Jerusalem but the military and the church and visiting pilgrims, leaving behind three building projects that form a visible legacy in the public sphere: Bethgibelin Castle, the convent of Bethany, and the covered market street in Jerusalem known as *Malquisinat,* the Street of Bad Cooking. Portuguese queens were also noteworthy patrons of urban construction projects. Not only did this endear the queen to her local subjects, but as Rodrigues and Santos Silva observe, they could closely scrutinize local officials, listen to their subjects' complaints, respond quickly, and thus reinforce their fidelity. They ate the local food, drank local wine, and sold the surplus at the market or stored it until the prices went up. In my chapter, I trace the shifting fortunes and wealth, both personal and official, of Aragonese queens whose husbands used their fiscal resources as a reserve fund that could be tapped when necessary to replenish a depleted treasury. The strategies used by Aragonese kings, especially Alfonso V (d. 1458), to deprive queens of the fiscal resources so crucial to the exercise of demonstrate the precariousness of money and wealth when it came to women.

The chapters in this collection depict the various spaces of opportunity afforded to women by wealth, no matter how that wealth was acquired—inheritance, work for wages or payment in kind, donation, patronage, rents from property—and whether real or depicted in imagined spaces of a work of literature. Medieval women engaged in a wider range of economic practices than we previously understood—at the most lofty economic domain of royal women, aristocratic landholders, and merchants of luxury good as well as the bottom of the economic stratus occupied by anchorites and construction workers. As attitudes and practices toward the making and spending of money changed, and as women's role in the economics of gender changed, women's access to wealth bore powerful social and cultural meanings that reflects a dynamic late medieval society in flux, uncertain of the meaning of women and wealth.

## Notes

1. For the classical formulation of wealth, see Aristotle, *Politics,* trans. Benjamin Jowett (New York: The Modern Library, 1943). For an overview of medieval Christian attitudes toward money and wealth, see Lester K. Little, *Religious Poverty and the Profit Economy in Medieval Europe* (Ithaca,

NY: Cornell University Press, 1978). Adam Smith's *The Wealth of Nations* (1776) made the decisive turn to modern economics as a quantitative inquiry based on monetary indices of income (Oxford: Clarendon Press, 1979).

2. Lewis Hyde, *The Gift: Imagination and the Erotic Life of Property* (New York: Random House, 1979); Marcel Mauss, *The Gift: The Form and Reason for Exchange in Archaic Societies*, trans. W. D. Halls (New York and London: Norton, 1990); Marshall Sahlins, *Stone Age Economics* (Chicago: Aldine-Atherton, 1972); *The Social Life of Things: Commodities in Cultural Perspective*, ed. Arjun Appadurai (Cambridge: Cambridge University Press, 1986).
3. Christopher Dyer, *Standards of Living in the Later Middle Ages: Social Change in England, 1200–1320* (Cambridge: Cambridge University Press, 1989); Michael McCormick, *Origins of the European Economy: Communications and Commerce, A. D. 300–900* (Cambridge: Cambridge University Press, 2001); and John Day, *The Medieval Market Economy* (Oxford: Blackwell, 1987).
4. John W. Baldwin, "The Medieval Theories of the Just Price," *Transactions of the American Philosophical Society* 49:4 (1959): 1–94 (rpt. in *Pre-Capitalist Economic Thought*, New York: Arno, 1972); Jacques LeGoff, *Your Money or Your Life: Economy and Religion in the Middle Ages*, trans. Patricia Ranum (New York: Zone, 1990).
5. Victoria De Grazia and Ellen Furlough, *The Sex of Things: Gender and Consumption in Historical Perspective* (Berkeley and Los Angeles: University of California Press, 1996).
6. J. L. Bolton, *The Medieval English Economy, 1150–1550* (London: J. M. Dent and Sons, 1987); Fernand Braudel, *Capitalism and Material Life, 1400–1800*, trans. Miriam Kochan (New York: Harper and Row, 1973); Carlo Cipolla, *Before the Industrial Revolution: European Society and Economy, 1000–1700*, 3rd edition (New York: Norton, 1994); Robert S. Lopez, *Medieval Trade in the Mediterranean World* (Oxford: Oxford University Press, 1955); Harry A. Miskimin, *Cash, Credit and Crisis in Europe, 1300–1600* (London: Variorum Reprints, 1989); Henri Pirenne, *Economic and Social History of Medieval Europe*, trans. I. E. Clegg (New York: Harcourt Brace Jovanvich, 1956; first French edition 1933).
7. Norman John Greville Pounds, *An Economic History of Medieval Europe*, second edition (London: Longman, 1994); Peter Spufford, *Money and Its Use in Medieval Europe* (Cambridge: Cambridge University Press, 1988); Spufford, *Power and Profit: The Merchant in Medieval Europe* (New York: Thames and Hudson, 2003).
8. Alice Clark's *The Working Life of Women in the Seventeenth-Century* (New York: Dutton, 1919) focused on a later period and is older but still useful. Important newer works include Lindsey Charles and Lorna Duffin, eds., *Women and Work in Pre-Industrial England* (London: Croom Helm, 1985); Barbara Hanawalt, ed., *Women and Work in Preindustrial Europe* (Bloomington: Indiana University Press, 1986); Martha C. Howell,

*Women, Production, and Patriarchy in Late Medieval Cities* (Chicago: University of Chicago Press, 1986); Howell, *The Marriage Exchange: Property, Social Place, and Gender in Cities of the Low Countries, 1300–1550* (Chicago: University of Chicago Press, 1998); David Herlihy, *Opera Muliebria: Women and Work in Medieval Europe* (New York: McGraw-Hill, 1990); Madeleine Pelner Cosman, *Women at Work in Medieval Europe* (New York: Facts on File, 2000). The classic study of women and gilds, Marian Dale, "The London Silkwomen of the Fifteenth Century," *Economic History Review* 4:3 (October 1933): 324–35, was revisited by Maryanne Kowaleski and Judith Bennett in "Crafts, Gilds, and Women in the Middle Ages: Fifty Years after Marian K. Dale," *Signs: Journal of Women in Culture and Society* 14:2 (Winter 1989): 474–88. For the transition from late medieval to early modern Europe, see Carol L. Loats, "Gender, Guilds, and Work Identity: Perspectives from Sixteenth-Century Paris," *French Historical Studies* 20:1 (Winter 1997): 15–30; Merry Wiesner, *Working Women in Renaissance Germany* (New Brunswick, NJ: Rutgers University Press, 1986); and Daryl M. Hafter, ed., *European Women and Preindustrial Craft* (Bloomington: Indiana University Press, 1995).

9. William Chester Jordan, *Women and Credit in Pre-Industrial and Developing Societies* (Philadelphia: University of Pennsylvania Press, 1993); Sally McKee, "Women under Venetian Colonial Rule in the Early Renaissance: Observations on Their Economic Activities," *Renaissance Quarterly* 51:1 (Spring 1998): 34–67; Kathryn Reyerson, *Business, Banking and Commerce in Medieval Montpellier* (Toronto: Pontifical Institute of Mediaeval Studies, 1985); Reyerson, *The Art of the Deal: Intermediaries of Trade in Medieval Montpellier* (Leiden: Brill, 2002).
10. See, for example, Susan Mosher Stuard, "Marriage Gifts and Fashion Mischief," in *The Medieval Marriage Scene: Prudence, Passion, Policy*, ed. Sherry Roush and Cristelle L. Baskins, Medieval and Renaissance Texts and Studies, vol. 299 (Tempe: Arizona Center for Medieval and Renaissance Studies, 2005), pp. 169–85; Sarah-Grace Heller, "Anxiety, Hierarchy, and Appearance in Thirteenth-Century Sumptuary Laws and the *Roman de la rose*," *French Historical Studies* 27:2 (2004): 311–48.
11. Shelly Lundberg and Robert A. Pollak, "Bargaining and Distribution in Marriage," *Journal of Economic Perspectives* 10:4 (1996): 139–58.
12. Martha C. Howell, "The Gender of Europe's Commercial Economy, 1200–1700," *Gender and History* 20:3 (November 2008): 519–38, quotes on pp. 520 and 532.
13. Women who engaged in physical labor carried a stigma akin to prostitution. On the economic implications of prostitution, see Ruth Mazo Karras, *Common Women: Prostitution and Sexuality in Medieval England* (Oxford: Oxford University Press, 1996); Leah Lydia Otis, *Prostitution in Medieval Society: The History of an Urban Institution in Languedoc* (Chicago: University of Chicago Press, 1985); and Joëlle Rollo-Koster, "From Prostitutes to Brides of Christ: The Avignonese Repenties in the Late Middle Ages," *Journal of Medieval and Early Modern Studies* 32:1 (2002): 109–44.

14. Cary Nederman and Martin Morris, "Rhetoric, Violence, and Gender in Machiavelli," in *Feminist Interpretations of Niccolò Machiavelli*, ed. Maria J. Falco (University Park: Pennsylvania State University Press, 2004), pp. 267–86.
15. Jack L. Amariglio, "The Body, Economic Discourse, and Power: An Economist's Introduction to Foucault," *History of Political Economy*, 20:4 (Winter 1988): 583–613.
16. Sheilagh Ogilvie, *A Bitter Living: Women, Markets, and Social Capital in Early Modern Germany* (Oxford: Oxford University Press, 2003).
17. Sheila Delany, "Sexual Economics, Chaucer's Wife of Bath and *The Book of Margery Kempe*" in *Feminist Readings in Middle English Literature: The Wife of Bath and All Her Sect,* ed. Ruth Evans and Lesley Johnson (London: Routledge, 1994), pp. 71–87.
18. On the economics of religion and intercession, see also Katherine L. French, "Maidens' Lights and Wives' Stores: Women's Parish Guilds in Late Medieval England," *Sixteenth Century Journal: The Journal of Early Modern Studies* 29:2 (Summer 1998): 399–425.
19. For comparison, see Stuard, "Marriage Gifts and Fashion Mischief," pp. 169–85.
20. See also Therese Martin, "The Art of a Reigning Queen as Dynastic Propaganda in Twelfth-Century Spain," *Speculum* 80:4 (October 2005): 1134–71.

# CHAPTER 1

# *CONSTANT DU HAMEL*: WOMEN, MONEY, AND POWER IN AN OLD FRENCH *FABLIAU*

*Daniel M. Murtaugh*

In the Old French fabliau *Constant du Hamel*, three would-be suitors unsuccessfully try to turn money into the sexual favors of Ysabel, a rich peasant's beautiful wife, while she successfully turns their unfulfilled desire into money. She succeeds because she is the only one in the story who understands money and can keep accounts of it in her head. The role of money in the story is symptomatic of a new order controlled by negotiation and wit that replaces an old order based on coercion. The story turns on the delusion of its male characters who think that they participate in the new order, that they can make their way with money, but who instinctively fall back on coercive assumptions from the old order and on their confident misjudgment of their relative strength against Ysabel.[1] They cannot understand the solvent effect of money on their cherished sense of hierarchical status, much less its effect on the more fundamental power relations of gender.

The new order of money, which followed upon the centralization and rationalization of the production of coin by governments in France, England, and Italy, was in part a response to the "commercial revolution" that opened Europe more widely to world markets and that Robert Lopez has compared to the Industrial Revolution of half a millennium later in its transforming effect on the economy.[2] The development of markets and currency coincided with technological advances in agriculture—principally in the design of the plow blade and harness and the improved practice of crop rotation[3]—and a favorable climatic change between 1150 and 1300,[4] to produce the phenomenon, infrequent but significant, of the rich peasant. Georges Duby has described "[t]he growing disparity of wealth" that opened within peasant society. By 1300 "a man's economic condition" trumped "hereditary and juridical lines separating free men from unfree." Duby cites the movement of one village in the Sâone from substantial economic equality in 1180 to pronounced stratification a hundred years later, with five families prospering and extracting fixed rents from their neighbors. In upper Provence, a rich peasant dowered his daughter with expensive cloth and 75 *livres* (or pounds) in cash, a sum of which we will calculate the value shortly. Duby concludes that the few peasants capable of such bridal gifts "had almost risen to the level of the petty nobility."[5]

Homelier evidences of peasant wealth are found in archeological studies of villages, where nondocumentary evidence is often more trustworthy than fourteenth- or fifteenth-century tax rolls that come late and are, in the words of Robert Fossier, "the product of fraud, error, and forgetfulness."[6] One can find evidence of the successive expansion of peasant dwellings. The contents of the houses, recovered from trash heaps or recorded at the death of a householder or, in one case cited by Fossier, in the aftermath of a destructive military attack, also reveal strata of wealth. For example, one might find more than one hearth, or chests or simply keys that tell of valuables to protect, or a footed bed for one or two, perhaps enclosed by curtains or sliding panels, rather than a straw mattress laid across a wooden frame to accommodate five or six adults and children. Certainly the bath that figures so prominently in *Constant du Hamel* would count as such an index of wealth.

The peasant who controlled such a household was part of a lucky 5 or 10 percent of his class (which in turn was approximately 90 percent of the population). He led—and sometimes exploited—a village community in which 25 to 45 percent were not wealthy but were above subsistence, 40 to 50 percent were at the margin of subsistence or below (farming ten acres or less), and 10 to 15 percent were in the extremities of poverty.[7] One might say that the wealthy peasant was rare and yet that everyone knew one or more of his kind. He or his father had bought his freedom from a lord whose duties to his own splendor and martial prowess required cash more than labor service or whose desire to clear forests for productive use led him to settle the sons of his former serfs on the new land on favorable terms, as freeholders or leaseholders at rents fixed forever, a deal that would sour as inflation robbed cash of its value relative to the produce of the tenants' labor.[8]

Such a peasant got where he was by industry and cleverness, including a cleverness with money. One has no trouble crediting Constant du Hamel with industry, but the other quality is not in evidence. How did he earn his place, then? Or how does the *fabloer* justify putting him there, when tradition, at least the secular side of it represented by comedy and romance, had pretty nearly settled the question of the peasant's nature: he was bestial and stupid.[9] The two instances most often cited from romance are to be found in *Aucassin et Nicolette* (Chapter 24) and *Yvain* by Chrétien de Troyes (286–305). One of the four manuscripts of *Constant du Hamel* inserts a description of Constant's ugliness that seems to recall the passage in *Aucassin and Nicolette*. Scholars consider it inauthentic, but it shows what came to mind when one thought of a peasant as a literary character.[10] How could such a creature rise in the world? An enlightened response would overturn tradition, asserting the cleverness of the peasant that, at least sometimes, explains his prosperity.

The *fabliau* tradition, however, is not enlightened. It is merely alert. In this instance, it secures its protagonist's economic status by the wits of his wife, whose beauty, of course, is the other catalyst of its plot. This, however, involves its own conflict with tradition. A woman's beauty, in general, has an inverse relation to her virtue in the comic tradition, which never strays too far from the tradition of Christian antifeminism; and beauty's alliance with wit only aggravates its potential for trouble. This break with tradition, nevertheless, is one the *fableor* is willing to make. Apparently it is easier to extol a witty and beautiful woman's virtue than a rich peasant's wit. This accommodation in the interests of what we might term ideological decorum is made easier by the fact that social observation makes it quite plausible. The *fableor* and his readers could easily observe the highly competent participation of women in the economic life of villages and towns, particularly in the management of finance, an area in which, theoretically, women only acted under the close supervision of their husbands or other male authority figures but in which, in fact, they displayed a high degree of initiative. This, of course, is a central contention of many of the chapters in this volume and of recent scholarship that examines the role of women in medieval and early modern credit and investment activity.[11] And so an essentially defensive maneuver on behalf of a conservative cultural vision of a debased class rationalizes the puzzle of the wealthy peasant by appealing to his wife's skill in managing money.

As we have seen, Duby emphasized the new dependence of rank on money in the rural economy. To understand how this novelty works in *Constant du Hamel*, we need to understand how money worked, and, especially, how much it was worth. The European system of money was an invention of the Carolingian empire, and its basis was the *denier*, which the English called the pence or penny, while still keeping a "d" for its abbreviation until the metric conversion of the late twentieth century.

Twelve *deniers* made one *sou* (or shilling), a coin whose existence was largely notional until the thirteenth-century currency reforms mentioned earlier. Twenty *sous* made a *livre* or pound, a denomination that made an even rarer appearance as a physical, circulating coin until those reforms were well established. What were these worth?

The answer to this question must be conjectural, but the conjecture can be responsible. Knowing a year's wages in the thirteenth century, for example, can suggest a comparable figure today and thus a rate of inflation that joins the two figures. Knowing the function of a dowry as capital formation (rather than consumption spending) enables us to relate that figure in the same way to one that would measure up to that function today. Approaching the problem from a different and complementary angle, economic historians, cited in the next paragraph, have actually compiled several series of wages and prices year by year from the mid-thirteenth to the mid-twentieth centuries. These again yield an inflation rate, which is encouragingly close to that suggested by the longer range point-to-point comparisons. Fundamentally, these conjectures enable us to feel the weight of cash totals in the thirteenth century by comparing them to their equivalents today. That weight is an essential component of the symbolic structure of these *fabliaux*—a part of their imagery, if you will—and that justifies the somewhat literal-minded number-crunching of the recovery effort.

We can grasp a vagrant bit of data and build on it. Malcolm Barber observes that in 1248 the third-class fare by ship to the Holy Land had become rather widely affordable at 56 *sous*, since this represented 112 days' earnings of a Paris tailor.[12] If we assume 200 working days in a year, that tailor had an annual income of 100 *sous* or 5 *livres*. If he could contemplate a trip to the Holy Land (and it would get cheaper), his income might be described as moderate but above subsistence. Perhaps, that is, it was equivalent to 6,400 English pounds or $12,000 today (or nearly $6.00/hour). Such a figure, with an adjustment for the increase in workdays in modern times, would represent annual inflation over 756 years of approximately 0.9 percent.[13] This is, in fact, a reasonable extrapolation of the inflation estimate made by E. R. Phelps-Brown and Sheila Hopkins in a 1956 study.[14] So let us unwind 0.9 percent inflation from the present back to 1250. We would probably agree that a person making $6,000 a year (or 3,200 pounds) today was scraping by barely, if at all. In 1250 that would have been 3 *deniers* a day, or two and a half pounds a year, the wage of a common laborer.

With this background we can return to Duby's rich peasant dowry of 75 *livres* and see that it was worth nearly 69,000 pounds today, or $130,000. We can also come back to *Constant du Hamel* and find evidence of pricing incompetence among Ysabel's suitors. The priest offers her 20 *livres*, immediately, without negotiation. And we know that he is serious because he shows up at her house bending beneath its weight in *deniers* contributed over the years by his rural parishioners.[15] Twenty *livres* is four years' income for that Paris tailor and eight for a common laborer. It is 19,000 modern pounds or $35,000. The magistrate's offer of 10 *livres* is still extravagant, equal to two years of the tailor's earnings or $17,000 today.

We must remember that the priest and the magistrate represent the estates of the church and of knighthood, and that their exemplars of money management are the bishop and the lord. In public, these exemplars use money as symbols of their power, principally by its lavish expenditure. No matter that in private they are assiduous in its accumulation. The calculation, anxiety, and meanness of spirit that may be involved in that accumulation are not the expression of their status; they are its unacknowledged props. To their peers and to their dependents, they must be seen to live for their pleasures, with no concern for their costs, and to bind their allies, and occasionally their dazzled inferiors, to themselves with thoughtless munificence.[16]

Such an ethos was obsolete, even atavistic, in the thirteenth century, and yet it retained its hold on the aristocratic imagination until well after the century had ended. As represented in *Constant du Hamel* by the parasitic magistrate and priest, it confronts in Ysabel and her husband a contrary ethos that it does not understand or even perceive. For wealthy peasants money is at once the reward of productive labor and the basis of its increase. As such it is something that they have come to understand, or, in the skewed distribution of wit established by the *fableor* in this particular household, something that Ysabel understands. Instead of a deliberately unmeasured medium of expression, it is something that she counts.

The gamekeeper represents a different sort of obsolescence. His offer of a ring worth a mark (or maybe more) belongs to a more realistic register, but that only highlights the loony excess of the other two bids. A mark is two-thirds of a pound, and we might add a little to that since to say that the ring "bien valoit .i. marc" (107) indicates a minimum estimate. So let us call it 15 *sous*, or $1,300 in today's money. That is six weeks' pay for the Paris tailor and may be the market price today for a night with a particularly desirable call-girl. In the thirteenth century, it falls within the price structure of "Le Foteor," the eponymous hero of another *fabliau* who charges 5 *livres* (200 *sous*) to serve an ugly woman but only 20 *sous* (plus some creature comforts) to serve a beauty. One could argue that the gamekeeper depends upon his own attractiveness, attested to by the author (102–3) and by Ysabel's chambermaid and accomplice (610), to get him a discount and to keep him in a frame of reference that is, after all, that of romance. For what he offers Ysabel, beneath or behind its announced monetary value, is a love token.

With the magistrate, the gamekeeper represents the knightly estate, being a retainer of the local lord, even though he is working here for his own account. But unlike the magistrate, the gamekeeper represents that aspect of seigneurial power that lends itself to idealized depiction on a tapestry, the noble *otium* of the hunt, linked by the happy ambiguity of "venery" to the noble *otium* of romantic love. So his obsolescence in the face of Ysabel's skills as a money manager is tinged with a certain nostalgia that we cannot summon for the magistrate and the priest, whose *desmesure* suggest that of a pair of drunken sailors. Their bids are in the register of the rich peasant's dowry reported by Duby, but the latter is a dowry after all, a capital base of future income.

So Ysabel's three suitors do not know the value of a *sou*. They do not, in fact, think in terms of power measured in fluid, numerical terms, and this puts them in the older feudal frame of reference where power comes from a fixed position in an estate fixed in a hierarchy. We see this when the three of them strategize over drinks. The magistrate proposes to the priest that one night with Ysabel would be worth a yearlong fast, translating the erotic into the religious and bypassing the monetary. The gamekeeper outbids him saying:

> Qui porroit sa bouche besier,
> Il en devroit souffrir la mort.
>
> [To have her lovely mouth to kiss
> One would agree to meet his death.]
> (ll. 160–61)[17]

And as this Tristan *manqué* escalates the ratio of price to reward—still with no monetary reference—we hear the dying echo of romance. The priest dismisses the two idealisms of his drinking partners:

> Qui de li se vueille entremetre
> de son chatel l'estuet jus metre
> tant que besoing, poverte & fain
> la face venire a reclaim.
> Ainsi doit on servir vilaine;
> fols est qui autrement s'en painne."
>
> [The man who's going to seduce her
> must rob her blind and thus reduce her

> to poverty and near starvation,
> then he'll have her cooperation.
> Now that's the way to treat a peasant—
> the man's a fool who says it isn't!]
> (ll. 169–74)[18]

This is the advice of the conspirator who bid four year's pay, unprompted, when confronted by Ysabel's dazzling beauty. The wickedness displayed here is complicated by foolishness displayed earlier, but, behind the regimes of seigneurial law and romance and religion, lurks mere coercion. The peasant's possession of money, to this seigneurial view, reveals not power but vulnerability. We control *him* (and her), the priest says, because we can take *it* away. There is no sense that we can *use* it, that is, money. Such recognition would give money the role of *intermediation* as a provider of *liquidity* (both terms of modern finance) that would require the further recognition of its solvent effect on the coercive prerogatives of rank.

One could, indeed, propose a more sophisticated, up-to-date approach to the conspirators' problem. They could arrange consciously (as do so many *fabliau* protagonists unencumbered by the blinders of privilege) to have their victim finance his own cuckoldry, extorting from him the bribes that Ysabel's beauty has extorted from them. One might even think that this is what the priest proposes, but a closer look at how the plot plays out reveals that it is not. With each of the suitors, the bribe extorted from Constant is one that Constant himself proposes, in a panic. It is, in this respect, a mirror image of the bribes offered to Ysabel. It is unplanned and irrational. The suitors take his offers even though the numbers do not match up. The priest bids 20 *livres* for Ysabel; Constant bids seven to bribe the diocese. The magistrate bids 10 *livres* for Ysabel; Constant bids 20 *livres* to bribe the lord's court. The gamekeeper bids 15 *sous* (in kind) for Ysabel; Constant offers 5 *livres* to settle the charge of poaching his trees. The two sets of bribes offset each other almost exactly, but they do so only in the aggregate and by accident, yielding no economically rational outcome to any individual.

Ysabel's plot to undo the three suitors has clear analogues in two other *fabliaux*, *Estormi* and *Le Prestre c'on porte*. In all three stories, the financial embarrassment of a nonnoble family provides an opportunity, apparently, to clerics or noble retainers to get at the beautiful woman of the house. *Constant du Hamel* sharpens the conflict by having the suitors cause rather than happily discover the financial embarrassment. All three stories feature exorbitant bribes for the ladies' favors. In *Estormi* it is 80 *livres*. In *Le Prestre c'on porte* it is 100 *livres*, or more than 173,000 of today's dollars. In all three the wife recognizes more clearly the value of the money and conceives a plot, but it is here that *Constant du Hamel* departs most decisively from its analogues. In each analogue, the wife confides in her husband, telling him what the priests want and what they will pay and suggesting a ruse, never fully defined, to secure the latter without yielding the former. We might expect that the details of the ruse are withheld as a narrative strategy, but, in fact, they never play out because at the crucial moment the husband breaks in and brains the would-be lover(s).

Thus sheer self-assertion in an act of violence aborts a design of wit. The husband simply cannot stand by, cannot suspend his status as head of the household and master of his wife, while she secures cash by shrewd manipulation. John, the husband in *Estormi*, even threatens his wife with his cudgel when he sees her shock at the first of three murders that he will commit. In response, "Cele se test"—she quiets down—and, in doing so, she cedes agency in generating the plot (in both senses) of this story. From here on it will be a matter of brute strength strategically allied with a kind of heroic stupidity in a victorious effort to move the dead weight of three incriminating corpses.[19]

John's dark self-assertion has a kind of idealized, separate embodiment in his nephew Estormi. I say idealized because Estormi is a creature of pure aggression, only aware, it seems, of the point at which his physical strength meets resistance. He has no interior consciousness and perceives none in others. His struggle with the miraculously reappearing corpse is simply a test of his strength that he must meet or suffer shame:

> Dont a il le deable el cors?
> Qui l'ont raporté ça dedenz?
> & s'il en i avoit .ii. cenz,
> si les enforrai je ainz le jor!"
> A cest mot a pris sanz retor,
> son pic & son sac & sa pele,
> puis a dit: "Ainz mes n'avint tele
> aventure en trestout cest monde!
> A foi, dame Dieus me confonde
> se j'enfouir ne le revois.
> Je seroie coars revois
> se mon oncle honir lessoie."

> [What? Has the fiend himself possessed
> his body? Who carried him, then?
> If there were two hundred of them,
> before day breaks I'd have them buried!
> Then, having said as much, he hurried
> to take his shovel, sack and hoe,

saying "There never has been so
strange a case in the universe!
May I incur the Lord God's curse
if I don't bury him again!
I'd be a base, fainthearted man
to let my uncle suffer shame."]
(ll. 370–81)[20]

This is a heroic boast—it could have been spoken by Beowulf—that commits the hero to a self-defining deed. When, in the second line, Estormi asks who has brought back the corpse, heroism seems threatened by the dawn of analysis. That is, he seems to look for a rational explanation for an apparently supernatural event. But the question is rhetorical. It serves merely to stage this event as a wonder and as a direct affront to his prowess. In the likeable modern formula, this is "all about him." He explicitly invokes the shame culture of heroism in his last line, after rather wittily embodying it in a rich rime on "revois." He will go back—"revois"—to rebury the body lest he be traitorous—"revois"—to his uncle.

Guillaume and Ydoine in *Le Prestre c'on porte* show a much higher degree of collaboration than John and Yfame, and the task of transporting the persistent corpse is shared out to the community in a way that dissipates heroic self assertion into more general social satire. But the agency in generating the plot is wrested just as decisively from Ydoine, and the ethos that displaces it could be said to have Estormi as its patron saint.

This is not, however, the way to get on in a money economy. It is true that John and Guillaume and their spouses get the money in the end, but they incur unacceptable levels of risk, rely too much on luck, and leave a residue of inert fleshly matter to haul away. The very essence of money's agency, on the other hand, is to catalyze transactions and leave no trace. This is the boast of the *Denier* to the Ewe, in a curious *debat* contemporary with our three stories.[21] The clutter of inert matter seeking exchange in a barter economy strangles markets, says the *Denier*:

Se failloie, marchiez faudroit:
Que sauroit chascuns qu'il vendroit?
L'en donroit brebis por cheval,
Et grosse toile por cendal,
Buef por asne, fuerre por fain.
Trestoz li mons morroit de fain
S'on donoit blanc pain por charbons
Et les jagleus por les poissons.

...Lus por harens, prunes por pomme?
Il n'est el monde si haut homme
Qui sanz moi puist monter en pris,
Quar je sui por toute rien pris.
Si sui cil qui tout taut et done.

[If it weren't for me the market would fold;
how would each vendor know what he sold?
One would give a ewe for a horse,
another fine silk for cloth that's coarse,
a steer for an ass, or fodder for grass.
A world-wide famine would come to pass
if white bread were offered a swap for charcoal
and fresh gladioli for filet of sole.
...Should a pike buy a herring, a plum buy an apple?
In all of this world there is no man who's happil-
y placed at the top not supported by me.
For each little thing I advance him the fee.
For all I'm the levy and the donation.]

The *Denier* boasts that he is the solvent of the distinctions that obstruct exchange. The paradox of money is that in doing so it is the only reliable arbiter of value. The *Denier* airily dismisses the Ewe's accusations of amorality. As comfortable with criminals as with cardinals, adaptable as *Faux Semblant* in *Le Roman de la Rose*, the *Denier* inhabits the same *demimonde* as the fabliau minstrel and in his very duplicity reveals a truth that can be counted, that is digital, and that dissolves the truth that is unique to a person or to a status.

As I said at the beginning, Ysabel, besides being beautiful, is the only character in her story or its two analogues who can count and carry sums in her head. When Constant begins to tell her his woes, she notes the numbers involved, the accounts payable, and runs them against numbers she has heard earlier from her husband's tormentors, numbers that now become accounts receivable. And, as she alone realizes, they balance. This knowledge informs her serenity as she assures her husband that there will be no net loss. Apparently Constant *could* pay the sums he promised, but doing so would impoverish him. The secret receivables of Ysabel's beauty, on the other hand, can make the transactions a wash. And Constant does not inquire into his wife's secrets.

The economy of wit established by the *fableor* in Constant's household does not exclude a touching teamwork between Constant's brawn and Ysabel's brain. It is featured twice, in analogous positions after two upsetting encounters with Ysabel's suitors, establishing a structural rhythm in the fabliau. After Ysabel rejects of the overtures of the priest, the magistrate, and the gamekeeper, we first learn of Ysabel's policy of benign secrecy with her husband:

> Me sire Constant du Hamel
> ne savoit mot de tout cest plet.
> Or oiez que la dame a fet:
> a son ostel en vint errant,
> s'a fet mangier le païsant,
> puis l'envoia en son labor
> ou il seut aler chascun jor.
>
> [But back to Constant du Hamel
> who of all this was ignorant,
> and to his wife, who simply went
> back home as quickly as she could
> and gave her working man his food
> and sent him to his daily toil
> of planting crops and tilling soil.]
> (ll. 138–44)

Later, after Constant's confrontations with the same three suitors, with their varied extortions, Ysabel calms him about the money he owes, money she knows that her beauty can extort from the extortionists, and the comforting routine of eating, sleeping, and working is reasserted (ll. 413–17).[22]

We see in these passages a productive enterprise, tied to routine and cooperation that is the legitimate source of wealth. The enterprise is one of transmutation. The labor that Constant *habitually* performs ("il seut aler" to the fields, i.e., he had the habit [*souloir*] of going) starts the process. The meals that Isabel prepares draw upon and sustain that labor. Her wit, finally, turns what exceeds that sustenance into money, which admits the household to the further opportunities of a market exchange economy. This peasant household steadily produces new wealth, in contrast the predations of the representatives of the clerical and lordly estates, which can only appropriate wealth already produced. The *fabliau* reveals in these passages a general sense of how the two privileged estates were parasitic on the peasant estate, the sole source of any new wealth. This perception is one that credibly emerges in a period of relative peace, when attention turns from the need for physical protection, which justified the seigneurial claims of the knightly class, to the means of maintaining and increasing wealth, that is, to the area of social activity in which the knight/lord cannot as readily justify his existence.[23] As Brian Stock notes, "The old formulae" that privileged the chivalric virtues "retained their appeal, but they less and less accurately described everyday economic exchange. The economy, although not recognized as such, became one of producers and consumers."[24]

In defense against this parasitism, Ysabel produces not a wash of payables and receivables, not the mere avoidance of loss, but a pure profit, because she is able to cancel the accounts payable while cashing the accounts receivable. That balance of payables and receivables allows her to embark on this last triumph in a benign state of "asymmetric risk." This term of modern financial analysis defines the position of an investor who, for example, buys for three dollars an option (or the right but not the obligation) to buy a stock for its current price—let us say $40.00—for a specified period. By doing so he limits his risk of loss during the term of the option to the price of the option. That is, if the stock drops even to zero he has only lost the three-dollar cost of his *right* to buy it at $40.00, a right he would, of course, not exercise. His ability to profit from the stock's rise, on the other hand, is unlimited, even though it is lessened by that same cost of the option. The calculation behind Ysabel's serenity is of essentially the same kind. Before she starts her highly profitable maneuvers against the three suitors, her potential losses are already covered.

The succession of tricks, the machinations of her "chanbriere" Galestrot, the reduction of the three naked suitors to commodities (and feathers at that) stored in a basket, are a rich comic invention, but I would like to focus on complementary procedural choices made by Ysabel and her opponents that make it all possible. The priest, the magistrate, and the game keeper accept payment in arrears, that is, they proceed on the basis of promises, with the promised service (e.g., dismissing a charge in the ecclesiastical court) preceding the promised payment. For the priest's promised disposal of charges against him, Constant promises 7 *livres* "next Wednesday," and the priest is satisfied. Constant promises 20 *livres* to the magistrate, not even specifying a date, and the magistrate is satisfied. He promises 5 *livres* to the gamekeeper "next Thursday," and the gamekeeper is satisfied. Constant is sincere in his promises, for this is how honest *men* deal with one another. His tormentors are, of course, insincere in their promises of relief from penalties that do not exist, but they are curiously punctilious in their acceptance of payment in arrears.

Ysabel, in contrast, requires payment in advance and puts herself at the fringe of patriarchial propriety. Money payment, always a morally risky matter in church teachings,[25] was thought to be more likely to be culpable if received in advance of the goods or, especially, the services that they compensated. That bad sort of payment is part of the significance of William Langland's Lady Meed in *Piers Plowman*, written in England a century or so later. In that poem Meed ("Reward") is reproached by Conscience because "Mede many tymes men yeveth before the doynge," a procedure "that is nother resoun ne ryhte."[26] Payment beforehand brought with it the obvious temptation to underperform when the money was already in hand or, hardly less culpable, the unwarranted assumption (cited specifically by Conscience) that one would be well enough or long-lived enough to take on a large task in response to (rather than in expectation of) a large payment. Payment in advance could also be a covert form of usury, when it introduced a difference between the price paid now rather than later when the goods purchased are delivered; this is the rationale of what we now call a futures contract.[27] There was, in general, a baleful logic to such a transaction in that it put the monetary value before the intrinsic value of what it paid for, logically prior because chronologically prior. The world of intrinsic value is the older feudal world of promises that bind and rewards that follow promises fulfilled. It is to this world that the male characters in *Constant du Hamel* are faithful, even the corrupt characters. This is how men (real men, true men) deal with each other. Money in advance, on the other hand, means that money itself, not a promise made and fulfilled, *makes things happen*. Too much of that and soon one will accede to the *Denier*'s claim to the Ewe that he is essential to a high status that should have an intrinsic moral basis. Money accepted in arrears shows a proper deference to the value that it imperfectly represents.

Ysabel will have none of this. Perhaps because she has learned from her three suitors that in their eyes money is a perfectly adequate representation of her intrinsic worth, the question of priority is settled in a purely practical way. Her procedure—cash in advance, please—is the same as that of "Le Foteor"—or any professional in the field to which the feudal assumptions of her three suitors have, in fact, assigned her. As John A. Alford has noted, "Payment in advance was required, typically, by those who operated on the fringes of the law—shysters, quacks, prostitutes. Because the law did not recognize contracts that were contrary to morals…, such persons had no legal recourse if their clients were dissatisfied and refused to pay."[28] She is, perforce, a practitioner of the new money economy, while the suitors and her husband remain in the old. That old economy insists on intrinsic human values expressible only in acts, not in cash, answerable only to qualitative not quantitative evaluation, and most heroically rendered in the strong arm that swings the sword or the cudgel. Ysabel must hold this old order in abeyance until she has secured the awards only available to the new money economy. When she has done so, she reveals all to Constant and releases the anarchic force represented elsewhere by Estormi, a force that she understands and therefore controls.

That display of force is the most trying episode for the modern reader. At the urging of the fair and virtuous Ysabel, Constant successively rapes the wives of the magistrate and gamekeeper and the mistress of the priest as their humiliated consorts watch, cowering, from the basket of feathers. As so often in the *fabliaux*, we confront the distance between the story's ethos and our own, between what made its audience laugh and what might make us laugh.[29] Another marker of that distance is the explicitly performative dimension of the closing episode. The rapes are presented for an audience of three, Constant's tormentors hidden in the basket of feathers (as Constant knows). This audience is then turned naked out of the barrel, which has been set afire by Constant, to unwillingly perform the ordeal of being mauled by Constant's dogs, for the benefit of an audience of the entire peasant village. Their vows, witnessed by this audience and indemnifying Constant and Ysabel, confirm what their performance has already demonstrated.

The combination of elaborate performance and an oath that glosses that performance recalls the survival into a literate age of preliterate symbolic acts that solemnized oaths committing one to a change in status. An instance from the eleventh century cited by R. W. Southern involved "a certain man . . . called William" who committed himself to a monastery as a serf and, to make "this gift . . . more certain and apparent, . . . put the bell-rope round his neck and placed four pennies from his own head on the alter of St. Martin in recognition of serfdom" an act witnessed by a dozen men. Though accompanied by an oath in words, Southern argues that the act itself was "an essential part—perhaps *the* essential part of the business," requiring "publicity" that would impress "the occasion and its significance on the memory."[30]

If we apply the same sort of analysis to the closing acts of *Constant du Hamel*, we find that they too, in their way, mark a change in status. Constant's tormentors all assumed that their rank made Ysabel available to them because she was a peasant's wife. The crude force of this assumption is clearest in the priest's speech to his co-conspirators over drinks. In raping each of their women as they look on, Constant shows instead that their women are absolutely available to him. In turning out, first, the naked wives and then the feathered, naked husbands into the public street, Constant demonstrates to the witnessing community that the earlier demonstration has been enacted. The indemnifying oaths of the three merely confirm the testimony of their nakedness, their subhuman coat of feathers, and their being chased down like game by Constant's dogs.

They had threatened Constant with ensnarement in a legal system that was literate, a matter of written law only dimly available to his powers of defense. In each case, his promised pay-off is meant to keep him out of this alien system. The encroachment of writing on the field of law in the Middle Ages, by which writing came not merely to memorialize obligations but to enact them, has been the subject of some of the more notable medieval scholarship of the last three decades.[31] A common theme that this scholarship shares with Southern is the resistant survival of preliterate ritual enactment into the new age of scribal enactment. This is what we see in the conclusion of *Constant du Hamel.*

The *fabliau* episode also seems remarkably class conscious. The witnessing villagers suggest a solidarity extending beyond the household of the protagonist, on behalf of a preliterate self-assertion, expressed in a gesture of brute strength and crudity more startling than that of Estormi with his hoe but very much of its kind. But that solidarity of class is not finally determinative here. Constant's three rapes are a performance—they are "staged"—in more than one sense. Underlying, or undermining, the enacting power of Constant's gesture is the sheerly manipulative power of Ysabel's trickery that made that gesture possible. Her role as impresario makes the action no more substantial than the liquidity of the *Denarius*, who dissolves all solidarities and clears all markets. The protests of the Ewe, and of medieval orthodoxy in general, against this solvent power were oddly echoed some 500 years later by Karl Marx and Friedrich Engels in their description of the triumph of the *Denarius* (or the "cash nexus") in bourgeois capitalism:

> All fixed, fast-frozen relations, with their train of ancient and venerable prejudices and opinions, are swept away, all new-formed ones become antiquated before they can ossify. All that is solid melts into air, all that is holy is profaned, and man is at last compelled to face with sober senses, his real conditions of life, and his relations with his kind.[32]

The extremity of bourgeois turmoil that Marx and Engels saw was, of course, for them a symptom of a coming collapse of the old order, beyond which they confidently foresaw the new order of a classless society established by a victorious proletariat. They shared with medieval orthodoxy an aversion to the solvent power of money. Its "uncertainty and agitation" were not for them the dust kicked up by a socially creative daemon. The fact that it could never achieve rest was enough to discredit such an idea and to mark it as a symptom of sin, though they would not use this term. For Marx and Engels, like medieval theologians, looked forward to a state of stability and rest in which public power was no longer political because the antagonisms of class that bring politics into being would have been abolished. They looked—to be sure, in a different place—for a paradise remarkably like that of Dante. Upon achieving their "association, in which the free development of each is the condition for the free development of all," one could say with the souls (apparently) in Dante's sphere of the moon, "essere in carità è qui *necesse*" (to live in disinterested love is here a necessary condition).[33]

That, however, is not the way of comedy as we use the term in discussing the fabliaux, a genre that gives the best lines and the last word to the *Denarius*. Its delight in the sweeping away of "fixed, fast-frozen relations, with their train of ancient and venerable prejudices and opinions" is an end in itself. To take the next step into the earthly or heavenly paradise would put an end to laughter, not the business of a "conte à rire."[34] In the *fabliaux*, the prize of the reader's favor goes to the character who best controls the agents of disorder that drive its plot, and in many *fabliaux* (most strikingly in *Constant du Hamel*) the agent is money. Ysabel's mastery of money enables her to subvert not only the hierarchies of feudal status but that last and most stubborn hierarchy of gender.

## Notes

This chapter grew out of a paper given in 2003 in an NEH Seminar on the fabliau and the medieval sense of the comic, directed by R. Howard Bloch at Yale University. I hope that, in its present form, it conveys some of the intellectual stimulation of that happy colloquy.

1. References to *Constant du Hamel*, *Estormi*, and *Le Prestre c'on porte* are to texts with translation by Nathaniel Dubin, to be published by the University of Pennsylvania Press and reproduced here by his kind permission. I have compared Professor Dubin's OF text with that of the *Nouveau receuil complet des fabliaux (NRCF)*, ed. Willem Noomen and Nico van den Boogaard (Assen, Netherlands: VanGorcum, 1983), and noted differences from their critical texts (presented along with diplomatic texts of each manuscript of each fabliau).
2. See Robert S. Lopez, *The Commercial Revolution of the Middle Ages, 950–1350* (Cambridge: Cambridge University Press, 1976 [1971]), esp. pp. vii, 27–48, 56–60, 70–79. On the development of money see John F. Chown, *A History of Money: From AD 800* (London: Routledge, 1994), pp. 1–40; an unfinished early treatment is Marc Bloch, *Esquisse d'un histoire monétaire de l'Europe* (Paris: Librairie Armand Colin, 1954). On the role of money as "a necessary pre-condition for" the commercial revolution of "the long thirteenth century," see Peter Spufford, *Money and Its Use in Medieval Europe* (Cambridge: Cambridge University Press, 1988), pp. 240–63. More recently, Joel Kaye, *Economy and Nature in the Fourteenth Century: Money, Market Exchange, and the Emergence of Scientific Thought* (Cambridge: Cambridge University Press, 1998) has argued that the more pervasive monetization of Europe in the thirteenth and fourteenth centuries encouraged a quantitative analysis that anticipated modern scientific thought as the discernment of unchanging essences yielded to the measurement of dynamic processes.

3. On technology, see Georges Duby, *Rural Economy and Country Life in the Medieval West,* trans. Cynthia Postan (Columbia: University of South Carolina Press, 1968), pp. 108–11; Werner Rösener, *The Peasantry of Europe*, trans. Thomas M. Barker (Oxford: Blackwell, 1994), pp. 42–43, 53–56; Robert Fossier, *Peasant Life in the Medieval West*, trans. Juliet Vale (Oxford: Blackwell, 1988), pp. 98–101.
4. On climatic change, see H. H. Lamb, *Climate, History and the Modern World,* second edition (London: Routledge, 1995), pp. 177–82, and *Weather, Climate & Human Affairs* (London: Routledge, 1988), pp. 40–74; and the editors' introduction to T. M. Wrigley, M. J. Ingram, G. Farmer, eds., *Climate and History: Studies in Past Climates and Their Impact on Man* (Cambridge: Cambridge University Press, 1981), pp. 3–50, which refers to the "Medieval Warm Epoch (MWE)."
5. Duby, *Rural Economy,* pp. 282–84.
6. Fossier, *Peasant Life*, p. 76. Other information in this paragraph draws on pp. 74–77.
7. Fossier, *Peasant Life*, p. 146.
8. Landlords eventually shifted to fixed term leases more frequently in the course of the thirteenth century. See Duby, *Rural Economy*, pp. 74–81 (on clearing), 237–39 (on fixed rents); M. M. Postan, ed., *The Cambridge Economic History of Europe*, second edition (Cambridge: Cambridge University Press, 1966), pp. 323–27 (in a chapter by F. L. Ganshof and A. Verhulst); Fossier, *Peasant Life*, pp. 142–45; Spufford, *Money and Its Uses*, pp. 243–45. A subtly argued account of the conditions and motivations that led to the high rate of manumission of serfs in thirteenth-century France is found in William Chester Jordan, *From Servitude to Freedom: Manumission in the Sénonais in the Thirteenth Century* (Philadelphia: University of Pennsylvania Press, 1986).
9. A comprehensive treatment of this traditional contempt, with extensive bibliography, is in Paul Freedman, *Images of the Medieval Peasant* (Stanford, CA: Stanford University Press, 1999), esp. the introduction and Chapter 6.
10. Manuscript B (Berne, Bibl. De la Bourgeoisie, 354, fol. 80c–88d) describes Constant's ugliness in ll. 731–43. See *NRCF*, I, 85, and the note on 338–39. The interpolation begins at a point parallel to l. 744 in MS A (Paris, Bilb. Nat. fr. 837), followed by Dubin, and to l. 678 in the critical edition of *NRCF*.
11. See, for example, William Chester Jordan, *Women and Credit in Pre-Industrial and Developing Societies* (Philadelphia: University of Pennsylvania Press, 1993), pp.11–82; Kathryn L. Reyerson, "Women in Business in Medieval Montpellier," in Barbara A. Hanawalt, ed., *Women and Work in Preindustrial Europe* (Bloomington: Indiana University Press, 1986), pp. 117–44. In the present volume the most relevant chapters (which deal with members of the upper aristocracy) are those of Ana Maria S. A. Rodrigues and Manuela Santos Silva, Theresa Earenfight, and Helen A. Gaudette.
12. Malcolm Barber, *The Two Cities: Medieval Europe 1050–1320* (London: Routledge, 1992), p. 74.

13. There are some complications in this calculation that should be laid out candidly. The work-year of only 200 days reflects the large number of religious holidays and "rest days," (in addition to Sundays) that were observed in the Middle Ages. See Edith Rodgers, *Discussion of Holidays in the Later Middle Ages* (New York: Columbia University Press, 1940), pp. 10–11. A straight comparison of the five-pound annual income to an equivalent income in 2004 would yield an average annual rate of increase of nearly 1.0 percent, but this would obscure the important compensation received in holidays by the medieval worker, in comparison to his modern counterpart. Another way of understanding that nonmonetary compensation would be as time released from wage-earning labor for the direct production of food that was the peasant's main source of nourishment, food that his modern counterpart would purchase rather than grow. So I have "grossed up" the medieval income to its 260-day equivalent, or six and a half pounds, before comparing it to the modern income. The result is an annual rate of change of 0.916 percent over 756 years. In subsequent calculations, I have used 750 as the compounding period (for a multiple of 933.3 times 1250 prices) and rounded numbers to the nearest hundred or thousand. I have assumed that the British pound (the best-credentialed descendent of the Carolingian pound) will buy 1.85–1.88 U.S. dollars today. This, of course, is the most perishable of my assumptions. In fact, as this goes to press, the pound has gotten costlier, but there are plausible reasons to consider this anomalous.
14. E. R. Phelps-Brown and Sheila Hopkins, "Seven Centuries of Building Wage," *Economica* 22 (1955): 195–206, reprinted in *A Perspective on Wages and Prices* (London: Methuen, 1981), pp. 1–12. Phelps-Brown and Hopkins survey wage rates, in pennies, of a craftsman in Southern England from 1264 to 1954 (pp. 11–12). I used their figures through 1949 so that I could join them with two other series: (1) a composite of the Implicit GDP Deflators for the United Kingdom, France, and the United States from 1950 to 1980, as found in *World Tables: The Third Edition* (Baltimore: Johns Hopkins University Press, 1983) and (2) changes in the U.S. Consumer Price index from 1981 to 2003 available online at Inflation Data.Com http://inflationdata.com/inflation/default.asp (accessed on 27 March 2009).
15. Philippe Ménard argues, in *Les Fabliaux: Contes à rire du Moyen Age* (Paris: Presse Universitaires de France, 1983), pp. 73–74, that the chronic venery of country priests in the *fabliaux* was probably not factual but that their generally assumed wealth probably was.
16. Compare the "*largitas*" of the "Crusader Queen" Melisende, with its apparent extravagance backed by actual calculation, in the discussion by Helen A. Gaudette in this volume.
17. Dubin follows the copy text A (Bibliothèque Nationale, francais 837) in reading "porroit" in the first line, while NRCF substitues "vorroit" of D (Bibl. de la Bourgeoisie, 354) in its critical edition (l. 157).
18. Dubin follows A; *NRCF*'s critical edition (ll. 160–70, 176–79) introduces variants from the other MSS.

19. An interesting deconstructionist reading of *Estormi* focuses on the embarrassment of these corpses. See Gregory B. Stone, "The Insistence of the Body in the Old French Fabliau Estormi," *Exemplaria* (1990): 449–73. See also Marie-Thérèse Lorcin, "Les Revenants dans les Fabliaux," *Reinardus* 2 (1989): 91–101.
20. *Estormi* appears only in A, and so there is no disagreement between Dubin's text and that of the *NRCF.*
21. *Du Denier et de la Brebis* from MS 7218 Bibliothèque Royale is found in *Noveau receuil de contes, dits, fabliaux et autre pieces,* ed. Achille Jubinal, vol. 2 (Paris: Chez Callamel, 1842), pp. 265–72. This edition does not number lines; the passage quoted here is on p. 272 and is the *Denier*'s triumphant last word in the *debat.* The translation is mine. The French tradition of satires featuring the personified *Denier* (or *Dan Denier*) is described and documented in John A. Yunck, *The Lineage of Lady Meed* (South Bend, IN: University of Notre Dame Press, 1963), pp. 211–6. A strikingly similar instance, *De dom Argent,* is quoted on p. 215.
22. In *NRCF* critical edition, ll. 398–412, with some variants.
23. In the fabliau *Le Chevalier qui fait parler les cons,* the title character's peculiar talent makes his fortune in a time "when all war gave out...and tournaments were forbidden" (ll. 35, 37), leaving him with an obsolete profession and a range of unmarketable skills.
24. Brian Stock, *The Implications of Literacy: Written Language and Models of Interpretation in the Eleventh and Twelfth Centuries* (Princeton, NJ: Princeton University Press, 1983), p. 86. Stock aligns the effects of what we now call "numeracy" with those of literacy in isolating values and concepts in an impersonal code (p. 85). On the same effect of advancing literacy in England, see M. T. Clanchy, *From Memory to Written Record: England 1066–1307,* second edition (Oxford: Blackwell, 1993).
25. A sentiment attributed to Pope Leo the Great (440–61) that it is difficult to avoid sin in the course of buying and selling (*difficile est inter ementis vendentisque commercium not intervenire peccatum*) was repeated through the centuries, down to the twelfth and thirteenth, when canon lawyers struggled to rationalize these activities in a monetized age. They were never able to conclude a final peace between theology and an activity that necessarily involved one party trying to get the better of another. Their efforts contended with assertions such as that of Peter Damian (1007–72) that avarice (not pride) was "radix malorum." See the discussions in John W. Baldwin, "The Medieval Theories of the Just Price," *Transactions of the American Philosophical Society* 49:4 (1959), pp. 12–15, 67–68; and Lester K. Little, *Religious Poverty and the Profit Economy in Medieval Europe* (Ithaca, NY: Cornell University Press, 1978), pp. 29–41.
26. William Langland, *Piers Plowman: The C Version,* ed. George Russell and George Kane (London: Athlone Press, 1997), III. 293–94. I have substituted "th" and "y" for their Middle English graphs and have changed the Middle English alternation of "u" and "v" to modern orthographic practice. For the background of Langland's passage, see Andrew Galloway,

*The Penn Commentary on Piers Plowman*, vol. 1 (Philadelphia: University of Pennsylvania Press, 2006), pp. 334–36; and John A. Alford, *Piers Plowman: A Glossary of the Legal Diction* (Cambridge: Brewer, 1988), p. 120 (defining "Pre Manibus" payments, or payments in advance).

27. On contracts that featured advance or delayed payment, see Baldwin, *Medieval Theories*, pp. 49–50 and Lopez, *Commercial Revolution*, pp. 70–79, 103–6. Thomas Aquinas argues that advance payment (or payment "pre manibus") at a discount to the fair price can constitute usury: "[I]f a buyer wishes to buy goods at a lower price than what is just, for the reason that he pays for the goods before they can be delivered, it is a sin of usury; because again this anticipated payment of money has the character of a loan, the price of which is the rebate on the just price of the goods sold. On the other hand if a man wishes to allow a rebate on the just price in order that he may have his money sooner, he is not guilty of the sin of usury" *Summa Theologiae*, IIa, IIae, qu. 78, art. 2, *respondeo*, at http://www.newadvent.org/summa/3078.htm, accessed 23 July 2008. Two things are notable here. First, everything seems to turn on intention; formally identical deals are usurious or not depending on what the buyer or seller wants and on whose wish initiates the deal. Second, the reasoning about the discount constituting a loan at interest is precisely that used in constructing a modern futures contract, except that the latter is not considered sinful; the price of such a contract when sold is determined in part by the prevailing rate of interest.
28. Alford, *Piers Plowman: A Glossary*, p. 120.
29. An intelligent rationalization of this concluding episode is offered by Gabriel Bianciotto, "De *Constant du Hamel*," *Renardus* 6 (1993): 15–30. His most interesting argument is that the audience of *Constant* would recognize an allusion to *Le Roman de Renart* in the violence of the episode, a recognition that would qualify and somewhat anesthetize its response.
30. R. W. Southern, *The Making of the Middle Ages* (New Haven, CT: Yale University Press, 1953), pp. 99–100.
31. See Stock, *Implications of Literacy*, pp. 12–87; Clanchy, *From Memory to Written Record*; and Richard Firth Green, *A Crisis of Truth: Literature and Law in Ricardian England* (Philadelphia: University of Pennsylvania Press, 1999), which links the regime of written law to the semantic shift of English "truth" and "true" from integrity ("I'll be true to you") to the adequation of concept and thing ("What you say is true").
32. *The Communist Manifesto*, with an introduction by A. J. P. Taylor (Hammondsworth, UK: Penguin, 1967), p. 83.
33. Marx and Engels, *Manifesto*, p. 105; Dante, *La commedia secondo l'antica volgata*, ed. Giorgio Petrocchi. 4 vols. (Milan: A. Mondadori, 1966–1967).
34. The famous definition of fabliau by Joseph Bédier, in *Les fabliaux: Etudes de littérature populaire et d'histoire littéraire du moyen age*, 6th edition (1893; repr. Paris: Champion, 1964), p. 39.

# CHAPTER 2

# TAKE ALL MY WEALTH AND LET MY BODY GO

*M. C. Bodden*

Money is the great signifier of exchange. In the narratives, "The Franklin's Tale," "The Wife of Bath's Prologue," and *The Book of Margery Kempe*, money is exchangeable with permissible rape, with the right to recalculate the marriage debt, with the right to qualify the terms of *soveraynetee*, the right to redemption of status; it is exchangeable with moral superiority, with despair, with enjoyable sex, with circulation of the self, and in "Franklin's Tale," it is literally exchangeable with franchise[1] and with *trouthe*. Even for a man—in this case the chicken-hearted knight in the "Wife of Bath's Tale" who pleads with the loathly hag, "Taak al my good [wealth] and lat my body go"—money is viewed by him as interchangeable with his (aristocratically privileged) sexuality.[2]

But when women have more money than their husbands, money as a signifier of exchange takes a remarkable form. There, in the above-mentioned narratives, a startling pattern is revealed: all three women, Dorigen, the Wife of Bath, and Margery Kempe, are married to men who need money or who need the distinctions that are maintained by money. Due to their husbands' or suitors' actions, all three women are subject to arbitrary tempests of probable economic loss or the loss of symbolic capital, that is, the prestige, status, and social control perceived as redeemable in economic terms.[3] All three women, however much their wealth, are compelled to negotiate their way to their freedom challenged by lovers or proscribed by husbands. Each is forced to use her resources to transact her freedom. What is significant, however, is that in order to transact her freedom, each chooses to transact her identity. All three redefine themselves as a woman, and thus negotiate their freedom by negotiating their identity. They successfully do so, in varying degrees.

First, by testing and imagining identities of the past. Second, by placing the construct of the public identities of noble women or women of means at the center of their debate with the past. Third, by repositioning what a woman is. In the process of these endeavors, they shift from being docile recipients of masculine knowledge to being disrupters of that same knowledge, interrogating its terms and redefining them—thereby "plotting" their own reality, and frequently their own public identity, with a new, positive inflection of money and power. In this chapter, I focus on "Franklin's Tale," somewhat on "Wife of Bath's Prologue," and, finally, very briefly on *The Book of Margery Kempe.*

## S/he Who Has Most Money "is most fre"

In "The Franklin's Tale" more so than in the other two narratives, money controls the discourse and the power relations between women and men. First, because she has wealth, position, and prestige Dorigen does not need to be saved through anyone's chivalric deeds. In fact, her money, combined with her symbolic capital, serves to delegitimize the ideology of the chivalric tradition. This becomes evident in the opening characterization of Arveragus, the knight who wishes to win her. Although Arveragus is introduced as engaged in years of "many a labour, many a greet emprise,"[4] we realize almost immediately that these labors are not the usual chivalric exploits intended to save widows or orphans, or rescue Dorigen or protect her environs. Chivalry is not even the issue. Rather, the concern being forefronted is Arveragus's anxiety about Dorigen's lineage: she "comen of so heigh kynrede."[5] And because she is of so high a lineage, Arveragus cannot bring himself even to address her. Then, too, such high lineage would assure symbolic capital for him. But he must first accrue some such capital for himself to better position himself. So, he sets about accumulating a reputation through deeds. Dorigen's nobility, however, is no mere set piece. Not only are her wealth and status the signifiers of prestige, power, and authority, and not only do they control the entire discourse of the tale, but they also shape the two fundamental themes underlying the tale. The first theme is expressed in the famous question at the end of the tale, "who is most fre?"—that is, who is most magnanimous or generous of spirit and money? The second, related, theme asks how one navigates *soveraynetee* and servitude in marriage. It should be noted that acute sensitivity to hierarchical markers asserts itself in every character, Arveragus, Aurelius, and the magician, and even in Dorigen. Each attempts to locate her-/himself within the spectrum of rank and reputation. This is the reason for the famous question at the end of the tale, "who is most fre?" Most scholars view that question as a narrative twist at the tale's end, but in fact Chaucer establishes it as a central theme from the tale's beginning. Of the first seventy-two lines of "Franklin's Tale," all but thirteen concern the effect of hierarchical markers on power relations in marriage. That subject sets up the tale's other, related theme: how to relinquish *soveraynetee* in a marriage and yet maintain the fiction of *soveraynetee*? Chaucer's strategy of devoting so many of the opening lines to the problem of navigating *soveraynetee* and servitude has led critics to regard the tale as his representation of what constitutes a balanced marriage. However, this ignores the fact that Chaucer deliberately problematizes the issue of balance by making the wife, Dorigen, of greater lineage and status than her husband. In other words, her identity as wife is linked to her wealth. And this matters. In marital relations, *soveraynetee* should be her husband's by law, but it was hers by lineage, breeding, and very likely economic wealth (judging from her leisure activities—the games of the wealthy—during Arveragus's two-year absence).

Renouncing "maistrye" and pledging mutuality in "lordshipe and servage" in their marriage vows would seem to resolve the question of *soveraynetee* and servitude for Arveragus and Dorigen.[6] But, in fact, *soveraynetee* and servitude are precisely what challenge Dorigen's freedom and her identity early in her marriage. Shortly after they are married, Arveragus, intent upon labors and deeds abroad, what he calls his "prosperitee," absents himself for two years. In that interim, Aurelius, a squire who is part of the circle of Dorigen and her friends, declares his love for Dorigen. She flatly rejects his declaration. Minutes later, as a way of softening the blow, she tells him that when the rocks, an endless threat to Arveragus's ship, are no longer along the coastal waters or seen along them, she will love Aurelius. Aurelius realizes that the task she sets him is meant to be an adamant refusal of him because he labels it an "inpossible," meaning that by nature it was a physically impossible situation. Two years of dolor and lamentation later, Aurelius, with his brother, engages the services of a magician/illusionist who, through astrological tables and lunar calculation, makes the rocks appear to disappear beneath a tide. Aurelius now confronts Dorigen with his claim to her. His "quest" to win her is clearly one that views Dorigen's body as goods that may be valued and exchanged, demonstrating thereby that the discourse of chivalry is the discourse of sexual economy.[7]

Dorigen's freedom is literally under siege. Her first response is to wholly forfeit her freedom by committing suicide. As she deliberates upon the classic stories of noble (and wealthy) women of the past who chose to commit suicide rather than permit violation of their bodies, Dorigen confronts the inherited model of gender identity: the Hieronimic tradition of the suffering ideal of womanhood.[8] The fact that she does not act upon the ideology of the suffering woman has been perceived by critics as a failure of resolve. She has spent two days deliberating upon this lengthy list of exempla, they say, and then does nothing. My view is that her ability to deploy the material as a form of assessing and critiquing esteemed women of the past,[9] an ability privileged by her status and wealth that provided her the education and leisure to read, was part of the transaction of her freedom. Her two days of dialoguing with the tradition were also two days of interrogating it. In doing so, she not only exposes the oppressive patriarchal values that counsel innocent women to kill themselves, but as she imagines their public identities she imagines her own. In contrast to those women who uncritically leapt to their death, she presents herself as a conflicted woman. Her own identity, in contrast to their singular self-annihilating response, is a more personal, complex identity. Repeatedly, as she imagines set after set of women who chose death over (the patriarchal construct of) dishonor, Dorigen asks herself "Why sholde I thanne to dye been in drede?" (l. 1386) or "Wel *oghte* a wyf rather hirselven slee/ Than be defouled, as it thynketh me" (ll. 1397–98, emphasis mine), or, again, "I wol conclude that it is bet for me/ To sleen myself than been defouled thus" (ll. 1422–23). What seems to emerge in her debate with these female identities is their *historical* identities—detached, largely, from their cultural identities. Intensity of absolute will characterizes each self-immolating woman (a masculine trait, interestingly enough), yet nuanced emotional, cognitive, or experiential qualities are absent. These are women of a Roman past, subjected to the consequences of war and forced marriages. None of the rapists are courtly lovers who courted their victims, none of them won their victims by apparently achieving the task set by the victim. None of them seems to have had a marital relationship contingent on openness and mutuality. If Dorigen is the type of woman who could confront the nature of the marriage-vow tradition and reinterpret it with an eye toward balance in marriage, would she not also be a woman who would critically confront female identities of the past and attempt to reinterpret them with an eye toward justice and harmony?

Then, too, in order for the patriarchal value of chastity to motivate any woman to engage in self-immolation, chastity must needs be stressed as *the* singular heroic path for women to take.[10] However, what captures the reader's attention as Dorigen reviews the women's heroic acts is the fact of their innocence, their faultlessness; the reader/audience is confronted as forcefully with the *innocence* of the women as s/he is with their suicides. And this is where constructing the public identities of noble women or women of means as the center of her debate with the past yields an interesting effect. The act of ticking off faultless woman after faultless woman produces the cumulative effect of confronting the audience (and, very likely, Dorigen) with the staggering senselessness of the deaths of innocent women. But it also accounts for Dorigen's repositioning of herself as a woman. She openly debates the extremes of the women's performance. The length of her pondering has been argued by critics to be absurdly long, even excessive.[11] I think that it is deliberately absurd, deliberately over the top—the very extravagance of the willful loss of life by innocent women has a way of distancing it from natural human responses. It problematizes their actions as any sort of model of an authentic resolution to a dilemma constructed by men for men's sake. The issue is not simply Dorigen "doing nothing." It is Dorigen not accepting the inherited construct of gender identity. It is Dorigen negotiating her identity; transacting her freedom.

Strangely enough, when Dorigen reveals to Arveragus, on his return, the condition of her troth or "trouthe" with Aurelius, Arveragus does not inquire into two significant features of the condition of that "trouthe." First, he does not inquire into the fact, much less raise an objection, that her pledge was openly intended to be no genuine pledge. Aurelius had immediately grasped that when he called it an "inpossible." Second, Arveragus does not inquire into the glaring fact that an illusion, or the occurrence of the tide, is not actually an honoring of Dorigen's request, however bizarre that request. Here, then, when the chivalric code would have dictated that he *should* have prevented her from violation by Aurelius, Arveragus instead proposes that her "trouthe" is more important than her fidelity in marriage, and demands that she give herself to Aurelius. Not only has he reasserted the sovereignty that he had renounced in their vows (thus failing in his own "trouthe"), but he has put his symbolic capital, Dorigen, into circulation. As did Aurelius's suit, Arveragus, too, has reduced Dorigen's symbolic capital—her prestige, status, economic wealth—to sexual economy. Whether out of despair or unreflected recklessness or the budding impulse to resist coercive hegemonic practices, Dorigen's next step is to disobey Arveragus. He has forbidden her, on pain of death, to speak to anyone of this pledge to Aurelius. Yet, Dorigen takes the busiest and most visible path through town, making her grief obvious to all who see her as she meets Aurelius. This is not at all the ideal suffering woman. She has gone public with the expression of her feeling. The wildness of her grief moves Aurelius (although he is more impressed with Arveragus's willingness to turn Dorigen over to him for the sake of keeping her pledge). In his recognition of her grief and of Arveragus's commitment to "trouthe," Aurelius cancels the "debt." In turn, the magician cancels Aurelius's debt of 500 pieces of gold.

If money is the great signifier of exchange in this narrative, then the final question, "who is most fre?" really means "Who has the most money? Or most symbolic capital?" For one thing, the question equates the act of forgiving a monetary debt with the act of turning one's wife over to another man. And we have already seen that Arveragus's franchise is exchangeable with Aurelius's gold[12] that, in turn, is interchangeable with the magician's covenant ("trouthe"). But this is all hilariously complicated by the issue of the relationship between money and illusion itself. Dorigen's promise to "love" is to be redeemed in the medium of an illusion, namely, the removal of the rocks. The frank intention of Aurelius and the magician was to secure Dorigen's body by means of that illusion. Arveragus exchanges his *trouthe* (his franchise) for an illusion and willingly exchanges his wife's body for an unquestioned illusion. Complicating all of this is the fact that the illusion of the removal of the rocks is to be redeemed in the medium of a second illusion, namely, money—which, as Jochen Hörisch says, is "not covered by anything other than itself."[13] Since money is itself merely a sign and its relation to what it stands for is both arbitrary and symbolic, and since truth and franchise are interchangeable with money, then, ultimately what Chaucer is saying is that "trouthe" and franchise are arbitrary and symbolic. It is, however, characteristic of him to plant within that theme an ironic subtext: "S/he who has most money is most fre."[14]

## "...a lusty oon,/ And faire, and riche, and yong, and wel bigon"

As I mentioned earlier, the primary focus of this chapter is Dorigen, with a secondary look at the Wife of Bath and an even briefer look at Margery Kempe.[15] The plentiful evidence for the Wife of Bath's use of land and resources to establish her social, marital, and economic identity would easily constitute a separate monograph elsewhere. Here I am interested largely in a particular aspect of that identity, namely the relationship between the Wife of Bath as businesswoman and her marital prosperity. Clearly, the Wife of Bath's way of getting and amassing money is inseparable from her impulse to construct her public identity and to reposition what a woman is. A woman's public identity was not, largely, an economic or political identity in medieval England. Her public identity was as a wife, a widow, or an unmarried woman—but that's precisely what the Wife of Bath contests.

When we meet her, Alisoun, the Wife of Bath, has been four times widowed. And while widowhood could "open doors of choice" it was also the surest way for a woman to lose her identity and certainly the most precarious way for her to negotiate her freedom.[16] In fact, where widows were concerned, each marriage and remarriage, "recast her identity"—explicitly giving to her "a new surname." Indeed, the consequences of each remarriage were multiple and momentous even if, at times, profitable. Not only did each remarriage gave to her a "new family of primary obligation," but also "a new male cover figure"[17] changing her legal status thereby making it impossible for her to enter contracts or assert or defend [her] rights in court, except with the consent and assistance of [her] husband.[18] Each change of identity presented the widow/wife with new kinships, with a new home to manage, and with "potential rivalry and jealousy from other members of her deceased husband's family."[19] Anna Dronzek's chapter in this volume contends, in fact, that "the stronger a woman's family identity was, the less frequently such a woman would face legal challenges to land held by right of that family identity."[20] Moreover, if a widow remarried, her "in-laws might well challenge her continued guardianship of her children" from her previous marriage.[21] Then, too, each remarriage faced her with new interpersonal relationships, new businesses to interact with, and even a new burial site. Perhaps of most concern to a remarrying widow were the changes to her property claims. So important was "real property (or land)" as the "basis for affluence, power, and authority," Dronzek stresses, that any examination of medieval women's agency remains incomplete without addressing women's relationship to land.[22] Not only did a widow's property come under the control of her husband when she remarried, but she also could be "abruptly stripped of status and resources almost immediately after her husband's death—indeed, the new widow could count herself lucky if she kept anything more than her clothing and personal adornments."[23] Further, on the day that she remarried, "any existing will or testament became invalid."[24] And although widows could inherit a third of the estate (of their deceased husband) they could scarcely bequeath it to whom they might if they remarried, because, by the fifteenth century, it had become so customary for men to make the wills insofar as they saw themselves as controlling the property that married women rarely made wills. The fact is that making wills after the death of each husband was a labor-intensive task reflecting "webs of social control" while honoring relationships forged over "decades of domestic life."[25] Most widows, it appears, had "no practical choice but to remarry"—given the likelihood of facing poverty or at least seriously reduced circumstances.[26] Yet, neither Jerome in the fourth century nor the very influential Juan Vives of the early-sixteenth century found economic necessity a viable reason for remarrying. Vives keeps Jerome's views fresh before his public: "Or if lust is not the stimulant, what madness is it to prostitute your chastity like a whore so that you can add to your wealth, and that for a worthless and perishable thing a precious and permanent possession, your chastity, is defiled?"[27] Studies indicate that remarriage enjoyed general socioeconomic approval.[28] Nevertheless, "the condemnation of all remarrying widows"—a theme which the Wife of Bath interrogates—remained a strong, common theme into the seventeenth century.[29] Then, too, if a widow remained unmarried for more than five years, there was little likelihood of remarriage.[30]

On the other hand, widows, if they remained widows, could "enter into contracts alone, sue for debt, run her business, till her land, and marry off her children."[31] Widowhood offered a "space for mobility," for "independence or autonomy."[32] Thus, for the English widow "the potential for power and separateness embedded in her new status might allow her to disrupt the flow of wealth, social control, and ideology that normally ran unchecked in masculinized channels of expression and transmission."[33]

If this is true, if the social, economic, and religious practices controlling widows' remarrying were so oppressive, and the potential of remaining a widow so attractive, why does the Wife of Bath choose to remarry a further four times? Two compelling reasons: increased real estate and mercantile power—both of which ensured increased marital power/authority. In fact, Chaucer, as pilgrim-narrator, makes that very connection in his opening lines about the Wife of Bath:

> A good WIF was ther OF biside BATHE,
> But she was somdel deef, and that was scathe.
> Of clooth-makyng she hadde swich an haunt
> She passed hem of Ypres and of Gaunt.
> (*General Prologue*, ll. 445–48)

She is deaf, "beten for a book,"[34] whose leaves she tore out because, as she says, she could no longer endure Jankyn's reading "on this cursed book al nyght."[35] This book, the "Book of Wikked Wives," detailed the woes of marriage, railed against subversive wives, and reproached woman as "the los of al mankynde."[36] It is a book about Alisoun's identity, at least in Jankyn's mind and in many a cleric's. At bottom, the book is about *maistrye*. And property is the basis of *maistrye*.[37]

So, too, while Alisoun's "Prologue" appears to be about *maistrye*, it is equally about mercantile authority and property. However, "[j]ust as the text of the Wife of Bath includes but supersedes the fabliau cliché (women are lecherous, lying, ostentatious, and self-destructing), so it reproduces but ironizes the socioeconomic situation of women's power."[38] In fact, Chaucer has prepared us for the Wife of Bath some eighty lines earlier where he has already "ironized" the socioeconomic situation of women's power and marital prosperity. At lines 361–64 in the *General Prologue* he describes a group of pilgrims:

> AN HABERDASSHERE and a CARPENTER,
> A WEBBE, a DYERE, and a TAPYCER—
> And they were clothed alle in o lyveree
> Of a solempne and a greet fraternitee.

Their livery—ornamented with silver knives and equipment "fressh and newe"—signified far more than guild membership; it pointed to economic status, to the culture of their mercantile life, to multiple and privileged relationships within the economic community and the state. Chaucer's aristocratic audience keenly attuned to the visual codes of dress saw the incongruity immediately: these lesser guild members were common tradespeople. And, as Gastle notes, that audience would have "most probably found such sumptuous dress subject for derision. They were dressed like aldermen, but could never be aldermen."[39] Given the 1363 statute that allowed only burgesses with goods worth over £500.00 to wear knives of gold or silver, David Hinton's question would have hovered in the mind of the audience: "Did each of these guildsmen really have enough in "wisdom, goods and rents to sustain the status of alderman?"[40] Even more significant are the final lines of this passage. There Chaucer tackles the guildsmen's wives, who are not present on the pilgrimage.

> For catel hadde they ynogh and rente,
> And eek hir wyves wolde it wel assente;
> And elles certeyn were they to blame.
> It is ful fair to been ycleped "madame,"
> And goon to vigilies al bifore, And have a mantel roialliche ybore.
> (ll. 373–78)

The couplet not only links "catel" with "wyves" as property of the husbands, but also rhymes "rente" and "assente" asserting a direct relationship between property and marital prosperity. Wives and cattle increase the husbands' economic value; in turn, both husbands and wives increase their claim to status and its cultural practices, livery. Indeed, the wives go one step better than their husbands: they appropriate the title, "madame," reserved for higher ranks, and have their mantles carried royally as they precede others at church vigils. There is an edge to Chaucer's amusement if Sylvia Thrupp is correct. Not all merchants were allowed these titles: "the wives of Aldermen seized upon the title of Lady, which was used by the wives of knights and esquires, and clung to it to the end of their lives, even when widowed or remarried to men who held no office."[41] And the wives of Chaucer's list of guildsmen were not the economic elite, they were not alderman's wives. Nevertheless, their appropriation of these material practices testifies to an impulse by women of the mercantile class to delineate their public identity in defiance both of the sumptuary laws and of professional and class boundaries.

It is this rigidity of boundaries and laws constructing one's public identity that Alisoun likewise challenges. By the time that we first meet her, "she has amassed a great deal of land and fee" and she has also amassed a great deal of experience.[42] She is a clothier, a capitalist entrepreneur. Not only her lands, but the cloth business itself very likely also came to her from her husbands.[43] As was true of most business women and men marriage was less about marriage as, rather, about marriage prosperity. Yet long before she had achieved her position as a capitalist entrepreneur, Alisoun's view of marriage was, from the first, candidly about marital-financial gain. Of her first three husbands, she declares, in her prologue "the thre were goode men, and riche, and olde"[44] Of all five husbands, she boasts, "I have pyked out the beste, / Bothe of here nether purs and of here cheste."[45] For Alisoun, marriage is the economics of body and resources. Later, speaking of their sexuality and their conjugal expectations, she admits

> They had me yeven hir lond and hir tresoor;
> Me neded nat do lenger diligence
> To wynne hir love, or doon hem reverence.
> (ll. 204–6)

"Lond" and "tresoor" equate property with sexuality. Clearly, for both men and women, the "root of marital 'maistrye' is economic control."[46] Although the wife of Bath views her own body as the site of exchange (when she feels an arm over her side) she withholds sex until the "raunson" is paid. The irony is that "raunson" is actually a criminal practice, a form of extortion for an abduction; it is not an exchange. (Is this Chaucer's playfulness or a critique on marriage as a socio-legally approved form of abduction?)

Yet, as Mary Carruthers rightly points out, "Alisoun is no simple acquisitive machine. Chaucer's brilliant stroke is to give her a streak of romance that blossoms in direct proportion to her accumulated wealth."[47] She can grow amorous, warmly nostalgic remembering her "yowthe" and her "jolitee."[48] She can "have ... [her] world as in [her] tyme"[49] because she can afford it. She was, as she says, "As help me God, I was a lusty oon,/ And faire, and riche, and yong, and wel bigon." The degree of her financial independence has changed.[50] When she meets Jankyn, she marries him not for money but for love. And she gives him all her "lond and fee."[51] She has given him economic control and thus *maistrye.* When he abuses it, refusing to give her any of the fruits of that land (rents, etc.) to which she was entitled, and despotically subjects her to tale after endless tale of "wicked wives," she is compelled to choose economic power over love. Her ability to repeat some seventeen abbreviated narratives and proverbs of "wicked" women from Jankyn's book, her exposure of the inconsistencies of clerical writings opposing remarriage, and her well-rehearsed replies to the Church's stances on virginity suggest that she has long placed the public identity of the ideal woman at the center of her debate and has rejected it. The fact that it cost her her hearing is underscored by Chaucer's referencing it as his opening statement introducing Alisoun, and his closing paragraph of her prologue where it contributes to her final triumph.

Alisoun reports that when she realized that Jankyn was never going to finish "To reden on this cursed book al nyght,/ Al sodeynly thre leves have I plyght/ Out of his book, right as he radde, and eke/ I with my fest so took hym on the cheke/ That in oure fyr he fil bakward adoun."[52] Certainly, there is wife abuse of husband going on as well as a husband's excessive "governing" of a wife's conduct. However, we know that Jankyn is not criminally liable for physically mistreating Alisoun because both conduct literature and legal judgments justify his physically keeping her in line (he can exercise "appropriate chastisement"). On the other hand, Alisoun is liable to public punishment; she can be put in the stocks, she can be brought to a court. Yet, what is remarkable is that in the middle of this violent situation—even in the midst of their making up (itself an extreme emotional situation)—she has enough presence, and is intimate enough with financial and legal arrangements, to convert a moment of violence and emotion into a moment of financial security. She uses the moment of emotional arousal as a moment to secure a contract: they "fille acorded." And "He yaf me al the bridel in myn hond,/ To han the governance of hous and lond,/ And of his tonge, and of his hond also;/ And made hym brenne his book anon right tho."[53] She has converted a situation that would have been legally construed as abuse of a husband and open to public disgrace, to, instead, grounds for reconstructing their financial and legal relationship. In the end, economic power not only secures marital prosperity, but it also reduces the hazard rate[54] of Alisoun's sensitive assets (if I may pun) and ensures socioeconomic asymmetry for her. After all, she now has not only the governance of "hous and lond," but also of Jankyn's "tonge," and "hond."

## Margery Kempe, "a lay wife and mother struggling all her life for redefinition"

Michael J. Braddick's and John Walter's observation about negotiating power in early modern England could just as well describe the situation in late medieval England: the disadvantaged "navigated their way in a world" whose resources favored the advantaged.[55] "But in negotiating their way around these potential dangers they did not lack negotiating powers of their own."[56] Both her gender and her married status somewhat disadvantaged Margery Kempe. Her negotiating power—money—is her chief means to transact her freedom, and, ultimately, to transact her identity. Born into a well-to-do family and having married John Kempe, who is likewise wealthy, she is keenly aware of money.[57] She is particularly aware of the way it supports her public identity and status. It is the first subject about which she speaks after recalling her first vision of Christ and the recovery of her reason. She writes, "And when this creature had thus through grace come again to her right mind, she thought that she was bound to God and that she would be his servant. Nevertheless, she could not leave her pride and showy manner of dressing"—wearing a headdress of gold mesh and wire and cloaks that "were underlaid with various colors between the slashes so that she would be all the more stared at, and all the more esteemed."[58] In fact, she specifically takes up the business of brewing because, as she puts it, she "craved more and more" worldly goods, and the need "to maintain her pride."[59] Sheila Delany does not hold back: "With Margery Kempe, one is kept constantly aware of the 'cash nexus'; it pervades her consciousness as it pervaded her world, part of every human endeavor and confrontation."[60]

Money is crucial for two endeavors in particular. In the first instance, money "recalculates" the marriage debt. Kempe had long sought to live a chaste marriage with her husband, John, but for years he refused his consent. Finally, in 1413, on their way back from York to Bridlington, John turns to the subject of their sleeping together. He sets up a three-point proposition: first, continue to sleep together in bed; second, pay my debts before you go to Jerusalem; third, eat and drink with me on Fridays as you once did.[61] Margery turns to prayer during which, she reports, God abrogated her formal agreement to fast because its intention was, as God assured her, that she "should the sooner obtain [her] desire," namely, to be free to live chastely.[62] Kempe then reframes her husband's proposition, introducing into it a momentous concept for a woman whose life "was inextricably bound up with mercantile concerns" and whose "autobiography…begins rooted in fellowship and secular concerns."[63] She negotiates consent for her life-long bodily autonomy. To be free from their conjugal debt, she agrees to pay John's debts. But, she adds, in exchange for eating and drinking with him on Fridays at his bidding, you are to "make my body free to God, so that you never make any claim on me requesting any conjugal debt after this day as long as you live."[64] The legal-doctrinal consequences of this are significant, but the sociosexual consequences are even more profound. Marriage theology (supported by canonical jurisprudence) held that the conjugal debt had a scriptural basis in Paul's teachings on marriage and the sexual rights of the spouses. "The husband must give the wife what is due her, and equally the wife must give the husband his due. The wife cannot claim her body as her own; it is her husband's. Equally the husband cannot claim his body as his own; it is his wife's."[65]

The sociosexual consequences of Margery's negotiation for bodily autonomy are even more extraordinary. It virtually changes Kempe's classification as a wife in terms of her sexuality; it radically repositions what a woman is because it challenges the fundamental social taxonomy of women as wife, widow, virgin, and it enables her to explore her worthiness to be included in the ranks of married women mystics.

The second endeavor—domestic travel and pilgrimages—is even more transformative: Kempe "uses travel to recontextualize her life and to place her behaviors and self-concept in a larger frame of reference that challenges the narrow ideological framework in which the English church authorities operate."[66] Travel literally provides a liminal experience for Kempe to test boundaries. Judith Adler writes that travel as performed art is "undertaken and executed with a primary concern for the meanings discovered, created, and communicated."[67] The meanings that Kempe wishes to discover, create, and communicate are the identities of the past that lie on the other side of those boundaries. In physically retracing the footsteps of the pilgrimage of St. Bridget (1303–73), Kempe spiritually and literally "resituate[s]" her own life, linking her identity to that of Bridget, a mystic who was both mother and widowed.[68] In using travel to reenact the "via dolorosa" of Christ, Kempe more deeply links her self-concept to that of Christ, furthering the identity of her place within the Holy Family. And in attaching "herself to a wider community of respected figures, Kempe mitigates her status as a deviant and grotesque anomaly."[69] By imaginatively reconstructing her social and spiritual identity, Kempe challenged received norms of what constitutes a "holy" woman. She has redefined the terms.

All three women, Dorigen, Alisoun, the wife of Bath, and Margery Kempe have plotted their own reality, their own public identity, and (in the case of Kempe, despite her anxious awareness of money) they have done this with a new positive inflection of money and power.

## Notes

1. Franchise (*fraunchise*) refers to the social status of a free person, but in this tale, more specifically to "nobility of character, generosity of spirit." *The Riverside Chaucer*, ed. Larry D. Benson, third edition (Boston: Houghton Mifflin, 1987), glossary. All references to "The Franklin's Tale" and "The Wife of Bath's Prologue" are from this edition.
2. "The Wife of Bath's Tale," l. 1061.
3. Symbolic capital refers to any ability or asset considered as being valuable by a given group of people. The primary forms of symbolic capital are labor and landed property, which may be converted "to gain advantages in the form of additional wealth, power, allies and marriage partners." Rebecca Bliege Bird and Eric Alden Smith, "Signaling Theory, Strategic Interaction, and Symbolic Capital," *Current Anthropology* 46:2 (April 2005): 221–48, quote on p. 223. Because symbolic capital implies differences between status and identities, its value lies in the cost of the investment in terms of time, energy, or wealth. Pierre Bourdieu, *The Logic of Practice* (Cambridge, MA: Polity Press, 1990), pp. 112–13.
4. "The Franklin's Tale," l. 732.
5. "The Franklin's Tale," l. 735.
6. However, the narrator cautions that this can work only if each has patience and forbearance. And although "forbearance" ("suffrance") is precisely what Arveragus swears as part of his betrothal vow to Dorigen (l. 788) it is also precisely what he transgresses—as well as transgressing *trouthe*, the other part of his vow.
7. It may be added that the inadequacies of the chivalric code are further exposed in the nature of Aurelius's courtly love pursuit of Dorigen: he doesn't *win* Dorigen; he deceives her.
8. "Dorigen's complaint summarizes six chapters of Jerome, *Adversus Jovinianum*.... Gatherings of such lists of exempla were common." *The Riverside Chaucer*, p. 900.
9. *The Riverside Chaucer*, p. 900, notes that although "Chaucer follows Jerome closely, he places his examples in a different order." The same endnote adds that Donald C. Baker, "A Crux in Chaucer's Franklin's Tale: Dorigen's Complaint," *Journal of English and Germanic Philology* 60 (1960): 56–64, "argues that the exempla are organized into women who commit suicide to avoid rape (1367–1404), women who commit suicide after being raped (1405–38), and notably faithful wives (1439–56)."
10. Jane Tibbetts Schulenberg is instructive on this issue in her "The Heroics of Virginity: Brides of Christ and Sacrificial Mutilation," in *Women in the Middle Ages and the Renaissance*, ed. Mary Beth Rose (Syracuse, NY: Syracuse University Press, 1986), pp. 29–72.
11. A list of scholars' charges against Dorigen's speech is found in James Sledd, "Dorigen's Complaint," *Modern Philology* 45:1 (1947): 36–45, esp. pp. 36–40. Sledd's argument is itself forward looking, with a postmodern touch to it: he sees a certain performing self-consciousness in Dorigen's

complaint, calling it "a deliberate bit of rhetorical extravagance, intended actually as an assurance that all shall yet go well" (p. 42). On the other hand, he disallows an intelligent seriousness to Dorigen's meditation, remarking that "when Dorigen indulges in her exempla, no audience can take them altogether earnestly" (p. 45).

12. So, too, is Dorigen's *trouthe.*
13. Jochen Hörisch, *Heads or Tails: The Poetics of Money*, trans. Amy Horning Marschall (Detroit: Wayne State University Press, 2000), p. 15.
14. That Chaucer clearly understood the relationship between the literal and figurative levels of language is evident in his parody of Januarie's pastiche of "The Song of Songs" in "The Merchant's Tale." The Song was itself already an allegorical figuring of a bride's intimate sexual love. In Januarie's lust-driven version, the symbolic language of the Song becomes more sexually encoded and meaning becomes more and more subject to the contingencies of senile self-titillation and foolish idealization of a wife as "paradys." Or, again, the motto of "Amor vincit omnia" on the Prioress's broach, the deliberate play on sex as commerce, as a debt in a "queynte world" (l. 236) in "The Shipman's Tale," and the dialogue of the three thieves in the tavern in "The Pardoner's Tale" are further examples of Chaucer signaling his knowledge of language and speech as symbolic.
15. "The Wife of Bath's Prologue," ll. 605–6.
16. Joel T. Rosenthal, "Fifteenth-Century Widows and Widowhood," in *Wife and Widow in Medieval England*, ed. Sue Sheridan Walker (Ann Arbor: University of Michigan Press, 1993), pp. 33–58, esp. p. 34.
17. Rosenthal, "Fifteenth-Century Widows," p. 38.
18. Tim Stretton, *Women Waging Law in Elizabethan England* (Cambridge: Cambridge University Press, 1998), p. 22.
19. James Brundage, "The Merry Widow's Serious Sister: Remarriage in Classical Canon Law," *Matrons and Marginal Women in Medieval Society*, ed. Robert R. Edwards and Vickie Ziegler (Woodbridge, UK: Boydell, 1995), pp. 33–48, esp. p. 34.
20. Anna Dronzek, "Women in Property Conflicts in Late Medieval England," p. 188.
21. Brundage, "The Merry Widow's Serious Sister," p. 34.
22. Dronzek, "Women in Property Conflicts," p. 188.
23. Brundage, "The Merry Widow's Serious Sister," p. 33.
24. Stretton, *Women Waging Law*, p. 23.
25. Rosenthal, "Fifteenth-Century Widows," pp. 40–41.
26. Edwards and Ziegler, *Matrons and Marginal Women in Medieval Society*, p. viii.
27. Juan Luis Vives, *The Education of a Christian Woman: A Sixteenth-Century Manual*, ed. and trans. Charles Fantazzi (Chicago: University of Chicago Press, 2000), Book Three: Chapter Seven, p. 323.
28. In Walker, *Wife and Widow in Medieval England*, see the volume's essays by Rosenthal, "Fifteenth-Century Widows and Widowhood"; Barbara Hanawalt, "Remarriage as an Option for Urban and Rural Widows in Late Medieval England," pp. 141–64; and Janet Senderowitz Loengard,

"*Rationabilis Dos*: Magna Carta and the Widow's 'Fair Share' in the Earlier Thirteenth Century," pp. 59–80.

29. James Brundage comments on the moral and social dilemmas widows faced: they could remarry but canon law disallowed priests to bless their marriage. Widows of modest means were "advised not only to remarry but also to do so speedily. But at the same time, civil authorities threatened to punish them if they did so within a year, while Church officials promised to nullify the civil penalties." "Widows and Remarriage: Moral Conflicts and Their Resolution in Classical Canon Law," in Walker, *Wife and Widow in Medieval England*, pp.17–31. See also Barbara J. Todd, "The Remarrying Widow: A Stereotype Reconsidered," in *Women in English Society 1500–1800*, ed. Mary Prior (London: Methuen, 1985), pp. 54–92, esp. p. 54.
30. A large fraction of remarriages "were contracted within a year or two of a husband's death and only a few after much more than five years of widowhood." Rosenthal, "Fifteenth-Century Widows," p. 42.
31. Hanawalt, "Remarriage as an Option," p. 141.
32. Rosenthal, "Fifteenth-Century Widows," pp. 34–35.
33. Rosenthal, "Fifteenth-Century Widows," pp. 34–35.
34. "The Wife of Bath's Prologue," l. 712.
35. "The Wife of Bath's Prologue," l. 789.
36. "The Wife of Bath's Prologue," l. 720.
37. Mary Carruthers, "The Wife of Bath and the Painting of Lions," *Proceedings of the Modern Language Association* 94:2 (1979): 209–22, esp. p. 213.
38. Mark Amsler, "The Wife of Bath and Women's Power," *Assays* 4 (1987): 67–83, esp. p. 69. Amsler cites Theodor Adorno's and Michael Riffaterre's work on the textual function of the cliché—namely, its resistance to being intended as entirely (in this case) negative (note 6).
39. Brian Gastle, "Chaucer's 'Shaply' Guildsmen and Mercantile Pretensions," *Neuphilologische Mitteilungen* 99:2 (1998): 211–16. All citations are from paws.wcu.edu/bgastle/SHAPLY.HTML. Gastle writes, "Wealth, social status, and membership in a reputable guild was a pre-requisite for holding a position of power such as alderman. Thrupp notes that, of over 260 London aldermen elected in the fourteenth century, 'only 9 were citizens of lesser companies,' and those nine had clear merchant ties and were likely moving into merchant activities of the greater guilds themselves. In the following century, not one sheriff or alderman was elected in London who was not one of the greater merchant guilds."
40. David Hinton, "'Closing' and the Later Middle Ages," *Medieval Archaeology* 43 (1999): 172–82, esp. p. 176.
41. Sylvia I. Thrupp, *The Merchant Class of Medieval London 1300–1500* (Ann Arbor: University of Michigan Press, 1989), cited in Brian Gastle, "Breaking the Stained Glass Ceiling: Mercantile Authority, Margaret Paston, and Margery Kempe," *Studies in the Literary Imagination* 36:1 (Spring 2003): 123–47, esp. p. 128–29.
42. Carruthers, "The Wife of Bath and the Painting of Lions," p. 211.

43. Carruthers, "The Wife of Bath and the Painting of Lions," p. 210.
44. "The Wife of Bath's Prologue," l. 197.
45. "The Wife of Bath's Prologue," ll. 44a–b.
46. Carruthers, "The Wife of Bath and the Painting of Lions," p. 215.
47. Carruthers, "The Wife of Bath and the Painting of Lions," p. 215.
48. "The Wife of Bath's Prologue," l. 470.
49. "The Wife of Bath's Prologue," l. 473.
50. Carruthers, "The Wife of Bath and the Painting of Lions," p. 215.
51. "The Wife of Bath's Prologue," l. 630.
52. "The Wife of Bath's Prologue," ll. 789–93.
53. "The Wife of Bath's Prologue," ll. 813–16.
54. "Hazard rate," as I understand it, is a concept in survival analyses that works out models for estimating the probability of default. The mathematical model of credit score cards that try to predict a customer's behavior regarding their credit situation is a basic example.
55. Joel Fredell, "Margery Kempe: Spectacle and Spiritual Governance," *Philological Quarterly* 75:2 (Spring 1996): 137–66, quote on p. 140.
56. All but one of the essays in their volume address early modern England. Michael J. Braddick and John Walter, *Negotiating Power in Early Modern Society: Order, Hierarchy and Subordination in Britain and Ireland* (Cambridge: Cambridge University Press, 2001), pp. 1–2.
57. Sheila Delany, "Sexual Economics, Chaucer's Wife of Bath and *The Book of Margery Kempe*" in *Feminist Readings in Middle English Literature: The Wife of Bath and All Her Sect*, ed. Ruth Evans and Lesley Johnson (London: Routledge, 1994), pp. 71–87, quote on p. 76.
58. *The Book of Margery Kempe*, trans. B. A. Windeatt (Harmondsworth, UK: Penguin Books, 1994), p. 43. All references will be from Windeatt's edition.
59. *The Book of Margery Kempe*, p. 44.
60. Delany, "Sexual Economics," p. 80.
61. *The Book of Margery Kempe*, p. 59.
62. *The Book of Margery Kempe*, p. 60.
63. Gastle, "Breaking the Stained Glass Ceiling," p. 136.
64. *The Book of Margery Kempe*, p. 60.
65. 1 Corinthians 7:3–5 cited in Lillian Bisson, *Chaucer and the Late Medieval World* (New York: St. Martin's Press, 1998), p. 224.
66. Terence N. Bowers, "Margery Kempe as Traveler," *Studies in Philology* 97:1 (2000): 1–28, quote on p. 15.
67. Judith Adler, "Travel as Performed Art," *American Journal of Sociology* 94:6 (1989): 1366–91. Adler adds, "Performed as an art, [and Kempe's pilgrimage was both self-conscious imitation and liturgically driven] travel becomes one means of 'worldmaking' (Goodman 1978) and of self-fashioning," p. 1368.
68. Bowers, "Margery Kempe as Traveler," p. 16.
69. Bowers, "Margery Kempe as Traveler," p. 15.

CHAPTER 3

# "CONSIDER, I BEG YOU, WHAT YOU OWE ME": HELOISE AND THE ECONOMICS OF RELATIONSHIP

*Sally Livingston*

"Perpende, obsecro, quae debes," Heloise writes in her first letter to Abelard, reminding him of the debt that he owes her. She has just received a copy of his *Historia calamitatum* and is incensed not only that he has not written her, but also that he has omitted her side of the story in his consolation letter to a friend. What is this debt that Heloise believes Abelard owes her and why does he have this obligation? It is not simply the Pauline marital debt, I believe, but a far deeper one. Using economic metaphors and language that play on the connection between marriage and ownership, Heloise cajoles Abelard into paying attention to her. By associating marriage with the profane, she argues that it is ownership, not desire, that is the occasion for sin. Abelard's marital debt thus becomes an obligation to satisfy her psychological need for recognition of the "love freely given" they once shared.

As Glenda McLeod has noted, the word "debitum" would have implied the marriage debt to a twelfth-century reader.[1] Taken from St. Paul in I Corinthians 7.3, "uxori vir debitum reddat," this conjugal sexual obligation gave each partner the unlimited right to demand sexual intercourse. The wronged party could appeal to an ecclesiastical court if the debt was not fulfilled.[2] As Peter Dronke has pointed out, this debt is permanently binding and prohibits either partner from making a unilateral declaration of continence.[3] Dyan Elliott notes that the Old Testament's reproductive function of marriage, "increase and multiply" (Gen. 1.28), becomes transformed by Paul. Advocating the avoidance of all sex (I Cor. 7.1), he allows that men and women may have one partner if sexuality cannot be completely avoided (I Cor.7.2 and 9).[4] The early Church Fathers, Elliott contends, had "a growing awareness that marriage and procreation were best defended if they were admitted as a part of God's original plan."[5]

St. Augustine in *De bono conjugali*, for example, distinguishes three levels of guilt in intercourse. If procreation is its purpose, there is no sin. If intercourse is performed with a spouse to satisfy lust, then it is only a venial sin. However, sex with someone to whom you do not have a commitment (his definition of marriage) is adultery or fornication and therefore a mortal sin. Abstinence, he stresses, is preferable to all of these.[6] Augustine argues that something good comes out of the evil of lust:

> carnalis uel iuuenalis incontentia, etiamsi uitiosa est, ad propagandae prolis redigitur honestatem, ut ex malo libidinis aliquid boni faciat copulatio coniugalis, deinde quia reprimitur et quodam modo uerecundius aestuat conupiscentia carnis, quam temperat parentalis affectus.
>
> [carnal or youthful incontinence, which is admittedly a defect, is applied to the honorable task of begetting children, and so intercourse within marriage engenders something good out of the evil of lust. Moreover, the lustful tendencies of the flesh are kept in subjection, and their hot passion becomes more seemly, for parental love contains it.][7]

Marriage, in fact, becomes a safeguard against fornication and adultery, a legal way to contain lust: "nuptiae tamen ab adulterio seu fornicatione defendunt." Augustine sees the purpose of marriage not only to procreate, but also to bear responsibility for each other's sins of the flesh:

> Debent ergo sibi coniugati non solum ipsius sexus sui commiscendi fidem liberorum procreandorum causa, quae prima est humani generis in ista mortalitate societas, uerum etiam infirmatis inuicem excipiendae ad illicitos concubitus euitandos mutuam quodam modo seruitutem…
>
> [So married couples owe fidelity to each other not merely in performance of the sexual act to bring forth children—and this is the primary compact between the human species in this mortal life of ours—but also in ministering, so to say, to each other, to shoulder each other's weakness, enabling each other to avoid illicit sexual intercourse.

For Augustine, a spouse must consent to intercourse, even if the demand appears to be too great:

> in eo ipso, quod sibi inuicem coniuges debitum soluunt, etiamsi id aliquanto intemperantius et incontinentius expetant, fidem tamen sibi pariter debent.

> ...in the very act, in which married partners pay the debt they owe to each other, even if they demand this too passionately and too lustfully, they owe equal fidelity to each other.][8]

In other words, marriage provided a "remedy for lust," as Philip Lyndon Reynolds has termed it, an outlet for a sexuality that is not merely for procreative purposes.[9] The marital debt was not one-sided; it applied equally to men and women. As James A. Brundage has pointed out, medieval canon law placed women in an inferior position to men except in matters of sex, where they were equal in committing sexual offenses.[10]

Given the importance of the marital obligation in the twelfth century, it is likely that Heloise makes use of the concept, albeit it in a different way. Her reference to Abelard's debt can be seen as a legitimate invocation of his marital responsibilities, which, although impossible for him to fulfill on the physical level, is still required on an emotional level.[11] Indeed, the concept of debt is one of the central features of Heloise's first letter to Abelard. At first it appears that she is simply asking for some word from him. He has discharged his debt to friendship by writing the *Historia calamitatum* as a solace to his friend. It is a greater debt, she contends, that binds him to her and her nuns:

> quas non tam amicas quam amicissimas non tam socias quam filias convenit nominari vel si quod dulcius et sanctius vocabulem potest excogitari. Quanto autem debito te erga eas obligaveris non argumentis non testimoniis indiget...
>
> [whom it is fitting to be called not friends as much as dearest friends, not comrades but daughters, or a name sweeter and holier that can be devised. How great the debt, moreover, by which you have obligated yourself to us needs neither argument nor testimony.][12] (Heloise to Abelard, Letter 2)

By using "we" she refers not only to her nuns, but more importantly to herself. McLeod has argued that when she uses the first person singular, Heloise speaks in her private role as Abelard's wife, while the second person plural indicates her public role as abbess.[13] I would suggest, rather, that here, as in the succeeding letters, Heloise often conflates the two, allowing her an easier transition into speaking of her private heart. This is clear when she segues into the use of the singular "I":

> Qui tanta hostibus largiris quid filiabus debeas meditare. Atque, ut ceteras omittam, quanto erga me te obligaveris debito pensa ut quod devotis communiter debes feminis unicae tuae devotius solvas.
>
> [You who give so abundantly to your enemies, consider what you owe to your daughters. Apart from everything else, repay the debt you owe

> a community of devoted women by discharging it more dutifully to her who is yours alone.] (Heloise to Abelard, letter 2)

In other words, Heloise tells Abelard that he should repay his debt to the nuns by discharging his debt to her. Clearly, this is not the Pauline marital obligation. He is bound to her by the tie of marriage but he is also deeper in her debt, she states, "because of the love by which I have embraced you, an unrestrained love, as is clear to all" ("quo te semper ut omnibus patet immoderato amore complexa sum"). In this sentence Heloise insists that the bond of love is more important than the bond of marriage. He is even more in her debt, she continues, because she obeyed his orders to become a nun and in doing so, she has allowed him to own both her body and her spirit:

> Et solus es qui plurimum id mihi debeas et nunc maxime cum universa quae iusseris in tantum impleverim ut cum te in aliquo offendere non possem me ipsam pro iussu tuo perdere sustinerem. Et quod maius est dictuque mirabile, in tantam versus est amor insaniam ut quod solum appetebat, hoc ipse sibi sine spe recuperationis auferret, cum ad tuam statim iussionem tam habitum ipsa quam animum immutarem ut te tam corporis mei quam animi unicum possessorem ostenderem.

> [And it is you alone who owes me a higher debt, greater now when I have satisfied all that you ordered, so that when I could not oppose you in anything, by your order I found strength to ruin myself. And what is more, strange to say, my love turned to such madness that immediately on your order I changed my clothing and my mind so that I might show that you alone possessed my body as well as my soul.] (Heloise to Abelard, letter 2)

Not only did Heloise not want to enter the convent, she also did not wish to marry Abelard in the first place. In what is perhaps the most widely discussed discourse in the letters, she distinguishes between marriage and concubinage. She is angry because he omitted from the *Historia calamitatum* the reasons for her refusal to marry, or in her words, "for preferring love to wedlock and freedom to chains" ("sed plerisque tacitis quibis amorem coniugio libertatem vinculo praeferebam"). She vehemently rejects marriage:

> Non matrimonii foedera, non dotes aliquas expectavi, non denique meas voluptates aut voluntates sed tuas, sicut ipse nosti, adimplere studui. Et si uxoris nomen sanctius ac validius videtur, dulcius mihi semper exstitit amicae vocabulum aut, si non indigneris, concubinae vel scorti.

> [I did not expect a compact of marriage, no marriage portion, and further I sought to satisfy not my pleasures or wishes but yours, as you know. And

if the name of wife seems more holy or powerful, sweeter to me always will be the word friends, or if you are not offended, concubine or whore.] (Heloise to Abelard, letter 2)

In the *Historia calamitatum* Abelard has only used the word "amica" to describe her. It is obvious that Heloise's concept of their relationship is far more than that. As Claire Nouvet has persuasively argued, by preferring to be Abelard's whore, she is demonstrating "a disinterested love which attempts to 'unbind' itself from the conjugal notions of possession and contractual obligation."[14] The use of the word "whore" is, however, more than this. Heloise takes a longstanding custom, that of the clerical concubine, and privileges it over marriage. By Abelard and Heloise's time the church was consolidating its formal control over marriage, which had previously been a civil act. Although it had struggled with clerical marriage since its early days, the fervor to prohibit the practice increased in the eleventh and twelfth centuries. Even with these restrictions, priests continued to have concubines. Concubinage was an established tradition and presumed monogamy. James A. Brundage has noted that Gratian viewed it as a relationship that had conjugal affection without the legal formality of marriage.[15] By confining the sexual act to marriage, the church reinforced Augustine's distinction between wife and concubine.

Thus Heloise, in insisting that she does not want to be his wife, denies the notion of the *marital* debt, preferring instead a debt based on "love freely given." In this, she stands in defiant opposition to church doctrine by playing on the idea of clerical concubinage. Although Abelard can no longer provide a sexual outlet for Heloise, her understanding of their debt to one another implies an emotional commitment central to the medieval notion of concubinage. Having both taken holy orders, she can provide solace to him and believes she has every right to demand it back from him.

Marriage, for Heloise, appears to be an economic not a sacred arrangement. In a bold critique of the "good" marriage, she writes,

Nec se minime venalem aestimet esse quae libentius ditiori quam pauperi nubit et plus in marito sua quam ipsum concupiscit. Certe quamcumque ad nuptias haec concupiscentia ducit, merces ei potius quam gratia debetur. Certum quippe est eam res ipsas non hominem insequi et se, si posset, velle prostituere ditiori.

[And if she marries a richer man more readily than a poor one, and covets her husband more for his possessions than for himself, she deems herself not least of all to be on sale. Certainly any woman who comes to marry

> through these desires deserves pay rather than gratitude. Certainly she is pursuing these things rather than the man, and she would, if possible, prostitute herself to a richer man.] (Heloise to Abelard, letter 2)

This connection that she makes between marriage and property, so central to the reality of life in twelfth-century France, is startling, to say the least. By equating marriage to prostitution—different from concubinage in Heloise's eyes—she attacks the secular idea of wedlock. She names her desire in words (*concubina* and *scortum*) that are deliberately bold and provide a stark contrast to wife (*uxor*). In describing marriage she uses an equally graphic word (*prostituere*). Although the three may seem to be related, Heloise actually makes a clear distinction. Even using the word *scortum* she is calling herself *Abelard's* whore. The relationship is based on mutual love and cannot be limited by what she sees as the restrictions of marriage. As Ruth Mazo Karras has observed, priests' concubines were often referred to as whores, which could simply have meant a sexually active single woman.[16] A prostitute, in Heloise's model, is promiscuous and sells her services to the highest bidder. In this discourse, it is the wife who is the prostitute. This formulation allows her to argue that her relationship with Abelard is justified precisely because it lies outside the bounds of marriage.

She extends the financial metaphors when she accuses him of holding her "cheap" (*vilitatem*). Because he has ignored her, she questions his motives for their relationship, again referring to Augustinian distinctions between lust and love:

> Dic, inquam, si vales aut ego quod sentio immo quod omnes suspicantur dicam. Concupiscentia te mihi potius quam amicitia sociavit, libidinis ardor potius quam amor. Ubi igitur quod desiderabas cessavit quicquid propter hoc exhibebas pariter evanuit.
>
> [Tell me, I say, if you can, or I will tell you what I think or rather what everyone suspects. Desire, rather than friendship bound you to me, the heat of lust rather than love. When, therefore, what you desired ended, any show of feeling you used to show vanished at the same time.] (Heloise to Abelard, letter 2)

Lust thus becomes equated with holding her "cheap," making her an object of exchange. Heloise uses this kind of language at the end of her first letter: "Consider your injustice, if when I deserve more you give me less, or rather, nothing at all" ("Quae vero tua sit iniquitas perpende si merenti amplius persolvis minus, immo nihil"). She has become the prostitute who has not even been paid. She concludes with "I beg you, think what you owe me" ("Perpende, obsecro, quae debes"). Thus this letter both begins and ends with the idea of debt, and the discourse in the middle in which she calls herself Abelard's "whore" redefines the conjugal debt as one based not on marriage, but on consent freely given and unencumbered by external forces. He "owes" her because she has selflessly given him her love, expecting only his—her version of the marital debt—in return.

The tone of Abelard's reply to her first letter is detached and completely ignores her discourse on debt and marriage. He tells her that she herself has the God-given power to comfort her nuns and does not really need him at all. But, he says, if she really needs his instruction in matters pertaining to God, she should write him and he will reply as God permits ("prout mihi Dominus annuerit"). In this fashion, he carefully circumscribes the terms under which he will communicate with her. Peggy Kamuf has called his tone "too-reasonable." He is, she says, responding selectively to Heloise's request for communication in order to avoid being drawn into her "flagrant transgression of conceptual limits," what he sees as inconsistencies in her logic.[17] Martin Irvine has taken this reading a step further: by deflecting desire onto a "love triangle formed of Abelard, Christ, and Heloise," Abelard actually continues desire through a divine source.[18] Although this interpretation is intellectually seductive, it has Heloise arguing from her body, thus trapping her in her own passions and dichotomizing feminine irrationality with Abelard's rational thinking. As Catherine Brown has boldly pointed out, this comes "perilously close to reinscribing previous generations' naïve oppositions without challenging their ideological underpinnings."[19]

I would suggest that the dichotomy is between Heloise's insistence on a personal relationship with Abelard and his insistence that Christ be the mediator. In preserving a direct line to Abelard, she keeps open the emotional interpretation of the marital debt, while he asserts their relationship only has validity because of their common denominator, Christ. By inserting Christ, Abelard frees himself from any direct obligation to Heloise.

This difference is clear in the salutations of their letters. In her first letter Heloise writes, "Domino suo immo patri, coniugi suo immo fratri, ancilla sua immo filia ipsius uxor immo soror, Abaelardo Heloisa" ["To her master, rather father, her husband, rather brother, his handmaid, rather daughter, his wife, rather sister; to Abelard, Heloise"]. In line with the conventions of medieval letter-writing, Heloise puts Abelard's name before her own, but only after she recounts the various roles they have played in each other's lives. This salutation links their private and public roles, but ultimately stresses their intimate connection. Abelard responds in his *salutatio*, "Heloisae, dilectissimae sorori suae in Christo, Abaelardus, frater eius in ipso" ["To Heloise, his most beloved sister in Christ, Abelard, her brother in him"]. Clearly, Abelard is correcting her. They are only brother and sister, connected by their relationship to Christ. Although he places Heloise's name first in the salutation, which denotes that she is his superior, he puts her in that role only in the circumscribed situation of their common bond in Christ.

In her second letter, Heloise skillfully manipulates his use of Christ: "Unico suo post Christum unica sua in Christo" ["To her one and only after Christ, she who is his one and only in Christ"]. Peter Dronke reads this phraseology to mean that she confirms that he follows Christ in her heart, while acknowledging that it contradicts the rest of the letter.[20] She is, however, positing two separate relationships to Christ: by the use of "post" for her and "in" for him, she says that her love for Abelard stands quite apart from her love of Christ, while for him, they are tied.[21]

She excludes Christ even further in the first line of this letter in which she calls him "unice meus," [my only one]. Abelard's response again stresses that they are related only through Christ: "Sponsae Christi servus eiusdem" ["To the bride of Christ, his own servant"]. By calling her Christ's bride, he is shifting the marital relationship, subtly negating her insistence on his debt to her. Abelard continues to place her title before his own in the salutation and proceeds to tell her why:

> Te vero extunc me superiorem factam intelligas quo domina mea esse coepisti Domini mei sponsa effecta.
>
> [You must understand that you were made my superior, from that point when having been made the bride of my Lord, you began to be my lady.] (Abelard to Heloise, letter 5)

But marriage for Heloise does not carry the spiritual significance that it does for Abelard. Rather, marriage has doomed them:

> Dum enim solliciti amoris gaudiis frueremur et, ut turpiore, sed expressiore vocabulo utar, fornicationi vacaremus, divina nobis severitas pepercit. Ut autem illicita licitis correximus, et honore coniugi turpitudinem fornicationis operuimus, ira Domini manum suam super nos vehementer aggravavit, et immaculatum non pertulit torum qui diu ante sustinuerat pollutum.
>
> [For while we enjoyed the delights of an uneasy love and, to use a fouler but more expressive word, abandoned ourselves to fornication, divine sternness spared us. However, when we reformed our illicit acts with licit ones and covered the disgrace of fornication by the honor of marriage,

> the anger of the Lord laid his hand heavily upon us and did not bear a chaste union though he had tolerated an unchaste one for so long before.] (Heloise to Abelard, letter 4)

After blaming Fortune for her woes, she then blames herself, as his wife, for his: "Quod fornicatoribus suis adulterae, hoc propria uxor tibi contulit" ["what adulterous women brought upon their paramours, your own wife brought upon you"]. As a wife she is responsible for his downfall; they were protected from the devil when they were lovers:

> Et callidissimus tentator hoc optime noverat quod saepius expertus fuerat, virorum videlicit ruinam in uxoribus esse facillimam . . . Qui denique etiam usque ad nos consuetam extendens malitiam, quem de fornicatione sternere non potuit, de coniugio tentavit.
>
> [The cleverest tempter knew well what he had often experienced, that clearly the easiest ruin of men is from their wives . . . At last, extending his usual malice even to us, he was not able to destroy whom through fornication he attacked though marriage.] (Heloise to Abelard, letter 4)

By the time he was castrated, she points out, they were married and living relatively chaste lives. Although Heloise here appears to accept medieval misogynistic and misogamistic ideas, I would suggest that she actually turns these beliefs to her own ends. To support her own desires, she uses the fact that marriage for a cleric like Abelard is worse than fornication. As his wife, not his lover, she has ruined him, she argues, thus implying that if they had never married, things would have turned out differently. The sin was not in their sexual relationship, but in their marriage.

She further rebels against medieval ideas of marriage by admitting that her mind still retains the will to sin and is on fire with its old desires. She cannot let go of them, even when she is supposed to be praying:

> Quocumque loco me vertam, semper se oculis meis cum suis ingerunt desideriis. Nec etiam dormienti suis illusionibus parcunt. Inter ipsa missarum solemnia, ubi purior esse debet oratio, obscena earum voluptatum phantasmata ita sibi penitus miserrimam captivant animam ut turpitudinibus illis magis quam orationi vacem.
>
> [Wherever I turn they always thrust themselves before my eyes. And they do not spare me from illusions even in sleep. During the very celebration of the Mass, when prayer ought to be purer, those obscene fantasies of pleasure so captivate my most unhappy soul that I apply my mind to those disgraces rather than to prayers.] (Heloise to Abelard, letter 4)

She refuses to allow her sexuality to be contained by religious doctrine. She remains Abelard's "whore," if only in thought.

In his letter in response, Abelard acknowledges their personal relationship more fully. He tries to explain why God punished them when they were married:

> Nosti post nostri foederationem conjugii cum Argenteoli cum sanctimonialibus in claustro conversareris, me die quadam privatim ad te visitandam venisse, et quid ibi tecum meae libidinis egerit intemperantia in quadam etiam parte ipsius refectorii, cum quo alias videlicet diverteremus, non haberemus. Nosti, inquam, id impudentissime tunc actum esse in tam reverendo loco et Summae Virgini consecrato. Quod, et si alia cessent flagitia, multo graviore dignum sit ultione.
>
> [You know that after our marriage, when you were living in the cloister with the nuns at Argenteuil, I came one day to visit you privately, and what the intemperance of my desire did with you there, actually in a corner of the actual refectory, since we had nowhere else to go. I repeat, you know how shamelessly we behaved then in so revered a place consecrated to the most high Virgin. And if our other shameful behavior ended, this one deserved much graver punishment.] (Abelard to Heloise, letter 5)

Castration, he declares, was a fitting punishment for him.

He also turns around the medieval misogamistic argument that marriage and children distract men from their higher duties to persuade Heloise that their marriage was a good thing for her and even better now that they are separated:

> Si enim mihi antea matrimonio non esses copulata facile in discessu meo a saeculo vel suggestione parentum vel carnalium oblectatione voluptatum saeculo inhaesisses...Quam lamentabile incommodum, si carnalium voluptatum sordibus vacans paucos cum dolore pareres mundo, quae nunc multiplicem prolem cum exsultatione parturis coelo! Nec esses plus quam femina nunc etiam viros transcendis et quae maledictionem Evae in benedictionem vertisti Mariae.
>
> [For if you had not been previously joined to me in matrimony, you might have easily clung to the world in my withdrawal from it, either at the suggestion of your relatives or in enjoyment of carnal delights. What lamentable trouble if abandoning yourself to the defilement of carnal delights, you had brought forth in suffering a few children for the world, when now you have delivered in exultation numerous progeny for heaven! And you would not have been more than a woman, whereas now you rise above men, and have turned the curse of Eve into the blessing of Mary]. (Abelard to Heloise, letter 5)

In this letter he also finally acknowledges their intimate relationship, but sublimates it into a spiritual one. He takes Heloise's physical longing for him and transforms it into a long digression on the Song of Songs, thus continuing the theme in his salutations. He writes, "It was a happy transfer of your married state, for you were previously the wife of a poor mortal and now are raised to the bed of the King of kings" ("Felix talium commercium nuptiarum ut homunculi miseri prius uxor nunc in summi regis thalamis sublimeris"). The early Church Fathers needed to desexualize a text that makes no direct mention of God and instead, as Ann W. Astell has termed it, "celebrates the passionate joys and sorrows of unnamed lovers."[22] The lover in the Song of Songs becomes in the twelfth century the "bride of Christ." Such nuptial imagery was not only an ungendered description of the relationship of the church with God, but also a common description of a religious woman. In transferring his own wife's allegiance to God, Abelard, in effect, rejects her.

By using the word "commercium" (whose many meanings in Lewis and Short's *A Latin Dictionary* include "trade," "traffic," "commercial intercourse," "a mercantile right," and more interestingly, "forbidden intercourse, illicit commerce"),[23] Abelard "trades" her to Christ, thus once again placing Christ between them. Heloise's salutations to Abelard, as detailed earlier, make clear that she rejects the name of Bride of Christ, as well as anything but a personal relationship with Abelard. Does Abelard use the word "commercium" precisely because of its multiple meanings? It appears in his *Theologia Scholarium* to describe the intercessory nature of prayer, which, he notes, is the only connection between God and man.[24] However, "carnale commercium" was widely used to denote sexual intercourse. This passage, in which the exchange is from Abelard, the human male, to Christ, the divine male, is thus cloaked in ambiguity.

He insists that God has bound them in marriage so that He could save the two of them together:

> ipse, inquam, clementer disposuit in uno duobus consulere quos diabolus in uno nitebatur extinguere. Paululum enim antequam hoc accideret, nos indissolubili lege sacramenti nuptialis invicem astrinxerat.
>
> He, I say, gently arranged to take care of two people in one, the two whom the devil tried to destroy in one. For a little while before this happened, he had mutually bound us by the indissoluble law of the marriage sacrament. (Abelard to Heloise, letter 5)

By joining their salvation together, Abelard once again returns to the theme of Heloise as the bride of Christ. She should always think of Him, not Abelard, as her true spouse: "Hunc semper, soror, verum tuum et totius Ecclesiae sponsum prae oculis habe, mente gere." ["Bear in mind, sister, Him as your true spouse and the spouse of the whole Church"]. Through their marriage he can share in her closeness to Christ: "Unum quippe sumus in Christo, una per legem matrimonii caro. Quidquid est tuum, mihi non arbitror alienum." ["For we are certainly one in Christ, one flesh through the law of matrimony. Whatever is yours I do not judge alien to me"].

The "one flesh" comes curiously close to a sexualized union, not between the two of them, but with Christ as the mediator of their desire. The marital debt is paid only by the presence of a third party. He asks her to become his intercessor to Christ, for through her, Christ's bride, he can receive that which he cannot get on his own ("Unde et de tuo nobis apud ipsum patrocinio amplius confidimus ut id obtineam ex tua quod non possum ex oratione propria"). He has enacted his own "commercium:" no longer the husband of Heloise, he is now triangulated into a divine relationship with Christ.

The last letter in which there is any kind of personal correspondence is letter five, from Heloise to Abelard, and in this letter the tone changes significantly.[25] She still attests to the primacy of her emotions, but they are now longer part of what she seeks from him:

> Revocabo itaque manum a scripto in quibus linguam a verbis temperare non valeo. Utinam sic animus dolentis parere promptus sit quemadmodum dextra scribentis.
>
> [I will therefore call back my hand from writing that which I cannot control my tongue from speaking. Oh, that a grieving heart would be prompt to obey the way of a writing hand!][26]

She will now focus her attention on other things, the care of her nuns. She asks Abelard for two things: a history for the authority of their order and a rule suitable for women. The continuing correspondence between Abelard and Heloise after these letters shows a continuing devotion to each other.[27] Her relationship to him becomes translated through the community of nuns of which she is a part. Heloise has, in effect, chosen silence—it has not been demanded of her. Indeed, it can be argued that by "institutionalizing" her relationship with Abelard, she is less marginalized from a public perspective: as nun and monk, their relationship is legitimate. She now speaks in his language and does not give voice to her private emotions.[28]

Does this mean, then, that Abelard has paid his debt? I would suggest that, in a sense, Heloise has gotten what she wants—a response to her pleas for attention, a fulfilling of the emotional component of the conjugal debt. Although their views on their marriage differ—she will always see it as both disgraceful and degrading—he finally acknowledges what has passed between them. Her grieving heart will not obey her writing hand, but having received Abelard's acknowledgment and recognition, it can allow itself silence.

## Notes

1. Glenda McLeod, "'Wholly Guilty, Wholly Innocent': Self-Definition in Héloïse's Letters to Abélard," in *Dear Sister: Mediveal Women and the Epistolary Genre,* ed. Karen Cherewatuk and Ulrike Wiethaus (Philadelphia: University of Pennsylvania Press, 1993), p. 66. Robert R. Edwards notes that the word *debitum* is also from the parable of the unforgiving servant (Matthew 18:23–35): the servant is forgiven an enormous debt by his master, but then demands a smaller debt repayment from another servant. Robert R. Edwards, *The Flight from Desire: Augustine and Ovid to Chaucer* (New York: Palgrave Macmillan, 2006), p. 75.
2. John W. Baldwin, "Consent and the Marital Debt: Five Discourses in Northern France around 1200," in *Consent and Coercion to Sex and Marriage in Ancient and Medieval Societies,* ed. Angeliki E. Laiou (Washington: Dunbarton Oaks Research Library and Collection, 1993), p. 251.
3. Peter Dronke, *Women Writers of the Middle Ages: A Critical Study of Texts from Perpetua (†203) to Marguerite Porete (†1310)* (Cambridge: Cambridge University Press, 1984), p. 137.
4. Dyan Elliott, *Spiritual Marriage: Sexual Abstinence in Medieval Wedlock* (Princeton, NJ: Princeton University Press, 1993), p. 22.
5. Elliott, *Spiritual Marriage*, p. 31.
6. Augustine of Hippo, *De bono coniugali, De sancta virginitate*, ed. and trans. P.G. Walsh (Oxford: Clarendon Press, 2001), p. 14.
7. Augustine, *De bono coniugali,* pp. 6–8.
8. Augustine, *De bono coniugali,* pp. 8–9.
9. Philip Lyndon Reynolds, *Marriage in the Western Church: The Christianization of Marriage during the Patristic and Early Medieval Periods* (Leiden: E.J. Brill, 1994), p. 255.
10. James A. Brundage, "Sexual Equality in Medieval Canon Law," in *Medieval Women and the Sources of Medieval History,* ed. Joel T. Rosenthal (Athens: University of Georgia Press, 1990), pp. 67–69.
11. McLeod, "'Wholly Guilty, Wholly Innocent,'" p. 66.
12. The Latin text is from J. T. Muckle, "The Personal Letters between Abelard and Heloise," *Mediaeval Studies* 15 (1953): 47–94. All translations are mine. The letters are hereafter referred to by M. T. Clanchy's system, beginning with the *Historia calamitatum* as Letter 1.
13. Muckle, "The Personal Letters," p. 65. Nancy A. Jones has argued, quite accurately, I believe, that "these shifts between the first person singular and first person plural pronouns reveal the intensification of her private

feelings about Abelard and their mutual past." See her "By Woman's Tears Redeemed: Female Lament in St. Augustine's *Confessions* and the Correspondence of Abelard and Heloise," in *Sex and Gender in Medieval and Renaissance Texts: The Latin Tradition*, ed. Barbara K. Gold, Paul Allen Miller, and Charles Platter (Albany: State University of New York Press, 1977), p. 28.

14. Claire Nouvet, "The Discourse of the 'Whore': An Economy of Sacrifice," *Modern Language Notes* 105 (1990): 750–73, esp. p. 758.
15. James A. Brundage, "Concubinage and Marriage in Medieval Canon Law," in *Sexual Practices and the Medieval Church,* ed. Vern L. Bullough and James Brundage (Buffalo: Prometheus Books, 1982), pp. 118–28, esp. p. 120.
16. Ruth Mazo Karras, *Sexuality in Medieval Europe: Doing Unto Others* (New York: Routledge, 2005), p. 104.
17. Peggy Kamuf, *Fictions of Feminine Desire: Disclosures of Heloise* (Lincoln: University of Nebraska Press, 1982), pp. 20–21.
18. Martin Irvine, "Heloise and the Gendering of the Literate Subject," in *Criticism and Dissent in the Middle Ages,* ed. Rita Copeland (Cambridge: Cambridge University Press, 1996), 87–114, esp. p. 102.
19. Catherine Brown, "*Muliebriter*: Doing Gender in the Letters of Heloise," in *Gender and Text in the Later Middle Ages,* ed. Jane Chance (Gainesville: University Press of Florida, 1996), 25–51, esp. p. 27.
20. Dronke, *Women Writers*, p. 121.
21. McLeod has described it in this way: "For Abélard, Hélöise's past has been obliterated and Hélöise's present absorbed into the love of Christ, but Hélöise's private love for Abélard continues to impinge on her public role as bride of Christ." McLeod, " 'Wholly Guilty, Wholly Innocent,' " p. 73.
22. Ann W. Astell, *The Song of Songs in the Middle Ages* (Ithaca, NY: Cornell University Press, 1990), p. 1.
23. Lewis and Short, *A Latin Dictionary* (Oxford: Clarendon Press, 2002), p. 378. It is interesting that Radice translates it as "transfer." Betty Radice, *The Letters of Abelard and Heloise* (London: Penguin Books, 1974), p. 138.
24. Peter Abelard, *Opera theologica: Corpus Christianorum Continuato Mediaevalis XIII* (Turnholt: Brepols, 1987), p. 402.
25. Heloise's response to this letter has generated considerable scholarly debate. Although its tone is so different from the first two, Glenda McLeod rejects the idea that she has undergone some kind of conversion. " 'Wholly Guilty, Wholly Innocent,' " p. 77. As Peter Dronke has explained, there is, in fact, significant continuity in her letters: her desire for a monastic rule reflects her "ceaseless quest for complete and honest understanding" *Women Writers*, pp. 138–39. Linda Georgianna suggests that it is an "institutionally-centered version of what she has asked of Abelard all along: consolation and guidance for an unruly heart." "Any Corner of Heaven: Heloise's Critique of Monasticism," *Mediaeval Studies* 49 (1987): 221–53, esp. p. 247. For Peggy McCracken, Heloise's third

letter continues McCracken's interest in the representation of the female body. See her article, "The Curse of Eve: Female Bodies and Christian Bodies in Heloise's Third Letter," in *Listening to Heloise: The Voice of a Twelfth-Century Woman,* ed. Bonnie Wheeler (New York: St. Martin's Press, 2000), 217–30, p. 227. Others, however, argue for a conversion—Abelard's, not Heloise's. Katharine Wilson and Glenda McLeod claim that she has won their rhetorical debate. See their "Textual Strategies I the Abelard/Heloise Correspondence" in Wheeler, *Listening to Heloise,* pp. 121–42, esp. p. 122. Barbara Newman views Heloise's last letter as the silencing of her desire as well as her feminine voice. See her chapter, "Authority, Authenticity, andn the Repression of Heloise" in *From Virile Woman to WomanChrist: Studies in Medieval Religion and Literature* (Philadelphia: University of Pennsylvania Press, 1995), 74. Jane Chance also contends that Heloise is the "magistra" in her "Classical Myth and Gender in the Letters of 'Abelard' and 'Heloise': Gloss, Glossed, Glossator" in Wheeler, *Listening to Heloise,* pp. 161–85, esp. p. 177. Joan Ferrante has argued in a similar vein: Heloise has directed Abelard's thought from the beginning of the correspondence, which continues on an intellectual rather than emotional level in her third letter. See her *To the Glory of Her Sex: Women's Roles in the Composition of Medieval Texts* (Bloomington: Indiana University Press, 1997), p. 59.

26. The Latin text of this letter is from J. T. Muckle, "The Letter of Heloise on Religious Life and Abelard's First Reply," *Mediaeval Studies* 17 (1955), 240–81.
27. In addition, other words of Abelard, including the *Hymnarius Paraclitensis,* the dedicatory letter to the *Expositio in Hexaemeron* and the prologue to the book of sermons have dedications to Heloise. See Jan M. Ziolkowski, *Letters of Peter Abelard, Beyond the Personal.* (Washington, DC: The Catholic University of America Press, 2006).
28. Clanchy refers to Heloise's entrance into religious life as the "silencing of Heloise," which he calls a "prelude to the silencing of academic women as a class for the next eight centuries." This statement is somewhat misleading, since she went on to pursue her intellectual interests after she had become a nun. M. T. Clanchy, *Abelard: A Medieval Life* (Oxford: Blackwell, 1997), p. 46.

# CHAPTER 4

# MONEY ISN'T EVERYTHING: CONCUBINAGE, CLASS, AND THE RISE AND FALL OF SIBIL·LA DE FORTIÀ, QUEEN OF ARAGON (1377–87)

*Núria Silleras-Fernández*

Sibil·la de Fortià became queen of the Crown of Aragon upon her marriage to Pere the Ceremonious (r. 1337–87) in 1377. The fifty-eight-year-old king ruled one of the most powerful kingdoms of the Western Mediterranean, an aggregate that spanned the principality of Catalonia, and the Kingdoms of Aragon, Valencia and Mallorca, Corsica, Sardinia, and the Duchies of Athens and Neopatria. Sibil·la was a Catalan, a member of the lower nobility, who married Pere after having been his concubine for some time and having given him a daughter, Isabel. She was remarkable because typically, a queen should have been a woman of royal lineage or of the highest nobility whose family could provide a considerable dowry and with whom a marriage alliance would offer political advantages. Women of such families tended to be raised with the aim of marrying them well; it was important that they be cultivated, sophisticated and of virtuous repute. They were frequently betrothed as infants, and married off soon after puberty.[1] Sibil·la, thus, represents one of the few examples of an illiterate member of the lower nobility who ascended to the rank of queen after having served her future husband openly as a concubine. This chapter examines Sibil·la's trajectory from concubine to queen, the opportunities and challenges that her rank and status presented her with, and the resistance she faced from the established elite.

Sibil·la was from Fortià, a town some 35 kilometers north of Girona, in northern Catalonia, the youngest of three children of Berenguer de Fortià and Francesca de Vilamarí. In 1371 she married Artal de Foces, a minor noble many years her senior. For Sibil·la this marriage was a step up and would convey her from provincial obscurity to the royal court. Her new husband was chamberlain in the household of Elionor de Sicilia, the third wife of Pere the Ceremonious, and was knighted by the king in appreciation for his service.[2] It was thus that the young and beautiful Sibil·la came to set foot in royal circles. In April 1375 Elionor died. Pere was left a widower, a condition he would share with Sibil·la, when Artal himself died soon after. Evidently the king and the young widow found mutual consolation; just seven months after the queen's death, Pere gave Sibil·la her first royal assignation, 2,000 *florins* to help her to support her household—they had become lovers.[3] When news of the affair reached the king's heir, Joan, the prince was delighted. He wrote to a trusted courtier, Joan Janer, in 1376, asking him to reassure Sibil·la that for his part he did not want his father to start looking for a new wife.[4] There was no reason for the royal heir to wish his father to marry again, and it was clear that it never occurred to him that Pere would consider using Sibil·la as anything but a lover.

By this time Pere the Ceremonious had survived three wives. In 1338 he married María de Navarra, in 1347 Elionor de Portugal, and in 1349 Elionor de Sicilia, the latter of whom gave him his long-awaited male heirs, Joan and Martí, who would eventually inherit the Crown in turn. As was typical in the Middle Ages, Pere's three marriages were driven by purely political goals. Each of the king's three wives brought him a considerable dowry and each had helped to seal important political alliances. By the time of his third bereavement Pere was fifty-six—an old man by medieval standards. The political situation in the Crown was stable and secure, he had "the heir and a spare"—a healthy adult successor and a second son also fit to rule. There was no need to contemplate remarriage.

Prince Joan, who expected to inherit the throne soon, certainly had no desire to see his father married again. A new marriage would mean a further reorientation of the Crown's foreign policy—an alliance with whichever dynasty the new queen had come from—and Joan had very different political ideas from those of his father. Pere had embarked on a very aggressive Mediterranean policy, reincorporating the Kingdom of Mallorca in the Crown of Aragon, fighting the rebellious Sardinians, battling Genoa as an ally of Venice and Byzantium, and annexing the Duchies of Athens and Neopatria. With Elionor de Sicilia's death, Pere was determined to bring her island homeland also under his control.[5] Given the direction of the king's policy, rumors that Joanna I, Queen of Naples in her own right (r. 1343–82) and the childless widow of Jaume IV of Mallorca, wanted to marry the king caused much concern.[6] Such a union would have brought Naples under control of the Barcelona dynasty and end any possibility of

Mallorca's separation, but at the cost of a considerable military campaign. It was unlikely that the Neapolitan nobility would submit willingly to a foreign prince, and France and the Papacy would never tolerate such a dangerous expansion of the Aragonese Crown.[7]

And indeed, Joan and Pere's political differences centered precisely on their approaches to France and the Papacy. Joan greatly admired both French culture and French women. In 1380 he earned the implacable ire of his father by disobediently marrying Violant de Bar, a niece of Charles V of France (1364–80).[8] As king, Joan would adopt many Gallic customs and affectations, and he was widely disdained as having become "Frenchified." While Pere the Ceremonious was careful not to officially support either the Roman or the Avignose popes during the Schism, Joan would formally throw his lot in with the French-controlled *curia* at Avignon.[9]

From the prince's perspective, even worse than the prospect of a fresh marriage was the possibility that Pere would sire children by a new wife. Should this occur, Pere would undoubtedly provide them generous support, assignations in the form of alienations of the royal patrimony that would otherwise be shared only by Joan and his brother Martí. But the political consequences of a new child might also prove disastrous. Joan and Martí were on excellent terms. The heir had no need to fear the ambitions of his younger brother, but a son by a new queen would be particularly dangerous, as his mother might convince the aging king to favor him over his earlier sons. Moreover, a child could be used as a figurehead by nobles hoping to legitimize a rebellion by proclaiming a pretender. Indeed, Pere the Ceremonious had lived through this very situation. After the death of his mother, Teresa d'Entença, Pere's father Alfons the Benign (r. 1327–36) remarried and produced two sons, Ferran and Joan, by his second wife, Elionor de Castilla. Elionor did all she could to alienate and disempower Alfons's previous offspring. Although she could not prevent Pere from coming to the throne, with her encouragement her sons each in turn led the *Uniones*, the rebellion of Aragonese and Valencian nobles that threatened the kingdom until 1348, and each betrayed him by going over to his arch-rival Pedro the Cruel of Castile during the brutal "War of the Two Peters" (1356–75).[10] Thus, Joan and his younger brother Martí were probably quite happy with the idea of their father taking a concubine, a companion in his old age and a distraction from any plans to find a legitimate spouse. Nor were they troubled in 1377 when Sibil·la gave birth to the king's new daughter, Isabel.[11] Bastards—if they were treated well and remained loyal—could be an asset to a dynasty.

In the thirteenth and fourteenth centuries, the illegitimate children of kings and magnates were certainly not pariahs; in fact, they customarily carried their pedigree with pride. The kings of the Barcelona dynasty were anything but chaste—the chronicles of the Crown are peopled by a parade of royal bastards. In the case of the royal family, these unofficial offspring were considered to be lesser members of the dynasty but members nonetheless. Although excluded from succession and the main part of the inheritance, particularly in the presence of legitimate children, they could expect to receive a small inheritance, a position in the Church or the administration, and a noble title or substantial dowry. Normally they married well, as their link to the royal house made them attractive matches. There was a certain gender dimension to their status in that the fortunes of these "natural children" depended essentially on the intention of the father to support them and acknowledge their relationship—and in this case, King Pere did recognize Isabel.[12] Moreover, as the experience of Isabel reflects, a child could be fully legitimized in the eyes of both the law and the Church. One strategy was for the parents to marry. Hence, although Isabel had been formally acknowledged as Pere's daughter, she did not become an *infanta* ("princess") of Aragon until Pere and Sibil·la had wed. But legitimate or not, the birth of a daughter was a boon for Sibil·la, who was now not merely a concubine, but the mother of the king's daughter. It was at this point that she and the child were assigned permanent accommodation at his royal palace in Barcelona, the *palau major.*

But the *infant* Joan was not the only one who was pleased with Sibil·la. Her relationship with the king was well known to the court and to his subjects, and her unofficial status did nothing to dent her popularity. Thus, as the "concubine-queen" of a widowed monarch she drifted into the roles typically played by queens. For example, in the fashion of Virgin Mary or of the Old Testament Queen Esther, she served as an intercessor between the king and his subjects.[13] Those who sought the king's favor, including members of the administration and the aristocracy—even members of the royal family—gave presents or money to Sibil·la and asked her to help them in their various causes.[14]

Marriage was, in theory, an indissoluble partnership, in which husband and wife enjoyed fundamentally equal rights guaranteed by Church and law.[15] Concubinage, on the other hand, was a sexual relationship of convenience—a private affair with minimal legal status, no religious legitimacy and no public ceremonial. Such relationships were often lengthy, but the female lover did not enjoy any type of institutional protection for herself or her children.[16] At the mercy of her lover, she had no dowry that she might threaten to reclaim, while the open nature of her sexual impropriety could make it difficult to marry well after the affair ended. And yet, Sixth Commandment of Catholicism notwithstanding, royal concubinage was extremely common in medieval Europe, even among married kings. Men demanded fidelity of their wives but took their own pleasure where they would. There was no lack of examples among King Pere's own line. His great-great-grandfather, Jaume the Conqueror (r. 1213–75) was well-known to be as prodigious in his conquests in the bed-chamber as on the battlefield. Married kings sometimes allowed their paramours to become parallel queens, displacing and marginalizing their legitimate queen-consorts. Queens who had been spurned in favor of lovers saw their capacity as intercessors or advisors to the king decrease, moreover they could no longer maintain the networks of influence and patronage that were typically the foundation of queenly power.[17] Two examples from contemporary Castile dramatically illustrate the influence concubines could have.

In 1328 when King Alfonso XI (1312–50) married his cousin, María de Portugal, he already had an "official concubine," Leonor de Guzmán. She was a member of the Castilian nobility, who like Sibil·la, had lost her husband at a young age. By the time of Alfonso's marriage, she had already borne the king several children and he was clearly in love with her.[18] The king approached the dilemma that faced him by setting up two households: one for his wife, who duly produced an heir, Pedro, and another for his concubine, who produced no less than ten children. Although María was the rightful queen, it was Leonor who continued to receive the king's attention and who accompanied him, whether in court or on campaign. Thanks to the valuable concessions that Alfonso granted her children, the royal patrimony declined, while her family became the most powerful feudal line of Castile. But the wheel of fortune turned for Leonor in 1350 when her patron and paramour died. With no formal position, and bearing the hatred of the dowager queen and the young heir, Pedro, each of who had felt humiliated by her successes, she was absolutely vulnerable. One year later she was imprisoned and executed. As enamored as Alfonso may have been, it never seems to have occurred to the king to simply marry Leonor in the first place; she may have been his lover but he did not regard her as proper material for a queen.

Despite his own experiences, Pedro in his turn surpassed his father's conjugal irresponsibilities. He too had taken a concubine before his marriage, the beautiful young noblewoman María de Padilla. Three days after his legal matrimony to the French princess Blanche de Bourbon, Pedro abandoned his bride, leaving her a prisoner in the fortress of Toledo following allegations of her infidelity and questions as to whether her dowry would be paid as promised. She would remain a prisoner for her remaining eight years, despite the fact that Pedro would declare his marriage to her void and briefly take another wife, Juana de Castro.

Through almost all of this time María de Padilla lived as Pedro's queen in all but name, until in 1361 the king ordered Blanche's assassination to clear the way for their marriage. Blanche was duly disposed of, but María died of natural causes before a wedding could take place. Nevertheless Pedro elevated her posthumously to the rank of queen, disavowing his other wives and children, and declaring his son by María, Alonso, to be his heir. But Alonso would not reign. In 1369 Leonor de Guzmán's eldest surviving son by Alfonso XI, Enrique de Trastámara, returned to Castile and with the support of Pere the Ceremonious murdered his half-brother and declared himself King of Castile. This marked the beginning of the Trastámara dynasty, which would not only dominate Castile, but also the Crown of Aragon after the extinction of Pere's own line in 1410.[19] Alfonso XI could hardly have foreseen that his devotion to his concubine Leonor would spell the destruction of his dynasty in such short order. Alfonso understood that it was not the role of king to marry for love, but rather for politics, and hence he chose the candidate who had the best dowry at her disposal and had the most to offer for the future expansion of his realms. In any event, as far as he was concerned, his beloved concubine Leonor would remain for him to enjoy irregardless of whom he married.

## Queen Sibil·la

Thus, it was an exceptional event when on 11 October 1377 King Pere the Ceremonious married his lover Sibil·la de Fortià. From a pragmatic point of view—and Pere was a person whose ruthless pragmatism was tempered only by his choleric tendencies—the king had nothing to gain. His marriage to Sibil·la would bring him no dowry and would establish no new alliance. The only apparent motives were his great love for her, his determination to fully legitimize their daughter, Isabel, and his desire to protect them, perhaps, from the fate of Leonor de Guzmán. But these were hardly reasons for a king to marry.[20] This was certainly how Pere's most important subjects felt. The upper nobility roundly rejected the notion of Sibil·la as queen, undoubtedly feeling slighted that an illiterate child of the lowest provincial nobility should rise above them in such a manner. The king's Pygmalionesque efforts to transform Sibil·la into an educated woman—the queen was immediately assigned two nuns to teach her to read and write—would have done nothing to appease their sense of righteous indignation.[21] For the nobility such a marriage represented a subversion of a divinely ordained social hierarchy.

Naturally, the fiercest resistance to this union came from within the royal family itself. Pere's children, Joan, Martí, and the *infanta* Countess

Joana d'Empúries were particularly vocal in their rejection. For Joan and Martí this marriage represented a threat to "their" royal patrimony, and for Joana, it was unthinkable that one of her own vassals should be transformed into her stepmother. On the contrary, it was those people who stood to gain from Sibil·la's new station who were happiest with the union. Foremost among these were members of her family, who suddenly saw their own status rise as a consequence of acquiring membership to the royal family. Moreover, they were such a motley bunch that individuals far too unseemly to pass as nobility were now claiming to be associates of royalty. For example, Andreu Salt, a peasant from the town of Inca in Mallorca presented himself to all who would listen as a cousin of the queen, in order to inspire fear and respect. Pere was understandably angry at such an imposture, which could only feed the criticisms aimed at his new wife, and set out to have the malefactor punished. But in tacit acknowledgment of the substance of those same classist objections that were aimed at Sibil·la by her enemies, Pere first commissioned the Governor of Mallorca to verify that Salt was not indeed a relative before having him punished—given his wife's background, anything was possible.[22]

## The Coronation

It was extremely unusual for a queen of the Crown of Aragon to be formally crowned as such; in fact Sibil·la was only the third royal consort to be given such an honor, having been preceded by Constança de Sicilia (1276) and Elionor de Sicilia (1352).[23] Elionor, Sibil·la's predecessor, had been granted the ceremony by King Pere as a reward for giving him the male heir, Joan, which he had long despaired of producing.[24] The fact that Sibil·la was spurned by the most important elements of the nobility made it important for Pere to formally reaffirm her title and position, and to publicly confirm the authority that she was entitled to as his legitimate wife. Thus, Sibil·la de Fortià was crowned queen at the Cathedral of Zaragoza on 31 January 1381 in a ceremony at which Pere expected the royal family and the leading members of the nobility of his realms to attend. The coronation was a spectacle in which their role was not merely to observe, but to participate; it was to be at once a celebration of the marriage and confirmation of the authority of the king.

Given this, the refusal of the great majority of the kingdoms' elite to attend was a humiliating affront to the king and queen. Most notable in their absence were Pere's own sons, Joan and Martí, whose resentment toward Sibil·la had only deepened in the four years since she legally became their stepmother. The one important noble who did attend was

Maria de Luna, the *infant* Martí's wife and one of the most wealthy and powerful seigneurs of the Crown in her own right. Along with her came her mother, Brianda d'Agout, and other women of the Luna household. Here they had the honor of carrying Sibil·la's crown, orb, and scepter—the ensigns of her queenly rank, in procession.[25] But Maria attended for the simple reason that she desperately needed a favor from King Pere, and she knew that he would not grant it to her unless she accepted the invitation. At the root of the problem was Maria's sister, Brianda de Luna, who five years earlier had provoked a scandal that had pushed the Crown of Aragon to the brink of civil war. This had occurred in 1377, when the seventeen-year-old Brianda had abandoned her legitimate husband, Lope Ximénez de Urrea, and fled to the arms of another magnate, Luis Cornel.[26] Maria de Luna feared that the king would send her sister back to Lope Ximénez to brake the feuding that had resulted; if there was going to be any hope that the affair would be settled in Brianda's favor, Maria could not afford to offend her father-in-law.

There were few other "A-list celebrities" at the event—the handful who came were representatives of the great families who were traditionally loyal to the royal family, as well as a sprinkling of major clergy.[27] Most of those in attendance were individuals who hoped to benefit from Sibil·la's rise, members of the scorned lower nobility and, in particular, the new queen's relatives and clients. To mark the occasion and to demonstrate Sibil·la's influence, Pere knighted her brother-in-law, Berenguer Barutell, and named him to the post of *alguacil*.[28] In sum, for the royal couple the coronation must have been at once a source of satisfaction and disappointment—on the one hand Pere had celebrated his love for his wife with a very public honor, but on the other, the fact that his most powerful subjects had boycotted the event undermined its prestige and reflected poorly on Pere and Sibil·la's authority.

## Sibil·la's Household

From the time of their marriage to that of her coronation, Sibil·la went from lover to wife and lady to queen, a metamorphosis that was reflected in the transformation of her household and her financial situation. Since the beginning of their relationship the old king had wanted to take good care of his beloved and gave her sufficient resources to maintain a household appropriate for a noble lady. Thus, in the house where she resided in Barcelona her staff and entourage amounted to twenty or so individuals. Her ladies-in-waiting Blanca de Foix, Blanca de Castanys, Constança d'Antillo, Francesca de Serra and Ponçeta Ferrera, were of a status and rank similar to her own. After the birth of her daughter Sibil·la was also provided with a nurse maid, Margalida, who was the wife of the king's own porter.[29] It was, thus, a modest household, but it was as such far bigger a staff that she could have dreamt of having before her relationship with the king. Nevertheless, this was only the beginning. Once Pere had married her in 1377 it was necessary for her to have a household and income that reflected her new status. No sooner had the vows been said that her household more than doubled in size.

Since the reign of Jaume II (r. 1291–1327) the queens of the Crown of Aragon had kept their own households, independent from that of their husbands. They also had their own income, mostly in the form of feudal rents and rights that were generated by the assignations that were agreed upon as a condition for the marriage.[30] As time went by these tended to grow, both as a consequence of occasional gifts on the part of the king, and as a growing family increased the budget that the queen required. Naturally, as Sibil·la established her queenly court she incorporated her most trusted servants in it, promoting them or assigning them to new positions.[31] The rest of the court was new, and as queen Sibil·la required many more attendants to fill the offices she now required. At the outset of her reign nearly two dozen positions were added, including chamberlain and major-domo, a large kitchen-staff, as well as porters, grooms, messengers, and squires.[32] She was now entitled to have her own chapel, which had a permanent staff of four, and a secretarial team that included a head secretary, several scribes, and a keeper of the seal.[33] As queen, Sibil·la's contingent of ladies-in-waiting was also expanded, and came to include members of the nobility such as her sister and her mother, as well as Beneyta, Violant and Estefania Carroç, and Blanquina de Talari, and various up-and-coming commoners, including Marquesa de Torroella, Francina de Palau, and Blanca de Castanys.[34]

Now that Sibil·la was queen, Pere the Ceremonious assigned her additional incomes and patrimony to support her "queenly dignity"—assignations that totaled the considerable figure of 150,000 *sous* per year.[35] To generate this type of income, Pere bought a number of castles and towns for her, for the most part in Valencia.[36] Roca has calculated that in order for her household to function the queen required a yearly income of 135,000 *sous*, to which a further 15,000-*sou* budget for clothing and personal expenses had been added by the king.[37] This was no mere frivolity; both Pere and Sibil·la understood that if one hoped to be treated like a queen, one had to look like one. Hence, in addition to these formal assignations the king showered her with a stream of gifts of expensive jewelry. Thus, Sibil·la enjoyed the resources necessary to maintain the luxurious lifestyle befitting a queen. But she did not spend all of her income on herself and her court, she also understood that the power of a queen lay in the extent and prestige of her network of patronage, and thus she was careful to generously reward her faithful dependents, to support members of her own family, as well as to patronize the Church.

## Keeping It in the Family

Queens, when they enjoyed the favor and/or affection of their husband, were in an excellent position to create such webs of affinity and patronage that consolidated their own position and contributed to the extension of their power.[38] Not only did they control a substantial patrimony of their own, from which they could make assignations and gifts as they pleased, but their household had a prestige that was matched only by that of a king. To be asked to serve as a functionary or lady-in-waiting in the queen's court was seen as a passport to wealth and station not only for the recipient but for his or her family as well—a further motive for subjects to ingratiate themselves with the queen.[39] Most queens, however, were foreign-born princesses, themselves the scions of royal families or lineages of the upper aristocracy. As such they had access to a source of wealth and prestige that was rooted in their own family and that was independent from that of their husband, the king. Sibil·la being from a local dynasty of the lower nobility lacked this crucial ingredient of queenly power. Hence, her ability to act on both a "national" and an "international" scale was limited. She was further disadvantaged by the fact that Pere was an old man when they married, and that he had two hale and healthy sons by an earlier marriage. Thus, Sibil·la would never have the chance to serve as lieutenant-general, as many of her counterparts did, or to enjoy the revered status of queen-mother.[40]

Given her particular situation it was crucial for Sibil·la de Fortià to protect and promote her immediate family, not only the children she had by King Pere, but her mother, her brother and sister, and their children.[41] Her ascent to the throne presented an opportunity to ennoble her family and increase their fortune, and in the absence of the support of the aristocracy of the realm it was crucial for her to build her own network of patronage from scratch. Thus, all of her closest relatives were incorporated into her royal household, and given generous assignations for food and clothing. But it was her brother who received the most favor. Bernat became Sibil·la's special project; he received rents and properties and, thanks to his sister's influence, entered the king's confidence. Within a short time he was given the prestigious offices of royal chamberlain and governor-general of Catalonia. Thanks to Sibil·la, Bernat had gone from being a provincial nobody to a highly placed courtier in record time.

Not surprisingly this led to tensions, not only because the established aristocracy would have seen this as an encroachment on their turf, but because Bernat did not hesitate to throw his weight around. He soon began to have run-ins with other members of the establishment; at one point he attacked a member of the Barcelona city council and did not shy from provoking powerful noblemen, such as Galceran de Vilanova.[42] For his part Pere found such behavior alarming; the last thing he needed was to have this *parvenu* provoking his ever-rebellious subjects. In the meanwhile, Bernat comported himself as a textbook example of the *nouveau riche*, trailed by an ever-increasing entourage of servants and hangers-on. Eventually the situation became embarrassing for Sibil·la, and she was forced to request that he let go four of his domestics, including the personal falconer whom he had employed.[43]

The next step in securing her brother's future would be to use her influence to marry him into the most prestigious family she could manage.[44] Having cast around for potential mates, Sibil·la settled on Timbor de Prades, the daughter of Count Joan de Prades and Sança Eiximenis d'Arenós, and a great-granddaughter of King Jaume II through paternal descent. The Count was well aware of Sibil·la's desperation to marry off her brother and the limited pool of possibilities she would have and, therefore, began to drive a very hard bargain. As a condition of the betrothal he demanded a sizeable gift of 700 gold *florins* in cash as well as a string of ecclesiastical benefices for his son Luis, not the least the position of Metropolitan of Tarragona—the highest Church office in the Crown of Aragon.[45] It is a testament to Sibil·la's influence and the concessions she could extract from the king that the marriage very nearly took place. The betrothal contract was drawn up by March 1383, but the constantly escalating demands of Joan de Prades, who seems to have been counting on Pere expiring before he had to fulfill his end of the bargain, ultimately sabotaged the negotiations.[46] After all Sibil·la had offered, the Prades's rejection would have been a further humiliation, but the queen soldiered on. The next candidate she set her sights on was Isabel, the sister of Juan I of Castile, but these negotiations also failed to yield success.[47]

Meanwhile, the presumptuousness of other members of Sibil·la's family not only aggravated tensions between the queen and the aristocracy, but pushed the kingdom into war. The most serious episode occurred when Bernat Alemany d'Orriols, a relative of Sibil·la, resolved to defy his overlord, Count Joan of Empúries, by refusing to comply with his feudal obligations. When the matter was put before Pere to resolve, instead of taking the side of his daughter and son-in-law (who seemed to be the injured parties), he instead forced them in 1381 to conclude a humiliating truce that favored Bernat Alemany. Emboldened by this, three years later Bernat again defied Joan, refusing to render the tribute he owed for the Castle of Foixà. Thus provoked, the Count took to arms and attacked

Bernat's territory—an act that violated the truce that had been mandated by the *corts* (Estates-general).

Pere was now obliged to uphold his authority as sovereign by force. He gathered his own troops and with Sibil·la at his side, marched on the count's lands in the Empordà. Joan responded to what he undoubtedly saw as a betrayal by appealing to the King of France, the Dukes of Berry and Armagnac, the Viscount of Castellbó, and the Avignonese pope. Joana, for her part, worked to defuse the conflict by seeking an audience with her father. But Pere's famous anger had been roused, and when his daughter appealed to him to support her husband, the king responded by slapping her face in the presence of the entire court. It would be the last time Pere saw Joana, who having returned to Empúries, died soon after. Meanwhile an invasion force of up to 2,000 French men-at-arms crossed the Catalan frontier, forcing the king and his ever-more resentful heir, Joan, to close ranks to repel the attack. This having been accomplished, in 1386 Pere took his revenge on what he saw as Count Joan's rebelliousness by appropriating the County of Empúries and incorporating it into the royal patrimony.[48] It was an episode that patently illustrated the queen's influence over the king, but consequently put the king's judgment in question and undermined his authority. It would have done nothing to endear them to the rest of the upper elite on which Pere's power ultimately depended. Only a year later, the king was obliged to restore Joan to his county.

## All That Glitters...

The fundamental problem for Sibil·la was that it took more than wealth and title for a woman to be recognized as queen. Lineage was also of fundamental importance as a social marker, and in this respect the queen, the daughter of provincial rustics, suffered an irremediable handicap. Normally the queen's court was the most sought after destination for the daughters of the nobility of the realm. To be invited to serve as a lady-in-waiting was a mark of great prestige and created favorable possibilities for marriage and for the family in question to integrate themselves into the royal household. But the established aristocracy resented Sibil·la as a lower-class *parvenu*, and presented with the choice of pleasing an aged king or his soon-to-be-successor, they sensibly chose the latter. As a result Sibil·la was subject to the public disdain of her aristocratic peers. The most notable episode took place in 1386 when the queen invited Lady Constança d'Aragó to attend her court.[49] Constança refused to come, stating that she had no intention of serving someone who was of lower status than herself. Naturally Pere was incensed by what was not only a grave insult to his queen, but by extension an affront to his own authority. Constança took refuge in Zaragoza, where she was supported by the city council and received the protection of the *infant* Joan. The old king was left sputtering; in an angry dispatch he sent to the municipality of Zaragoza he referred to her as "that dark (*negra*) evil woman, the Devil's daughter, Lady Constança."[50] But Constança's defiance was taken as an example by the women of the other established noble houses. Those who did come were members of the lower-nobility and bourgeoisie, who saw in Sibil·la an opportunity to better their own fortunes and to enter royal circles that otherwise they would not have.

The episode of Constança d'Aragó also proved to be a catalyst for the complete breakdown of relations between the king and his heir. Pere already held a deep grudge against Joan for having defied him by marrying Violant de Bar, and for the old king his son's disrespect of Sibil·la was the final straw. Joan, for his part, well understood that old as he may have been Pere was still king and had the power to undermine or derail the succession. Therefore he decided to attempt a reconciliation and journeyed to Barcelona for an audience to pay his respect to his father. But Pere would have none of it; through June and July 1386 Joan was kept waiting in Martorell, just outside Barcelona, as he begged his father's permission to enter the city. The king refused and Joan, having been publicly rebuked, withdrew to his Duchy of Girona.[51] By this point there was no disguising the conflict between the king and his son. Joan struck back at his father later that year. Pere and Sibil·la hoped to obtain a crown for their daughter Isabel and had been negotiating to marry her to Louis II d'Anjou, King of Naples, but Joan used his influence in the papal court at Avignon and Clement VII scuttled the process.[52] As far as Pere was concerned this was the end of the line for Joan. In the tradition long-established in the Crown of Aragon, Joan had been serving as Pere's lieutenant-general in preparation for his eventual ascent to the throne. Now, driven by suspicion and vindictiveness, the king determined to deprive him of this position, and to give it to none other than Bernat de Fortià, Sibil·la's brother. Given the hostility that the Fortiàs were faced with by the nobility of the realm, such a proposal could hardly be implemented; but, at any rate, Pere would not live to carry it out. The king died on 5 January 1387 at the venerable age of sixty-eight and having ruled his sprawling empire through war, plague, and rebellion for half a century.[53]

## A Queen on the Run

By that point Sibil·la was no longer at her husband's side. Pere had been ill for some time before his death, and it was clear for Sibil·la and her entourage that he was not long for the world. Fearing retribution at the hands of the soon-to-be-king Joan, two weeks before his death she packed up all of her belongings, including her clothing and jewelry and, gathering her family members, most trusted servants and a few loyal followers, fled.[54] It was a curious parallel to the case of Pere's father, Alfons the Benign. Three months before his death in 1336, his second wife, Elionor de Castilla, took her sons Ferran and Joan and fled to the court of her brother Alfonso XI of Castile.[55] Her motive was the same—she feared the vengeance of the new king (in her case, Pere the Ceremonious), for having single-mindedly promoted her children at the expense of the royal patrimony. Through her patronage she had assembled a powerful political party, and her sons were seen as possible pretenders by the restive nobility. Later, in 1396 Sibil·la's successor as queen, Joan's wife Violant de Bar, would face a similar predicament after her husband died. In the view of the new rulers, Martí and Maria de Luna, she and her unpopular courtiers had bankrupted the kingdom and pushed it to the brink of ruin; moreover, she had attempted to derail Martí's succession with a spurious claim to pregnancy.[56] Although Violant did not flee (Joan's death had come by surprise, and Violant had been effectively placed under arrest soon after), she did dispatch letters to her powerful relatives in France, who let it be known to Martí and Maria that they would brook no ill-treatment of their dowager cousin.[57]

Sibil·la's decision to abandon her husband must be considered in this light; she was about to lose her sole protector and be left at the mercy of her sworn enemies. But compared to other dowagers she was at a serious disadvantage because of her humble, local origins. Both Elionor de Castilla and Violant de Bar had powerful families that were based outside the Crown of Aragon and therefore, could provide refuge or protection. Sibil·la's family members, on the other hand, were subordinates of the Aragonese dynasty, and their power and status was a consequence of her position, rather than the other way around. Nevertheless, there was nowhere else to go, and therefore, the soon-to-be dowager fled to St. Martí sa Roca in Catalonia, one of the castles that belonged to her brother Bernat.

But the king's sons were hard on her heels, and the *infant* Martí mustered his forces and laid siege to the castle where Sibil·la had taken refuge. Resistance was futile, and the day after the death of her husband, the king, Sibil·la opened the gates of the castle to the prince and threw herself at his mercy.[58] She, her brother, and their various supporters were placed under arrest. She and Bernat were immediately stripped of the towns, castles, and other properties that they had acquired during her reign and King Joan handed most of these over to his own wife, Violant de Bar.[59] This was merely the prelude to a formal trial in which she and her partisans were accused of abandoning the king and of stealing from the royal patrimony.[60] Finally, came the greatest humiliation—the former queen was accused of using sorcery. Pere's passion for her was seen as so absurd and his decision to marry her so perverse that it could only have been the result of witchcraft. Moreover, after Pere's death, King Joan had fallen ill, and this too was held to be a consequence of Sibil·la's black art.[61] These last charges reflect the beginnings of a fundamental change in European attitudes toward women; a process that would culminate in the "witch-craze" of the sixteenth and seventeenth centuries. Women who exercised what was seen as undue influence over men, or who had transgressed the narrowing boundaries of social and sexual behavior to which they were subject, would henceforth be suspected of being instruments of the Devil. But she did have her title; it was undeniable that she had been queen of the Crown of Aragon and had been crowned before the eyes of God and Man in the Cathedral of Zaragoza. To put a queen, even a disgraced dowager to death or to trial accused of being a witch, would have set a dangerous precedent in this age of Jacqueries and Peasants' Revolts.[62]

Thus, the resentment of Joan, Martí, and the aristocracy was vented on Sibil·la's lesser followers, several of whom were put to death. The queen, however, along with her brother and their most prestigious supporter, Count Huc Roger II of Pallars, were set free.[63] Nor would it reflect well on the new monarchs to have a former queen living in misery, and so Sibil·la was granted an annual pension of 25,000 *sous* for life, while Bernat received a similar assignation of 12,000 *sous*. Several of their properties and castles were restored to them. As for the *infanta* Isabel, whatever her mother's sins may have been, she was the daughter of a former king and was, therefore, welcomed into the royal court. She was provided with her own household, and an income worthy of her station as princess of the blood, and was eventually married to Count Jaume d'Urgell, a direct descendant of Alfons the Benign through the male line.[64] Sibil·la's own allowance, while sufficient, was a far cry from the 150,000 *sous* she had at her disposal as queen, and for her remaining nineteen years she lived rather modestly, renting a house next door to her former palace in Barcelona from her ex-treasurer, Bartomeu de Relat. It was there where she died on 25 November 1406; having had taken the vows of a Franciscan tertiary, she was laid to rest in the order's convent of Barcelona.[65]

## Conclusions

The rise and fall of Sibil·la de Fortià demonstrates that while a queen's power and authority was based almost entirely on the wealth and influence she derived from the publicly expressed esteem and confidence of the king, this alone was not enough to ensure a successful and secure reign, particularly one that would outlive that of her husband. If a queen did not have the support of the upper nobility, or a significant portion of that elite, she could not hope to effectively exercise power. Queenly power depended also on the recognition of her subjects. This was particularly true, as in the case of Sibil·la, when the queen in question had no independent powerbase. Her experiences also reveal that the authority of the king was far more consensual than is often imagined; by going against the will of his subjects—and in particular the members of his own family and the upper aristocracy—Pere risked humiliation and revolt.

The fact that Sibil·la and Pere had been openly adulterous was not a concern. High society was prepared to turn a blind eye to the most blatant violations of established sexual morality on the part of kings, as long as their actions did not threaten the established political and social order. Thus, concubines, like bastards, were tolerated and even welcomed as long as they did not attempt to usurp the legitimately born by daring to assume formal power. The problem with Sibil·la was not that she had been Pere's lover before their marriage, but that she was a member of the "lower class" (or lower upper-class), who had overstepped her bounds. And it was well understood that the queen and her household became a powerful conduit for the redistribution of the wealth of the royal patrimony. Consequently, the members of the established elite would do everything possible to undermine her; a state of affairs that would force Sibil·la in turn to close ranks with the few supporters she had and favor them excessively. The class barrier was very real in both a theoretical and a practical sense; if Sibil·la was not a "bad" queen to start with, the upper aristocracy would ensure that she would become one, at least in their eyes. There would be no Cinderella stories in the medieval Crown of Aragon—however much wealth a king might shower on his beloved, it simply would not be enough if she were not already recognized as a member of the aristocratic "club."[66] Simply put, money was not everything.

## Notes

For historical context, see Thomas N. Bisson, *The Medieval Crown of Aragon: A Short History* (Oxford: Clarendon, 1986); J. N. Hillgarth, *The Spanish Kingdoms, 1250–1516*, 2 vols. (Oxford: Clarendon Press, 1976–78); and Ramón Menéndez Pidal, ed. *Historia de España*, 42 vols. (Madrid: Espasa-Calpe, 2005). Abbreviations used in this article include ACA (Arxiu de la Corona d'Aragó), CSIC (Consejo Superior de Investigaciones Científicas), and RP (Reial Patrimoni).

Personal names are given in the vernacular linguistic variant closest to that which the individuals in question would have used, with the exception of popes, whose names are given in English.

1. Between 1256 and 1266 Alfonso X, King of Castile (r. 1252–84) compiled a legal code known as "The Seven Parts" (*Las siete partidas*). The section of the treatise that relates to queen outlines four characteristics a queen must possess—good lineage, beauty, good education, and wealth—and specified that good behavior and noble lineage were most important. [*Las siete partidas del rey Don Alfonso el Sabio* (Madrid: Real Academia de la Historia, 1972), 3 vols., vol. II, Partida 2,6,1, pp. 41–42.] See John C. Parsons, "Family, Sex, and Power: The Rhythms of Medieval Queenship" in *Medieval Queenship*, ed. John C. Parsons (New York: St. Martin's Press, 1993), pp. 1–12.
2. Josep Maria Roca, "La Reyna empordanesa," *Memorias de la Real Academia de Buenas Letras de Barcelona* 10 (1928): 9–212, p. 14. Roca includes an extensive appendix of edited documents. See also Alberto Boscolo, *La Reina Sibil·la de Fortià* (Barcelona: Rafael Dalmau, 1971), p. 17.
3. Pere gave her 2000 gold *florins* annually taken from the feudal rents of the village of Algezira and the taxes (*peatge*) of the city of Calaç. ACA: RP, reg. 506, f. 1r (11–20–1375). See also Roca, "La Reyna," p. 21. Soon after she began to receive other types of gifts from the king, such as 200 gold *florins* to pay for clothes and jewels that she had bought. ACA: RP, reg. 506, f. 1v (4–1376). The gold *florin*, a coin introduced by Pere the Ceremonious, was valued at 13 *sous* (see below, n. 35).
4. Roca, "La reyna," p. 17.
5. When his son Joan was widowed in 1378 Pere unsuccessfully tried to force him to marry Maria, the daughter of Federico III of Sicily and Constança d'Aragó, and heir to the throne of Sicily.
6. Roca, "La reyna," p. 17; Rafael Tasis, *Joan I, el rei caçador i músic* (Barcelona: 1959), p. 73; Boscolo, *La reina*, pp. 21 and 99–100.
7. After Pere the Ceremonious's great-grandfather, Pere the Great, captured Sicily in 1282, the French led an invasion of Catalonia sanctified as a Crusade by Pope Martin IV.
8. Before marrying Violant de Bar, Joan had been betrothed to Jeanne de Valois, daughter of Philip IV, but she died in 1371 while on her way to Perpignan for the marriage. Two years later Joan married Matha d'Armagnac, the daughter of the Count of Armagnac who died in 1378. Tasis, *Pere el Cerimoniós*, pp. 147–56. See note 6.
9. Andrés Ivars,"La 'indiferencia' de Pedro IV de Aragón en el Gran Cisma de Occidente (1378–1382)," *Archivo Ibero Americano* 29 (1921): 21–97.
10. Pere had Ferran assassinated, while Elionor and Joan were put to death on orders of Pedro the Cruel.
11. Roca, "La Reyna," p. 22.
12. Thomas Kuehn, *Illegitimacy in Renaissance Florence* (Ann Arbor: University of Michigan Press, 2005), p. 8.
13. Lois Huneycutt, "Intercession and the High-Medieval Queen: The Esther Topos," in *Power of the Weak*, ed. Jennifer Carpenter and Sally-Beth MacLean (Urbana: University of Illinois Press, 1995), pp.126–46; Janet Nelson, "Medieval Queenship," in *Women in Medieval Western European*

*Culture*, ed. Linda E. Mitchell (New York: Garland, 1999), pp. 179–207, esp. p.186.

14. ACA: RP, reg. 506, f. 1v (2–28–1376); f. 17r (12–5–1376). Roca, "La reyna," p. 21.
15. The Church did not permit divorce, but recognized that a marriage could be annulled in certain circumstances such as impotence, lack of physical consummation, and consanguinity. The notion of equality of men and women in marriage was a fiction, especially concerning expectations regarding chastity, fidelity, and sexual continence. See D. L. D'Avray, *Medieval Marriage: Symbolism and Society* (Oxford: Oxford University Press, 2005); Christopher Brooke, *The Medieval Idea of Marriage* (Oxford: Oxford University Press, 1989), pp. 130–42.
16. Pauline Stafford, *Queens, Concubines and Dowagers: The King's Wife in the Early Middle Ages* (London: Leicester University Press, 1998), pp. 62–63.
17. Eleanor of Aquitaine presents a rare exception. Confined in castles by her chronically unfaithful husband Henry II (r. 1154–89) for over fifteen years, she continued to be an important political actor thanks to her great personal wealth and her influence over their sons.
18. María Jesús Fuente, *Reinas medievales en los reinos hispánicos* (Madrid: La esfera de los libros, 2003), pp. 272–95.
19. In 1410 Martí I, second son of Pere the Ceremonious, died without a surviving legitimate heir. In 1412 in a verdict known as the "compromise of Caspe," a council gave the throne to Fernando I de Antequera, a member of the Trastámara dynasty of Castile and son of Juan I of Castile and Elionor of Aragon, and therefore grandson of Pere the Ceremonious. Jaume Vicens Vives, *Els Trastàmares* (Barcelona: Editorial Teide, 1956), pp. 78–85.
20. Marriages for love were very rare among the royalty and the nobility in the Middle Ages. The best-known example is Eleanor of Aquitaine who chose to marry Henry, Duke of Normandy and later King of England, in 1152, motivated partly by personal affection. It was a marriage that had rather serious "issues" (see above, n. 17). Elizabeth Brown, "Eleanor of Aquitaine Reconsidered: The Woman and her Seasons" in *Eleanor of Aquitaine. Lord and Lady,* ed. Bonnie Wheeler and John C. Parsons (New York: Palgrave Macmillan, 2003), pp. 1–54.
21. Roca, "La reyna," pp. 13 and 159 (1–4–1382).
22. Roca, "La reyna," pp. 26–27 and 166 (12–8–1377).
23. After Sibil·la only two other queens received formal coronations: Maria de Luna (1399) and Elionor de Albuquerque (1414). Jaume Riera Sans, "La coronació de la reina Elionor (1352)," *Acta Mediaevalia* 26 (2005): 485–92, esp. p.485.
24. In his memoir of 1347 he remarked that it seemed "by the will of God, We will have only daughters [. . .]" Pere III el Cerimoniós, ed. *Crònica*, A. Cortadellas (Barcelona: Edicions 62, 1995), p. 178.
25. Josep Maria Roca, "Johan I d'Aragó," *Memorias de la Real Academia de Buenas Letras de Barcelona*, 11 vols (Barcelona: Institució Patxot, 1929), pp. 432–34, doc. XI; Boscolo, *La reina*, pp. 58–60.

26. Pedro Garcés de Cariñena, *Nobiliario de Aragón, anotado por Zurita, Blancas y otros autores*, M. I. Ubieto Artur, ed. (Zaragoza: Anubar, 1983), p. 262; Jerónimo Zurita, *Anales de la Corona de Aragón* (Zaragoza: Consejo Superior de Investigaciones Científicas, 1978), IV: 670 [X:XXIX]; Esteban Sarasa Sánchez, *Sociedad y conflictos sociales en Aragón, siglos XIII–XV. Estructuras de poder y conflictos de clase* (Madrid: Siglo XXI, 1981); Esteban Sarasa Sánchez, "Mitos y ritos feudales en Aragón. El caso de doña Brianda de Luna," *I Congreso de Aragón de Etnología y Antropología* (Zaragoza: Consejo Superior de Investigaciones Científicas, 1979), pp. 127–32; Salvador Sanpere Miquel, *Las damas d'Aragó* (Barcelona: Impresa de la Renaixensa, 1879), pp. 89–105, and Núria Silleras-Fernández, *Power, Piety, and Patronage in Late Medieval Queenship: Maria de Luna* (New York: Palgrave McMillan, 2008), pp. 67–72.
27. Other noblemen in attendance included the Viscount of Rocabertí, Bernat de Cabrera, Antón de Luna, Pere de Prades, Pere Ferrandez Dixer, Bernat de Pinós, Huc d'Anglesola, Blasco d'Alagó, Arnau d'Orcal and Ot de Montcada. Members of the upper clergy included Archbishop Lope Fernandez de Luna of Zaragoza, Archbishop Giovanni (II) of Sassari, Bishop Hernando Peréz Muñoz of Huesca, the Abbot of the royal monastery San Juan de la Peña, the Abbot of Montearagón, and the Commander of the Military Order of Montesa. The cities of Barcelona, Lleida, Mallorca, Tortosa, Perpignan, and Zaragoza also sent representatives. Roca, "Johan I d'Aragó," pp. 432–34, doc. XI.
28. Roca, "Johan I," p. 432. The *alguacil* was a judicial official.
29. ACA: RP, reg. 506, ff. 1r, 11r, 11v,12v, 13v, 21v, 24r, 43r. Also Roca, "La reyna," 21.
30. In the Crown of Aragon, the fiscal manifestation of the queen's household was known as the *cambra de la reina* ("the queen's chamber"). See Theresa Earenfight's essay in this volume for an examination of the fifteenth-century queen, María of Castile's *cambra*.
31. For Bernat de Foix see ACA: RP, reg. 507, f. 50r (1–1–1378).
32. Roca, "La reyna," pp. 27–28.
33. ACA: RP, reg. 507, ff. 1r, 43r, 43v, 46v, 47v, 52v, 62v, 63v, 64v, 84r, 86r, 86v, 87v, and 99r.
34. ACA: RP, reg. 507, f.51r (1– 31–1378).
35. Sibil·la's feudal rents included 27,000 *sous* from Algezira, 20,000 *sous* from Noella and Mola, 40,000 *sous* from Cocentaina, 50,000 *sous* from Jafuda, 8,000 *sous* from tolls (*peatge*) of Calatayud and 6,000 *sous* in hospitality tax (*cena*). Pere added to these assignations after Sibil·la complained that they were no sufficient. ACA: RP, reg. 507, ff. 1r–v, 2r, 6r, 7r, 7v, 8r, 8v and Roca, "La reyna," pp. 29–30. The *sou* (*sueldo*, *solidus*, shilling), the standard coin of the realm, represented one-twentieth of a silver pound or twelve *diners* (*dineros*, *denarii*, pennies). Compare these figures to those given by Earenfight for María of Castile, and by those given by Rodrigues and Santos for Portuguese queens, also in this volume.
36. Roca, "La reyna," pp. 28–29.

37. Roca, "La reyna," p. 29.
38. See Ronald G. Asch, "Court and Household from the Fifteenth to the Seventeenth Centuries," in *Princes, Patronage, and the Nobility: The Court at the Beginning of the Modern Age, c.1450–1650*, ed. R. G. Asch and A. M. Birke (Oxford: Oxford University Press, 1991), pp. 1–38; Erin Jordan, *Women, Power, and Religious Patronage in the Middle Ages* (New York: Palgrave, 2006), pp. 62–63; Rita Gomes, *The Making of a Court Society: Kings and Nobles in Late Medieval Portugal* (Cambridge: Cambridge University Press, 2003), pp.152–53; Diana Webb, "Queen and Patron," in *Queens and Queenship in Medieval Europe*, ed. Anne J. Duggan (Suffolk: Boydell, 1997), pp. 205–22. See also Helen A. Gaudette's chapter in this book on Melisende of Jerusalem.
39. For the political role of queens, see Ernst Kantorowicz, *The King's Two Bodies: A Study in Medieval Political Theology* (Princeton, NJ: Princeton University Press, 1967), pp. 381–83; Michel Foucault, *History of Sexuality*, 2 vols. (New York: Pantheon, 1978), I: 92–102; Theresa Earenfight, "Partners in Politics" in *Queenship and Political Power in Medieval and Early Modern Spain*, ed. T. Earenfight (Aldershot, UK: Ashgate, 2005), pp. xiii–xxviii, esp. pp. xiv–xvi.
40. The lieutenant acted as a deputy for the king when he was absent from his kingdoms, during war or other times of crisis, or when he was needed in one specific kingdom. Absent an heir, the position normally went to the queen. See Jesús Lalinde, "Virreyes y lugartenientes medievales en la Corona de Aragón," *Cuadernos de Historia de España* 31–32 (1960): 98–172, esp. pp. 111, 121; Theresa Earenfight, "Absent Kings: Queens as Political Partners in the Medieval Crown of Aragon," in Earenfight, *Queenship and Political Power*, pp. 33–51; Núria Silleras-Fernández, "Spirit and Force: Politics, Public and Private in the Reign of Maria de Luna (1369–1406)," in Earenfight, *Queenship and Political Power*, pp. 78–80.
41. In addition to Isabel, Sibil·la and Pere had a son and named him after his father in 1378, but he died the following year. See Tasis, *Pere el Cerimoniós*, p. 112.
42. Roca, "La reyna," pp. 198 (4–10–1380) and 197–8 (5–8–1383).
43. Roca, "La reyna," p. 198 (2–11–1380).
44. For comparison, Maria de Luna supported her bastard half-brother, Ferran López de Luna, when she was queen (r. 1396–1406). Ferran was less troublesome than Bernat, but Maria employed him in key administrative positions, arranged a favorable marriage and a title for him, despite allegations of negligence and incompetence. Silleras–Fernández, *Power, Piety and Patronage*, pp. 73–75.
45. Roca, "La reyna," pp. 199 (10–14–1381 and 11–4–1381), 199–200 (4–2–1383), and 200 (12–2–1382).
46. Roca, "La reyna," pp. 111–5 and 200 (3–16–1383). Timbor was married to the Viscount Bernat IV de Cabrera, Count of Modica and Osona.
47. Roca, "La reyna," pp. 119–26.

48. Santiago Sobrequés Vidal, *Els barons de Catalunya* (Barcelona: Editorial Teide, 1957), pp. 146–49.
49. Roca, "La reyna," p. 165 (11–2–1377).
50. Roca, "La reyna," pp. 203–4 (2–20–1386).
51. Daniel Girona Llagostera, *Itinerari del Rei en Joan I (1387–1396)* (Barcelona: Extret de la Revista d'Estudis Universitaris Catalans, 1931), p. 1.
52. Roca, "La reyna," p. 129; Boscolo, *La reina,* pp. 121–22. Isabel married Jaume d'Urgell, grandson of King Pere's brother Jaume, an unsuccessful claimant for the throne of the Crown of Aragon at Caspe in 1412. Louis II d'Anjou married Joan's daughter, Violant.
53. *Diccionari Biogràfic*, 4 vols. (Barcelona: Albertí, 1969), III: 473.
54. Sibil·la escaped with her mother, her brother, Contança d'Erill, Count Hug de Pallars, Berenguer and Nicolau d'Abella, Bartomeu Llunes, Huget d'Angesola, Berenguer de Senesterra, Pere de Planella, Pere de Vall (the king's treasurer), Beneta d'Arborea, and other family members, including Bernat Ramon de Vilamarí, Botafoc and Bernat Barutell, and Berenguer de Vilaragut. Zurita, *Anales*, IV: 716–22 [X: 40]; Roca, "La reyna," p. 142, Boscolo, *La reina*, p. 126.
55. Tasis, *Pere el Cerimoniós*, p. 7.
56. Núria Silleras-Fernández, "Queenship en la Corona de Aragón en la Baja Edad Media: estudio y propuesta terminológica," *La Corónica. A Journal of Medieval Spanish Language and Literature* 32:1 (2003), pp. 120–25.
57. Silleras-Fernández, "Queenship," pp. 127–28; Silleras-Fernández, *Maria de Luna*.
58. Zurita, *Anales*, IV: 718 [X:XL]; Roca, "La reyna," p. 143.
59. Roca, "La reyna," p. 142; Boscolo, *La reina*, pp. 127–28 and 132.
60. Zurita, *Anales*, IV: 717 [X:XL]; Roca, "La reyna," pp. 143–44.
61. Zurita, *Anales*, IV: 718–19 [X:XL]; Roca, "La reyna," p. 145; Boscolo, *La reina*, pp. 131–33. In 1460, Jaume Roig, a Valencian who was official physician of María of Castile (r. 1416–58), queen of Aragonese King Alfonso the Magnanimous (r. 1416–58) wrote a misogynistic satire known as the *Spill* ("The Mirror") or the *Llibre de les dones* ("The Book of Women"). Roig recounts the story of Sibil·la and alleges that she was judicially tortured along with her accomplices, an opinion the sixteenth-century Aragonese historian Jerónimo Zurita agreed with. This is unlikely and probably represents an embellishment on the part of Roig.

    For Joan to attribute sickness to sorcery was completely in character. Not only was he frequently ill, but also he was superstitious. When his fiancée Jeanne de Valois died in 1371 at Beziers en route to their wedding ceremony (see above, n. 8) he arrested Bonanada, a midwife who served in the household of his mother, Elionor de Sicilia, because it was rumored she had killed the princess using sorcery. Queen Elionor intervened. In an angry letter she defended Bonanada's innocence, demanded her immediate release, discredited the woman's accusers as liars, and shamed Joan by saying that was inappropriate for a future king to give credence to obviously fantastic tales. See the document in Roca, "Johan I," pp. 372–3 (10–6–1373). See also Robin Briggs, *Witches and Neighbors: The Social and Cultural Context of European Witchcraft* (New York: Penguin, 1998), pp. 61–63.

62. Pedro "the Cruel" of Castile did indeed put two queens to death: his aunt Leonor de Castilla, the dowager of Alfons the Benign of Aragon (1336) and Blanche de Bourbon, his own wife (1361). Both of these, however, were extrajudicial killings.
63. Berenguer d'Abella and Bartolomé Limes were executed on 19 April 1387, Zurita, *Anales*, IV: 719 [X:XL]; Roca, "La reyna," p. 143.
64. Zurita, IV: 720 [X:XL]. Pere named Sibil·la as one of the executors of his will and specified that she was to have the care of their daughter Isabel and any other children they might have (the queen was pregnant when the document was drafted), and confirmed various donations and properties he had given her. The will is edited in Antoni Udina Abelló, *Els testaments dels comtes de Barcelona i dels reis de la Corona d'Aragó* (Barcelona: Fundació Noguera, 2001), pp. 340–54 (8–17–1379). See also Roca, "La reyna," pp. 147–54.
65. Roca, "La reyna," pp. 154 and 158.
66. Astute members of the elite understood this. After the death of Martí in 1410, his second wife, Margarida de Prades, became enamored of her chamberlain, Joan de Vilaragut. She married him and had a child but kept the relationship in absolute secrecy to her death. Núria Silleras-Fernández, "Widowhood and Deception: Ambiguities of Queenship in Late Medieval Crown of Aragon," in *Shell Games. Studies in Scams, Frauds, and Deceits (1300–1650),* ed. M. Crane, R. Raiswell and M. Reeves (Toronto: Centre for Reformation and Renaissance Studies, 2004), pp. 185–87 and 196–207.

CHAPTER 5

# MERCHANT WOMEN AND THE ADMINISTRATIVE GLASS CEILING IN THIRTEENTH-CENTURY PARIS

*Sharon Farmer*

With a population that approached 200,000 around the year 1300, Paris was the largest city in Western Europe.[1] Like other major cities, it had a stratum of wealthy bourgeois merchants who also dominated the local urban government. Paris differed from other French towns, however, because it was the center of royal government and because virtually every major aristocrat and high church leader in France and Flanders had a residence there.[2] The special status of the city offered unique opportunities to the leaders of the Parisian merchant class.

Boris Bove described these opportunities in his recent study of the forty-three merchant families that produced the municipal leaders of Paris between 1260 and 1350. According to Bove, commercial success in Paris frequently resulted in appointments to royal and aristocratic administrative offices. Men of the Parisian upper bourgeoisie who started their careers as drapers (merchants of wool cloth), mercers (merchants of silk cloth and mercery goods), and furriers soared to the heights of wealth and power when they were granted positions such as master of the royal mint, treasurer of the realm, or master of the royal forests and waters. On an even more intimate level vis-à-vis the king, some of these men ended up serving as officers of the royal court itself, as master of the royal stables, chamberlain, king's *pantler*, or king's *argentier* (the officer in charge of purchases of luxury textiles for the king's clothing and that of his family).[3]

A number of the women in these prominent Parisian families were well-known retailers in their own right. Indeed, because Parisian inheritance customs favored dividing an inheritance equally among siblings or among all those of the same degree of kinship, women inherited their family businesses along with their brothers.[4] And because Parisian inheritance practice favored widows, a number of widows in this group took over their husbands' businesses, even if they had children. Often, Parisian widows would share a business with their children, but the widow had the larger share in the business and the children eventually moved on, leaving the widow to run the business on her own.[5] A number of women, moreover, maintained separate businesses even while their husbands were alive. Some, like Erembourc of Moustereul and Genevieve la Fouacière, were independent textile merchants; others—including at least two women from families of Parisian alderman—drew on the capital from their husbands' businesses to lend money at interest.[6]

Nevertheless, even when they rose to the highest echelons of Parisian taxpayers, merchant women in Paris experienced a glass ceiling: they never held municipal office, nor do we see them entering the ranks of the powerful royal and state administrative offices that were held by the men in their families. The financial rewards for top royal administrative positions—especially royal gifts of lucrative rents on administrative offices—greatly enhanced the financial success of the men of Parisian alderman families; the women, however, enjoyed those rewards only indirectly, as wives, widows, and heiresses.[7]

The Statutes, or *Ordonnances,* of the French Royal Household—written rules defining the rights and privileges of various individuals who had access to the king—create an even broader impression of the glass ceiling that excluded women. For instance, a list of Statutes from the reign of King Charles IV (1322–28) mentions over thirty Parisian merchants who had special privileges at the royal court; all of those merchants were men.[8]

Women merchants in Paris experienced a glass ceiling because of restrictions on their access to political and administrative office; and if we are to believe the prescriptions of the *Ordonnances* of the French royal household, they even experienced exclusion from commercial contact with the court. Their apparent exclusion from administrative office and from the royal court fits into a pattern that historians of medieval women have emphasized again and again: with the advent of royal bureaucratic government in the twelfth century and with the growth of urban government, women found themselves increasingly excluded from centers of political power.[9]

Nevertheless, if we adjust our sites, focusing not on the very highest administrative offices, but on the next notch down in the hierarchy of official and unofficial administrative and courtly positions, and if we look at actual practice rather than at royal prescriptions, we find that a number of women became extremely influential as furnishers to royal and aristocratic courts and that commercial contact with royal and aristocratic courts could lead to official positions at the royal court and in royal and aristocratic administrations.

In the rest of this chapter, I will discuss three groups of merchant and administrative women who gained access to and privileges at royal and aristocratic courts in the late thirteenth and fourteenth centuries. First, I will discuss merchant women who sold luxury goods to royal and aristocratic households, focusing especially on three women who dominated their fields in the late thirteenth and early fourteenth centuries. I will then turn to a handful of women who gained recognition as official purveyors of luxury goods to the French royal household. Finally, I will discuss over a dozen women—many of whom probably started out as merchants of luxury goods—who attained administrative positions as concierges of royal and aristocratic residences.

While my analysis incorporates evidence from the 1270s to the 1450s, most of the evidence comes from two categories of sources from the years 1292–1328. First, there was a series of seven tax assessments for levies that King Philip IV imposed on the citizens of Paris. The assessments were made in 1292, 1296–1300, and 1313. The assessments of 1296–1300 constituted the last five years of an eight-year period when the king collected 10,000 Parisian pounds (*livres parisis*) each year from between 9,000 and 11,000 Parisian heads of household. These assessments seem to have been based on the estimated value of each taxpayer's business income, inventory, and investment. Manual laborers who were paid by the day or week, people who were too poor to pay taxes, religious professionals, and the nobility were not included on the lists. The assessments for 1293, 1294, and 1295—the first three years of the eight year run—have been lost, as has that part of the 1296 assessment that listed the more modest tax payers, or *menu peuple*, who paid a tax of between 2 and 5 *sous*.[10] The assessment for 1292 includes many more taxpayers—c. 14,500—than are included in the assessments of 1297–1300, largely because taxpayers deemed capable of paying only 1 *sou* were included.[11] Although the precise purpose of the 1292 assessment is not clear, the dominant theory among historians of Paris is that it was drawn up in preparation for the levy that ran from 1293 to 1300.[12] The assessment of 1313 is not quite comparable to the other assessments, because its function was different—it was drawn up for the knighting of the king's oldest son. This assessment included fewer taxpayers than the others—approximately 6,000. Moreover, the 1313 levy occurred after the currency had been devalued, so it is difficult to draw comparisons between taxes paid in 1313 and those paid earlier.[13]

Despite the differences among the various assessments, they provide remarkable data for a twenty-one year period in the life of Parisian merchants and artisans. Because each taxpayer was listed by parish and street, and because many of them had last names or other consistent markers of identity, in addition to their first names, it is sometimes possible to trace an individual's rise to financial prominence and to analyze the transmission of family businesses from one generation to another. It is also possible to calculate the relative importance of women within a given profession. Overall, women constituted 13.8 percent of the heads of household who were assessed in the tax assessments of 1297–1300 (the years for which we have the most comparable data).[14] Because of the emphasis on heads of household, working wives usually disappear in these assessments. Moreover, not every taxpayer was identified by profession, and the assessors recorded men's professions more often than they recorded those of women—so all attempts at statistical analysis of various professions are only approximations.[15] Nevertheless, by comparing the percentage of women among the heads of household who were identified as practicing a particular profession to the percentage of women taxpayers overall, we gain some insight into professions that included high proportions of women and professions that included very few women.

The other records that are important for this study are the account books that were kept by royal and aristocratic households. In these accounts, administrators who worked for kings, queens, and aristocrats attempted to keep track of the expenses that their employers incurred to maintain their lavish lifestyles. The accounts thus list, usually in separate categories, disbursements for food, clothing, jewelry, and plate, and for the maintenance of furnishings and horses.[16] Among the surviving household accounts that overlap with the tax assessments of 1292–1313, the richest and most complete for what they reveal about Parisian merchants are the accounts of Count Robert II of Artois and his daughter, Countess Mahaut of Artois, covering the years 1292–1328. The count probably generated two to three household account books each year between 1292 and 1302; his daughter apparently generated three household account books each year between 1302 and 1328. Out of approximately one hundred household account books that the count and countess originally generated between 1292 and 1328, thirty-three have survived to the present day.[17] In addition, the archival sources from Artois include not only the household account books themselves but also thousands of supporting documents, including receipts from Parisian merchants and accounts kept by the concierges of several Artois residences.[18]

Royal and aristocratic household account books indicate that between 1278 and 1450 at least twenty women sold textiles to royal and aristocratic households. There were three woman drapers, who sold high-end woolens; there was one woman who sold tapestries; there were three individual mercers plus another cluster of unnamed mercers, who sold silk cloth, silk products, and mercery goods; and there were thirteen women who sold fine linens, including table linens, towels, altar cloths, and linen fabric for stockings and underwear.[19] The predominance of linen merchants in this group conforms to what the tax assessments from 1297 to 1300 tell us about women's relative importance in this profession—women constituted 50 percent of the linen merchants who were identified in those tax assessments.[20]

The prominence of women among the linen merchants of medieval Paris, and women's strong presence among the mercers (20 percent in the tax assessments of 1297–1300)[21] also fits a long-term trend: scholars of early modern Paris have recently demonstrated that women mercers—including merchants of fine linen—played a major role in the luxury fashion markets of eighteenth-century Paris.[22] There is evidence for such women in the seventeenth century as well.[23] Although I have not had the opportunity to examine evidence from the sixteenth century, my guess is that the prominent women mercers of seventeenth- and eighteenth-century Paris were the heirs to a pattern that had been set by the end of the thirteenth century and that persisted right up to the French revolution of 1789.

But overall numbers and percentages tell only part of the story, for there were some women who clearly attained unrivalled positions as the leading Parisian merchants of a given category of goods. And what we have to remember is that being at the pinnacle of the retail market in thirteenth- and early fourteenth-century Paris put an individual at the pinnacle of the retail market in Northwest Europe: every aristocrat in France and Flanders had a residence in Paris. Paris served as a focal point for their itineraries and was frequently the place where they spent the most time.[24] It was in Paris, moreover, that they did most of their luxury shopping—for just about everything except woolen cloth. Paris was the best place to purchase jewelry, gold and silver plate, imported silks, saddles, harnesses, and spices. Moreover, it was a major center—along with Reims and Rouen—for the production of luxury linens; its tapestries were rivaled only by those of Arras; and its embroidered textiles and alms purses were highly prized as well. Even the English kings and queens regularly sent their buyers to Paris to purchase these goods.[25]

One of the women in the group of unrivaled women merchants—Ysabel of Tremblay—was from the highest stratum of Parisian bourgeois society: her husband served twice as a witness, or *prud'homme*, for the municipal government of Paris, her aunt's husband, Etienne Haudry, served both as a *prud'homme* and as an alderman, and her son served as an alderman.[26] Ysabel's husband, Jean, was a major draper who supplied fine woolens to the household of the Count of Artois.[27] When Jean died, Ysabel took over the family business. Her grown son and her son-in-law lived nearby and were also identified in the 1313 tax assessment as drapers, but the two younger men were clearly less established than Ysabel. In that year, Ysabel paid an enormous tax of 75 *livres tournois* (or 60 *livres parisis*), while her son-in-law, who was taxed with her, paid a tax of only 9 *livres tournois*, and her son, whose business was either part of hers or nearby on the same street, paid a tax of 18 *livres tournois*.[28] Ysabel's favored position vis-à-vis those of her son and son-in-law was not at all unusual: Parisian widows usually took over family businesses, and while many adult children started out working under their widowed mothers, most eventually moved on, leaving the widow with full charge of the family business.[29]

Nevertheless, the Parisian tax assessments suggest that Ysabel's role as a major female draper was extremely unusual: in the years 1297–1300 less than 2 percent of the taxpayers who were identified as drapers were women.[30] I suspect, however, that more women participated in this profession than the assessments reveal. The 1292 tax assessment listed over twenty taxpaying women from alderman families—which dominated the draper profession—but no profession is named for any of those women.[31] This was probably because the families were so well-known that no other source of identification was needed. Since these women appear in the assessments it is clear that they headed some kind of business, we simply do not know what it was. I also suspect that because these women were so wealthy and their families were so well known they did not remain in a widowed state for very long unless they wanted to. Once they remarried they may well have continued practicing a profession, but in most cases only their husbands appeared in the tax assessments. Still we do catch occasional glimpses in the tax assessments of working wives in this group. Indeed, the assessment of 1313 indicates that two women who had married into the family of Ysabel of Tremblay's husband were prominent moneylenders.[32]

Whether there were more women drapers than the tax assessments would lead us to believe, it remains the case that Ysabel of Tremblay was extremely unusual. Indeed, the size of the tax that she paid in 1313 placed her among the top sixteen tax payers—or the top .27 percentile—of people who were assessed in that year.[33] That group included no other women. Ysabel was also unusual because for at least six months, if not longer, she held a virtual monopoly on the sale of luxury woolens to the French royal household. In the second half of 1316, a period for which we have one of the rare surviving records of the *Argenterie*, or French royal wardrobe accounts, Ysabel supplied the French royal household with virtually all of its wool cloth—including purchases for All Saints' Day (November 1), when winter clothing was disbursed to household members, Christmas, the installation ceremony of Pope John XXII, and the coronation ceremony of King Philip V and Queen Jeanne of Burgundy. The wool that Ysabel sold to the royal household in 1316 was used to make garments for the king, the queen, and the royal children, and it was given away as gifts and liveries to approximately 120 people. The total value of Ysabel's sales to the royal household in 1316 added up to more than 2,215 *livres parisis*, which was a huge sum of money.[34]

The next two prominent merchants whom I want to discuss dominated the aristocratic linen market in Paris for almost fifty years. The first of those two was Jeanne la Fouacière, who first shows up in an account of purchases made by the English royal household in 1278, when agents for the English king were sent to Paris to purchase luxury goods in preparation for a tournament at Windsor castle.[35] The agents purchased a total of 130 *livres* worth of fine linens at that time, all of them from Jeanne la Fouacière. In the rare French royal accounts that record purchases of linen cloth, we find Jeanne two times, in 1307 and 1308.[36] In each of those cases, the linen purchases involving Jeanne are the only ones that are mentioned. Jeanne also shows up as a frequent supplier of fine linens to the household of the Countess of Artois between 1302 and 1310, although she is not the only linen merchant in those records.[37]

When she wrote her last will and testament in 1313, Jeanne la Fouacière identified herself as a widow, but we are never told the name of her husband, nor what profession he may have exercised.[38] In her testament, Jeanne also mentions her sister, Genevieve, who, like Jeanne, shows up in the Artois accounts as a linen merchant. Genevieve's husband, William of St.-Marcel, was a mercer.[39]

Jeanne la Fouacière also appears in the late thirteenth-century Parisian tax assessments, although she is never identified in those assessments as a merchant of linen cloth. Her tax assessments were well above those of most women who sold linen cloth: whereas the average tax for women who were linen merchants was under 3 *livres*, Jeanne paid between 12 and 16 *livres*.[40] These tax payments put her in the range of the average taxes of the Parisian aldermen—whose members included the wealthiest of the Parisian bourgeoisie.[41] Indeed, Jeanne's social connections overlapped with those of alderman families—one of the executors of her will was a priest who served as executor for Jeanne Haudry, wife of the alderman

Etienne Haudry.[42] There is no evidence, however, that Jeanne was, herself, related to any aldermen.[43]

After Jeanne la Fouacière died in 1313, Erembourc of Moustereul emerged as the leading Parisian furnisher of fine linens. She shows up both in the accounts of Countess Mahaut of Artois and in the French royal accounts.[44] The Artois accounts also indicate that Erembourc provided services for the Pope in Avignon: in 1327 and 1328 she took charge of shipping to Avignon the clothing, saddles and harnesses that Pope John XXII delivered to his knights during his Easter and All Saints' livery ceremonies.[45] It made sense for a linen merchant to take on these responsibilities: silks, especially, were always wrapped in linen for shipment.

The tax assessments indicate that Erembourc rose to prominence as a linen merchant from a relatively modest background. Between 1298 and 1300 she was listed in the tax assessments as a mere linen weaver, paying an annual tax of 10 *sous*, which was half a *livre*.[46] This was below the average tax for the overall population, which was just under a *livre*. By 1313, however Erembourc's fortunes had changed dramatically. She does not appear in the tax assessments herself that year, but her husband does, paying a relatively large tax of 6 *livres tournois*, which was close to three times the size of the average tax paid in that year.[47] What is particularly striking, however, is the fact that Erembourc's husband is listed in relationship to her, as "Fee Baudichon, husband of Erembourc of Monteruel." In Erembourc and Fee's case, the tax assessors conformed to the usual norm of listing only the male head of household in the tax assessment, but they acknowledged, nevertheless, that it was Erembourc who earned the more significant income.

One privilege that was available to prominent merchants who furnished the French royal household was the opportunity to participate in the process of compiling an inventory of the possessions of recently deceased members of the royal family and the opportunity to purchase some of those possessions. In 1328, Erembourc of Moustereul was the only person who purchased linens that had belonged to the recently deceased Queen Clemence of Hungary.[48] Jeanne la Fouacière must have been offered a similar opportunity to purchases linens from the estate of Queen Margaret of Provence, widow of King Louis IX, who died in 1295. When she wrote her own will in 1313, Jeanne bequeathed to the main hospital of Paris (the *Hôtel Dieu*), "my best bed set, with a coverlet, which once belonged to Queen Margaret, the widow of King Louis IX."[49] We can well imagine that between 1295 and 1313 the bed linens of Queen Margaret held pride of place in the shop of Jeanne la Fouacière, reminding Jeanne's customers of her special relationship with the French royal court.

The second group of prominent Parisian women merchants that I want to discuss consists of those who gained recognition as the French king's official purveyors of particular commodities. In the scattered royal and aristocratic household accounts from 1278 to 1450 I have located four of these women: Peronnelle, who was the king's spice merchant or spice specialist (*Espicière le roy*) between 1299 and 1307; Peronnelle de Crepon, who was identified as the king's tapestry merchant or tapestry weaver in 1374; another Peronnelle, who was the purveyor of the king's gloves between 1368 and 1375; and Jeanne of Dammartin, purveyor of the king's gloves in 1387.[50] My discussion focuses on Peronnelle the spice merchant because the Parisian tax assessments enable us to piece together the evolution of her career.

Peronnelle l'Espicière first shows up in the Parisian tax records in 1292, when she was identified as a spice merchant.[51] By 1299, however, and again in 1300, she was identified in the tax records as *Espicière le roy*, a position that she apparently held until at least 1307.[52] Peronnelle's role as the king's favored furnisher of spices was not a monopoly—the French royal court did not allow that—nor did her relationship with the royal court prevent her from doing business with other customers.[53] Indeed, we can assume that in identifying Peronnelle as the official furnisher of spices to the king, the royal court enhanced her business reputation, and thus her circle of customers.

Spice dealers sold a variety of goods, most of which arrived in Paris via long distance trade. Their merchandise included spices from the Far East; sugar, rice, cotton, and silk cocoons from the Mediterranean basin; as well as wax, nuts, pigments, and dyes.[54] Apparently because spices were often used for medicinal purposes, spice specialists could attain prominent positions in royal and aristocratic courts. Indeed, according to the statutes of the French royal household written in 1316, the king's spice specialist at that time was one of the king's three "valets de chambre," along with his barber and his tailor.[55]

Overall, women were slightly underrepresented among merchants of spices: in the Parisian tax assessments of the years 1297–1300, women who were heads of households constituted 11 percent of spice dealers paying taxes, which was just less than women's overall representation in the tax assessments (13.8 percent).[56] This is about what we would expect, since women who were spice merchants paid a tax that was slightly above the average tax, and women's representation within a given profession tended to decrease as the average income of the profession increased. In the years 1297–1300, the years for which we have the most comparable data, women spice merchants paid an average tax of 1.7 *livres*; the average tax payment during those years was just less than 1 *livre*.[57] As we might expect for the woman who came to be known as the king's spice merchant, Peronnelle did even better than most women within her profession: between 1297 and 1300 Peronnelle's assessments ranged from 6 *livres* to 8.75 *livres*.[58]

Already in her earliest appearance in the tax assessments, in 1292, Peronnelle's place both within her profession and within her family is striking: it appears that she and her brother had inherited a family business, but that she was now the one who was in charge. In that year Peronnelle paid a tax of 7 *livres*, while her brother paid one of only 2.5 *livres*. Moreover, her brother appeared on the tax assessment immediately after her, and he was identified as "Pierre, her brother."[59] Peronnelle was assessed each year between 1296 and 1300. In 1296, 1298, 1299, and 1300 she was listed as the first taxpayer on the Petit Pont, the bridge between the left bank and the Île-Notre-Dame, where the king resided. Of over a dozen spice merchants on the Petit Pont, Peronnelle paid the highest tax. Peronnelle's brother Pierre was assessed only in 1296 and 1299. In both cases, he was identified as Peronnelle's brother, and in both cases, his tax was considerably lower than hers: in 1296 he paid a tax of 58 *sous* while she paid a tax of 6 *livres*, 10 *sous* (a total of 130 *sous*); in 1299 she paid 8 *livres*, 15 *sous* (or 175 *sous*) while he paid only 20 *sous*.[60]

Peronnelle thus provides an example of a woman who enjoyed a favored position over her brother in inheriting a family business. This was unusual: the Parisian tax assessments indicate that while daughters often inherited a business, it was relatively rare for a sister to gain precedence over her brother.[61] Even more unusual is the fact that Peronnelle emerged, within a profession dominated by men, as the king's favored furnisher of spices.

As prominent purveyors of luxury goods, women like Ysabel of Tremblay, Jeanne la Fouacière, Erembourc of Moustereul and Peronnelle l'Espicière had the kinds of experiences that could lead to administrative positions: they were literate and numerate, so they could keep accounts; they knew luxury products and luxury markets; and they had connections in high places. It is for this reason that so many of the male drapers, mercers, and furriers of Paris ended up serving as administrators to aristocrats and kings.

The same was true, I believe, for some of the women merchants of Paris. At least a dozen women in and around Paris served as concierges of aristocratic and royal residences in the years 1292–1328.[62] I do not know the backgrounds of most of these women, but the evidence indicates that some concierges started out as merchants of luxury goods: one male concierge for the Parisian residence of the Count of Artois was also a goldsmith, and a woman spice dealer who did a lot of business with the Countess of Artois ended up working as her concierge as well.[63]

Concierges did not enjoy an intimate relationship with their employers: along with their household entourage, kings and aristocrats led a peripatetic life, moving several times a month from one residence to another; concierges by contrast were tied to one particular residence. Nevertheless, the concierge of a rural chateau or urban aristocratic residence was more than a simple guardian. Moreover, the concierge of an aristocrat's Parisian residence had extra responsibilities, because on multiple occasions when the lord or lady of the residence was not in town the concierge would be asked to make important purchases of luxury goods. We know from the surviving accounts kept by several concierges of the Count and Countess of Artois that their duties encompassed acting as property managers, contractors, rent collectors, interior designers, and tailors. In the 1270s the concierge of the Artois residence in Paris collected rents on eighteen rental properties that the count owned on the adjacent rue Pavée.[64] In 1302 an unnamed concierge, probably a woman, paid to repair the porter's room, which had been damaged by fire, and had the rabbit warren repaired to keep the rabbits away from ditches and trees in the garden.[65] In 1303 the Artois concierge, Madame Bienvenue, paid to repair the kitchen, several doors, several pieces of furniture, the fountain, and the stables at the Artois residence in Paris. She also employed a gardener to tend to the grapevines, bought silk to cover a book that had belonged to the queen, and commissioned a silk embroidery for the chapel.[66]

The records of Count Robert of Artois and his daughter indicate that at least ten individuals served as concierges for the Artois residence in Paris between 1292 and 1328.[67] Three of the ten were women. One of the three—Jeanne of Léry—served as concierge for the Artois residence for at least six years, from 1297 to 1301, and again in 1302–3.[68] This is one of the two longest periods of service that I have identified for any single concierge in the Artois records.

As concierge of the Parisian residence of the count of Artois, Jeanne of Léry was paid a daily wage of 1.5 to 2 *sous* a day. 2 *sous* per day was a typical wage for the literate clerks who worked for the state bureaucracy. For instance, that was the wage that was paid in 1313 to the clerks who assisted in compiling the Parisian tax assessment for the knighting of the king's oldest son. However, clerks who worked for the state were not paid on Sundays or holidays.[69] More important, I suspect that the official wages of concierges constituted only icing on the cake—a supplement to the free housing that they received, to whatever business income they continued to generate on the side, and to perks that they folded into expense accounts submitted to their employers. Jeanne of Léry's tax payment of 1 *livre* was about the same as the average overall tax in Paris; it was above average for a woman's tax.[70]

In addition to these two women whose work for the Artois household was limited to the role of concierge, a third woman—Jeanne l'Espicière, who was indeed a spice merchant—seems to have provided multiple services to the Artois household. Jeanne l'Espicière first appears as a supplier of spices to the Artois household in 1308,[71] but by 1310 she was providing other services as well. We find her in that year, together with Pierre the Tailor, who was identified as the concierge of the Artois residence in Paris, buying linen from Jeanne la Fouacière, which was used to make bed sheets in the Artois residence and clothing for members of the Artois household.[72] In 1315, the Artois household reimbursed Jeanne in her capacity as concierge for payments that she had made to masons, glaziers, and tile cutters who had worked on the residence and its fountain and for her purchases of linen cloth and linen towels.[73] In 1317 she shows up again, along with another man who is identified as the concierge, as a witness when the countess's treasurer removed funds, in an official capacity, from the Artois treasury in Paris.[74] Throughout the period that she provided these services for the residence, Jeanne and her husband, Pierre le Vaillant, continued to sell spices to the Artois household.[75]

There is no question that elite women merchants of the thirteenth through the fifteenth centuries experienced an administrative glass ceiling in Paris. They were not awarded valuable positions as masters of the royal mint, as officers of the royal forests, or as treasurers of the realm. Nevertheless, a number of women gained unsurpassed reputations as merchants of fine luxury goods, and through those reputations they gained favor in the courts that they served. Moreover, while these women could not hold the highest offices in royal, aristocratic, and state administrations, they could hold some offices, such as that of concierge of a major royal or aristocratic residence; and a number of them were recognized as officially named purveyors of goods and services to the royal household. Even without an official title, moreover, some prominent women retailers came to hold near monopolies in supplying royal or aristocratic households with a particular category of luxury goods, and their favored relationships with those households could lead to favored opportunities, such as the chance to own and display luxury goods that had once belonged to members of the royal family.

The evidence of aristocratic and royal household accounts indicates that women merchants of Paris continued to hold prominent positions as purveyors of fine linens, silks, and mercery goods well into the fifteenth century. Indeed, it appears that the gendered patterns that were established in the thirteenth and fourteenth centuries continued into the early modern period as well. By the end of the thirteenth century, women were strongly represented among the mercers and linen merchants of Paris; two of those women dominated the Parisian market in fine linens for nearly fifty years. By 1378 several women mercers had attained highly prestigious stalls in the gallery of the Palais Royale in Paris; women mercers and merchants of fine linens and laces were still well established in the Palais Royale in the seventeenth and eighteenth centuries, although in the eighteenth century many of those mercers relocated to the Rue St. Honoré once it become a center for shops specializing in luxury fashions.[76]

During the reign of King Louis XVI, the dressmaker Rose Bertin held so much sway over Queen Marie Antoinette that many called her "the minister of fashion." Rose was only one of a whole group of women merchants who set fashion trends in eighteenth-century Paris. According to Jennifer Jones, "from seamstresses and linen drapers to female hairdressers and *marchandes de modes,* women played an important role in the Parisian fashion trade" in the eighteenth century.[77] Women's prominence in these trades, Jones argues, is indicative of an eighteenth-century feminization of fashion, which resulted from a growth in the numbers of women among the working poor as well as from a perception, on the part of social reformers, that access to work in the clothing trades could provide single women and widows with a respectable way to support themselves.[78]

But how much of this was really new in the eighteenth century? As I have argued elsewhere, singlewomen and widows already constituted a significant proportion of the working poor in thirteenth-century Paris.[79] It is clear, moreover, that many of those women contributed to the production of luxury textiles and fashion accessories: the seven female guilds that were created in Paris between c. 1260 and 1300 were all connected with the creation of silk fabric, silk accessories, embroidered accessories, and women's hats; and women constituted approximately 90 percent of the silk weavers in late thirteenth-century Paris.[80] Moreover, by the end of the thirteenth century, merchant women in Paris were well established as purveyors of linen and silk textiles. Already in the thirteenth and fourteenth centuries, in the prominent careers of women like Jeanne la Fouacière and Erembourc of Moustereul, we see the precursors of Rose Bertin and the other eighteenth-century *marchandes de mode.* Moreover, in the careers of Peronnelle L'Espicière, who became the king's purveyor of spices, and Jeanne L'Espicière, who served the Countess of Artois both as a supplier of spices and as concierge, we see the ways in which medieval women managed to cross the gender barrier between commerce and administration.

## Notes

1. See Sharon Farmer, *Surviving Poverty in Medieval Paris: Gender, Ideology and the Daily Lives of the Poor* (Ithaca, NY: Cornell University Press, 2001), p. 17, note 19 for general discussion of the debates surrounding the size of the population of Paris.
2. Josef Semmler, "Die Residenzen der Fürsten und Prälaten im mittelalterlichen Paris (12.–14. Jahrhundert)," in *Mélanges offerts à René Crozet*, ed. Pierre Gallais and Yves-Jean Riou, 2 vols. (Poitiers: Société d'études médiévales, 1966), 2:1217–36.
3. Boris Bove, *Dominer la ville: prévôts des marchands et échevins parisiens de 1260 à 1350* (Paris: Editions CTHS, 2004), pp. 69–105, 269–91.
4. Le Roux de Lincy, *Histoire de l'Hotel de Ville de Paris* (Paris: J. B. Dumoulin, 1846), pt. 2, pp. 121–22 (Sentences of the Parloir aux bougeois from 1293).
5. Janice Archer, "Working Women in Thirteenth-Century Paris (PhD Dissertation, University of Arizona, 1995), p. 142. See the discussion of Ysabel of Tremblay in this chapter, p. 94. Ysabel was a widowed draper whose share in her husband's business was much larger than those of her son and son-in-law. Another widow from the alderman class who went into business with her son, but had the greater share in the business, is Peronnelle, "widow of Jehan Augier," who, in 1297 paid a tax of 11 *livres* 5 *sous*. Next to her on the tax assessments and sharing a valet and *chambriere* with her was Jehan Augier, apparently her son, who paid a tax of 7 *livres* 16 *sous*. Karl Michaëlsson, *Le livre de la taille de Paris, l'an 1297* (Göteberg: Elanders Boktryckeri Aktiebolag, 1962), p. 33. Peronnelle or her deceased husband also had two daughters (Agnes, "daughter of the deceased Jehan Augier" and Jeanne, "daughter of the deceased Jean Augier") who had moved to another street, where they had a joint business with a combined value that was almost equal to the combined value of the business of their mother and brother Michaelsson, *Le livre de la taille . . . 1297*, pp. 26–27.
6. The tax assessment of 1313 included marginal notes concerning ten men of various occupations (draper, spice merchant, innkeeper, maker of armor, etc.) whose wives were identified as "monnoieres"; two of those women were married to men in the de Tremblay family, which included several aldermen (see discussion of Ysabel of Tremblay, below). While the term "monnoier/e" could refer either to a person who minted money or to a person who changed or lent money, the context for these women suggests that they lent money: most of the marginal notes for these wives indicate that the wife's share of the tax burden was one-half of the total tax burden for the household; the assumed relationship between the value of the husbands' businesses and the value of the wives' businesses suggests that the women were money lenders and that the money that they had to lend was generated by their husbands' businesses: Karl Michaëlsson, *Le livre de la taille de Paris, l'an de grace 1313* (Göteberg: Wettergren & Kerbers Förlag, 1951), pp. xviii–xix.

7. On institutional rents, which were much more lucrative than rents on urban properties, see Bove, *Dominer*, pp. 106–14.
8. Bibliothèque Nationale de France, ms. Clairambault 833, fol. 736–737, 739.
9. Jo Ann McNamara and Suzanne Wemple, "The Power of Women Through the Family in Medieval Europe, 500–1100," in *Women and Power in the Middle Ages*, ed. Mary Erler and Maryanne Kowaleski (Athens: University of Georgia Press, 1988), pp. 83–102; Marian F. Facinger, "A Study of Medieval Queenship: Capetian France, 987–1237," *Studies in Medieval and Renaissance History* 5 (1968): 3–47; Lois Huneycutt, *Matilda of Scotland: A Study in Medieval Queenship* (Rochester, NY: Boydell, 2003); Martha C. Howell, *Women, Production and Patriarchy in Late Medieval Cities* (Chicago: University of Chicago Press, 1986).
10. For general discussion of the 1293–1300 assessments, see Archer, "Working Women," pp. 77–80, 152–53. All five of the assessments from 1296 to 1300 are contained in ms. KK 283 in the Archives Nationales in Paris (henceforth AN KK 283). The assessments of 1296 and 1297 have been published: Karl Michaëlsson, *Le livre de la taille de Paris, l'an 1296* (Göteberg: Elanders Boktryckeri Aktiebolag, 1958); Michaëlsson, *Le livre de la taille . . . 1297*. I am grateful to Janice Archer, who shared with me her alphabetized printout of all of the women in the 1292, 1296–1300, and 1313 tax assessments.
11. Hercule Géraud, *Paris sous Philippe-le-Bel d'après des documents originaux et notamment d'après un manuscrit contenant 'Le Rôle de la Taille' imposée sur les habitants de Paris en 1292,* rept. ed. (Tübingen: Max Niemeyer Verlag, 1991); David Herlihy, *Opera Muliebra: Women and Work in Medieval Europe* (New York: McGraw-Hill, 1989), p. 135; Archer, "Working Women," p. 82.
12. Archer, "Working Women," p. 79.
13. Archer, "Working Women," p. 78.
14. Archer, "Working Women," p. 110.
15. Archer, "Working Women," pp. 80, 106; Caroline Bourlet, "L'anthroponymie à Paris à la fin du xiiie siècle d'après les rôles de la taille du règne de Philippe le Bel," *Genèse médiévale de l'anthroponymie moderne*, ed. Monique Bourin and Pascal Chareille, vol. 2–2 (Tours: Publications de l'Université de Tours, 1992), pp. 16, 23.
16. For a general introduction to aristocratic and royal household account books see Malcolm Vale, *The Princely Court: Medieval Courts and Culture in North-West Europe* (Oxford: Oxford University Press, 2001), pp. 69–80.
17. For a list of the surviving accounts of Robert II and Mahaut of Artois see Robert-Henri Bautier and Janine Sornay, *Les Sources de l'histoire économique et sociale du moyen âge: Les états de la Maison de Bourgogne* (Paris: Editions du CNRS, 1984), pp. 256–60.
18. Supporting documents are in Series A of the Archives départementales de Pas-de-Calais (Henceforth PdC A); most have been catalogued by Jules-Marie Richard, *Inventaire-Sommaire des Archives departementales antérieures à 1790, Pas-de-Calais, Archives Civiles—Série A*, 2 vols. (Arras: Imp.

de la Société du Pas-de-Calais, 1878, 1887). See below at notes 64–66 for accounts kept by concierges.

19. On the draper Ysabel of Tremblay, see the discussion in this chapter on pp. 93–95. Other drapers were Genevieve de Lille and La Dame de Trumelières: Bove, *Dominer*, p. 650; L. Douët-d'Arcq, *Comptes de l'argenterie des rois de France au xiv$^{e}$ siècle* (Paris: Jules Renouard et C$^{ie}$, 1851; rpt., New York, London: Johnson Reprint Corporation, 1966), p. 86. On the tapestry merchant, Peronnelle de Crepon see below at note 50. The mercers were Martine la Thierrie (1368–76); "une merciere de Paris" (1368); "Mercieres du Palais de Paris" (1378); and Ysabiau la Cauchoise (1386): Bernard Prost, *Inventaires mobiliers et extraits des comptes des ducs de Bourgogne de la Maison de Valois (1363–1477)*, 2 vols. (Paris: E. Leroux, 1902–1904), 1:116, 124, 150–151, 158, 166, 495; 2:22, 583. On the linen merchants Jeanne la Fouacière, Genevieve la Fouacière and Erebourc of Moustereul, see below at notes 35–49. The others were Jeanne la Fructiere (1304); Jeanne la Pareirere (1315); Guillemete de la Pomme (1352); Jeanne de Brie (1387); "une marchande de linge de Paris" (1371); Amaline la Haronne (1368); Asselot, lingiere (1401); Jeanne la Buoise (1383); Jamecte Buynarde (1450); and Marguerite Bourdelote (1450): PdC A 199, fol. 93; PdC A 329, fol. 18v; L. Douët-d'Arcq, *Comptes de l'argenterie*, pp. 93–96, 143, 297; L. Douët-d'Arcq, *Nouvelle recueil de comptes de l'argenterie des rois de France* (Paris: Librairie Renouard, 1874), pp. 241, 260; Prost, *Inventaires* 1:106, 158, 257; 2:149, 225, 330–31, 334.
20. Archer, "Working Women," p. 180.
21. Archer, "Working Women," p. 325.
22. Jennifer Jones, *Sexing La Mode: Gender, Fashion, and Commercial Culture in Old Regime France* (Oxford: Oxford University Press, 2004).
23. See, for instance, the seventeenth-century engraving by Abraham Bosse depicting the Gallery of the Palais Royale. One of the commercial booths in the gallery is that of a woman selling fine linens and laces: Linda Levy Peck, *Consuming Splendor: Society and Culture in Seventeenth-Century England* (Cambridge: Cambridge University Press, 2005), p. 54.
24. Vale, *Princely Court*, 145–52; M. Le Comte de Loisne, "Itineraire de Robert II, Comte d'Artois," *Bulletin philologique et historique (jusqu'à 1715) du Comité des travaux historiques et scientiques* (1913): 362–83.
25. On aristocrats and kings shopping in Paris: Vale, *Princely Court*, pp. 351–54; Samuel Lysons, "Copy of a Roll of Purchases Made for the Tournament in Windsor Park, in the Sixth Year of Edward the First," *Archaeologia* 17 (1814): 297–310; Frédérique Lachaud, "Textiles, Furs and Liveries: A Study of the Material Culture of the Court of Edward I (1272-1307)" (DPhil: Oxford, 1992), 121–22; Françoise Piponnier, *Costume et vie sociale: La cour d'Anjou xiv$^{e}$-xv$^{e}$ siècle* (Paris: Mouton, 1970), pp. 27, 41; *De Rekeningen der graven en gravinnen uit het Henegouwsche huis*, ed. J. Smit, 3 vols. (Amsterdam and Utrecht: J. Müller, 1924–39), 1:178–9, 521–2, 558; PdC A 132/3; PdC A 151/91; PdC A 263, fol. 21v; PdC A 270, fol. 25v; Brussels, Archives géner-ales du Royaume, CC 1, membrane 19; Ghent, Rijksarchief, Inventaire

Gaillard, 52, membrane 5, 7; Ghent, Rijsarchief, Inventaire St.-Genois, 668. On luxury goods produced in Paris: Marian Campbell, "Paris, miroir ou lumière pour l'orfèvrerie anglaise vers 1300?," in *1300: L'art au temps de Philippe le Bel*, ed. Danielle Gaborit-Chopin and François Avril (Paris: Ecole du Louvre, 2001), 203–18; Sharon Farmer, "*Biffes, Tiretaines* and *Aumonières*. The Role of Paris in the International Textile Markets of the Thirteenth and Fourteenth Centuries," in *Medieval Clothing and Textiles*, vol. 2, ed. Robin Netherton and Gale R. Owen-Crocker (Woodbridge: Boydell, 2006): 75–89.

26. Bove, *Dominer*, pp. 644, 646 (under Haudry, Tremblay). For an explanation of the function of prud'hommes, see pp. 230–35. On Ysabel's relationship to Jeanne Haudry, the first wife of Etienne Haudry, see Jeanne Haudry's testament: Boris Bove, "Vie et mort d'un couple de marchands-drapiers parisiens, d'après les testaments de Jeanne et Étienne Haudry (1309, 1313)," *Paris et Île-de-France, Mémoires*, 52 (2001): 71.
27. Bove, *Dominer*, p. 648.
28. Michaelsson, *Livre de la taille . . . 1313*, p. 202. Ysabel's role as head of the family business is partially discussed by Bove, *Dominer*, p. 407.
29. Archer, "Working Women," pp. 139–51.
30. Archer, "Working Women," p. 254. I have calculated the percentage from her estimated numbers for all four years.
31. They are Agnes, daughter of the deceased Bertaut Arrode; Alison Arrode and her sister; Perronnelle Arrode; Jehanne Arrode and Gilete her daughter; the daughter of Jehan Augier; Perronnelle, sister of Antoine Boucel; Alice, widow of Etienne Bourdon (taxed with her unnamed four children); Marie, mother of Adam and Jacquet Bourdon; Dame Edeline of Dammartin; Marie la Marcele; Genevote, niece of Raoul of Pacy; Perronnelle of Pacy; the widow of Philippe Paon; Dame Jehanne la Piz-d'Oe (taxed with her unnamed three children); the widow of Thomas Piz-d'Oe and Marote her daughter; Dame Agnes la Sarrazine; Dame Jehanne la Sarrazine; the sister of Jehannot of Tremblay; Ameline of Tremblay; Jehannete, daughter of Guillaume Toussac; Marie, widow of Guillaume Toussac: Géraud, *Paris sous Philippe-le-Bel*, pp. 16, 17, 18, 25, 29, 30, 35, 38, 63, 67, 71, 72, 90, 91, 99, 137.
32. See note 6 above.
33. I have derived the list of sixteen taxpayers paying 75 *L tournois* or more from Michaëlsson's list of those paying 20 *L tournois* or more in 1313: *Le livre de la taille . . . 1313*, pp. xvi–xviii. There were 5979 tax paying units in that year: Michaelson, p. xiv.
34. Douët d'Arcq, *Comptes de l'argenterie*, pp. 5–6, 20–22, 27–28, 37, 40, 45, 52–54, 63, 67.
35. Lysons, "Copy of a Roll of Purchases," 305.
36. Robert Fawtier and François Maillard, editors, *Comptes royaux (1285–1314)*, vol. 2 (Paris: Imprimerie Nationale, 1954), #23992, 24078.
37. PdC A 178; PdC A 189/3; PdC A 192; PdC A 263, fol. 18; PdC A 270, fol. 22; PdC A280, fol. 20.

38. Paris, Archives Nationales, L 938/46.
39. PdC A 151/34.
40. Jeanne's tax assessments: Michaëlsson, *Livre de la taille... 1297,* p. 30; AN KK 283, fols. 100, 160, 238v. The average tax assessment of linen merchants ("chanevaciere," "vendeur de toiles,") in the 1297–1300 tax assessments is based on my own calculations of listings of linen merchants in the 1297–1300 tax assessments: AN KK 293, fols. 39, 45, 60, 105, 156.
41. Bove, *Dominer,* p. 60. Aldermen who were active between 1292 and 1313 paid an average tax of 14 *L parisis.*
42. Paris, Archives Nationales, L 938. The executor was Bernard de Pailly. For his role as executor for Jeanne Haudry, see Bove, "Vie et mort d'un couple," 71.
43. While the aldermen of Paris included mercers, Jeanne la Fouacière's brother-in-law, Guillaume of St.-Marcel, was not a member of any of the alderman families.
44. Douët-d'Arcq, *Comptes de l'argenterie,* p. 36; PdC A 357; PdC A 361; PdC A 368; PdC A 374; PdC A 379; PdC A 387; PdC A 403; PdC A 396, fol. 14v, 15; PdC A 448, fol. 26; PdC A 458, fol. 32.
45. PdC A 461, fol. 30v; PdC A 470, fol. 21v; PdC A 474, fol. 15.
46. Paris, AN KK 283, fol. 112, 189, 265v.
47. Michaëlsson, *Le livre de la taille... 1313,* p. 118. The total amount collected in the Paris levy of 1313 was 10,000 *livres parisis,* which amounted to 12,500 *livres tournois.* Tax payers were assessed in *livres tournois.* There were 5979 tax paying units, so the average tax (12,500/5979) was 2.09 *livres tournois.* I have calculated this average from the figures given by Michaëlsson, pp. xiii, xiv.
48. Douët-d'Arcq, *Nouvelle recueil de comptes de l'argenterie,* p. 77.
49. Paris, Archives Nationales L 938.
50. On Peronnelle the king's spice merchant, see discussion that follows. For the other three women see Prost, *Inventaires,* I:193, n. 3, 364, 385, 428; Douët d'Arcq, *Nouvelle recueil,* p. 215.
51. Géraud, *Paris sous Philippe-le-Bel,* p. 139 (fol. 62a).
52. Paris, AN KK 283, f. 210v, 285v.
53. Bove, *Dominer,* pp. 86–87.
54. Francesco di Balduccio Pegolotti, "Spices," trans. from *La prattica della mercatura* by Robert S. Lopez, *Medieval Trade in the Mediterranean World* (London: Oxford University Press, 1955), pp. 109–14. See also W. Heyd, *Histoire du commerce du levant au moyan âge,* trans. into French by Furcy Raynaud, 2 vols. (Leipzig: Otto Harrassowitz, 1923, 1936), 2: 563–711.
55. Bibliothèque Nationale de France, Collection Clairambault, ms. 832, pp. 529, 571.
56. Archer, "Working Women," p. 325.
57. Archer, "Working Women," p. 325.
58. Michaëlsson, *Le livre de la taille... 1297,* p. 181; AN KK 283 fol. 121v, 210v, 285v.

59. Géraud, *Paris sous Philippe-le-Bel*, p. 139.
60. Michaëlsson, *Le livre de la taille... 1296*, p. 202; Michaëlsson, *Le livre de la taille... 1297*, p. 181; AN KK 283 fol. 121v, 210v, 285v.
61. Archer, "Working Women," pp. 150, 275–314. In Archer's appendix concerning the transmission of family businesses, I find only one sister winning out over her brother: p. 303.
62. Women concierges in the Parisian tax assessments: Adeline, concierge of the Count of Ponthieu; Ameline, concierge of Mon. Godefroy; Cateline, concierge of the Bishop of Chartres; Isabel la concierge; Isabel, concierge of the Seigneur of Beaumont; Jacqueline, concierge of the Seigneur of Coucy; Jeanne of Léry, concierge of the Count of Artois; Perrine, concierge of the Duke of Burgundy: Géraud, *Paris sous Philippe-le-Bel*, p. 159; Michëlsson, *Le livre de la taille... 1296*, p. 20; Michaëlsson, *Le livre de la taille... 1297*, p. 274; AN KK 283, fol. 103v, 166, 163v, 201v, 225v, 242, 245, 258, 275v, 277v. Parisian women concierges in other sources: Marguerite, concierge of the King; Bienvenue, Concierge of the Count of Artois; Jeanne l'Espicière, Concierge of the Count of Artois: Bove, *Dominer,* 282–83; PdC A 187/1; PdC A 329—these last two are accounts by Bienvenue and Jeanne l'Espiciere, partially edited by Jules-Marie Richard, "Documents des xiiie et xive siècles relatifs à l'hôtel de Bourgogne (ancien hôtel d'Artois) tirés du trésor des chartes d'Artois," *Bulletin de la société de l'histoire de Paris et de l'Île-de-France* 17 (1890): 140, 152–4. Concierge outside of Paris: Jeanne, concierge of the Count of Artois at Conflans: PdC A 176/1 (account by Jeanne).
63. Mahy of Arras, goldsmith/mercer and concierge of the Count of Artois: PdC A 28, PdC A 32. On Jeanne l'Espiciere see below at notes 71–75.
64. Richard, "Documents," pp. 138–39.
65. PdC A 181/4.
66. Richard, "Documents," pp. 152–54; PdC 187/1.
67. They are Mahy of Arras, goldsmith/mercer, 1283, 1286: PdC A 28, PdC A 32; Nicolas Renaud, 1292: PdC A 133; Jacques de la Fouriere, 1296: PdC A 140; Robert, 1297: Michaëlssom, *Livre de la taille... 1297,* p. 51; Jeanne of Léry, 1297–1301, 1302–3: Michaëlsson, *Livre de la taille... 1297,* p. 274; AN KK fols. 103v, 166, 245; PdC A 158; PdC A177; PdC A193; *Le compte general du receveur d'Artois pour 1303–4*, ed. Bernard Delmaire (Brussels: J. Duculot, 1977), p. 181, #3093; Bienvenue, c. 1302–3: Richard, "Documents," p. 140, 15–3; PdC A 184, A 187, A 192, A 193; Pierre le Tailleur 1307–13: PdC A 232; PdC A 242; PdC A 280; PdC A 316; Quentin Messier, 1314: PdC A 325; Richard Langlois, 1326: AN KK 393; Richard, "Documents," p. 142; Jeanne l'Espiciere: Richard, "Documents," p. 140.
68. See previous note.
69. Michaëlsson, *Livre de la taille... 1313*, p. xi.
70. AN KK 283, fol. 103v, 166, 245.
71. PdC A 243, #13.
72. PdC A 280 (and A 242 for Pierre's identity as concierge).

73. PdC A 316 fol. 2, 20; A 334 fol. 33v.
74. PdC A 351, fol. 1.
75. Jeanne alone: PdC A 280 fol. 20v, 21; PdC A 273; PdC A 293; PdC A 298, fol. 20v. Jeanne and Pierre le Vaillant: PdC A 303; PdC A 448, fol. 25v. Pierre le Vaillant: PdC A 357, fol. 22v-23; PdC A 374, fol. 26; PdC A 378, fol. 14, fol. 22; PdC A 396, fol. 13v; PdC A 403; PdC A 458; PdC A 483.
76. Prost, *Inventaires*, 2:22; Carolyn Sargentson, *Merchants and Luxury Markets: The Marchands Merciers of Eighteenth-Century Paris* (London: Victoria and Albert Museum, 1996), pp. 18–23, 136. On the seventeenth century, see note 23 above.
77. Jones, *Sexing la Mode*, p. 96.
78. Jones, *Sexing la Mode*, pp. 96–98.
79. Farmer, *Surviving Poverty*, pp. 136–40.
80. Farmer, *Surviving Poverty,* p. 142, n. 14. On silk weavers: Archer, "Working Women," p. 252, numbers for "carier de soie," "fabricante de tissu," "ouvriere de soie," "fabricant de draps de soie," "fabricant de velours," "tisserand de soie"; and on p. 270, "fabricant de draps d'or."

CHAPTER 6

# "APPROPRIATE TO HER SEX"? WOMEN'S PARTICIPATION ON THE CONSTRUCTION SITE IN MEDIEVAL AND EARLY MODERN EUROPE

*Shelley E. Roff*

The construction site, supported by numerous trades and material suppliers, was an important factor in the economy of cities in medieval and early modern Europe. When reading the literature on the history of architecture, construction, and the related trades, one has the impression that women made virtually no contribution to the built environment other than as aristocratic patrons of the art. Although it is true that the majority of day laborers and craftsmen at any given site were male, there is evidence in many regions of Western Europe that women were commonly employed alongside the men, albeit in the most menial of tasks. Poor women and slaves worked as day laborers on construction sites, and women of better means were employed in the workshops of the various building-related crafts. One might not expect to find a woman in the historically male position of master of a craft, much less as a master of the works, or architect. The training and professional licensure required for these positions legally barred women from their attainment, and socially it was not permissible for a woman to be in this kind of a position of knowledge and leadership.[1] However, aristocratic women were in a position to personally influence and guide the design of the projects they patronized, and there are cases where women have managed the design and construction of their own homes. Illuminating women's participation on the construction site has implications for understanding women's relationship to money. The construction site provides an opportune lens through which to observe societal attitudes toward women whose livelihood was secured through wages, rather than the socially sanctioned route of inheritance and to bring out of the shadows women's work or "support" that was continually a vital part of the economy.

Defining women's contribution to the built environment is a task where one will encounter many forms of occlusion. A typical example can be found in women's help in the shop with production, often by cleaning and providing food for the husband and apprentices, which has not been recognized as part of the economy of the building trades or of any other craft. The married couple was the foundation of the craft workshop, and a fundamental unit of the urban economy. In some cities in Europe, a man could not establish a shop if he was not married.[2] With wives and daughters present in almost all workshops, female "support" of varying levels existed in all trades. Merry Wiesner has noted that women's work was often simply not seen as work, thus was never recorded for tax or other purposes. She explains, "City and state governments often suggested that guilds and other occupational groups overlook the production of a small number of items by widows and other poor women because this was not really 'work,' but simply 'support,' and the women would otherwise need public assistance."[3] As long as the woman did not overstep her boundaries by becoming more successful than a guild member, she might be allowed to continue her "support." Women's positive contributions in the craft workshops have been and continue to be overlooked, due to a continued tendency to diminish women's work.

## Historiography

The omission of women from descriptions of the construction site has historical origins. Medieval and early modern writers acknowledged women's participation in certain crafts that they deemed acceptable for the female constitution and physique. However, they fell silent or inferred opposition to women's employment that did not fit their ideology. The assumptions of these writers are not unique to their times; these attitudes have filtered into modern historiography. A parallel to this situation can be seen in the study of medieval warfare, where modern historians have failed to recognize the evidence of women's participation.[4] When encountering women's appearance in male-dominated crafts and as day laborers in historical documents, historians have previously rationalized this as an exceptional phenomenon to be attributed to social or economic crises, when war or disease produced a shortage of men, or when the discrepancy of the wage rate between men and women was great enough to make female labor financially desirable.

A vivid example of the social crisis rationalization can be found in the early twentieth-century work of the Spanish historian Ramón Carande.[5] Carande justified the numerous accounts he had found in the archives of women doing heavy labor in fourteenth-century Seville by hypothesizing that this was the result of the Black Plague, which had decimated the population and left a great predominance of women over men. He also attributed women's employment to the increase in a population that he labeled "disfavorable," such as the many handicapped, mutilated, leprous, and insane, also being employed at these sites. Carande believed this imbalance in the population alone accounts for such an unusual situation where women were engaged in work that, as he put it, "today [...] is considered inappropriate to her sex."[6] Although he was correct in pointing out the effects of the plague on the population of Seville, the multitude of examples in Spain and in many regions of Europe of women working on construction sites points to a habitual practice of employing women. Socioeconomic crises may have served only to increase the instances and number of women employed for a period.

Carande's disapproval of female day laborers represents a long-standing cultural attitude that had become even more rigid by the nineteenth and early twentieth centuries. What incited his comments on the "unusual" and "inappropriate" activity of female day laborers was the belief that women were not capable of hard manual labor, much less should they be found working outside of the home. The implication is that women should not earn their own money, nor should they have access to or control over money, because it would give women independence from the family and the power to direct their own lives. The fear of Carande and others is that this would upset the traditional social balance, one in which men worked for money and women served men and the family.

Graphic imagery and historical documentation from the time are also fairly silent. Images of building construction sites in paintings and engravings from the medieval and the early modern period never, to my present knowledge, depict women working on these sites. Most of the images that have come down to us are manuscript illuminations, which were commissioned for aristocratic, bourgeois, or religious audiences and were intended for purposes other than historical documentation. However, women do appear in these images as patrons (figure 6.1). To find women working in this context, one must investigate a wide variety of historical documents, such as municipal rolls and accounts of expenditures, documents of court cases, wills, inventories of wages paid on construction sites, prison records, hospital records, and records revealing cause of death. These sources provide a general indication of the frequency of women's participation, albeit with only a minimum of information recorded. Scribes and clerks who recorded daily transactions often registered women's presence only with the word *mulier, mullyer, dona, femme*, or *wench* when recording their wages. Tax records often only recorded the head of household with an occupation.[7] The contribution of a wife or her occupation was not usually mentioned unless she was a widow. This presents a challenge to uncovering women's participation in construction and in the building trades.

I have organized the material of my investigation, drawn from a variety of published primary and secondary sources, into two categories of work: women working as day laborers and those working in the building crafts. The following survey presents a broad overview of typical cases in Western Europe, in order to build a case for the pervasiveness of women's participation in this field. Their participation can vary tremendously between cities, and the reasons for the differences are difficult to assess. Certainly, the discontinuities encountered in archival records and the intermittent recording of women's employment precludes an accurate statistical study. Cultural differences, such as the greater cohesiveness of the extended family and the younger age of marriage in southern Europe, especially in Italy,[8] may attest for the lack of evidence for female day laborers in that region.

The survey focuses on the thirteenth to the seventeenth centuries, beginning with the early records of municipal governments and ending before the Industrial Revolution, when changes occur in the materials and technology of building and in social attitudes. The discursive terms "medieval" and "early modern," devised by historians to define a paradigmatic shift in Western thought and culture, are not natural delimiters for this study. The status of medieval women, regulations curtailing their employment and remuneration, and ideals of feminine conduct do not necessarily change with the advent of the Renaissance. The expansion of urban centers starting in the thirteenth century set off a trend of increasing female employment for day laborers and in the crafts, which only began to contract on occasion for women working in the crafts in the sixteenth century with ensuing economic crises.

## The Construction Site

There is no typical construction site in this study; however, there are a few factors they all share in common. Most sites were directed by a master of the works who organized and scheduled the work of a hierarchy of day laborers, material suppliers, craftsmen, and clerks. This work occurred both on and off the construction site. The rate of pay for each job responded to this skill-based social hierarchy. Women and children could enter this work hierarchy, but did so usually at the lowest level, meaning on a temporary basis and at a reduced rate of pay. Women's ease of access to thi' hierarchy depended on her social class but to an even greater degr~ on her family connections.

The organization of a construction site was complex and required the management of a master of the works or his administrative equivalent. Most construction projects required the timely coordination of various artisans' work, and usually a large number of people had to be hired, directed, and paid. In addition, the work for one project could extend for many months to many years depending on the size of the project.[9] The seasonal and itinerant nature of construction work limited women's opportunities to work on these sites. Seasonal or temporary work is a condition in which poor women often can be found employed. In the winter, building activities on the site would come to a halt. The work in progress would have to be covered and protected from the weather, and portions of the building would continue to be made within the shelter of a masters' workshop.[10] Those hired as day laborers had no option but to seek other work. Women working in building craft workshops, such as those of glaziers or sculptors, had more year-round continuity in their work than those working for stone masons or plasterers. In the case of large-scale buildings, the work force often consisted of traveling bands of masons, stuccoists, glass makers, mosaicists—not an approved lifestyle for a woman, since women who traveled were often associated with prostitution. These groups would travel to a major site, set up for business, and begin hiring local people to help as they were needed.[11] Women also might find employment in the services of their master who was hired for a particular project.

## Women Working as Day Laborers

Only the poorest women in search of daily wages to supplement their family income or to ensure their own personal survival looked to the construction site for employment. The labor these women engaged in was strenuous and was comparable to work in the fields to which women in the countryside undertook. The most common task women engaged in was the transportation of water and materials such as sand, lime, gravel, and mortar to the site. They can also be seen digging ditches for foundations and roads and operating "man"-powered wood and metal machinery. There may have been on occasion a woman strong enough to equal the tasks of a man; certainly there are cases documented in agricultural labor.[12] However, the women working on construction sites varied greatly in age, and most likely in abilities. Without a doubt, women must have managed the heaviest of tasks by breaking down the weight of materials into smaller units. As Donald Woodward has suggested in his study on male laborers in early modern England, the buckets, spades, shovels, and wheelbarrows used on site could carry either large or small loads.[13]

How did these women find employment on the construction site? Some women may have fallen into this work because they knew someone already involved, or another family member was hired. Some women may have come to the city from rural areas looking for work, accustomed to the hard physical labor of the fields. Many may have looked for work by going to an early morning hiring, usually held on a main plaza or fairground or a specific landmark in a city. Paris had several such labor markets serving different trades.[14] The Place de Grève was well-known as a labor market for the building trades and unskilled laborers.

The earliest documented cases I have encountered of women working in construction for wages are in thirteenth-century Spain, where women found employment helping in the construction of stone and wood structures in Navarre.[15] They were hired as day laborers along with men to repair a millhouse and its adjoining wood dam in Coreylla. In Peralta, they were also hired as day laborers to build another dam, a road to the palaces and to help rebuild the arches and columns of a building that had fallen into disrepair. Also in Navarre, there are records of Jewish women taking part in the heavy labor of construction on royal palaces and fortresses.[16] The extent of the women's involvement in these projects is not recorded.

In the next century, when the city of Seville ordered the surrounding walls and their battlements to be repaired, they hired female as well as male day laborers to serve the masters of the various crafts.[17] By 1383 the number of crews of women that worked on construction sites had become quite large. In 1385, these laborers were hired for the project as hod carriers and construction workers, although at lower wages than men. A hod carrier is a worker who assists a bricklayer, plasterer, or stonemason by carrying bricks or mortar to them in a wooden trough on their shoulders. In 1386, women were also hired as part of a crew to work on a marble-faced bridge, and in 1393 there is an account of women working on a site to help mend a water channel for a mill, to build a basin from which animals could drink water, and to mend and clean a road.[18] Near this location they also dug trenches for the foundations of part of the city wall. In this same year, the rebuilding of the arches around the city was completed from a supply of bricks in part purchased from a female tile- and brick-maker, Sol Martines.[19] Many similar accounts of women in these roles can be found in the municipal accounts of Seville in the fourteenth century.

In fifteenth-century Toledo, women worked on the construction of the cathedral. Usually just one or two were hired, and not necessarily every day.[20] Since their names were not recorded, we cannot know if the same women were hired each day, or if it varied. They did work similar to that of the male laborers: they swept the cathedral, gathered lime, and worked on the roof. They were paid about half of the rate for male day laborers, but about the same as the young boys who worked for the masters.

There are numerous occasions of women working on construction sites and in the building trades in France. At Perigeux after 1350, women did most of the labor carrying sand, water, and lime on construction sites and often made the mortar for the constant work on the city's fortifications.[21] These women were paid considerably less than men for the same work. Men usually directed the carts with pack animals to carry materials long distances, for example, carting stone to the masons. However, women often helped with the animals. The verb, *aider,* or to assist, is usually used in the municipal documents to indicate the women's secondary role. In Toulouse, almost half of the construction laborers employed to build the Périgord college from 1365 to 1371 were women.[22] On this site, men helped the women place baskets of stones and bricks on their heads, and the women carried the stones to troughs that were later transported by men. Women also helped demolish walls and dig out ditches. Their wages, as is often the case, were well below that of the male laborers. In fifteenth-century Paris, women worked right beside men clearing the land and constructing the foundations of buildings.[23] Hod carriers of both sexes transported gravel and earth.[24] In sixteenth-century Lyon, adult women were a prominent source of semiskilled labor at construction sites, doing road repair and other labor along with the men.[25]

In England, women were engaged in working with a variety of building materials. Eighty-six women were hired in 1555 to carry moss and gravel to the Weir dam in Durham, England.[26] In the 1560s, the city council of Chester hired women to power the treadwheel of a "great crane of iron" used on the construction site of new stone quay on the river near Neston. In the countryside, the thatching of roofs was a job routinely done by women. A woman named Katherine Rolf was hired by the nuns at St. Radegund's in Cambridge to do a great variety of tasks, including helping the thatchers to thatch the roofs of two tenements.[27] In another case in Kendal in 1639, a woman and her husband together thatched the roof of the town kiln. Both male and female prisoners were hired at an equal rate of pay to produce large amounts of cement at the House of Corrections in Hull in the seventeenth century.[28]

In German cities there are extensive accounts of women working on building sites. Periodically, women from the lower classes often took on the heavy physical work of construction, such as mortar mixing and roof-making.[29] In Frankfurt-on-Main women were hired to make clay walls and to work in the lime works. In fifteenth-century Mulhausen, there is a report of a female clay transporter and another woman who was injured while lifting clay from a pit.

Women's relatively easy access to the construction site as day laborers may be due to several factors. There were no legal barriers to women engaging in manual labor during this period since no guild organizations existed for this type of work. Also, one must consider that the temporary and often short duration of the jobs and the low rate of pay made the hiring of great numbers of female laborers a cost-effective solution. In almost all accounts surveyed, women were paid lower wages than men for similar work. Woodward succinctly explains that women's lower rate of pay "reflected deeply embedded male attitudes relating to the economic and social inferiority of women which were buttressed by biblical authority."[30] The documentary evidence from Durham, Chester, Newcastle, Lincoln, and Beverley informed him that, the rate of pay for women in proportion to those of men follows the 3:5 rate recommended in the Bible (Leviticus, 27, 3–4), with some variation. Woodward also observed that it was only occasionally that women appeared on the construction site in northern English towns, and the women usually constituted a small proportion of the workers. Greater numbers were hired, at times in large gangs, when a surge in the demand for labor coincided with a decreasing wage rate for women.

Despite the substantial number of cases of female day laborers on construction sites across Europe, not much can be known about them individually. Rarely is a name, age, or marital status recorded in the cases surveyed.[31] Most often they are simply listed as female or as a gang of women. At times women worked as part of a team or in some cases they worked alongside male family members. However, the case of women laborers of Stiffkey in Norfolk documented by Woodward gives a sense of the potential range women involved: "fifteen unmarried women living with their families, five widows, three wives of husbandmen or craftsmen, and thirteen wives of day labourers."[32] Their ages ranged from under twenty to older women, possibly over seventy.

## Women Working in the Building Crafts

Building craft workshops and their guilds were part of a community of such craft organizations that were quickly gaining political and social importance in thirteenth-century European cities. The economy of medieval Europe depended on the family business or workshop for its vitality. In these family workshops, the master's wife, daughters, and maids often worked alongside his journeymen and apprentices, which accounts for women working in many trades that were believed to be exclusively male.[33] This practice was condoned by Christine de Pisan, who gave advice regarding the proper conduct of women at different social levels in *The Treasury of the City of Ladies* (1405). A craftswoman, whom she assumes will be married, "should learn all the shop details so that she can properly supervise the workers when her husband is away or not paying attention."[34]

In her article on craftswomen in sixteenth-century Lyon, Natalie Davis has given us a detailed glimpse into the workshops of this period.[35] Women of the middle classes were expected to be involved in work at home or in other families' shops as wage earners. Davis has found that in large workshops of the building trades women with skills could be found doing peripheral jobs.[36] She also points out some constraints on the ways in which wives may have been involved in their husband's shops. Women who worked in the same trade as their husbands were often confined to the realm of the workshop. Work regularly performed on sites away from the house would rarely have involved wives as helpers. Also, the wife's involvement in the work within the shop may have been determined by how much time she had free from other household tasks, which would have included the preparation of food for the journeymen and apprentices, and from childbirth and nursing. Davis brings in an additional constraint of a peculiarly medieval character:

> In Catholic artisinal families, the "state of pollution" which clung to a new mother may have kept her out of the shop until she had her churching ceremony, the *relevailles*, lest her glance bring everybody bad luck. And popular beliefs about the dangers of menstruating women to technical and natural processes, which we know were current in the sixteenth century, may have barred the wife from some workshops at certain times of the month, lest she rust iron and brass, dull cutting instruments, jeopardize the already hazardous process of casting, and so forth.[37]

In contrast, Davis points out that the help of the wife was needed for the survival of the family, and often her work was recognized by the community as her identity in partnership with her husband.

In most locations across Europe, women were denied official apprenticeships of the guild and excluded from becoming masters; nevertheless, their contribution within the workshop itself may have been more essential to its livelihood than just that of a cheap source of labor.[38] By the fifteenth and continuing into the seventeenth century, guild and civic regulations began to oppose women working in the crafts. The existence of these bans is a good indication that women were already working in that particular industry, and it is evident from the number of times in which such regulations had to be reissued that these laws were not strictly adhered to.

Wiesner has observed that in German cities, especially in the sixteenth and seventeenth centuries, there were guild and civic regulations against women working in most crafts, although these were not always strictly obeyed.[39] For example, in Frankfurt in 1597, the journeymen cordmakers filed a complaint to the city council against the masters of their newly formed guild, because they were supposedly still hiring only young women and girls, although this was not tolerated by most guilds. In 1605 the city council of Memmingen had to consider the case of a wife and daughter of a glazier who had been doing work outside of their own home. The glazier conceded that his wife should be confined to work within the boundaries of their home, but was pleading the case for his daughter to be allowed to work with him outside until she became married.[40]

In the seventeenth century, there was a movement throughout many cities by the journeymen of craft guilds to have women barred from working in their families' workshops, for the journeymen felt that there was too much competition for jobs.[41] By the late seventeenth century, most of the metal crafts had totally forbidden the use of single women. Wiesner concludes that these bans were introduced as a solution to unemployment among male craftsmen, distressed by competition from cheaper female labor, and other economic factors. The banning of women from these occupations underscores the point that it was common practice for women to be acquiring the skills of a trade in the setting of the family workshop, even those trades that operated within the realm of the construction of buildings.

Craftsmen on the site were defined by the kind of material they used, such as wood, plaster, tiles, stone, glass, or iron. By far the most commonly employed craftsperson to be found would be those who worked with wood.[42] The heavy weight of materials and the strenuous or dangerous nature of the work involved in some crafts did limit women's involvement. Trades where the majority of the work took place on the construction site, such as masonry and carpentry, appear to have been less accessible to most women. Often the skill levels of each gender were used as a reason to exclude women from certain trades. Although in Nuremburg there are numerous records of female glaziers,[43] in other

German cities women were barred from glass-cutting due to their supposed clumsiness and lack of skill. Yet, as Wiesner has pointed out, these same women were capable of making lace and silk thread, requiring steady hands and an eye for exacting detail.[44]

Another reason for the exclusion or limitation of women in the building trades may stem from the "mystery" of some crafts, which were an essential part of building practices in the Middle Ages.[45] Membership in the guilds was usually through inheritance: father to son. This was a method of protecting the trade secrets of the master craftsmen's procedure, and ensured that only those that were part of the guild could practice their trade. Apprenticeship was the means by which one would learn these trade secrets and was a requirement for acceptance into the guild. In some cities, widows were encouraged to marry a journeyman of her former husband's trade to "keep things in the family."[46]

Nevertheless, there are many cases in which women were not excluded from these crafts on site. Municipal records in both London and Paris indicate that, from the fourteenth to the seventeenth century, numerous women worked in the building trades as masons, carpenters, doormakers, and other crafts that required the worker to be present on the site.[47] In the *Livre des Métiers* (1270) of Etienne Boileau, a compilation of the statutes of the principle guilds of Paris, construction workers, woodworkers, and metalworkers are listed among the occupations of female head of households.[48] The Spanish historian Ramón Carande has also noted that there were female guilds related to the building trades in Paris.[49] One study of Paris's municipal tax records in 1296 and in 1313 lists two female masons, a tiler and a plasterer.[50] Outside of Paris, other records reveal women working as masons. An account in Strasbourg explains that two women joined the mason's guild from 1452 to 1453 and, by doing so, were granted the right to town citizenship.[51]

Women were also engaged in a variety of occupations other than the building trades but related to construction. In London in 1383, Katherine Lightfoot is recorded as the supplier of 2,000 painted tiles to the King for his bath at Shene Palace.[52] This woman may have been the wife of Henry Yevele, an architect and master builder, however I cannot ascertain whether this was the same woman. As cited earlier, another woman was recorded as a brickmaker and supplier in Seville. Also in London, a woman received payment from the churchwardens at St. Mary at Hill for doing "gilte" and painting the tabernacle of the church.[53]

However, this participation does not hold true for all medieval cities. For example, the municipal accounts in fourteenth-century Shrewsbury indicate that women contributed their labor within the family workshops, but no references have been discovered testifying to women's participation in the woodworking, building, or metal industry. Widows of these craftsmen did not carry on their husband's trade afterward, and indeed it is possible that they may have been prohibited from doing so.[54] In the city of Lyon, there are no recorded instances of women working in skilled trades, although it is likely that they did; a woman imprisoned for a crime in 1548 was recorded as Catherine Fromment, cabinetmaker.[55]

Despite laws regulating women's participation in the trades in some cities, women who worked in their husband's workshop did on occasion continue to do this work as widows.[56] A statute of 1271 addressed to masons, plasterers, carpenters, and other woodworkers in Basle ruled that women could become members of a guild in the building trade of their husband and could remain in the guild as widows, providing they did not remarry.[57] However, in this case it is not clear as to whether these female members were engaged in professional work or simply social duties. In seventeenth-century German cities, workshops run by widows and other women often make up as much as 10–15 percent of some crafts, although this does not appear to be typical of other regions of Western Europe.[58] Even in the heaviest industries, such as ironmaking and roofing, some cities allowed the masters' widows to run their shop for as much as fifteen or twenty years after the death of their husbands. However, this was not always the case as Wiesner has recorded:

> In 1624, a stonemason's widow asked to be allowed to continue working, as she had a large amount of stone left which her husband had purchased just before his death and which no one was willing to buy. Several stonemasons answered her with the comment that it was now the practice in Frankfurt and elsewhere that widows were allowed to work only four weeks after their husband's death.[59]

The city council wrote to Strasbourg to find out what their practices were, only to realize that they also limited their widow's work to four weeks. This shows that it was common for wives to be working in their husband's workshops and that they acquired enough skill to be running a shop on their own.

## Societal Attitudes toward Women Who Worked

The fate of women working in the crafts was substantially different from those laboring on the construction site. A woman's marital status was not always a determining factor in the location of her work or her poverty; certainly both single and married women worked for wages. However, single women who never married were often destined to a life of poverty, caught in a perennial cycle of working for limited wages or depending on charitable institutions for assistance.[60] Within the realm of the crafts, the financial welfare of women working as wives and daughters in workshops was secured by the success of the workshop, but even more so by access to conjugal property or dowries.

A woman's *endowed* status appears to be absolutely key to her financial survival and a secure entry into the craft economy. Single, married, or widowed, women were believed to be impoverished if they did not have the support of a dowry. A woman's family of origin was responsible for providing her with a premortem inheritance for her support upon her marriage.[61] Dowering a daughter became increasingly more expensive and important as a status symbol for families as the economic crises of the late Middle Ages ensued. A meager dowry could cause a drop in social status that could affect the family's own livelihood, and the inability to dower a daughter was a cause of shame.[62]

Dowries were required for marriage by law and might include cash and property, as well as shops. Indeed, in this study the widows observed running their own craft shops and material supply businesses may have inherited them originally as a dowry. During a marriage, the husband's duty was to administer and protect the dowry, at least according to law. Women received control of their dowries and other marriage gifts upon the dissolution of the marriage or the death of their husbands.

A woman without a dowry in the medieval and early modern world had no culturally accepted means of support. An unendowed woman's financial recourse was to resort to charity, working for wages, prostitution or criminal pursuits. Women who pursued work for wages found temporary employment in other workshops, in menial jobs or in manual labor. As Diane Owen Hughes has noted, Mediterranean societies were concerned with the problem an un-endowed woman could present to its moral steadiness.[63] This attitude may have spurned the increasing popularity of the dowering of young girls as a form of charity. If the family was too poor or the girl did not have a father, she might look for work outside the home in order to acquire a dowry for marriage. How were unendowed women, invariably those who worked for wages, perceived, in light of their counterpart?

Literary, theological, and legal sources discouraged women from working outside the home, especially from engaging in manual labor. Manual labor was one of the factors that made the construction site appear, at least in theory, inappropriate for female employment. Both medieval and early modern theorists drew upon ancient sources to argue that women's involvement in manual labor was more than inappropriate; it was against the natural order predestined by God. According to a late medieval canonist Antoninus, it was a mortal sin if an able husband did not provide for his wife.[64] In the story of Adam and Eve's expulsion from the Garden of Eden (Genesis, 3), their curse and their duty to each other are defined: Adam's punishment was to provide for their bread with the sweat of his brow and Eve was to suffer bringing forth children and to live under the rule of her husband. Aristotle was brought into this argument to demonstrate the difference between servants and women; the former were created for hard labor, whereas women were designed for domestic chores and the care of children. One early modern theorist admonished that a husband should "spare her weak body from all toil and labour of worldly employment exceeding her ability."[65]

This gendering of male and female labor, based on a paradigm of productive and reproductive labor, shows up consistently in clerical authors' works. According to Sharon Farmer, who has studied poor women in thirteenth-century Paris, this contributed considerably to working women's invisibility.[66] These authors spoke of women in their sermons as one body, categorizing endowed and lower status women together. They ignored the fact that married women worked, and insisted that men alone supported the family. They turned a blind eye toward the existence of both married and single women's productive labor that contributed to the city's economic welfare. Men were usually identified by their profession or social class; whereas women were identified by their sexual or marital status (nuns, virgins, married, or widowed). This trickled down to other forms of secular documentation, such as the tax records used in this study, where men and women are categorized in this manner, making it difficult to determine the nature of a woman's work.

Writers in the higher social classes insisted that women were not designed for hard labor but evidently had to make an exception for women in the lowest tier of the social order: slaves, peasants, servants, and the working urban poor. Those women who could not adhere to the prescriptive vision of proper female behavior were set as a class apart from other women, they were poor. Who were these women who did engage in manual labor? We cannot know much about them as individuals; however it is possible to understand their plight more clearly as a social class.

Despite the idealization of spiritual poverty proclaimed by religious orders in the High Middle Ages, by the fifteenth century the attitude toward poverty had become harsher.[67] Poverty was seen as a consequence and punishment for sin. This attitude had evolved by the sixteenth century toward a view that poverty was a social parasite, even a crime. This contempt for the poor has to be understood as a fear on the part of the middle and upper classes of the growing masses of vagabonds, paupers, beggars, and refugees who, fleeing the ravages of war, came to their cities in search of bread.[68] Indeed, the number of the poor in European cities increased dramatically between 1350 and 1500.[69] The charitable institutions established in earlier centuries continued to provide alms, but were at times overwhelmed by this growing unemployed sector. Those engaging in crime intermixed with honest paupers and the working poor, which led to a mistrust of indigence in general. The increasing number of popular rebellions transformed mistrust into outright fear.[70] Poverty aroused pity as well as disgust and fear.

How did poor women who earned wages for manual labor fit into this picture? Women encumbered by the harshness of poverty had few choices for livelihood. If they worked for wages, they were a step above the pauper, the beggar, and the prostitute. They were part of the working poor, defined by an inadequate income and at times an inability to find work.[71] The majority of poor women were hired for domestic work in other people's homes. Beyond this form of servitude, their alternative was to find a wage-earning job outside the domestic sphere. According to the contemporary ideology, the woman who worked for wages outside the home was a destitute and miserable soul, surely without the support of a father or husband, and likely to fall into begging, thievery, or prostitution.

Medieval society's contempt for the poor also extended to manual labor. A scene from a fifteenth-century manuscript, "The Fables of Bidpai" personifies this attitude toward the working poor that depicts two women and a man dressed in rags carrying wood into the city (figure 6.2).[72] Their activity is similar to the kind of work day laborers would have performed on construction sites. The women are barefoot, and their clothes are torn to reveal their gender and their bodies. Poverty was often expressed in visual imagery by the lack of clothing, but in this case, the male worker is fully clothed in contrast to the women. Are the women's clothes torn to demonstrate that, due to their labor, their poverty was greater than the man's? Or does it imply that, due to their labor and their poverty, they may be just one step away from prostitution? The iconography of the image suggests that these women's poverty may have forced them to engage in activities that do not befit their gender, therefore their condition warrants a loss of feminine modesty. The women's exposed, protruding bellies indicate possible pregnancy. One of the problems with low-wage jobs was that they often did not provide enough to survive on and they were easily expendable. The bourgeois of Paris observed in the fifteenth century that the low wages of laundresses, seamstresses, and other menial professions encouraged the development of prostitution as a side profession.[73]

Women's work could also have positive moral connotations. There is evidence from literary sources that certain kinds of crafts were not considered necessarily inappropriate for women. In 1361 Boccaccio wrote *De Claris Mulieribus*, a compendium of 104 biographical legends of Classical women.[74] This text may be read as a prescription for acceptable female activities, which included crafts such as weaving, sculpting, and painting. Boccaccio conjectured that these endeavors would occupy both the body and the mind, equating the banishment of idleness with the virtue of chastity. In the early fifteenth century, this text was translated into French and accompanying illustrations of women engaged in these activities were commissioned. Since women were encouraged to partake in these artistic endeavors, it is probable that the illuminations drew from actual female activities. Indeed, there are documented cases of women engaged in crafts related to the ornamentation of buildings. For example, the earlier cited case in London of a woman painting the tabernacle at St. Mary at Hill. Also, the weaving of tapestries used to decorate the interior of domestic buildings was a predominantly female craft.

A very well-known image depicting women building a city stone by stone is illustrated in Christine de Pisan's *Le livre de la cité de dames* (1405) (figure 6.3).[75] This painting represents a metaphorical city in de Pisan's book where women could create and conduct model lives, yet it also exemplifies a parallel with reality. The image is one of empowerment. In the image we see women taking control of the direction of their lives by actively building it themselves.

The management skills of noblewomen could at times be required for repair and new construction on their estate. The countess of Artois directed the renovation of her chateaux and a chapel and also the construction of a new hospital in the fourteenth century.[76] Just a century after de Pisan wrote her book, Jacquette de Montbron, an aristocratic dowager was recorded in her brother-in-law's book, the *Recueil des Dames*, as having designed and built her own home and renovated many other structures on her estate by her own hand.[77] She drafted her own plans and designed her home in the Renaissance style, following the trend of importing "modern" Italian design into France in the late sixteenth century. Her humanist education, her inheritance, and her widowed status allowed her the freedom to pursue her passion for building, and she was praised for her industriousness. Could she be the first recorded woman architect-builder? If one woman has been found engaging in the design of architecture, it is possible that other discoveries will follow.

Queens, who specifically controlled their own purse strings, could direct their money toward architectural projects as a means of enhancing their vocations. As Helen Gaudette eloquently presented in her study of Queen Melisende of Jerusalem in chapter seven of this book, this queen oversaw the construction of a fortress, a convent, and a covered market street, as a means of extending her political influence and demonstrating her religious piety. Other twelfth-century queens, such as Eleanor of Aquitaine and Blanche of Castile were involved beyond the extent of mere patronage; each was extensively involved with the design of their patron churches.[78] Women's patronage of architecture, at all levels of society, most often appeared as an act of piety.[79]

## Conclusions

Women's participation on the construction site has a history. It is not the recounting of great historical events and monuments, but a history of everyday life that, for the most part, exposes the working conditions of poor and middle-class women and the social prejudices against their plight in life. The social ideology of women's place in the economy, one that dates back to ancient times, did not change over the centuries. Despite the opposition toward women working outside the home or in any form of manual labor, women without substantial means of lifelong support were unable to adhere to the ideals of contemporary theorists and found a means of living doing just that. Women's participation in the building crafts in the early modern period became increasingly limited as opposition to female pressure on the job market grew and the professionalization of the crafts progressed. It is evident that the poorest women in search of work had the most liberal access to the construction site itself, whereas the opportunities for women in the crafts were tied to their family connection through birth, dowry, or marriage and most often limited within the confines of the home workshop. The birth, dowry, or marriage of an aristocratic woman put her in a position of greatest freedom. Although she might not appear on a construction site daily, with no husband present at her side she might wield the greatest authority over the design and construction of her patronized work.

Further evidence needs to be gathered before an accurate chronological history can be determined. However a general pattern has emerged with the evidence at hand. Beginning with the early Middle Ages, Lisa Bitel has observed that women's work in general did not change much from the fall of the Roman Empire until the eleventh century.[80] In the city, women were confined to domestic work in the home; in the country, their sphere enlarged only to the agricultural fields. The eleventh and twelfth centuries were characterized by an increasing number of women in the crafts and working outside of the home. Since crafts had not yet attained a high degree of organization, women more freely participated.

The nature of women's work began to change with the shift in demographics from the countryside to the growing urban centers and the expansion of the middle class beginning in the thirteenth century. In the cases observed in this study from the thirteenth to the seventeenth centuries, women's regular employment as unskilled day laborers appears to be fairly continuous. However, more focused regional studies are needed to clarify this trajectory. Only two points can be made with confidence. A primary factor in the continuity of their employment is the lack of legal barriers or bans against women working as day laborers; their work was unskilled, and there was no corporate organization overseeing or protecting male employment. Also, considering that the cycles of construction in any region were intimately linked with those of the economic cycle, women's participation in construction may have waxed and waned with the events of economic history.

In the cities reviewed in this study, the number of women recorded working in the building crafts increased between the thirteenth and fourteenth centuries. These numbers increased substantially by the fifteenth century, especially in Paris, Strasbourg, and Würzburg. Up until the second half of the fifteenth century, there appears to have been conditions that encouraged women's engagement in the crafts. After that point, increasing economic pressures and competition for jobs, which led to the professionalization of trades, began to make employment more difficult for women. To claim the title of a profession and to demand appropriate wages, formal training and proof of licensure became a standard requirement.[81] David Herlihy has also recognized the diminished participation of women in many crafts after the fifteenth century.[82] He reports that the guilds became more closed to women and a tendency can be seen in many parts of Europe to ban women from all but the most marginal participation. The reduced role of women in the economy continued to be the case until the twentieth century.

How pervasive was women's participation on the construction site? The numbers of women in proportion to those of men working on most sites is small and women's presence is only seen occasionally. Yet, consistently across Western Europe one can find construction sites bustling with the labor of both men and women. Philibert de l'Orme, a sixteenth-century royal architect and the son of a Lyon mason, was once quoted as saying: "Can anything be found which can employ and busy more people of either sex than building?... poor people, who otherwise would have to go beg for their bread?"[83]

**Figure 6.1** Husband and wife carry a keystone that will complete the vault of a church.

*Source*: Woodcut, printed by Peter Drach, Speyer, late fifteenth century.

**Figure 6.2** Wood carriers in rags entering the city.

*Source*: Miniature of the *Fables of Bidpai*, French, fifteenth century.

**Figure 6.3** Chistine de Pisan invites women to build an ideal city (detail).

*Source*: Miniature in Christine de Pisan, *Le livre de la cité des dames*. Manuscrits, français 1178, f. 3. Biblioteque Nationale, Paris, 1405.

## Notes

1. Women could be masters in crafts other than in the building trades, which were historically male-dominated.
2. Hilde van Wijngaarden, "The Role of Women in the Survival of Poor Families in the Seventeenth Century," in *Women in Towns: The Social Position of Urban Women in a Historical Context,* ed. Marjatta Hietala and Lars Nilsson (Stockholm: Stads- och kommunhistoriska institutet, 1999), p. 40.
3. Merry Wiesner, *Women and Gender in Early Modern Europe* (Cambridge: Cambridge University Press, 2000), pp. 104–5.
4. See Megan McLaughlin, "The Woman Warrior: Gender, Warfare and Society in Medieval Europe," *Women's Studies* 17 (1990): 193–209.
5. Ramón Carande, "Sevilla, fortaleza y mercado: Algunas instituciones de la ciudad, en el siglo XIV especialmente, estudiadas en sus privilegios, ordenamientos y cuentas," in *Anuario de Historia del Derecho Español,* vol. 2 (Madrid: Centro de Estudios Históricos, 1925), pp. 268–70.
6. Carande, "Sevilla, fortaleza y mercado," p. 269. Ellipsis inserted by the author and not from the original.
7. Donald Woodward, *Men at Work: Labourers and Building Craftsmen in the Towns of Northern England, 1450–1750* (Cambridge: Cambridge University Press, 1995).
8. Sharon Farmer, *Surviving Poverty in Medieval Paris: Gender, Ideology and the Daily Lives of the Poor* (Ithaca, NY: Cornell University Press, 2001), pp. 25–26.
9. John Fitchen, *Building Construction before Mechanization* (Cambridge, MA: MIT Press, 1990), 14–15.
10. Fitchen, *Building Construction,* p. 247, n. 3.
11. Spiro Kostov, *The Architect: Chapters in the History of the Profession* (New York: Oxford University Press, 1977), p. 76.
12. Woodward, *Men at Work,* p. 110.
13. Woodward, *Men at Work,* p. 110.
14. Michel Mollat, *The Poor in the Middle Ages: An Essay in Social History* (New Haven, CT: Yale University Press, 1986), p. 243.
15. J. Zabalo Zalegui, *El Registro de Comptos del Reino de Navarra de 1280* (Pamplona: Diputación Foral de Navarra, 1972), nos. 213, 240, 242.
16. Therese and Mendel Metzger, *Jewish Life in the Middle Ages: Illuminated Hebrew Manuscripts of the Thirteenth to the Sixteenth Centuries* (New York: Alpine Fine Arts Collection, 1982), p. 199.
17. Carande, "Sevilla, fortaleza y mercado," p. 393.
18. Carande, "Sevilla, fortaleza y mercado," pp. 397, 401.
19. Carande, "Sevilla, fortaleza y mercado," p. 400.
20. Ricardo Izquierdo Benito, "La vivienda en Toledo a fines de la Edad Media: Elementos constructivos," in *La ciudad medieval: De la casa al tejido urbano,* ed. Jean Passini (Cuenca: Ediciones de la Universidad de Castilla-La Mancha, 2001), pp. 281–301, esp. p. 283–84, n. 11.
21. Arlette Higounet, "La femme du Moyen Âge en France dans la vie politique, économique et sociale," in *Histoire mondiale de la femme,* vol. 2, ed.

Pierre Grimal (Paris: Nouvelle librairie de France, 1974), pp. 135–70, esp. p. 165; Higounet, *Les comptes de la taille et les sources de l'histoire démographique de Perigeux au XIVe siècle* (Paris: S.E.V.P.E.N., 1965).

22. Jean Verdon, "La vie quotidienne de la femme en France au bas moyen âge," in *Frau im spatmittelalterlichen Alltag* (Vienna: Veroffentlichungen des Instituts fur Mittelalterliche realienkunde Osterreichs, 1986), p. 365. First cited in Phillipe Wolff, *Commerce et marchands de Toulouse (vers 1350–vers 1450)* (Paris: Librairie Plon, 1954), p. 441.
23. Andrée Lehmann, *Le Rôle de la femme dans l'histoire de France au Moyen-âge* (Paris: Berger-Levrault, 1952), pp. 467–68.
24. Nathalie Baudoux-Jung, "La construction de tours de la ville d'Amiens d'après les 'marchés à tasque' (fin XIVe–début XVe siècle)," in *La ville au Moyen-Âge. I: Ville et espace*, ed. Noël Coulet and Olivier Guyotjeannin (Paris: Éditions du CTHS, 1998), p. 190.
25. Natalie Zemon Davis, "Women in the Crafts in Sixteenth-Century Lyon," in *Women and Work in Pre-industrial* Europe, ed. Barbara Hanawalt (Bloomington: Indiana University Press, 1986), pp. 167–97, esp. p. 177.
26. Woodward, *Men at Work*, pp. 110–11. In the first week of employment four married women were recorded, and Woodward assumes that the rest, who are named, were single and probably young.
27. Eileen Power, *Medieval English Nunneries* (London: Cambridge University Press, 1922), 157.
28. Woodward, *Men at Work*, p. 113.
29. Erica Uitz, *The Legend of Good Women: Medieval Women in Towns and Cities* (Mt. Kisco, NY: Moyer Bell Limited, 1990), p. 61.
30. Woodward, *Men at Work*, pp. 112–15.
31. This is true in most regions, except in England where many accounts often list the name and marital status of the woman.
32. Woodward, *Men at Work*, pp. 109–10. Woodward notes that it is on rare occasion a husband and wife or family were hired as a team to complete a specific job in Durham.
33. Merry E. Wiesner, *Working Women in Renaissance Germany* (New Brunswick, NJ: Rutgers University Press, 1986), p. 149.
34. Margaret Wade Labarge, *Women in Medieval Life: A Small Sound of the Trumpet* (London: Hamilton, 1986), p. 145.
35. Davis, "Women in the Crafts," pp. 167–97.
36. Davis, "Women in the Crafts," p. 187.
37. Davis, "Women in the Crafts," p. 174.
38. Diane Hutton, "Women in Fourteenth-Century Shrewsbury," in *Women and Work in Pre-Industrial England,* ed. Lindsey Charles and Lorna Duffin (London: Croom Helm, 1985), pp. 83–99, esp. 89. Also, see R. H. Hilton, *English and French Towns in Feudal Society: A Comparative Study* (Cambridge: Cambridge University Press, 1992), pp. 66–67.
39. Wiesner, *Working Women,* pp. 164–67.
40. Wiesner, *Working Women,* p. 151.
41. Wiesner, *Working Women,* pp. 164–65.

42. Heather Swanson, *Medieval Artisans: An Urban Class in Late Medieval England* (Oxford: Basil Blackwell, 1989), p. 83.
43. Uitz, *The Legend of Good Women,* p. 61.
44. Wiesner, *Women and Gender,* p. 105.
45. Wiesner, *Women and Gender,* p. 17. For example, the secrets of the masonic guilds' design principles were so closely guarded, usually in oral tradition alone, that little of what they practiced is known today.
46. Wiesner, *Working Women,* p. 162.
47. For Paris, see Lehmann, *Le Rôle de la femme,* 467–68; G. Fagniez, *Etudes sur l'industrie et la classe industrielle au XIIIe et au XIVe siècle* (Paris: 1877), 86–88. For London, see H. Littlehales, ed., *The Medieval Records of a London City Church 1420–1559 (St. Mary at Hill)* (London: Early English Text Society, 1905), pp. 64–65, 76, 94, 133, 138–39, 142, 152–53; A. H. Thomas, *Calendar of Plea and Memoranda Rolls Preserved among the Archives of the Corporation of the City of London at the Guildhall, 1413–1437* (Cambridge: Cambridge University Press, 1843), p. 229, Roll A57; Swanson, *Medieval Artisans.*
48. David Herlihy, *Opera Muliebria: Women and Work in Medieval Europe* (Philadelphia, PA: Temple University Press, 1990), p. 145.
49. Carande, "Sevilla, fortaleza y mercado," p. 296.
50. Higounet, "La femme du Moyen Âge," pp. 154, 156.
51. Uitz, *The Legend of Good Women,* p. 61. For examples in Burgundy see Verdon, "La vie quotidienne," p. 375.
52. M. Wood, *The English Medieval House* (London: 1965), 373, and Public Record Office, London C1/48/37 and C1/33/261, Exchequer Kings Rembrancer accounts 473.
53. Littlehales, *The Medieval Records,* p. 142.
54. Hutton, "Women in Fourteenth-Century Shrewsbury," pp. 89, 96.
55. Davis, "Women in the Crafts," p. 180.
56. Davis, "Women in the Crafts," pp. 151, 160–61. Also see A. Abram, "Women Traders in Medieval London," *Economic Journal* 26 (1916): 276–85, esp. pp. 276–78, 281, 284–85.
57. Uitz, *The Legend of Good Women,* p. 61.
58. Wiesner, *Working Women,* p. 151.
59. Wiesner, *Working Women,* pp. 160–61.
60. Single women in thirteenth-century France are a typical example presented in Farmer, *Surviving Poverty in Medieval France,* pp. 29–31.
61. Marion A. Kaplan, "Introduction," in *The Marriage Bargain: Women and Dowries in European History,* ed. Marion A. Kaplan (New York: Haworth Press, 1985), pp. 1–11, esp. 1–2.
62. Kaplan, "Introduction," pp. 33–43.
63. See Diane Owen Hughes, "From Brideprice to Dowry in Mediterranean Europe," in *The Marriage Bargain,* ed. Kaplan, pp. 13–58, for an excellent and very detailed account of ancient and medieval dotal practices.
64. Margaret R. Sommerville, *Sex and Subjection: Attitudes to Women in Early Modern Society* (New York: E. Arnold, 1995), p. 102.

65. Sommerville, *Sex and Subjection*, p. 102.
66. Farmer, *Surviving Poverty in Medieval France*, 107–22.
67. Mollat, *The Poor in the Middle Ages*, pp. 255, 297.
68. Mollat, *The Poor in the Middle Ages*, p. 31.
69. Mollat, *The Poor in the Middle Ages*, p. 233.
70. Mollat, *The Poor in the Middle Ages*, p. 251.
71. Mollat, *The Poor in the Middle Ages*, p. 295.
72. The "Fables of Bidpai" was a compilation of Hindu and Buddhist moralizing stories on politics and proper human conduct composed to instruct Indian princes under the title, "Panchatantra" (Five Principles). The fables spread across Persia and into Europe by the early Middle Ages. These were copied and translated into many European vernaculars from the medieval period through the twentieth century.
73. Mollat, *The Poor in the Middle Ages*, p. 245. Also see Ruth Karras, *Common Women: Prostitution and Sexuality in Medieval England* (Oxford: Oxford University Press, 1996), pp. 48–55.
74. Giovanni Boccaccio, *Concerning Famous Women,* translation of *De claris mulieribus* by Guido A. Guarino (New Brunswick, NJ: Rutgers University Press, 1963).
75. Christine de Pisan, *The Book of the City of Ladies,* translation of *Le livre de la cité des dames* by Earl Jeffrey Richards (New York: Persea Books, 1982).
76. Verdon, "La vie quotidienne de la femme," p. 375.
77. Madeleine Lazard, "Jacquette de Montbron, une bâtisseuse humaniste," in *Royaume de Fémynie: Pouvoirs, contraintes, espaces de liberté de femmes, de la Renaissance à la Fronde,* ed. by Kathleen Wilson-Chevalier and Éliane Viennot (Paris: Champion, 1999), pp. 17–26.
78. See Eleanor Greenhill, "Eleanor, Abbot Suger and Saint-Denis," in *Eleanor of Aquitaine: Patron and Politician,* ed. William Kibler (Austin: University of Texas Press, 1976), pp. 81–113; Henry Adams recounts in *Mont Saint Michel and Chartres* (Boston: Houghton Mifflin, 1933) that Blanche of Castile was involved in the design of the porch for Mont Saint Michel.
79. There are numerous studies of aristocratic women's patronage of architecture in Europe and in the Byzantine and Muslim world. Two noteworthy examples are Carolyn Valone, "Architecture as a Public Voice for Women in Sixteenth-Century Rome," *Renaissance Studies* 15:3 (2001): 301–27, and Ulku U. Bates, "Women as Patrons of Architecture in Turkey," in *Women in the Muslim World,* ed. Luis Beck and Nilda Keddie (Cambridge, MA: Harvard University Press, 1978), pp. 245–60. Also of interest are studies of women pursuing architectural patronage as a form of piety, such as Carolyn Valone's article on "Roman Matrons: Various Views of the Cloister Wall," in *The Crannied Wall: Women, Religion, and the Arts in Early Modern Europe,* ed. Mondon Craig (Ann Arbor: University of Michigan Press 1992), pp. 49–72. R. McKitterick, "Women in the Ottonian Church: An Iconographic Perspective," in *Women in the Church: Studies in*

*Church History*, ed. W. J. Scheils and D. Wood (Oxford: Blackwell, 1990), pp. 79–100 provides the most recent overview of female monastic patronage in German-speaking regions. In Norway, Birgit Sawyer has recorded an intriguing correlation between women, piety, and the building of bridges and rest houses for travelers in her article "Women as Bridge-Builders: The Role of Women in Viking-Age Scandinavia," in *People and Places in Northern Europe, 500–1600: Essays in Honour of Peter Hayes Sawyer*, ed. Ian Wood and Niels Lund (Woodbridge, UK: Boydell, 1991), pp. 211–24. There are numerous cases of provisions left by women of lesser means in their wills for the construction and mending of churches, roads, and bridges. For example, in F. Furnivall, ed. *The Fifty Earliest English Wills in the Court of Probate, London. A. D. 1387–1439,* vol. 78 (London: Oxford University Press, 1964), pp. 49–51, 85–86, there are cases such as Alys Chirche who in 1430 left provisions for Twykenham Bridge, Kingston Bridge, Wyke Causeway, and Harlington Church and Lady Peryne Clanbowe who in 1422 left provisions in her will to help mend bridges and bad roads.

80. Lisa M. Bitel, *Women in Early Medieval Europe 400–1100* (Cambridge: Cambridge University Press, 2002), p. 236. The author noted that the only shifts women benefited from occurred during periods of temporary shortages of men, when women had brief opportunities to acquire skills in work outside of the home.
81. Wiesner, *Women and Gender*, p. 104.
82. David Herlihy, *Women, Family and Society in Medieval Europe: Historical Essays, 1978–1991* (Providence, RI: Berghahn Books, 1995), pp. 91–95.
83. Davis, "Women in the Crafts," p. 177.

CHAPTER 7

# THE SPENDING POWER OF A CRUSADER QUEEN: MELISENDE OF JERUSALEM

*Helen A. Gaudette*

Royal honor and authority in twelfth-century Europe and the crusader states normally depended on personal generosity, patronage, and displays of wealth.[1] Every act of patronage or gift of support, lands, titles, and appointments made by a ruler to his or her subjects or vassals was charged with significance and part of an overall strategy of resource investment and spending policy to enhance his or her kingdom's power, influence, and defense.[2] At that time, the political power of all virtuous western European kings and queens, including those of the Latin Kingdom of Jerusalem, was ideally kept and exercised by securing the peace, prosperity, and piety of their realms. They strived to spend their kingdom's resources wisely, no matter how limited they were, in order to achieve these aims.

During her reign from 1131 to 1152, Queen Melisende of the Latin Kingdom of Jerusalem spent her kingdom's resources carefully and strategically to benefit her kingdom, her dynasty, and herself. Mostly, she patronized the kingdom's religious institutions because that was one of the most acceptable domains of patronage open to the participation of medieval noble women, and she used it to her advantage politically whenever possible.[3] Through the strategy of patronage, queens could extend their influence. They often had access to the formidable resources of their kingdoms and, through religious patronage, they could pursue a variety of political, religious, and social agendas. Thus, queens provided support or backing for artists, building projects, scribes, and church institutions in the form of gifts, money, positions, lands, political influence, and personal encouragement and assistance.[4] Patronage created a link between a queen and a particular person or religious institution that could become a mutually beneficial relationship and often also became the basis for friendship and political alliance. Examples of these connections abound in the twelfth century, but perhaps some of the most important include those between Eleanor of Aquitaine and Fontevraud Abbey,[5] Urraca of León-Castilla and the Church of Santiago of Compostela,[6] and Empress Matilda and Bec Abbey.[7] Spending was therefore an important strategy for Melisende because she was a woman and, ultimately, her gender defined the actions she could take to promote her position and wield authority as a queen regnant. Her charters depict the degree of her spending and indicate that she accessed power through patronage, ruling by the virtue of *largitas* or generosity, the female personification of which is prominently featured on the beautifully carved ivory front cover of the *Melisende Psalter*, produced for her by the Church of the Holy Sepulcher's scriptorium during the years 1135–36.[8] She spent her kingdom's resources to its benefit to be sure—but also spent them to increase public confidence in her queenship.

The eldest daughter of King Baldwin II of the Latin Kingdom of Jerusalem, Melisende was married to Fulk V of Anjou in 1129 and in the next year they had a son and heir whom they named Baldwin after his grandfather. On 14 September 1131, in accordance with her father's wishes, Melisende and Fulk were crowned and anointed co-rulers of the kingdom.[9] Fulk was crowned king as Melisende's husband, and her rights as a queen regnant were fully recognized by the nobles and churchmen of the kingdom's high court. They ruled together jointly until Fulk died in 1143 when he was thrown from his horse during a hunting accident outside the city of Acre. On Christmas day a few weeks later, their thirteen-year-old son Baldwin was solemnly anointed as King Baldwin III. Although he was crowned at his mother's side to rule jointly with her as his father had, he was under the legal age to rule so she took over the governing of the kingdom, and by all accounts, ruled wisely and judiciously, defying the gender norms of the time.[10] As Erin Jordan has observed in chapter eight of this volume, "a woman engaged in political activity during the thirteenth century challenged a number of gender norms entrenched in medieval society, particularly those that positioned women as subordinate to men, characterizing them as incapable of effective governance."[11] Later on, Melisende intentionally continued to deny Baldwin's demand to rule alone despite his coming of age in 1145 when he had turned fifteen. By 1150, this had become a source of strong frustration for him but Melisende managed to keep an incredible amount of political support at this time.[12] In 1152, Baldwin was forced to revolt against his mother, to gather an army, and conduct a civil war against her.

After she surrendered a few weeks later, her support evaporated and she was removed from the throne. She did, however, retain some influence as an advisor to him until her death in 1161.[13]

Regrettably, very little evidence about Melisende's life and reign has been preserved. The principal sources are William of Tyre's *A History of the Deeds Done beyond the Sea*, which he began in 1169, the royal charters issued in her name or with her consent and the witness lists that accompany them, and some material sources such as the *Melisende Psalter*.[14] There are no extant sources written by Melisende or anyone who knew her personally. Understanding her reign, however, is absolutely necessary if the history of the Latin Kingdom of Jerusalem is to be complete in any way. For twenty-one years, she wielded real power as queen regnant of the kingdom, yet there have been very few attempts made by historians to understand how she ruled and why she did the things she did because the evidence is so scarce.[15]

In this chapter, therefore, inspired by the theme of this book, I would like to examine the way Melisende wielded power through spending by assessing the impact and consequences of her involvement in three large construction projects in the kingdom, namely Bethgibelin Castle, the convent of Bethany, and the covered market street in Jerusalem known as *Malquisinat*, the Street of Bad Cooking.[16] As each required a tremendous amount of money to be completed, they reveal some of the circumstances of her reign and some of the political strategies behind her investments, especially in the areas of military defense policy, church building, and urban planning. They prove that the resources at her disposal as queen must have been substantial and have come mainly from the crown's income, which was derived from a variety of sources: the vast royal demesne, including her dower cities of Acre and Tyre, the monopoly over the minting of coins, taxes paid by Bedouin tribesmen and religious taxes of the kingdom's non-Christian subjects, customs and harbor tariffs on some imported and exported goods, and enemy possessions plundered in battle. Unfortunately, no record of her personal wealth has survived although it might have consisted of precious objects, jewels, relics, and books.

My first example of Melisende's spending power occurred during the period of her joint reign with Fulk. In 1136, the king and queen turned their attention to defending the south of the kingdom. Although it was rare to see a queen involved in planning military measures at this time, in the Latin Kingdom as well as in the West, Melisende's unique position as queen regnant guaranteed her some participation in determining the kingdom's military spending. Two years before, Fulk had attempted to discredit and exclude her from governing in the kingdom, but she had found two champions in Hugh of Puiset, the Count of Jaffa, and William, the Patriarch of Jerusalem, who had supported her authority as joint ruler and forced Fulk to back down. From then on, she had been included in almost every one of Fulk's public acts and charters.[17] Her participation here is an important indication of Fulk's continued acknowledgment of her position as queen regnant and the influence she had won in this crucial area of governing. Although she never fought in a battle during her reign, she was often left in charge of defending the kingdom while Fulk and later Baldwin III, her son, were away conducting wars. Also, it was she who ordered her constable Manasses with the army of Jerusalem to Edessa in the effort to defend in against Zengi in 1144, who hosted the war council of Acre in 1148 that decided on attacking Damascus during the Second Crusade, and who aided Baldwin of Lille in taking back a fortress in 1157 in Gilead on the Jordan River, while Baldwin III was campaigning in Antioch.[18]

After calling all of the people in the vicinity together as well as Patriarch William and the local lords for aid, Melisende and Fulk spent an enormous amount of money and effort to start building a large fortress at the ancient city of Beersheba where there was a great well for water. Called Bethgibelin, it would be located strategically at the foot of the mountains overlooking the plains twelve miles east of Ascalon to guard the approach road from Hebron to Ascalon and stop the disastrous incursions of the Fatimids into the kingdom from the south. Therefore, the decision made by Fulk and Melisende to build the castle in this location was determined by geographical factors and forever changed the rural landscape of the area by creating a new crusader military presence in the region.[19] Built as part of what Martin Hoch calls a "strategy of containment," Bethgibelin Castle would later function as one link in a chain of castles built around Ascalon to stop the raids conducted by the Fatimids. It would also serve as an administrative center for the area, and operate as a military base for a future attack on the city.[20] When the construction was completed, Fulk issued a charter with Melisende's consent that confirmed and transferred the lordship over it, from Hugh of St. Abraham or Hebron to Raymond of Puy, the Master of the Hospitallers or the Knights of St. John, a religious order dedicated to caring for the kingdom's sick citizens and visiting pilgrims.[21]

With this construction project, Melisende and Fulk changed the character of the Hospitallers into a military order.[22] They also appropriated and produced a space that would ensure the future safety of the monarchy and the kingdom.[23] William of Tyre wrote that Bethgibelin was a fortress, "surrounded by an impregnable wall with towers, ramparts, and a moat...when the fortress was finished and complete in every part, it was granted by common consent to the brothers of the house of the Hospital, which is at Jerusalem. They have guarded their charge with all due diligence, even to the present time; and from that day, the attacks of the enemy in that place have become less violent."[24] The Hospitallers must have been willing to take on these responsibilities and may even have asked for them. Alan Forey maintains that, "[t]he Hospitallers were being assigned direct control over strongholds and were not just receiving rights of overlordship. To have entrusted frontier strongholds in these circumstances to an institution which contained no military element would have been foolhardy, and it is difficult to believe that Fulk would have asked Hugh of St. Abraham to surrender his rights, or that the grant of Beit-Jibrin would have been made to the Hospitallers...if the hospital had been still purely a charitable institution."[25]

The charter recording the transfer was witnessed by a long list of the kingdom's clerics and barons, indicating that the conferring of military responsibilities on the Hospitallers was a widely accepted decision. The charter also included a gift to the Hospitallers made by Fulk and Melisende of four *casalia* or villages. It is likely that Fulk and Melisende gave the Hospitallers these four villages in order to provide them with added income to fulfill their new military duties. They would have understood how expensive the effort would be. William of Tyre wrote that a considerable amount of money and effort had already been expended during their reign before the castle had been built to supply the area with enough manpower, provisions, and weapons to keep the Fatimids of Ascalon at bay.[26] A few years later, the Hospitallers would take on even more military responsibilities and costs on the frontiers of the County of Tripoli in 1144 when Count Raymond of Tripoli gave them the fortress of Crac des Chevaliers, and four other castles in his county to man and defend.[27] Thus, from this time on, the Hospitallers became crucial to the survival of all of the crusader kingdoms against their enemies.

The convent of Bethany, my second example of Melisende's construction spending, was begun in 1138. At this time, she was still ruling jointly with Fulk, but he does not appear to have participated in the convent's planning or execution in any substantial way. William of Tyre maintained that it was solely Melisende's idea to found the convent "in order to provide for the healing of her own soul and those of her parents as also for the salvation of her husband and children."[28] It was viewed as her own personal spending project and a demonstration of her piety and religious patronage, and it would honor her parents, husband, and sons, sanctifying and promoting the new royal dynasty of Jerusalem. Melisende eventually placed her youngest sister Ivette, who had entered the convent of St. Anne in Jerusalem as a girl, in charge of the convent as its abbess; in fact, according to William of Tyre, it "was consideration for this sister which led the queen to undertake this enterprise, for she felt that it was unfitting that a king's daughter should be subject to the authority of a mother superior, like an ordinary person."[29] Her other sisters, Alice and Hodierna, had previously made advantageous marriages to the powerful princes of Antioch and Tripoli.

According to William of Tyre, "[a]fter much deliberation," Melisende chose Bethany as the place to found her convent.[30] Less than two miles from Jerusalem on the road to Jericho, Bethany was a small village on the southeastern slope of the Mount of Olives. It was secluded but its closeness to the city offered many advantages to the nuns, who could be more easily supported and protected by the queen. It was situated on the edge of the barren and wild hills that descended eastward to the Dead Sea, and its lands supported olive groves and sheep grazing. It seems that this site was chosen by Melisende, at least in part, for its ideal geographical location and nearness to Jerusalem. Moreover, it was in Bethany that each year on Palm Sunday, the faithful gathered for the procession to Jerusalem that imitated Christ's triumphal entry as described in the gospels.[31]

Bethany belonged to the canons of the Church of the Holy Sepulcher but Melisende, as demonstrated by an 1138 charter granted with Fulk, had convinced Patriarch William and the other canons to exchange it for Tekoah, a town south of Bethlehem near Hebron.[32] The founding of the convent was a widely supported initiative as the charter's witness list contains the names of most of the kingdom's barons and highest level churchmen. William of Tyre wrote that since the area was exposed to the kingdom's many enemies, Melisende, "at great expense caused to be built a strongly fortified tower of hewn and polished stone. This was devoted to the necessary purpose of defense, that the maidens dedicated to God might have an impregnable fortress as a protection against the enemy."[33] Through the exchange of lands, the patriarch therefore agreed with Melisende's initiative to found and protect this sacred place outside Jerusalem at the crown's expense. The many prominent names on the charter's witness list signified that Melisende's project was accepted by the barons and churchmen of the kingdom as a proper exercise of her role as queen with the power to spend royal funds as she saw fit. Besides its close proximity to Jerusalem, however, the basis for Melisende's choice of Bethany must also have been determined by its significance in the New Testament and its former inhabitants, Christ's friends Mary, Martha, and Lazarus.

One of the most important tasks of Jerusalem's monarchy was to protect and promote Christendom's holy sites within the kingdom. The gospels relate that Christ visited Bethany many times to stay with his friend

Lazarus, probably when visiting Jerusalem during feast days, and that each time he was there he was prominently served by women, his friend's sisters Mary and Martha. In the usual female role, Martha served Christ as a servant by waiting on him and presumably preparing meals to feed him and his disciples. On one occasion, Mary angered Martha by not helping her with the duties of hospitality and instead sitting at Christ's feet to listen to his teaching. To Martha's disappointment, Christ approved of Mary's contemplative role and preference to listening over housework and accepted her as one of his disciples.[34] Mary became venerated as a model for Christian women, who should not be concerned with earthly worries or distractions so it made sense that Melisende would consider Mary's home of Bethany as a perfect place for a convent of women dedicated to serving Christ through humble devotion and prayer. Bethany's real prominence, however, as related by John's gospel, was that it was the location for one of his most famous miracles, the raising of Lazarus from the dead.[35] Melisende would have been aware that a foundation and church dedicated to him and his sisters on this spot would attract many Christian pilgrims, who would spread its acclaim throughout Europe and Byzantium as well as help support her convent and its nuns financially with their donations. Lazarus was a very popular saint, who was venerated widely in the Latin as well as the Greek Orthodox Church.[36] Throughout her reign, Melisende made a sincere effort to support and patronize religious institutions of both traditions. She made substantial gifts to the Greek Orthodox Laura of St. Sabas and its monks, for example, at the same time that she was patronizing the Church of the Holy Sepulcher and its patriarch and canons, and the Abbey and Shrine Church of Our Lady of Jehoshaphat and its monks.[37]

William of Tyre reported that when the tower and church were finished at Bethany, Melisende established her sister and the nuns in their new home and placed over them an elderly, experienced abbess to guide them, with the intention for her sister to succeed her when she died. Then she generously,

> endowed the church with rich estates, so that in temporal possessions it should not be inferior to any monastery, either of men or women; or rather, as it is said, that it might be richer than any other church. Among other possessions which she generously bestowed upon this venerable place was the famous city of Jericho with its dependencies, situated in the plain of Jordan and very rich in resources of every kind. She also presented to the convent a large number of sacred vessels of gold and silver adorned with gems. She likewise gave it silken stuffs for the adornment of the house of God and vestments of every description, both priestly and levitical, as ecclesiastical rules required.

> On the death of the venerable woman to whom she had entrusted the charge of convent, the queen put her original intention into effect. With the sanction of the patriarch and the willing assent of the holy nuns, she made her sister the superior of the convent. On that occasion, she made many additional gifts, such as chalices, books, and other ornaments pertaining to the service of the church. As long as she lived, she continued to enrich the place by her favor, in the interests of her own soul and that of the sister whom she so tenderly loved.[38]

Although the convent of Bethany is now in ruins and none of these richly decorated objects have survived, William's description of them indicates that Melisende spared no expense in order to lavishly furnish and equip her foundation and support her sister.[39] It is also important to highlight William's record of her gift of books to the convent of Bethany. Here is evidence that she endowed the convent with manuscripts and was associated with the flourishing *scriptoria* in the kingdom such as the one in the Church of the Holy Sepulcher from which she could have commissioned these books. Her generous endowment guaranteed the success of her convent as well as her reputation as a devout and dutiful queen and must have won her the admiration of the kingdom's churchmen and citizens alike. Here too is evidence that Melisende used Bethany to construct a space that would ensure the prominence of her dynasty and the kingdom—a space that would also have been seen and understood as both royal and feminine.[40]

My third example of Melisende's spending power is *Malquisinat* Street, the covered market street in Jerusalem that she constructed in 1152, just before her son Baldwin overthrew her from power. Her purpose in building this street was probably politically motivated and, what Hans Eberhard Mayer has called "an attempt to woo the city," in order to win the support of its citizens for herself, instead of her son, during their political showdown.[41] Just before this time, Baldwin had demanded the right to rule on his own as king, however, the patriarch of Jerusalem, openly supporting Melisende's desire for the continuation of their joint rule, had refused to perform the coronation ceremony without her being present. Refusing to back down, Baldwin then unexpectedly appeared in public wearing a crown of laurel and called for a meeting of the high court. According to William of Tyre, after much deliberation, the barons compelled Melisende to divide the kingdom with him. She kept Jerusalem and Nablus, and he took Tyre and Acre.[42] At this time, in a charter for the Church of the Holy Sepulcher, Melisende waived a suit that she had brought against it over some Christian Syrian inhabitants of the village of Bait-Surik near Jerusalem.[43] The Holy Sepulcher was to be allowed to hold these people in peace as they had held them since the days of Godfrey's reign, just after Jerusalem was conquered in 1099. To them, she even added some other Syrians of the village of Calandria also near Jerusalem, as well as some in two other villages. She did all of this in return for the shop previously owned by a man named William the Bastard and a share in his two money-changing tables that she and Fulk had given the church back in 1138. With the income from this shop and tables, she would provide the city of Jerusalem with a new street.[44]

Known as *Malquisinat* Street or the Street of Bad Cooking, it was a place where vendors could sell cooked meals and bread to pilgrims. It was covered by a stone vault ceiling. Parallel to it on each side, were two other streets that Melisende may have built at the same time, known as the Street of Herbs and the Covered Street. These streets were centrally located within the city, suggesting that once again, Melisende chose the site for its ideal geographical location. *Malquisinat* Street was within walking distance to important Christian pilgrimage sites in the twelfth century, especially the Church of the Holy Sepulcher, St. John's Hospital, the Temple (Dome of the Rock), and the Abbey of St. Anne.[45] The three streets had passages that were six meters high and three meters wide. Their shops were no more than four meters square. There were square shaft openings above *Malquisinat* Street to let in light and air and let the smoke from the cooking fires out. Stone arches covered the openings to keep the rain from seeping in.[46] Today, there can still be seen some inscriptions carved into *Malquisinat's* arches that linked it to Jerusalem's convent of St. Anne, where Melisende's sister Ivette had lived as a nun before she moved to the convent of Bethany. The carved letters "SCA ANNA" might suggest that Melisende had arranged for the abbey to receive a share in the rents of the shops so inscribed and that she had not stopped patronizing St. Anne's after her sister had left.[47]

Melisende built *Malquisinat* Street to solve an urgent problem for her city. By the middle of the twelfth century, there had been a rapid growth in the number of pilgrims visiting Jerusalem from the West to pray at its holy places and shrine churches, including the Church of the Holy Sepulcher, the *Templum Domini*, and the tomb of the Virgin Mary at the bottom of the Valley of Jehoshaphat.[48] This was largely a result of the church building and beautification project at the Church of the Holy Sepulcher and other sites carried out mainly during her reign, from 1140 to 1149. In fact, Jaroslav Folda believes that Melisende must have been "heavily involved" in the rebuilding project at the Holy Sepulcher and that she and the patriarch of Jerusalem "were jointly involved in the major decisions made about the final phases of the church from 1146 on."[49] Unfortunately, there is no direct evidence or testimony that Melisende was involved in the funding or designs of the church. Pilgrims congregated in throngs all over the city's streets, especially in the spring, and, even though the malodorous smells of *Malquisinat* Street must have wafted far and wide (giving the street its name), there was a desperate need for vendors in the city that would sell them cooked food as they had no place to cook their own. Her construction of this street extended her influence and was a strategically timed move to demonstrate her capacity to effectively govern the city (as opposed to her son Baldwin's), solve its problems, and make the lives of its inhabitants better.[50] Perhaps she hoped to remind the city, and even the kingdom itself, that her rule would continue to guarantee its peace and prosperity.

These three examples of Melisende's spending power demonstrate her careful and strategic disbursement of the kingdom's resources. She and Fulk spent the money needed to build the castle of Bethgibelin to help provide for the defense of their kingdom, which faced a constant threat of attacks from the south. She lavishly spent money to build, fortify, and furnish her convent at Bethany to house religious women and promote the memory of her predecessors and the prestige of the royal dynasty as well as to make her sister Ivette an influential abbess, a position worthy of her royal birth. And in the final days of her reign, she spent money to endorse herself, as part of a bid to remain in power by building *Malquisinat* Street. This was constructed, in part, to win over her subjects and raise her public approval ratings, so to speak, by alleviating the logistical problems that faced her city. The merchants of her street provided for the needs of pilgrims, who were vital to the city's economy though they overwhelmed it each spring by their large numbers. William of Tyre wrote that Melisende was "a woman of great wisdom who had had much experience in all kinds of secular matters. She had risen so far above the normal status of women that she dared to undertake important measures. It was her ambition to emulate the magnificence of the greatest and noblest princes and to show herself in no wise inferior to them...she ruled the kingdom and administered the government with such skilful care that she may be said truly to have equaled her ancestors in that respect."[51] If these examples of Melisende's spending can be used to define her reign in any way, they reveal how she earned a reputation as a smart and ambitious ruler, who diligently strived to protect and promote her kingdom and its interests. They also show that during her reign she made every effort to protect her own position as queen regnant—and why she had been unwilling to relinquish the authority she had been born to wield.

## Notes

1. This chapter is based on a paper I was invited to give at the 39th International Congress on Medieval Studies, Western Michigan University, Kalamazoo, MI, on May 7, 2004, in a series of panels about women, power, and money

organized by Theresa Earenfight, whom I would like to sincerely thank for such an opportunity, as well as the Society for Medieval Feminist Scholarship, which sponsored them.

2. G. G. Coulton, *Five Centuries of Religion*, vol. 3, *Getting and Spending* (Cambridge: Cambridge University Press, 1936), pp. 1–86; Lester K. Little, *Religious Poverty and the Profit Economy in Medieval Europe* (Ithaca, NY: Cornell University Press, 1978), p. 8; Thomas N. Bisson, ed., *Cultures of Power: Lordship, Status, and Process in Twelfth-Century Europe* (Philadelphia: University of Pennsylvania Press, 1995); John L. La Monte, *Feudal Monarchy in the Latin Kingdom of Jerusalem, 1100–1291* (Cambridge, MA: The Medieval Academy of America, 1932); Steven Tibble, *Monarchy and Lordship in the Latin Kingdom of Jerusalem, 1099–1291* (New York: Oxford University Press, 1989).
3. Constance Berman, "Women as Donors and Patrons to Southern French Monasteries in the Twelfth and Thirteenth Centuries" in *The Worlds of Medieval Women: Creativity, Influence, and Imagination*, ed. Constance H. Berman, Charles W. Connell, and Judith Rice Rothschild (Morgantown: West Virginia University Press, 1985); Madeline H. Caviness, "Anchoress, Abbess, and Queen: Donors and Patrons or Intercessors and Matrons?" in *The Cultural Patronage of Medieval Women*, June Hall McCash, ed. (Athens: University of Georgia Press, 1996); William W. Kibler, ed., *Eleanor of Aquitaine: Patron and Politician* (Austin: University of Texas Press, 1976); Penelope D. Johnson, *Prayer, Patronage, and Power: The Abbey of la Trinité, Vendôme, 1032–1187* (New York: New York University Press, 1981).
4. McCash, *The Cultural Patronage of Medieval Women*, p. 4; recent studies of women's role in gift exchange in Western society have shown unequivocally that women not only give more gifts than men but are also the greatest recipients, see David Cheal, *The Gift Economy* (London and New York: Routledge, 1988) and Aafke E. Komter, "Women, Gifts, and Power," in *The Gift: An Interdisciplinary Perspective*, ed. Aafke E. Komter (Amsterdam: Amsterdam University Press, 1996), p. 129, who writes that the "fact that women in western society are the greatest gift givers, then, cannot be disentangled from, on the one hand, their more vulnerable societal and economic position compared with men and, on the other, from the power they are invested with by being society's prime intermediaries in creating and recreating social relationships by means of gift giving."
5. Jane Martindale, "Eleanor of Aquitaine," in *Richard Coeur de Lion in History and Myth*, ed. Janet L. Nelson (London: King's College London and the Centre for Late Antique and Medieval Studies, 1992), p. 23; Marie Hivergneaux, "Queen Eleanor and Aquitaine, 1137–1189," in *Eleanor of Aquitaine: Lord and Lady*, ed. Bonnie Wheeler and John Carmi Parsons (New York: Palgrave Macmillan, 2003); Lois L. Huneycutt, "*Alianora regina anglorum*: Eleanor of Aquitaine and Her Anglo-Norman Predecessors as Queens of England," in *Eleanor of Aquitaine: Lord and Lady*, ed. Bonnie Wheeler and John Carmi Parsons (New York: Palgrave Macmillan, 2003); Jean-Marc Bienvenu, "Aliénor d'Aquitaine et Fontevraud," *Cahiers de civilization medievale* 29 (1986): 15–27.

6. Bernard F. Reilly, *The Kingdom of León-Castilla Under Queen Urraca, 1109–1126* (Princeton, NJ: Princeton University Press, 1982), pp. 48 and 146.
7. Marjorie Chibnall, "The Empress Matilda and Bec-Hellouin," *Anglo-Norman Studies* 10 (1988): 35–48; Chibnall, *The Empress Matilda: Queen Consort, Queen Mother, and Lady of the English* (Oxford: Oxford University Press, 1993), p. 668.
8. *Melisende Psalter,* London, British Library, Egerton MS 1139; Helen A. Gaudette, "The Piety, Power, and Patronage of the Latin Kingdom of Jerusalem's Queen Melisende," (unpublished PhD. Dissertation, Graduate Center, City University of New York, 2005), pp. 169–81.
9. William of Tyre, *Chronicle,* in *Corpus Christianorum, continuatio mediaevalis*, vols. 63-63A, ed. R. B. C. Huygens, H. E. Mayer, and G. Rösch (Turnhout: Brepols, 1986); the English translation is William of Tyre, *A History of the Deeds Done Beyond the Sea*, vol. 2, trans. E. A. Babcock and A. C. Krey (New York: Columbia University Press, 1943), quoted throughout as WT followed by the book, chapter, and page in Babcock and Krey: WT 14.2, p. 51.
10. WT 18.27, p. 283.
11. Erin L. Jordan, "Exploring the Limits of Female Largesse: The Power of Female Patrons in Thirteenth-century Flanders and Hainaut," in this volume, p. 155.
12. WT 17.15, p. 207.
13. WT 17.14, p. 207; WT 17. 30, p. 233.
14. Melisende's charters are listed in Reinhold Röhricht, ed., *Regesta Regni Hierosolymitani* 1097–1291, 2 vols. (New York: Burt Franklin, 1960), quoted throughout as RRH plus the charter no.; *Melisende Psalter,* London, British Library, Egerton MS 1139.
15. The most important of these that have examined her reign are Hans Eberhard Mayer, "Studies in the History of Queen Melisende of Jerusalem," *Dumbarton Oaks Papers* 26 (1972): 95–182; Bernard Hamilton, "Women in the Crusader States: The Queens of Jerusalem (1100–1190)," in *Medieval Women*, ed. Derek Baker (Oxford: Oxford University Press, 1978), pp. 143–74; Jaroslav Folda, *The Art of the Crusaders in the Holy Land, 1098–1187* (Cambridge: Cambridge University Press, 1995); Lois L. Huneycutt, "Female Succession and the Language of Power in the Writings of the Twelfth-Century Churchmen," in *Medieval Queenship*, ed. John Carmi Parsons (New York: St. Martin's Press, 1993), pp. 189–201; Sarah Lambert, "Queen or Consort: Rulership and Politics in the Latin East, 1118–1228," in *Queens and Queenship in Medieval Europe: Proceedings of a Conference Held at King's College London, April 1995*, ed. Anne Duggan (New York: Boydell Press, 1997), pp. 153–69; Deborah Gerish, "Ancestors and Predecessors: Royal Continuity and Identity in the First Kingdom of Jerusalem," *Anglo-Norman Studies* 20 (1997): 127–50.
16. For a fascinating examination of the level of women's participation on the construction site, see Shelly E. Roff, chapter six in this collection: " 'Appropriate

to her Sex?' Women's Participation on the Construction Site in Medieval and Early Modern Europe."

17. WT 14.18, p. 76; RRH 164, 174, 179, 181, 210.
18. WT 16.5, p. 143; WT 17.1, p. 185; WT 18.19, p. 269; for more on fighting women during the crusades, see Keren Caspi-Reisfeld, "Women Warriors during the Crusades, 1095–1254," in *Gendering the Crusades*, ed. Susan B. Edgington and Sarah Lambert, (New York: Columbia University Press, 2002), pp. 94–107.
19. For more on the concept of "landscape" as a cultural process, see Eric Hirsch and Michael O'Hanlon, eds., *The Anthropology of Landscape: Perspectives on Place and Space* (Oxford: Clarendon Press, 1995).
20. See WT 11.22, p. 81; and Martin Hoch, "The Crusaders' Strategy against Fatimid Ascalon and the 'Ascalon Project' of the Second Crusade," in *The Second Crusade and the Cistercians*, ed. Michael Gervers (New York: St. Martin's Press, 1992), pp. 122 and 125; Adrian J. Boas, *Archaeology of the Military Orders: A Survey of the Urban Centres, Rural Settlements and Castles of the Military Orders in the Latin East (c.1120–1291)* (New York: Routledge, 2006).
21. Helen Nicholson, *The Knights Hospitallers* (New York: Boydell, 2001); Jonathan Riley-Smith, *The Knights of St. John in Jerusalem and Cyprus, c. 1050–1310* (London: Macmillan, 1967); E. E. Hume, *Medical Work of the Knights Hospitallers of St. John of Jerusalem* (Baltimore: Johns Hopkins University Press, 1940).
22. RRH 164; WT 14.22, p. 82.
23. For the seminal work on the social production and construction of space, see Henri Lefebvre, *La production de l'espace* (Paris: Anthropos, 1974; published in English as *The Production of Space,* Oxford: Blackwell, 1991). See also three geographers who have engaged Lefebvre's ideas: David Harvey, *The Condition of Postmodernity* (Oxford: Blackwell, 1990), Edward W. Soja, *Thirdspace: Journey to Los Angeles and Other Real-and-imagined Places* (Oxford: Blackwell, 1996), and Tim Unwin, "A Waste of Space? Towards a Critique of the Social Production of Space..." *Transactions of the Institute of British Geographers*, New Series 25:1 (2000), 11–29.
24. WT 14.22, pp. 81–82.
25. Alan Forey, *The Military Orders from the Twelfth to the Early Fourteenth Centuries* (Toronto: University of Toronto Press, 1992), p. 19.
26. WT 14.22, pp. 80–1.
27. Riley-Smith, *Knights of St. John*, p. 55.
28. WT 15.26, p. 132.
29. WT 15.26, p. 133.
30. WT 15.26, p. 133.
31. Matt 21: 1–11; Mark 11: 1–11; Luke 19: 28–44; John 12: 12–19.
32. RRH 174.
33. WT 15.26, p. 133.
34. Luke 10.39–42.
35. John 11.1–43.

36. John J. Delaney, *Dictionary of Saints* (New York: Doubleday, 1980), p. 351; see also Linda Seidel, *Legends in Limestone: Lazarus, Gislebertus, and the Cathedral of Autun* (Chicago: University of Chicago Press, 1999).
37. RRH 409, 268, 278, 313, 359.
38. WT 15.26, p. 133–4.
39. Sylvester John Saller, *Excavations at Bethany (1949–1953)*, Publications of the Studium Biblicum Franciscanum 12 (Jerusalem, 1957).
40. For more on the theory of feminine social construction of space, see Robert D. Sack, *Conceptions of Space in Social Thought* (London: Macmillan, 1980); Doreen Massey, *Space, Place and Gender* (Cambridge, MA: Polity Press, 1994); G. Rose and M. Ogborn, "Feminism and Historical Geography" *Journal of Historical Geography* 14 (1988): 405–9.
41. Mayer, "Studies in the History of Queen Melisende of Jerusalem," p. 167.
42. WT 17.13-14, pp. 205–6.
43. RRH 278.
44. RRH 278.
45. John Wilkinson, Joyce Hill, and W. F. Ryan, eds. and trans., *Jerusalem Pilgrimage, 1099–1185* (London: Hakluyt Society, 1988), pp. 276–308; Myriam Rosen-Ayalon, "Three Perspectives on Jerusalem: Jewish, Christian, and Muslim Pilgrims in the Twelfth Century," in *Jerusalem: Its Sanctity and Centrality to Judaism, Christianity, and Islam*, ed. Lee I. Levine (New York: Continuum, 1999), pp. 326–46.
46. Adrian Boas, *Jerusalem in the Time of the Crusades: Society, Landscape, and Art in the Holy City under Frankish Rule* (London and New York: Routledge, 2001), p. 147.
47. Boas, *Jerusalem in the Time of the Crusades*, p. 147.
48. Sylvia Schein, *Gateway to the Heavenly City: Crusader Jerusalem and the Catholic West (1099–1187)* (Aldershot, UK: Ashgate, 2005).
49. Folda, *Art of the Crusaders*, pp. 178, 186, 202–3. See also, Robert Ousterhout, "Architecture as Relic and the Construction of Sanctity: The Stones of the Holy Sepulchre," *Journal of the Society of Architectural Historians* 62.1 (2003): 4–23.
50. Thus "space is a social and political product." Quoted in "An Interview with Henri Lefebvre (interviewers G. Burgel, M. G. Dezes, and translated by E. Kofman)" *Environment and Planning D: Society and Space* 5.1 (1987): 30.
51. WT 16.3, pp. 139–40.

# CHAPTER 8

# EXPLORING THE LIMITS OF FEMALE LARGESSE: THE POWER OF FEMALE PATRONS IN THIRTEENTH-CENTURY FLANDERS AND HAINAUT

*Erin L. Jordan*

In his *Chronique Rimée*, first circulated in northern France in the late thirteenth century, Philippe Mouskes described the spending habits of Jeanne, the countess of Flanders and Hainaut, during her husband's twelve-year incarceration in Paris following the battle of Bouvines in 1214. According to Mouskes, Jeanne was so generous in her donations to religious communities that, upon his return in 1226, Ferrand found the county teetering on the verge of bankruptcy. As a result, Ferrand was forced to rescind many of the donations made by his imprudent and overly pious wife. Mouskes stated "tous les dons que la comtesse avait dounes fist resaisir, a son oes et a son plaisir." [all of the gifts that the countess had given were taken back, for his use and for his pleasure.][1]

Mouskes's description of the countess's actions provides an opportunity to explore the ability of women in the thirteenth century to obtain and spend money, an obvious indicator of their position in society and the extent to which they acted as lords. In the earlier quote, Mouskes suggests that although Jeanne had access to comital land and revenues during her husband's absence, her ability to dispense them was curtailed. His *Chronique Rimée* depicts Jeanne as ultimately powerless. She was able to act independently only during her husband's unexpected absence and, even then, her actions were merely pending, requiring his eventual consent to be considered binding. Mouskes implies that although it was

Jeanne who inherited the counties, the assent of her husband was required for her transactions to be considered legitimate, shedding light on the thirteenth-century understanding of the relationship between heiresses and the men they married. However, as the argument here hopes to demonstrate, further investigation into her experience indicates that Jeanne's position was considerably more complex than Mouskes would suggest, as was the relationship between women and power in the thirteenth century. This discussion seeks to investigate that relationship in greater depth by examining Jeanne and Ferrand's actions in conjunction with monetary donations to monastic foundations. It will measure the extent to which Jeanne, as hereditary countess of Flanders and Hainaut, possessed the ability to exercise lordship over her domains. As an heiress, Jeanne occupied a unique position, enjoying access to considerable wealth in her own right. However, the level to which she was able to alienate the land and dispense the resources that comprised her inheritance is questioned by Mouskes. According to the norms of feudal governance, fiefs were accompanied by a considerable amount of authority. Were heiresses like Jeanne able to exercise that authority? Was she able to freely dispense the resources she had inherited, or did all power ultimately pass to her husband upon their marriage?

By comparing the account of events provided by Mouskes with extant charter evidence, it is possible to assess the range of actions available to the countess as a religious patron, a clear measure of her authority. Her actions in this regard are extremely well-documented, with individual charters issued by Jeanne numbering in the hundreds. Although patronage has often been treated by scholars as an activity performed within the confines of the private sphere, this study argues otherwise. It is predicated on the notion that an assessment of these actions as a patron sheds light on her role as a political actor. Donations to religious foundations were very public acts, witnessed by a range of individuals, including members of the secular as well as the sacred community.[2] Although typically stemming from pious motives, they were ultimately public actions, functioning as visible, tangible symbols of the donor's power, wealth, and prestige. As such, they would have been regarded by individuals in the Middle Ages as serving a number of functions, some personal, some political, but all equally valid.[3] Hence, an examination of Jeanne as a religious patron is simultaneously an examination of her political action. Her ability to alienate land and dispense comital resources, whether on behalf of individuals or religious foundations, speaks to the extent of her authority as a lord, and provides a measure of the power she actually wielded.

The experience of Jeanne also provides an opportunity to assess the extent to which female rulers were viewed by their peers as viable participants in the realm of the political. Whether Mouskes's account of Jeanne and Ferrand's actions proves to be an accurate description of the limits of her authority, he does provide a glimpse of medieval attitudes toward women who ruled. Mouskes's view is particularly valuable because it expresses secular, rather than sacred, attitudes toward women. While the majority of narrative sources available for this period were produced by monks, clerics, or members of the church, Mouskes was part of a new group of secular authors.[4] According to Ronald Walpole, Mouskes was from a prominent French family that held several titles and land near the city of Tournai.[5] Writing for his own personal pleasure, Mouskes was "scarcely conscious of any responsibility as a historian." Although the factual mistakes that pepper Mouskes's account have led scholars to question its historical value, his ability to present attitudes typical of the time cannot be easily discounted. Walpole concludes that Mouskes is "certainly representative of his own age," qualifying that "he represents only a portion, not the whole of contemporary French society."[6] His views about women like the countess of Flanders were undoubtedly shared by many of his contemporaries, who were accustomed to a world in which men ruled and women occupied the periphery of politics. Mouskes was probably not alone in associating women like Jeanne with financial mismanagement, as reflected in his characterization of her as overly pious and generous to a fault in her donations. While women were considered more naturally inclined toward charitable acts, the emotions responsible for such actions were viewed as equally likely to lead them to excessive generosity. Charitable impulses in women, although encouraged, were to be "mediated and ultimately controlled by men."[7] This is precisely the relationship Mouskes envisions between Jeanne and Ferrand, and projects upon his account of their actions as patrons. Mouskes clearly sees Jeanne as subject to the will of her husband, even in the realm of religious patronage. This investigation into Mouskes's presentation of events will also gauge the extent to which perceptions of gender informed medieval narrative accounts and whether exclusive reliance on such accounts clouds our modern assessment of female agency in the thirteenth century.

Although Jeanne's overall record as a religious patron suggests that she was an extremely devout individual, dedicated to promoting her spiritual well-being by ensuring her own salvation through securing the intercession of others, her generosity was made possible by the unusual position she occupied in thirteenth-century Europe. As the eldest daughter of the celebrated Baldwin IX and Marie of Champagne, she inherited the counties of Flanders and Hainaut in 1206. Both of her parents were casualties of the Fourth Crusade. While Marie died in Acre in 1204/5, en route to join her husband in Constantinople, Baldwin died shortly after his coronation as First Latin Emperor, most likely at the hands of the Bulgarian king Ionnitsa.[8] These events elevated the six-year old Jeanne to a position of considerable significance. The count of Flanders had traditionally occupied a position of prominence among the vassals of the king of France, wielding power as a result of the strategic location of the county and the immense wealth generated by its burgeoning cloth industry. The addition of the county of Hainaut added a key source of agricultural wealth, and ties to the Holy Roman Emperor, the feudal lord of land east of the Scheldt River and traditional rival of the king of France.[9] In the years preceding his departure on the Fourth Crusade, Baldwin IX fought successfully to strengthen the position of Flanders and Hainaut vis-à-vis France, capitalizing upon the youth and inexperience of Philip II.[10] By allying with England, Baldwin was able to tip the balance of power in northern Europe in favor of the Anglo-Flemish coalition, winning a key victory against France in 1200, and gaining control of the cities of Aire and Saint-Omer, and the lordship of Guînes, Ardres, Lilliers, Richebourg, and Béthune through the treaty of Peronne.[11] Exulting in his triumph, the count declared his intention to join the Fourth Crusade, clearly sufficiently confident about his current situation to contemplate an extended absence from his domains. However, within a few short years of his departure for the Holy Land, the gains made by Baldwin IX would be reversed by the king of France, and his daughter Jeanne would become a pawn in the struggle for domination of northern Europe.

Once news of Baldwin's death reached France, Jeanne, as his eldest daughter and heir to both counties, was immediately claimed as the feudal ward of Philip Augustus. After securing physical control of the young countess through an alliance with her uncle, Philip of Namur, the king spirited her away to his court in Paris, where she remained until her marriage to Ferrand of Portugal in 1212.[12] Ferrand was young and foreign, both qualities that appealed to Philip II, who planned to control Flanders through a count chosen specifically for his dependence on France and sympathy to French interests. However, Philip's plans soon backfired when Ferrand joined the coalition spearheaded by John I of England. Philip had underestimated the young count, wounding his pride in 1212 by intercepting him and Jeanne on their return to Flanders from France following their marriage and demanding the return of the Saint-Omer and Aire, key cities lost to Baldwin IX a decade earlier. Facing the small but heavily armed force sent by the king, the defenseless Ferrand had no choice but to agree to the terms of the treaty of Pont-à-Vendun.[13] However, his resentment continued to fester. Ferrand eventually confronted Philip in 1213 at Gravelines, refusing to participate in the king's impending invasion of England unless the cities were returned to Flemish control. Philip refused, Ferrand withdrew, and when the king was forced to cancel his plans to invade England, he ordered his army to attack Flanders instead. French forces invaded the county of Flanders, ravaging the countryside around the city of Lille. The humiliated Ferrand appealed to John I for aid, agreeing to join the anti-French coalition led by the king of England, Renaud of Dammartin, count of Boulogne, and Otto of Brunswick, the aspiring Holy Roman Emperor.

Despite several initial victories, the coalition was resoundingly defeated by Philip at the battle of Bouvines in July, 1214.[14] Count Ferrand, along with approximately one-third of the leading nobles of Flanders, was taken to Paris to stand trial for treason. According to Mouskes, the young count was paraded through the streets of Paris in chains and subjected to the enthusiastic abuse of the crowds.[15] As soon as she was informed of the outcome of the battle and her husband's imprisonment, Jeanne departed for Paris, where she petitioned Philip Augustus for Ferrand's release. Although the majority of the Flemish prisoners were ransomed and released by 1216, the king remained deaf to her pleas, refusing to release Ferrand. His truculence had serious implications for Jeanne, who was charged with governance of the two counties until her husband's release could be secured.

While the particular circumstances that propelled her to a position of real power were unusual, Jeanne's initial position as heiress of Flanders and Hainaut was not. In the late twelfth and early thirteenth centuries, France witnessed a not insignificant number of fiefs pass to women like Jeanne.[16] While many of these women remain rather obscure figures in the historical record, the abundance of documentation available for the counties of Flanders and Hainaut provides an ideal opportunity to examine the position of such noblewomen in medieval society. This issue is particularly relevant for the high Middle Ages, considered an especially pivotal period in terms of the ability of women to exercise power. According to scholars, the centuries following the year 1100 witnessed a gradual reconfiguration of inheritance practices among the nobility, potentially altering the relationship of women to authority. The adoption of primogeniture in theory resulted in the political marginalization of all children but the eldest male, who inherited the patrimony intact.[17] When combined with the preference for the senior branch of the family, or the patrilineage, such shifts would have had a considerable impact upon the ability of women to access authority. Noblewomen already adversely affected by the centralization of monarchy, bureaucratization of royal administration, and church reform that occurred, were further marginalized by such shifts in inheritance practice. These phenomena combined to limit the ability of women to access public authority and restrict them to the newly emerged private sphere, devoid of power as it is traditionally understood.[18] However, while these changes worked in theory to disadvantage women, medieval reality often proved much more complicated and unpredictable. By altering the way land passed among generations, primogeniture and patrilineage could potentially benefit women, since in the absence of a male heir, fiefs on the continent would pass, intact, to the eldest daughter of the senior branch of the family.[19]

However, the question remains, to what extent were these heiresses integrated into feudal governance? Past scholars have often dismissed them as anomalous, representing a malfunction in a system intended to privilege males. This categorization justifies excluding them from discussions of the political system of the thirteenth century since they were merely aberrations.[20] However, the frequency with which they appear in the historical record, inheriting fiefs and exercising lordship, challenges this explanation. As mentioned earlier, the thirteenth century in particular saw a number of powerful principalities devolve to women. Continuing to dismiss them as exceptions to the norm of male power results in an inaccurate understanding of how feudal governance functioned during this period.

However, not all scholars confine these women to the footnotes of political histories by dismissing them as extraordinary. Others have acknowledged their importance as heiresses of key fiefs, but focused predominately on their role in transferring authority from generation to generation. However, while this approach does integrate women into the political narrative, it does not position them as independent actors in their own right; they function merely to legitimate the actions of the men around them.[21] Although this may have been the medieval ideal, a way to reconcile attitudes about the weaker sex with the reality of female inheritance, it does not adequately address the instances when women failed to conform to expectations, ruling in their own right. As the example of Jeanne demonstrates, some women did not remain mere placeholders, marrying to confer authority on the men who wielded power in their stead, but were independent political actors. The frequency with which women inherited in this period and the role that many played in events that would have been deemed political by their contemporaries begs an examination of their experience and a reassessment of their role in politics.[22] Careful examination of their individual experiences is required before the full complexity of feudal governance is appreciated and these women accurately integrated into our understanding of the political as it operated in the thirteenth century. By examining the experience of Jeanne and her actions in conjunction with money, measured here in the form of donations of rents or tithes in coin, it is possible to further this process.

Clearly, a woman engaged in political activity during the thirteenth century challenged a number of gender norms entrenched in medieval society, particularly those that positioned women as subordinate to men, characterizing them as incapable of effective governance.[23] This is clearly the attitude expressed in the chronicle of Mouskes, who, like many men of the period, considered women, at least in theory, more suited to domestic pursuits than political action. However, to what extent is Mouskes's attitude about proper roles for women mirrored by the reality of Jeanne's experience, as depicted in the charter evidence?

An examination of charters produced during the early years of her rule suggests that while Jeanne possessed authority, she seldom wielded actual power. She resided at the court of France for the first six years following her father's death in 1206. During her minority, Jeanne was completely excluded from the governance of Flanders and Hainaut, which was entrusted to her uncle, Philip of Namur. Once she attained the canonical age of majority, her position altered, but only slightly. Following her marriage to Ferrand in 1212, Jeanne was clearly recognized by her contemporaries as the repository of official authority in the fiefs she had inherited. Such recognition is illustrated by an incident that occurred immediately on their return to Flanders. In the course of touring his new domains without his wife, Ferrand was refused entrance into the wealthy city of Ghent and the townspeople threatened military resistance unless their young countess was produced and presented alongside him as proof of their union. Ferrand was forced to summon Jeanne from the city of Douai to appease the people of Ghent, who then relented and opened the city gates. To the people of Ghent, Ferrand wielded power as their new count, but his authority clearly stemmed directly from his marriage to their countess.

As I have argued elsewhere, authority and power were distinct concepts in the medieval mind and were understood as separate functions in the realm of governance.[24] This distinction is illustrated in the above example, and reflected in the early relationship between Jeanne and Ferrand more generally. In the years immediately following their marriage, Jeanne remained largely confined to the periphery of politics. Although she was recognized as the repository of authority, the extent to which she was expected to wield power was subject to negotiation. No doubt in part due to her age, power in her domains during this early period was exercised by her husband, who directed the affairs of the two counties in her stead. Examination of the charters produced between 1212 and 1214 indicate that her consent was not even required for his actions to be deemed legitimate; he made alliances with the English, granted liberties to towns, and defied his liege lord, the king of France, all seemingly without seeking or needing her consent.[25] To the extent that their movements can be traced during these years, they seldom seem to have been in the same place at the same time, suggesting that the count felt no compulsion to even consult his young wife, but made decisions autonomously.[26] The documentary evidence is equally silent concerning her actions as a religious patron; from 1212 to 1214, Jeanne issued a single charter in her own name, and that charter merely confirmed a previous donation made jointly by the couple.

As the earlier discussion makes clear, during the early years of their marriage, Jeanne possessed authority, but seldom wielded power. However, Ferrand's rebellion in 1214 dramatically altered both of their realities, effectively reversing their positions. While his imprisonment in the Louvre resulted in his relegation to the margins of political activity, it propelled Jeanne to the forefront of affairs, forcing her to play a much more prominent role in governing Flanders and Hainaut. Measuring the extent of her religious patronage during her husband's absence makes it possible to assess the degree to which his absence altered her position. During the period of Ferrand's incarceration (1214 to 1226), the countess orchestrated the foundation of the Augustinian abbey of Zoetendale and the Cistercian nunnery of Nieuwenbos, and contributed significantly to the establishment of the Cistercian community at Épinlieu. She was also instrumental in the foundation of several mendicant communities during this period, including that of the Franciscans at Valenciennes, created shortly before Ferrand's release in 1226.[27]

Overall, between 1214 and 1226, the countess issued 114 charters to various religious foundations in Flanders and Hainaut. A mere fraction of these conveyed donations of money. The Premonstratensian abbey of Vicoigne was one of the first to benefit from the countess's generosity, receiving an annual rent of 8 *livres* 5 *sous* in 1215.[28] The Cistercian abbey of Épinlieu, which Jeanne cofounded in 1216 with Beatrice de Lens, was granted an annual rent of 20 *livres blancs* in June 1217.[29] The Cistercian nuns of Fontenelle also received several donations from the countess, including a rent on land at Quesnoy in September 1219 and an annual rent of 12 *livres blancs* in August, 1222.[30] In January, 1221, she donated a tithe valued at 20 *libras Flandrensis* to the Benedictine monks of Saint-André in Bruges and an annual rent of 20 *livres* to the canons of Chateau l'Abbaye, a community that adhered to the order of Arrouaise.[31] The canons of the cathedral chapter at Courtrai were granted several rents between 1219 and 1223, specifically intended to provide four prebends to support four new chaplains.[32] While only ten of these donations conveyed rents or tithes in coin, such transactions are representative of wider patterns of activity, and can provide insight into the nature of her position. Based on this litany of donations, which represents a mere fraction of her actions as a patron, Mouskes's description of her as exceptionally generous rings true.

Although Jeanne's efforts to free her husband proved futile during the reign of Philip Augustus and his son and successor Louis VIII, she eventually secured his release in 1226. After numerous pleas to the French king and repeated requests for papal intervention failed, Jeanne's threat to secure an annulment of the marriage and find another husband finally forced the issue. Since 1215, rumors had been circulating about a possible marriage between Jeanne and Pierre Mauclerc, duke of Brittany. When faced with a possible alliance between Brittany and Flanders, the young Louis IX had no choice but to free the count.[33] Jeanne was summoned to Paris, where negotiations regarding her husband's release were finalized in the form of the Treaty of Melun, signed in April, 1226. Jeanne agreed to the exorbitant ransom of 50,000 *livres parisis*. She returned to her domains, spending the next six months gathering the required funds from various lenders, including a number of monastic and religious foundations.[34] In December, she returned to Paris, where she and Ferrand renewed their marriage vows, and pledged homage to King Louis IX. After a confinement of twelve years, five months, and nine days, Ferrand was finally free. He and Jeanne returned to Flanders in January of 1226.

According to the chronicle of Mouskes quoted earlier, the imprudent spending of his wife during his absence resulted in the recently liberated Ferrand's extreme displeasure. Mouskes suggests that Jeanne's excessive generosity to religious communities within her domains had left the counties of Flanders and Hainaut on the verge of bankruptcy. If Mouskes is correct in his depiction of events, and Ferrand did rescind many of the donations made by his wife, one could conclude that her actions during his absence were not considered binding without his consent. In other words, if the scenario presented by Mouskes is accurate, one could surmise that although Jeanne inherited authority along with the counties of Flanders and Hainaut, she was to function merely as a figurehead, incapable of serving in any official capacity as countess. Once she married, all authority passed to her husband, whose consent was required for her actions, even in the realm of religious patronage, to be considered legitimate. As a woman, albeit a noble one, Jeanne was to serve merely as a feudal placeholder, unable to alienate land or dispense resources independently of her husband.

However, to what extent can Mouskes's account be considered an accurate rendering of events, and hence a reliable assessment of the relationship between men, women, and power during this period? If events had, in fact, transpired as Mouskes described, one would expect to see a flurry of charters issued in the years immediately following Ferrand's return, either affirming Jeanne's earlier actions, and hence making them legitimate, or negating donations comprised of rents in coin and requesting that the recipients of her largesse return the money they had received. However, examination of the hundreds of charters issued by the count and countess failed to reveal a single document issued by Ferrand that rescinded or retracted a donation made by his wife. Hence, I have been unable to locate a single document that indicates that Ferrand did, as argued by Mouskes, rescind any of the donations made by Jeanne during his absence.

There is also no evidence to corroborate Mouskes's assertion that Jeanne's generosity as a patron had compromised the county's financial well-being during her husband's absence. In fact, any financial troubles the count might have faced upon his return most likely stemmed from his rebellion. To secure her husband's release, Jeanne was forced to pay the sum of 50,000 *livres parisis*. As evidenced in the charters, much of the money came in the form of loans from various monastic and religious communities in Flanders and Hainaut. If the counties of Flanders and Hainaut were, as suggested by Mouskes, teetering on the verge of bankruptcy in 1226, it was more likely the result of Ferrand's imprudent rebellion, rather than of Jeanne's piety. Furthermore, Jeanne's very ability to raise such an enormous sum of money attests to her effectiveness as a ruler during her husband's absence, as does her success in securing his release.[35] Her actions in this regard call to question the condemnatory tone of Mouskes's narrative and his depiction of Jeanne as an impulsive, imprudent, and ultimately inept, ruler.

Another determinant of the extent of the countess's authority would be whether or not her husband's consent was required to make charters issued during his absence legitimate. If this were the case, one would expect to see a number of charters issued in the months following his return that confirmed all donations made by Jeanne in the decade of his incarceration. However, examination of the hundreds of charters issued after Ferrand's return reveals only four documents that expressly confirm donations made previously by the countess. While these four charters do not specifically concern rents or donations of money, they do provide an indication of the extent to which her actions were binding without his consent. The first, issued in 1227, confirms a donation of an annual rent of 4,000 herrings a year made by the countess to the Abbey of Aywieres.[36] Count Ferrand issued three charters in 1228, one each to the abbeys of Nonnenbossche, Eename, and Saint-Pharailde, all specifically addressing and confirming donations made by his wife during his absence.[37] In addition to these four documents, a number of other charters were issued by the couple that did not explicitly mention earlier actions by the countess, but repeated the same donation. For example, in 1222, Jeanne had donated a rent of 10 *livres blancs* to the Cistercian monks of Vaucelles, to be paid from the revenues of the toll taken at the city of Lille.[38] In September, 1227, Ferrand, along with Jeanne, donated a rent of 10 *livres blancs,* also from the toll at Lille, to the abbey of Vaucelles. Both charters stipulated that the money was to be used to provide the bread and wine used at mass, suggesting that the second charter represented a confirmation of the earlier donation.[39] A similar pattern occurs in a series of charters issued concerning an annual rent of 8 *livres*, donated to the abbey of Notre-Dame de Boulogne to pay for the bread, wine, and candles used in mass. The first charter relating to this donation was issued by Jeanne in 1224. A second charter, with almost identical wording, was issued jointly by Jeanne and Ferrand in 1228. Again, the similarities suggest that the charter of 1228 did not, in fact, convey a second donation, but merely reiterated, and confirmed, the first.[40] Overall, of the 114 donations made by Jeanne during her husband's absence, only eight were either confirmed by Ferrand or reiterated earlier donations verbatim. These figures suggest that the vast majority of her actions during his absence did not require his consent, but were considered binding in their own right. This conclusion not only contradicts the narrative of Mouskes, but attests to the countess's agency during her husband's absence.

Mouskes's accusation that the countess had bankrupted the county as a result of her generosity is also belied by the numerous donations made jointly by the count and countess in the years following his return. Not only did Ferrand fail to recall the sums of money granted by his wife, but he became an equally avid patron, making donations of money and rents in coin jointly with her until his death in 1233. Jeanne and Ferrand made thirty-five donations to religious communities between 1226 and 1233, the year of his death. Of these, sixteen were rents or tithes, including an annual rent of 400 *livres* donated to the abbey of Marquette, founded jointly by the count and countess in 1224. Marquette would receive a total of sixteen donations from Jeanne and Ferrand between 1226 and 1233.[41] The abbey of Aulne received a rent of 80 *libras blancs* to sustain eight monks "in the service of god."[42] The Cistercian nuns of Ravensberg were the recipients of a donation in 1227 that included ten and one-half marks and eleven rams per year. The rent was to provide for a chaplain to perform the divine office on behalf of the count and countess.[43] These donations, along with the rest of those issued after Ferrand's return, suggest that Mouskes exaggerated in his indictment of the countess's generosity, and that the financial stability of the counties was more secure than his account would suggest.

Overall, examination of charters that record donations to religious communities, viewed here as an index of an individual's power, suggest a fairly complex situation. It is true that in the years after her marriage and preceding the battle of Bouvines, Jeanne conformed to the expected norm, remaining on the margins of political affairs in Flanders and Hainaut. Her peripheral position is illustrated by her overall inactivity as a patron. Whether the result of restrictions placed on her ability to access money or her lack of inclination, the countess did not direct a single donation to a religious community during this period. However, after Ferrand's capture, her position changed dramatically, as did her role in political affairs and her patronage of religious communities. She clearly did not feel constrained in dispensing the resources of the county, generously directing donations of money to favored communities throughout her domains. Although Ferrand did confirm several of the donations made by the countess during his imprisonment, he by no means confirmed all of them. Why his confirmation was considered necessary for some donations but not for others remains a question to be answered. One possible explanation for this disparity is the role of the recipients of these donations in seeking the count's confirmation. It is possible that in the instances where Ferrand issued confirmations, the impetus stemmed from the monks or nuns themselves, who sought additional reassurance that donations made by their countess would be honored by their count.

Examination of Jeanne's monetary donations to religious foundations throughout the course of her lifetime results in several interesting conclusions. Perhaps the most surprising is the fact that after Ferrand's release, Jeanne was not forced to fade into the wings, but rather continued to occupy center stage—the only difference in her position post-1226 was that she shared that stage with her husband. According to a traditional understanding of the position of women, one which privileges marital status in determining access to power, one would expect that her increased ability to make decisions and donations was conditional, attained at her husband's expense. In many ways, Jeanne's position during Ferrand's incarceration was similar to that of a widow, freed by the absence of a husband to act autonomously.[44] If this were the case, one would expect her to relinquish most of the power she had exercised following his return. Rather than returning to the margins of political affairs, the position she occupied in the years immediately following her marriage, Jeanne shared authority and power with Ferrand until his death. After Ferrand's return, Jeanne continued to make donations in her own name, indicating that her husband's presence was not, in fact, a check on her ability to wield power. Her experience suggests that while marital status was an important determinant of a women's ability to exercise power, it was neither the only, nor even in some instances the most important, determinant. Age, circumstance, and experience were clearly influential in determining the extent to which women could actually wield power. Examining Jeanne's actions after Ferrand's death in 1233, though it lies outside of the parameters of this discussion, supports this conclusion. The extent of Jeanne's religious patronage increased gradually over the years, seemingly regardless of her marital status, but rather proportional to her age, experience, and the security of her position. Between 1233 and her own death in 1244, Jeanne issued 197 charters to religious foundations, of which fifty-three were donations.

This study also emphasizes the importance of examining individual experience in attempting to further our understanding of the political role of women in the high Middle Ages. Although studies of individuals are often dismissed as inconclusive due to their very narrow focus, I would suggest that generalizations about the position of women and the various ways power operated in the thirteenth century can only be accurate if based on detailed case studies such as the one presented here. Such a narrow focus, although sacrificing breadth for depth, allows us to better appreciate the nuances of medieval society, and to form a more complex and sophisticated understanding of the nature of authority as it pertained to powerful men and women in the Middle Ages.[45] And, finally, this study demonstrates the problems associated with reliance on narrative sources for an accurate understanding of medieval society. Contrary to the indictment of Jeanne's actions presented by Mouskes, the reality of the situation as reflected in the charter evidence suggests that Jeanne proved to be a fairly competent ruler during her husband's absence. Ferrand did not rescind the donations made by his wife during his absence, and the county was financially stable enough to absorb the enormous ransom exacted by the king of France, as well as numerous new donations made to monasteries by the recently reunited couple. Was his alternative portrayal of her a result of a negative personal experience? Or could he have been projecting accepted gender norms onto the countess, reflecting the anticipated relationship between female rulers and their husbands, rather than the reality of her individual experience? Scholars have often warned of need to identify the differences between the ideal as presented in chronicles, which filter events through a personal, and often politicized, lens.[46] Here, the extant charters offer the possibility to glean the reality of female experience that differs considerably from what one might find if relying solely on narrative sources. Although this particular study addressed only four of the over 50,000 lines of text that comprise Mouskes's chronicle, one might wonder what similar attempts to corroborate other portions of his account concerning women might reveal.

However, equally revealing might be an alternative read of Mouskes. Of the donations explicitly confirmed by Ferrand after his return, several expressly concerned funds provided by the count and countess for the celebration of mass. In the case of the donation made to the abbey of Vaucelles, the rent donated was to be used to provide the bread and wine involved in the ceremony; in the case of the abbey of Boulogne, it was to pay for the bread, wine, and candles used at mass. This commonality suggests that Mouskes was referring to spiritual, rather than material, profit. Clearly, Ferrand wanted to ensure that he received credit for donations granted by his wife in the interest of salvation, allowing him to benefit equally from the spiritual returns on her material investment. Perhaps the problem with Mouskes's account of Jeanne's experience is not a product of his inaccurate rendering of events, but rather the result of the modern tendency to read gender bias onto a medieval source. It seems plausible that Ferrand's concern was less for the money spent by his wife during his absence, and more for his exclusion from the spiritual benefits her monetary donations would have accrued. In other words, for Mouskes, Count Ferrand and Countess Jeanne, it was not a question of financial matters, but of spiritual ones.

## Notes

The author would like to thank Paul Hyams, Ann Little, Thomas Bredehoft, Michael Kramp, and Brian Luskey for comments and suggestions on earlier drafts of this chapter.

1. *Chronique Rimée de Philippe Mouskes*, ed. Baron de Reiffenberg. vol. 1 (Bruxelles: M. Hayez, 1836), ll. 27789–90, p. 795.
2. Penelope Johnson, "Agnes of Burgundy: An Eleventh-Century Woman as Monastic Patron," *Journal of Medieval History* 15 (1989): 93–104. According to Johnson, Agnes turned to religious patronage because more mainstream avenues of exercising power were denied her due to her sex.
3. Miriam Shadis discusses the permeability of the boundary between sacred and secular as well as the political significance of religious patronage in "Piety, Politics, and Power: The Patronage of Leonor of England and Her Daughters Berenguela of Léon and Blanche of Castile," in *The Cultural Patronage of Medieval Women* (Athens: University of Georgia Press, 1996), pp. 202–27, especially pp. 202–3. See also Erin L. Jordan, *Women, Power and Religious Patronage in the Middle Ages* (New York: Palgrave Macmillan, 2006), pp. 84–85.

4. See Jacques Dalarun, "The Clerical Gaze," in *A History of Women in the West, Vol. 2. Silences of the Middle Ages*, ed. Christiane Klapish-Zuber (Cambridge: Cambridge University Press, 1992), pp. 15–42, p. 42. Dalarun argues that by the thirteenth century, the voices of clerics were not the only ones being heard. Joined by an increasing number of secular authors, the ensuing message about women heard by society was much more discordant, reflecting a new ambivalence about gender.
5. Ronald N. Walpole, *Philip Mouskés and the Pseudo-Turpin Chronicle* (Berkeley and Los Angeles: University of California Press, 1947), p. 392. Until recently, many scholars believed that the author of the *Chronique Rimeé* was Philip of Ghent, bishop of Tournai until 1283. However, more recent investigation has debunked that assumption.
6. Walpole, *Philip Mouskés*, p. 410. Fiona Tolhurst cautions against the tendency to view medieval chronicles generally as objective historical records, particularly in regards to texts produced in the high Middle Ages. See Fiona Tolhurst, "The Great Divide?: History and Literary History as Partners in Medieval Mythography," *Historical Reflections/Réflexions historique* 30 (2004): 7–27, here p. 27.
7. See Carla Casagrande, "The Protected Women," in *A History of Women in the West*, ed. Christiane Klapish-Zuber, vol. 2, pp. 70–104, especially p. 98. The appearance of Aristotle's texts in the eleventh and twelfth centuries fostered a new, scientific understanding of the role of women, one that emphasized her fragile and malleable nature. JoAnn McNamara argues that in the high Middle Ages, gender replaced class as the "basic organizing principle" of society, further restricting options for noblewomen who were previously able to use family connections to transcend the limitations typically placed upon women. McNamara, "Women and Power through the Family Revisited," in *Gendering the Master Narrative*, ed. Mary C. Erler and Maryanne Kowaleski (Ithaca, NY: Cornell University Press, 2003), pp. 17–30, 22–23.
8. For the career of Baldwin IX, see R. L. Wolff, "Baldwin of Flanders and Hainaut, First Latin Emperor of Constantinople: His Life, Death and Resurrection, 1171–1225." *Speculum* 27 (1952): 281–322. For the fourth crusade more generally see Michael Angold, *The Fourth Crusade: Event and Context* (New York: Longman, 2003).
9. For Flanders during this period, see Thérèse de Hemptinne, "Vlaanderen en Henegouwen onder de erfgenamen van de Boudewyns, 1070–1244," *Algemene geschiedenis der Nederlanden* (Haarlem: 1982), p. 372–98; David Nicholas, *Medieval Flanders* (New York: Longman, 1986); Gerard Sivery, *Structures agraires et vie rurale dans le hainaut à la fin du Moyen Age* (Lille: 1977). Events on the continent more generally are discussed by Gabrielle Spiegel, *Romancing the Past: The Rise of Vernacular Prose Historiography in Thirteenth-Century France* (Berkeley and Los Angeles: University of California Press, 1993); Jim Bradbury, *Philip Augustus: King of France, 1180–1223* (New York: Longman, 1998); Elizabeth M. Hallam and Judith Everard, *Capetian France, 987–1328*, 2nd ed. (New York: Longman, 2001);

and Robert Henri Bautier, ed., *La France de Philippe Auguste: le temps des mutations: actes du colloque international* (Paris: Éditions du Centre national de la recherche scientifique, 1982).

10. The tumultuous relationship between Flanders and France in the late-twelfth and early-thirteenth centuries is described in detail by John Baldwin, *The Government of Philip Augustus: Foundations of French Royal Power in the Middle Ages* (Berkeley and Los Angeles: University of California Press, 1986).
11. John Baldwin, "La décennie décisive: les années 1190–1203 dans le règne de Philippe Auguste," *Révue Historique* 266 (1981): 311–37; and Speigel, *Romancing the Past*, p. 39.
12. Philip of Namur's actions in regard to his nieces earned him the scorn of many of the Flemish people. According to terms of the treaty of Pont-de-l'Arche, which ceded control of the young heiresses to Philip of France, Philip of Namur was to marry the king's daughter Marie, elevating his status at the expense of his nieces. For the complete text of the treaty, see H. F. Delaborde, Elie Berger, C. F. Brunel, and Charles Samaran, eds, *Recueil des Actes de Philippe Auguste*, vol. 1 (Paris, 1916), nos. 1043, 1208, pp. 110–11. Ferrand of Portugal was the nephew of Mathilda, the widow of Philip of Alsace and dowager countess of Flanders.
13. Archives Départementales du Nord, Lille, *Inventaire Chronologique et Detaillé des chartes de la Chambre des comptes à Lille,* par Denis Joseph Godefroy, 2187, H 51, no. 276 (25 Feb 1212).
14. Philip's progress through the Flemish countryside is traced by Baldwin, *The Government of Philip Augustus*, p. 209. See also David Nicholas, *Medieval Flanders*, p. 152. For a detailed account of the battle and its participants see Georges Duby, *The Legend of Bouvines: War, Religion and Culture in the Middle Ages* (Berkeley and Los Angeles: University of California Press, 1990).
15. Mouskes, *Chronique Rimée,* 22203–09, p. 375: "Enkaines, comme lupars, Fu Ferrans et bien refieres De III pies; car desfieres. Avoit este trop longement pour lui saner, qu'il n'en ot point en toute Flandres en cel point."
16. Studies of several of these women are available, including Constance H. Berman and Mariam Shadis, "A Taste of the Feast: Reconsidering Eleanor of Aquitaine's Female Descendants," in *Eleanor of Aquitaine: Lord and Lady,* ed. Bonnie Wheeler and John Carmi Parsons (New York: Palgrave Macmillan, 2003), pp. 177–211; Yannick Hillion, "La Bretagne et le Rivalité Capétians-Plantagenets. Un Exemple: La duchesse Constance (1186–1202)," *Annales de Bretagne et du pays de l'Ouest* 92 (1985): 111–44; Erin L. Jordan, "The 'Abduction' of Ida of Boulogne: Assessing Female Agency in Thirteenth-Century France," *French Historical Studies* 30 (2007): 1–20. The county of Flanders in particular was no stranger to women occupying positions of power in the decades preceding the rule of Jeanne and her sister and successor, Marguerite, including Sybile of Anjou, Mathilda of Portugal, Margaret of Hainaut, and Marie of Champagne. For the countesses of Flanders between the eleventh and thirteenth

centuries, see Penelope Adair, "Countess Clemence: Her Power and Its Foundation," in *Queens, Regents and Potentates*, ed. Theresa M. Vann (Dallas, TX: Academia Press, 1993), pp. 63–72; Nicholas, "Women as Rulers: Countesses Jeanne and Marguerite of Flanders (1212–78)," in *Queens, Regents and Potentates*, ed. Vann, pp. 73–89; Nicholas, "Countesses as Rulers in Flanders," in *Aristocratic Women in Medieval France*, ed. Theodore Evergates (Philadelphia: University of Pennsylvania Press, 1999), pp. 111–37; and Jordan, *Women, Power and Religious Patronage in the Middle Ages*. Though most of Flanders's countesses during this period accessed authority through marriage, three inherited in their own right, including Margaret, the daughter of Thierry of Alsace, and Jeanne and Marguerite, daughters of Baldwin IX.

17. Most notably Georges Duby, *The Chivalrous Society*, trans. Cynthia Postan (Berkeley and Los Angeles: University of California Press, 1977) and *The Knight, the Lady and the Priest: The Making of Modern Marriage in Medieval France*, trans. Barbara Bray (Chicago: University of Chicago Press, 1994). Discussions of this shift in inheritance practice generally include Jane Martindale, *Status, Authority and Power: Aquitaine and France, 9th to 12th Centuries* (Aldershot, UK: Ashgate, 1997); Philippe Godding, "Le droit au service du patrimoine familial: les Pays-Bas Méridionaux (12e–18e siècles)," in *Marriage, Property and Succession*, ed. Lloyd Banfield (Berlin: Duncker and Humboldt, 1992), pp. 15–35; J. C. Holt, "Feudal Society and the Family in Early Medieval England: The Heiress and the Alien," *Transactions of the Royal Historical Society* 35 (1985): 1–28; and Jennifer Ward, *Women in Medieval Europe, 1200–1500* (New York: Longman, 2002), pp. 4–5.
18. This view is perhaps most effectively articulated by Jo Ann McNamara and Suzanne Wemple, "The Power of Women through the Family in Medieval Europe, 500–1100," in *Women and Power in the Middle Ages*, ed. Mary Erler and Maryanne Kowaleski (Athens: University of Georgia Press, 1988), pp. 83–101, p. 94. They argued that while women enjoyed considerable access to power during the more fluid, family-centered governance of the early Middle Ages, such access was curbed in the twelfth and thirteenth centuries by the emergence of monarchical states and the bureaucratization of government. For example, in her study of countess Clemence of Flanders, Penelope Adair argues that Clemence enjoyed access to comital resources denied her successors, who found their agency circumscribed by the emergence of bureaucratic administration, accompanied by the establishment of public and private spheres. See Adair, "Countess Clemence," pp. 63–64. In addition to looking before the twelfth century for examples of women exercising authority, authors in the volume, convinced they would find few "powerful" women after 1100, focused on redefining the terms and attempting to measure more ephemeral qualities like influence. However, as recent studies have shown, such shifts may not have occurred as uniformly as previously assumed, and may not have been as detrimental to women as

we have tended to believe. See also Holt, "Feudal Society and the Family in Early Medieval England," 1–28, and Ward, *Women in Medieval Europe*, pp. 4–5.

19. While in England such fiefs and the offices associated with them were divided among all female heirs, they devolved intact to the eldest daughter on the continent, producing a potentially powerful woman. Linda Mitchell, *Portraits of Medieval Women: Family, Marriage and Politics in England, 1225–1350* (New York, 2003), pp. 2–3; Scott L. Waugh, *The Lordship of England: Royal Wardships and Marriages in English Society and Politics. 1217–1237* (Princeton, NJ: Princeton University Press, 1988), p. 16. Jennifer Ward notes the regional differences that existed in medieval inheritance practices, and the ability of women to hold land as heiresses or as widows in a variety of places, including the Low Countries. See Ward, *Women in Medieval Europe*, p. 5. Scholars have begun to question the extent to which such changes actually occurred, revisiting in particular assumptions regarding the impact of such practices on women. See, among others, Theodore Evergates, *The Aristocracy in the County of Champage, 1100–1300* (Philadelphia: University of Pennsylvania Press, 2007); Amy Livingstone, "Diversity and Continuity: Family Structure and Inheritance in the Chartrain, 1000–1200," in *Mondes de l'Ouest et villes du monde: Regards sur les sociétés médiévales,* ed. Catherine Laurent, Bernard Merdrignac, and Daniel Pichot (Rennes), pp. 415–29; Constance Bouchard, "The Structure of a Twelfth-Century French Family: The Lords of Seignelay," *Viator* 10 (1979): 36–59; Stephanie Christelow Moers, "The Division of Inheritance and Provision of Non-Inheriting Offspring among the Anglo-Norman Elite," *Medieval Prosopography* 17 (1996): 3–44. A number of recent studies have challenged continued attempts to position these women at the margins of the political in the Middle Ages, arguing for a more complex view of their role in governance. Such views are succinctly outlined by Kimberly A. LoPrete, "Gendering Viragos: Medieval Perceptions of Powerful Women," in *Victims or Viragos?,* ed. Christine Meek and Catherine Lawless (Dublin: Four Courts Press, 2005), pp. 17–38. See also Frederic Cheyette, *Ermengard of Narbonne and the World of the Troubadours* (Ithaca, NY: Cornell University Press, 2001) and Amy Livingstone, "Noblewomen's Control of Property in Early Twelfth-Century Blois-Chartres," *Medieval Prosopography* 18 (1995): 55–72.

20. Kimberly LoPrete discusses the problems associated with categorizing women as exceptional in "The Gender of Lordly Women: The Case of Adela of Blois," in *Pawns or Players? Studies on Medieval and Early Modern Women*, ed. Christine Meek and Catherine Lawless (Dublin: Four Courts Press, 2003), pp. 90–110. For the dangers of assuming uniformity in past experience see Mitchell, *Portraits of Medieval Women*, p. 134.

21. Georges Duby, "Women and Power," in *Cultures of Power: Lordship, Status and Process in Twelfth-Century Europe*, ed. Thomas Bisson (Philadelphia: University of Pennsylvania Press, 1995), pp. 69–85, p. 74 and Lois Huneycutt, "Female Succession and the Language of Power in the

Writings of Twelfth-Century Churchmen," in *Medieval Queenship*, ed. John Carmi Parsons (New York: St. Martin's Press, 1993), pp. 189–201.

22. For another example of women who refused to conform to expected norms and share power with men, see Helen Gaudette's discussion of Melisende of Jerusalem in this volume.
23. See the discussion in Duby, "Women and Power." Jacques Dalarun describes the most prominent writers of the eleventh and twelfth centuries as "unabashed misogynists." Dalarun, "The Clerical Gaze," p. 42.
24. While authority denoted the legitimate right to act, grounded in one's possession of a feudal office or fief, power was a much more ephemeral concept, typically associated with the ability to impose one's will upon others. Imposing a clear distinction between these two concepts allowed medieval society to reconcile prevailing notions of male dominance in the political realm with the realities of feudal governance. As long as the practices of primogeniture and patrilineage prevailed among the nobility, the presence of women in the public sphere was inevitable since fiefs passed to daughters in the absence of male heirs. However, although the right of women to inherit powerful feudal offices well into the thirteenth century frequently resulted in their ability to access authority, the extent to which these women wielded power has yet to be fully determined. See Jordan, *Women, Power and Religious Patronage*, pp. 21–24 and Helen Maurer, *Margaret of Anjou: Queenship and Power in Late Medieval England* (Woodbridge: Boydell, 2005).
25. For example, after their marriage in 1212, Ferrand alone performed homage for the county of Flanders. See Delaborde, Berger, Brunel, and Samaran, *Recueil des Actes de Philippe Auguste*, no. 978, pp. 373–74.
26. Jeanne's relatively limited position in the political affairs of Flanders is revealed in a charter issued by Philip Augustus to the échevins of the city of Douai in June 1213. Philip prohibited the city's leaders from signing a peace treaty with count Ferrand or with the dowager countess Mathilda, but made no mention of the current countess. This charter confirmed the laws and customs previously established for the city by Philip of Alsace, and expressly prohibited them from forming peace with either Ferrand or Mathilda: "sine eis cum comite Fernando vel cum Regina comitissa Flandrie nullam pacem faciemus" Delaborde, Berger, Brunel, and Samaran, *Receuil des Actes de Philippe Auguste,* no. 1304, pp. 442–43.
27. Jean Francois Foppens, ed., *Diplomatum Belgicorum Nova Collectio sive Supplementum ad Opera Diplomatica Auberti Miraei*, vol. I (Brussels, 1734), no 78, p. 199. The charter was issued from the city of Lille.
28. ADN, 59 H 29/125 (1215).
29. Léopold Devillers, ed., *Cartulaire de l'Abbaye de Épinlieu* (Mons, 1867), no. 2, p. 179.
30. ADN, 32 H 5/1215 (September 1219); ADN 32 H 5/29 (6 August 1222).
31. Rijksarchief Bruges, no. bl. 7002 (27 January 1221); ADN 58 H 20/123 (December 1221)

32. Charles Mussely and Émile Molitor, eds., *Cartulaire de l'ancienne église collégiale de Notre Dame de Courtrai* (Gand, 1880), no. 47, 26 August 1219, p. 49; no. 48, October 1219, p. 50; no. 53, 2 July 1223, p. 53.
33. According to Jean Richard, there was a considerable element of truth to the rumors of Jeanne's betrothal. Richard argues that negotiations between Jeanne and the count of Brittany had progressed to the point of securing a papal dispensation from the Pope. Louis sent his papal legate, Romanus Frangipani, to secure the revocation of the annulment, and confirmation of Jeanne's marriage to Ferrand. See Jean Richard, *Saint Louis: Crusader King of France*, trans. Jean Birrell (Cambridge: Cambridge University Press, 1992), p. 15.
34. The text of the treaty was published in Alexandre Teulet, Joseph de Laborde, Elie Berger, Henri-François Delaborde, eds., *Layettes du Trésor des Chartes*, vol. 2 (Paris, 1863–1909), no. 1762, p. 77. Jeanne and Ferrand promised to remain loyal vassals, providing military service when requested. In addition to the 50,000 *livres*, to be paid in two installments, they agreed to refrain from constructing any new fortresses south of the Escaut River. Jeanne spent several months touring her domains to collect the guarantees and funds stipulated by the treaty. See Theo Luykx, *Johanna van Constantinopel, Gravin van Vlaanderen en Henegouwen, haar Leven (1199/1200–1244), haar Revgeering (1205–1244), vooral in Vlaanderen* (Antwerp: N.V. Standaard, 1946), pp. 259–60.
35. Similarly, Jeanne was forced to raise money during the episode of the false Baldwin, when a local hermit claimed to be Baldwin IX, fostering rebellion and driving Jeanne from power. Faced with revolt throughout much of her domains, Jeanne was forced to enlist the help of her cousin, King Louis. However, the king's intervention, although ultimately successful in quelling the rebellion, came at a steep price. Louis exacted 10,000 *livres parisis* as payment for his services. See Speigel, *Romancing the Past*, p. 52; and Jordan, *Women, Power and Religious Patronage*, pp. 47–48.
36. Maurice Vanhaeck, ed., *Cartulaire de l'Abbaye de Marquette* (Lille: S.I.L.I.C., 1937), no. 3 (1227), p. 7.
37. Léopold Van Hollebeke, ed., *L'Abbaye de Nonnenbossche de l'ordre de St. Benoit, pres d'Ypres (1101–1796)* (Bruges: Vandecasteele-Werbrouck, 1865), no. 43, 23 August 1228, p. 108; Charles Piot, ed., *Cartulaire de l'Abbaye Eename* (Bruges: De Zuttere-van Kersschaver, 1881), no. 164, May 1228, p. 133; Alphonse Wauters, ed., *Table Chronologique des Chartes et Diplômes Imprimés concernant l'histoire de la Belgique* (Brussels: Kiessling et Cie., 1903–12), no. 4 (1228), p. 71.
38. ADN, 28 H 19/712 (1222).
39. ADN, 28 H 19/716 (September 1227).
40. Édouard de Coussemaker, ed., *Inventaire Analytique et Chronologique des Archives de la Chambre des Comptes à Lille* (Lille: M. Quarré, 1865), no. 395, 1224, p. 173; no. 471, 1228, p. 197. A third charter, issued by the countess in 1233, after Ferrand's death, directed the bailiffs of Gravelines

to deliver payment of the rent promptly to the abbey, suggesting that the earlier instructions were being ignored; no. 203, 1233, p. 238.

41. Vanhaeck, *Cartulaire de l'Abbaye de Marquette*, no. 35, p. 29.
42. Foppens, *Opera Diplomatica*, no. 108, 1229, pp. 391–92.
43. Foppens, *Opera Diplomatica*, no. 4, November 1227, p. 102.
44. For the impact of marital status on women's experience, see Mitchell, *Portraits of Medieval Women*; Michel Parisse, ed., *Veuves et veuvage dans le haut moyen age* (Paris: Picard, 1993), Emmanuelle Santinelli, *Des femmes éplorées? Les veuves dans la société aristocratique du haut Moyen Age* (Villeneuve d'Ascq: Presses Universitaires du Septentrion, 2003) and Susan M. Johns, *Noblewomen, Aristocracy and Power in the Twelfth-Century Anglo-Norman Realm* (Manchester: Manchester University Press, 2003).
45. This attempt to develop a new approach to evaluating the role of women, one that avoids anachronism and rejects past tendencies to label powerful women as "surrogate men," hence dispensing with the need to actually explain their presence, echoes the views of others, including Kimberly LoPrete, "The Gender of Lordly Women: The Case of Adela of Blois."
46. Baldwin, *The Government of Philip Augustus*, p. 382; Mitchell, *Portraits of Medieval Women*, pp. 2–3; and Tolhurst, "The Great Divide." Tolhurst in particular stresses the need to account for the political nature of sources, and to understand the presentation of female figures as conditioned by the agenda of individual authors.

CHAPTER 9

# MONEY, BOOKS, AND PRAYERS: ANCHORESSES AND EXCHANGE IN THIRTEENTH-CENTURY ENGLAND

*Lara Farina*

For literary scholars, the question of how economic contexts influence literature is not a surprising one, given that we are now routinely familiar with both Marxist and New Historicist approaches to our subject.[1] Even so, we do not often ask the question, "How does economic history help us understand *devotional* literature?" much less the extra-disciplinary yet correlative one, "What does devotional literature have to offer economic history?" To take up this less familiar query (through which we might participate more fully in a cross-disciplinary fashioning of historiography), we need to consider that devotional materials might provide more than just representations that help to date economic changes. Devotional literature, like other kinds of literature, can also provide greater understanding of what economic practices *meant* to medieval people. After all, even the most scholastic of medieval writers did not discuss "the economy" as a self-contained structure but rather saw trade as imbricated in social and spiritual relations of many kinds. And, as Lianna Farber has recently argued, medieval thinking about the essential conditions of exchange also frequently arrived at "the absence of an external standard and the necessity of inscribing acts of imagination and fiction into the law."[2] Imaginative/fictional representation of social and spiritual relations is of course the subject of literature, so these observations suggest that medieval writing about economic issues could, or even had to, cross into "literary" genres easily. Following its divergent paths into imaginative representations of spiritual selves and communities may prompt us to reconsider what kinds of information economic history should take into account.

By "devotional literature," I do not just mean religious writing in general. Recent studies by Farber, Joel Kaye, and Jaques LeGoff, have already made extensive and often brilliant use of the theological archive in their studies of medieval economy and its attendant cultural discourses.[3] They have shown how articulations of church doctrine (whether in formal treatises, penitential manuals, or epistles) contain a wealth of information about medieval attitudes toward the uses of money, loaning at interest, fair and unfair trade, and similar subjects. Rather, I am proposing that we look also at genres that are generally overlooked in these better-known histories: "devotional literature" for me includes prayers, hymns, and tracts written for the specific purpose of prompting meditation and worship. Their perceived marginality to economic histories may be due to their often personal nature, their inability to legislate trade, or their expressions of disdain for worldly rewards. However, these qualities do not constitute serious obstacles to the questions I have proposed and are, in fact, equally present in the letters and treatises that do make their way into scholarly discussion of economic institutions and their meanings. Further, devotional writing can not only enrich our understanding of the language of exchange in the Middle Ages but also show how the material conveyers of language—books—signified as reminders of exchange relations. Even devotional literature aimed at withdrawn audiences, and even that of a seemingly "personal" nature, can contribute to this understanding, as my focus on vernacular anchoritic texts is here intended to demonstrate.

## Knowing a Bargain

Anchoritism is defined by enclosure. To embark on a religious career, the anchorite promised to spend the rest of his or her days confined in the space of an anchorhold, engaging in constant meditation and prayer. Though they could occasionally be found in small groups, most anchorites were solitaries, and many were female, especially in the thirteenth century, when anchoritism gained in popularity and visibility. Such confinement and solitude were obviously aimed at enabling the anchor's aesthetic discipline and absorption in prayer. Yet the amount of privation in anchoritic life could vary considerably. The anchorhold could be a cell, or it could be a house. The anchor could be truly alone, or she could keep servants. She might be entirely dependent on the community or a patron for financial support, or, if she were wealthy, she may have considerable resources of her own at her disposal. Affluent widows, in particular, may have found the life of an anchoress to be more appealing than remarriage or joining a monastic community. Further, some anchoresses took up or remained in advisory roles, keeping a hand in local, monastic, or dynastic politics. Even if the anchor's intent truly was to retreat from worldly concerns, her anchorhold would still be centrally located in her community, most often attached to or near a parish church, sometimes attached to a monastery.[4]

The social connectedness of anchors is apparent in their contemporaries' writing about them, such as Margery Kempe's well-known portrait of Julian of Norwich's role as a spiritual advisor.[5] But it is also evidenced by literature produced *for* them, as we see in thirteenth-century England during the greatest period of growth in the popularity of anchoritic careers. I refer here to the corpus of devotional literature known as the "AB" texts, so called because of their shared dialect, though their shared manuscript history is the more compelling reason for regarding them as a group aimed at a particular audience.[6] These texts were originally intended for female readers in the West Midlands, particularly (though not necessarily exclusively) for anchoresses. They include the Lives of female martyr saints Katherine and Margaret, the *Ancrene Wisse* (addressed to three women living together as anchors), the advisory tract *Hali Meiðhad,* the short allegory *Sawles Ward,* and the prayers of the "Wooing Group." Although some of these were meant to be read in meditative solitude, their collective existence points to anchorites' social connection with individuals and communities who could provide them with textual resources, and not only with copies of extant devotional texts but also with original, labor-intensive works that re-imagine devotional discourses to suit the needs of a newly prominent female readership.[7]

Reflection on the socioeconomic exchanges attendant on the practice of anchoritism and, in particular, on the provision of reading materials to anchors is handled in a particularly focused way in the subset of the AB texts known as the "Wooing Group" prayers. The group is composed of four prayers—*Þe Wohunge of Ure Lauerd, On Lofsong of Ure Louerde, On Ureisun of God Almihti*, and *Þe Oreisun of Seinte Marie*—that share form, language, and manuscript history.[8] Short enough to be recited frequently and clearly meant to be read aloud, the prayers were intended to be aids for contemplation of the Passion, for which they encourage their readers to imagine themselves as witnesses of the Crucifixion. Although they are often thought of as the most esoteric or mystical of the works in the AB collection, the Wooing prayers make pointed use of commercial metaphors to articulate the spiritual "debts" of their anchoress-readers.

The prayers choreograph an affective, charitable response to the Passion. This response, however, is predicated on a dramatization of the social status of the anchoress's career. Here, the texts draw on the well-known metaphor of "marriage" to Christ. The *Wohunge of Ure Lauerd*, in particular, stages the anchoress's engagement to Christ, who is portrayed—via a listing of his assets—as the ideal suitor, one modeled on the heroes of romance literature. The following passage shows an example of one quality in the list: generosity—which provides the *Wohunge* with an opportunity to discuss the logic of giving and returns.

> Þen ȝif I ani wile for largesce luue; luue iwile þe iesu crist largest ouer oðre. For oðre largemen giuen þise uttre þinges. bute þu swete iesu for me gef þeseluen. þ tin ahne heorte blod ne cuðes to wið halde. Derre druri ne gef neauer na lefmon to oðer. And tu þ erst me gef al þe seluen; þu hafdes me heht mi lefmon to þe giue al me seluen. to rixlen o þi rihthond crunet wið þeseluen. Hwa is ta largere þen þu. Hwa for largesce is betere wurð to beo luued þen þu mi luue lif. A swete iesu leue þ te luue of þe beo al mi likinge.[9]
>
> [So if I will love anyone for his generosity, I will love you, Jesus Christ, most generous of all. For other men of largesse give amounts of outer things, but you, sweet Jesus, gave your self for me, such that you could not withhold your own heart's blood. No lover ever gave a dearer gift. And you who first gave me all of your self, you have promised me, my lover, to whom I give all my self, to rule on your right hand, crowned beside yourself. Who is then more generous than you? Who is more worthy to be loved for generosity than you, my life-love? Ah, sweet Jesus, grant that love of you be all my desire.]

This meditation not only asks the anchoress to think about the value of gifts, it reasons through the "worth" of giving itself. Generosity, affirmed as an asset with dual functions (both the affiliation/identification of giver and recipient and the power to rule), is nonetheless one such asset in a list of many: Christ's strength, military prowess, gentility, wisdom, and beauty all receive similar treatment. The form of the list, which takes up 254 of the prayer's 658 lines, asks the reader to think about relative value, about what can be exchanged for what and at what gain or loss.[10] All of this fashions the anchoress's union with Christ, and thus her devotional occupation, as the best choice in a marriage market, in which suitor's qualities are quite clearly marked as social capital.

Given that the Wooing Group prayers were to be recited regularly, their readers may have thereby reflected near daily on the principles of trade. The texts put their readers through the paces of bargaining on their own behalf, never mind the fact that their anchoritic reader's "choice" has already been made, as is witnessed by her professional commitment to devout life. Consequently, the persona that the prayers construct for the anchoress is one defined by the practice of trade. The *Wohunge*, after considering the "wealth" that Christ offers, determines a profit motive for its persona, who declares "Ne mai I naman ȝive mi luue to sweeter biȝete" [I cannot give my love to any man for sweeter profit]. Similarly, the *Ureisun of God Almihti* follows its statement about the need for ascetic sacrifice with this thought about easy gains: "me nis he fol chapmon þe buþ deore awac þing & for forsakeþ a deor wurþe þing. Þ me beodeþ him for naut & bi hat him þer take mede. Forto nimen hit" [But is he not a foolish merchant who pays too high a price for an inferior thing, and refuses a priceless thing that someone offers him for nothing, and also promises him a reward for taking?].[11] Lines such as these shape the rhetorical "pitch" of the prayers, in which the anchoress reader is told that if she plays the part of a cagey bargainer, she can get something for nothing.

And the Wooing prayers do insist that their readers have nothing to make something of. The persona's lack of resources is stressed in the *Wohunge*, where she notes that "my born brothers have thrown me aside," as they are elsewhere in the Wooing Group in allusions to the reader's "unworthiness," such as one in the *Lofsong*: " Nabbich nowðer in me wisdom ne wurschipe & am redleas nab ich hwardemide leden mi life iþise worlde & am helples. Ich habbe on monie wise mislicunge of þonke & heorte sec of sorwe. Ne habbe hwoa me froure" [I have in myself neither wisdom nor honor and am without counsel. I do not have what I need to lead my life in this world and am helpless. My thoughts are full of unease and my heart is sick with sorrow and I have no one to comfort me].[12] Christ's extravagance is conveyed by the emphasis on the persona's lack: she has no wealth, no kin, no comfort, and further, no honor (the asset so fetishized by the economy of marriage). Since it is rather unlikely any actual anchoress would fit this profile, particularly in the thirteenth century when the institution seems to have been much more accessible to participants with financial resources and supportive social networks, the portrait of the destitute anchor was doubtless intended to heighten the pleasure of the "unbelievable deal" to be achieved through anchoritic life.

The profit from this deal is represented as "sweet," and it is thereby linked to the particular register of pleasures outlined in the AB texts as the reward of successful devotion. "Sweetness" is very often the ultimate good in anchoritic literature and in twelfth- and thirteenth-century devotional literature more broadly. The concept can be invoked as a metaphor, as it is in the *Ancrene Wisse's* description of hope as a "sweet spice in the mouth." But it also has more literal dimensions in the body-oriented world of the anchor. Christ's body itself is said to be soft and sweet, and the anchoress's body, according to the *Wisse*, should be both merged with and modeled after His.[13] The taste of Christ's body of course recalls the eucharist, which, in turn, recalls a whole repertoire of stories of miraculous eating, particularly apparent in the *Lives* of thirteenth-century holy women and in the period's hagiography.[14] In the AB text collection, both Katherine and Margaret are miraculously fed in their respective *Lives*. In *Katherine*, the heroine says of Christ, "Me swete lif se softeliche he smecheð me & smelleð Þ al me þunche sauure & softe Þ he sent me" [(He is) my sweet life, so sweetly he tastes and smells to me, that everything he sends me seems savory and delicate]. Further, a "sweet smell" issues from her cell to comfort the followers she has just converted through her preaching.[15] A particularly loaded term, "sweetness" thus points both to the pleasure of sensory intensification through ascetic training and to a quasi-sacramental authority gained from mystical union. By being "sweet" then, the anchor's profit is both total gratification and confirmation of her closeness to God.

## The Price of Profit

Of course, language describing God's "purchase" of souls through Christ's Incarnation and Passion has both scriptural sources and a long history of theological and literary use. The very naming of Christ as Redeemer invokes economic models, and scriptural passages such as the Parable of the Vineyard (famously addressed by the later West Midlands poem *Pearl*) and the Parable of the Talents were widely used by both devotional and secular literature to theorize the "economy of salvation." But I think it worth noting how emphatically the Wooing texts reference the reader's engagement in processes of barter, acquisition, and profit. The *Wohunge* insistently portrays the anchoress's love as bought, rather than given, and in its 658 short lines, forms of the verb "buggen" appear no less than seven times, usually accompanied by the adjectives "cheap" and "deore," and always as the center of an extensive remark about value and its measuring. The *Ureisun* and *Lofsong* are similarly punctuated with pithy observations about loss and gain, payments and profits, deals and debts.[16]

In fact, the Wooing Group's language appears to be part of an expanding vocabulary related to trade in the early thirteenth-century vernacular. Their word for profit, "biȝete," for example, while not new to English, acquires new meaning in the AB texts and in a few other, possibly related, contemporary Middle English texts. While the Old English precedent, "begitan," simply means to get, usually in the sense of taking, "biȝete" in the Wooing Group and in other contemporary religious writing denotes acquisition through exchange, as well as gaining of advantage.[17] Further, use of the term "biȝete" actually appears concentrated in devotional literature in late twelfth and early thirteenth-century Middle English writing. It appears, for example, in the early thirteenth-century prose dialogue edited as *Vices and Virtues*. There, the Parable of the Talents stresses that the Lord's loan to his servants is "for to biȝeten ðar mide" [to get profit with]. Interestingly, *Vices and Virtues* also shares the Wooing Group's connection of profit with the training and heightening of the senses. The Parable of the Talents actually begins the text's discussion of "ða fif wittes" [the five senses], and the talents are understood allegorically as the senses themselves. The senses, on loan from God, enable the multiplication of profit: God wants the return on his investment to be "wel imotet, and bi rihte wæiȝe wel i-wæȝien, and wel imered gold" [well coined, well weighed by correct weights, and of well refined gold].[18] This suggests that the Wooing texts, together with other early thirteenth-century devotional texts in the vernacular, were formative in crafting a new language of trade. This was a language connecting profitable exchange with both self-discipline and sensory pleasure.

But why? Why did a dramatization of bargaining and acquisition suggest itself as material for devotional, and particularly, anchoritic meditation? The work of the scholars I mentioned at the beginning of this chapter suggests one answer: simply that the ethics of commerce was very much on the minds of thirteenth-century religious writers. While scholars have rightly objected to characterizations of thirteenth-century Europe as witnessing the "rise" of capitalism, monetary transactions and new practices of exchange, investment, and accruing surplus did increasingly make their way into a variety of written records. Canonists, confessors, and sermon writers assessed the morality of monetary transactions, especially those in which merchants made a "shameful gain" (*turpe lucrum*) by buying cheap and selling dear or by loaning at interest. Theologians attempted a formulation of the "just price" and a condemnation of "enormous discrepancy" (*leasio enormis*) in profit. Even more significant: when trade and profit got the attention of theologians, the subject found its way into their writing about God. Peter Abelard, for instance, used the metaphor of minted money to explain the Trinity. Closer to the issues raised by the Wooing Group, the thirteenth-century Franciscan, Bonaventure, asked "whether God had loved mankind more than Christ, on the basis that if someone trades one thing for another, he values what he receives more than what he gives; only a fool would exchange a more valuable for a less valuable thing." Salvation theology had encountered the structure of profit, putting the Wooing Group's handling of the subject in sophisticated company.[19]

The above examples—the pitting of "shameful gain" against the "just price," the use of monetary metaphor in Abelard's unorthodox explication of the Trinity, and Bonaventure's struggle with the logic of commercial exchange—attest to the difficulty faced by the writers of religious tracts when attempting to reconcile an increasing dependence on and valuation of commercial economies with traditional Christian prohibitions against gaining at the expense of another. Getting this relationship wrong, for thirteenth-century religious women, could lead to heresy and damnation. Again, the Wooing Group's contemporary, *Vices and Virtues*, is helpful for seeing how this reconciliation—or lack of it—was being played out in the Group's immediate social context. The ethics of profit is topic of much interest in *Vices and Virtues*. Though the work uses the Parable of the Talents to conceptualize devotional practice as a kind of investment, it elsewhere goes so far as to say that "ealch miede is itheld for gauele" [every reward is reckoned for usury]. It blasts those who profit from fellow Christians as well as those who "befasteð here paneȝes ðe haðene menn, for to habben of them biȝeate" [trust their pennies to heathen men in order to profit through them]. It also singles out for blame landowners who collect rents from property leased to the church and the "chapmann ðe beið and selð mid unrihtwisnesse" [chapman who buys and sells with unrighteousness], saying that the latter "ne muȝen neure soðe scrifte don" [may never do true penitence].[20] *Vices and Virtues*'s approach to the subject of commercial exchange is to critique monetary practices it sees as already too much tolerated by "civil custom" and to deflect the acquisition of profit into the realm of the spiritual, by reshaping it as metaphor. It nonetheless attests to the presence of troubling commercial exchanges underlying the operation of the church itself, like church rental of properties and loans given out by clerics themselves, and to the monetary economy's infiltration of the meaning of devotional tropes.

The social conditions of English anchoritism in many ways further brought the economy of devotion to the surface of civic attention. To even begin a religious career, anchors needed financial support. If not wealthy enough to support themselves, anchors had to secure some form of patronage, which could come from secular clergy, monasteries, or laypeople. Though dependent on external support, the anchor was not quite reduced to beggary, however, for several things gave anchors some bargaining power. Monasteries could benefit from the status gained by being affiliated with an anchoritic holy man or woman (a good example of this is Christina of Markyate's presence at St. Albans). The boost to reputation could translate into increased lay support for the monastic house itself. Lay communities could anticipate pilgrims visiting the anchorhold and the market activity these brought. Indeed, anchorholds frequently became the site of market fairs. That the anchorhold was a place of financial investment is neatly suggested by the quaint fact that anchoritic cells were frequently used as "primitive banks," secure places to store valuables and legal documents.[21]

The financing of anchoritism was bound up with the larger thirteenth-century discourse on commerce in the practice of intercession. Intercession was spiritual service work, valuable labor that could be provided charitably or in exchange for remuneration of various kinds. LeGoff finds the idea of intercession, aided by an increasing reliance on the concept of Purgatory (in which the otherwise damned could work—or be helped—toward salvation), to be deeply influential in the thirteenth-century discourse about acquired wealth. He cites an *exemplum* from 1220 in which a "certain usurer of Liège" is helped through Purgatory by the devotions of his wife, who "hard by his grave...had a house made for herself, in which she shut herself up and by alms, prayer, and fasting and by watching day and night strove to please God for his soul's sake."[22] The anchoritic overtones of the wife's commitment are unmistakable. Anchoresses, however, could not always claim a purely charitable donation of their services, since their prayers were offered in return for financial support. Further, the public visibility of anchors, despite their practice of a privatized form of devotion, must have made their work somewhat difficult to imagine as part of an economy of pure charity. As Marc Shell has argued, unlike the public acts of largesse that so often sealed political allegiances, charity demands privacy; the truly charitable act expects neither public accolades, nor witnesses of expected returns.[23]

The AB texts address their readers' involvement in these quasi-charitable exchanges of spiritual services most pointedly in the texts' depictions of their own role in this exchange. The exchange of prayer for material support is nowhere more directly illuminated than in the postscripts of the *Wohunge* and the *Ancrene Wisse*, which comment on their writers' provision of the texts to their intended audiences:

> Prei for me mi leue suster. þis haue i writen þe for þi þ wordes ofte quemen þe heorte to þenken on ure lauerd. And for þi hwen þu art on eise carpe toward iesu & seie þise wordes. & þenc as tah he heng biside þe blodi up o rode. And he þurh his grace opne þin heorte to his luue & to reowðe of his pine. (*Wohunge*)
>
> [Pray for me, my dear sister. I have written you this because words often allure the heart to think on our Lord. And so, when you are at ease, talk to Jesus and say these words. And imagine that he hangs beside you, bloody, on the cross. And may he, through his grace, open your heart to his love, and to pity for his pain].[24]

> Of þis boc redeð...Ich hopie þ hit schal beon ow gef ge hit redeð ofte; swiðe biheue; þurh godes muchele grace. elles ich hefde uuele bitohe mi muchele hwile. Me were leouere godd hit wite do me toward rome; þen forte biginnen hit eft forte donne....Ase ofte as ge habbeð ired eawhit her on; greteð þe leafdi wið an aue; fo him þat swonc her abuten. Inoh meað-ful ich am þe bidde se lutel. (*Ancrene Wisse*)
>
> [Read from this book...I hope that it will be very profitable to you, if you read it often, through God's great grace—or else I have badly wasted my long hours. God knows, I would rather set out for Rome than start it over again!...As often as you read anything from here, greet our Lady with a Hail Mary on behalf of him who toiled over it. I am moderate to ask for so little].[25]

The commentary makes clear that the anchoresses' prayers are the payment for the writers' labor. The clarity of the expectation, however, belies the ambiguity of the relationship it establishes. Prayers would be meaningless if not given with charitable intentions, as the postscripts acknowledge by encouraging their readers to model their intentions toward the writers after Christ's charity. Given this context, the envois cannot demand or enact a contractual obligation. Yet, a kind of payback is expected, the emphasis on the labor involved in writing is anything but subtle in its depiction of the readers' debt.

While texts' representation of themselves as gifts demanding some kind of reciprocation is a common medieval trope, the Wooing Group prayers relate the giving of texts to the exchange of the bodies of Christ and the anchoress. As the *Wohunge*'s postscript records the giving of the text to the reader, it recalls Christ's giving of the "true love letters" within his body. In that prototypical gift, the distinction between text and body is difficult to draw and brings to mind a similar passage from the parable of the lover-knight in *Ancrene Wisse*: Christ gives a "love-greeting," a "gospel-like text" that is also His body.[26] The amatory nature of the "letters" emphasizes their charity, or caritas, and the various genres listed in the *Wisse*'s description recall the *Wohunge* itself: it is simultaneously a love letter, a representation of an event portrayed in the gospels, and a meditative prompt asking the reader to look into Christ's interior and imagine what she sees. Thus, the two textual exchanges (Christ/anchoress, writer/anchoress) overlap and characterize each other. By doing so, however, they also complicate the anchoress's role as an agent of exchange.

Although the anchoritic reader is represented as a barterer, negotiating on her own behalf and using the language of commercialism, she is also constructed as a recipient of gifts. Christ "buys" the anchoress's devotion, but he does so with gifts, like texts, which have no fixed price and establish a relation between the anchoress and His person, rather than a relation between commodities. Yet the anchoress is also "bought," like a thing more than a person, and Christ himself has thing-like qualities in his circulation as text. Further, the anchoress is the recipient of another gift, one modeled after Christ's, the gift of the text she reads. Here we do not see her bargaining, but rather indebted to the giver. Christ's gift to the anchoress is act of supreme charity, one that is offered as a model for the anchoress when returning the textual gift with a gift of prayer. But, since the textual gift is given with an expectation of return, it cannot be truly charitable, and the anchoress's "countergift" cannot be either. Finally, since the textual gift and Christ's gift are analogous, this raises the question of whether the anchoress's devotional commitment is itself an expected return on Christ's investment in her. If so, this required reciprocation would seem to cloud the understanding of charity.

Gift exchanges constrain as much as they benefit; they are "largesse" rather than "charity." Largesse is (public) giving with the expectation of returns. Shell has noted that the constraints of largesse were not lost on thirteenth-century writers, who observed that "the large giver... cupidinously demands a countergift, or is assumed by the recipient to expect a countergift; largesse... is merely a species of cupidity." Sarah Kay has further demonstrated that, in thirteenth-century *chansons de geste*, the genre most given to representing largesse, gift-giving is as much an expression of hostility as it is of generosity, since it can force the recipient into unwanted obligations.[27]

I am not suggesting here that the anchoresses' obligations to God are unwanted. But I will suggest that the anchoress-reader's trade with Christ is not easy for the Wooing texts to represent, either through the grammar of commerce or the discourse of gift-giving. As an analogue to dramatize the anchoress's mystical marriage, commercial exchange presents several difficulties. The most notable of these is the inequality of the exchange, raising the specter of unjust prices, uncontrollable profits, and God's seemingly irrational offer of everything for "nothing." Also a problem is the lack of a prior positive representations of the female merchant in advisory literature, hagiography, or romance—the genres from which the Wooing texts draw the most. Although thirteenth-century romance is rife with commercial language and commodity fetishism, its most notable "mercantile" women are figures like the Duenna in *The Romance of the Rose*, whose professed habit of financially draining multiple lovers is hardly offered as model behavior. But figuring the marriage as enacted through an exchange of gifts is also difficult, since that way the all-important representation of charity becomes haunted by its opposite, cupidity. Further, the textual trade that supports the anchoress's devotion is caught in this representational bind as well, whether we see the imagination of the textual gift as following from that of the anchoress's trade with Christ or we see the textual gift itself as the exchange through which the trade with Christ is understood.

While the prayers recited by enclosed solitaries may not seem the first place to turn for reflections on the thirteenth-century economy, the Wooing Group provides ample material suggesting the meaning of exchange relations and women's place in them. Not only were the prayers in this collection written at a time of intense church debate about the ethics of commerce, but they were aimed at an audience whose relatively new form of devotion required the thinking through of financial arrangements from the start. Their forging of a vernacular vocabulary of trade and profit points to the rhetorical uses and powerful appeal of commercial exchange, even for an audience intent on ascetic discipline. Yet the works also struggle with reconciling profit, gifts not paid for, and hopes for mutual benefit. Their ambitious content draws from diverse genres (the discourse on the Song of Songs and the *Sponsa Christi*, romance literature, and hagiography) to create the novel figure of the bartering bride, yet this figure raises as many questions about the place of the anchoress as it answers.

## Notes

1. The relation of medieval studies and Marxist analysis is the subject of *The Marxist Premodern*, a special issue of *The Journal of Medieval and Early Modern Studies* 34:3 (Fall 2004). For examples of recent work on the relation of economic history and medieval literature, see: D. Vance Smith, *Arts of Possession: The Medieval Household Imaginary* (Minneapolis: University of Minnesota Press, 2003) and Andrew Cowell, *At Play in the Tavern, Signs, Coins, and Bodies in the Middle Ages* (Ann Arbor: University of Michigan Press, 1999).
2. Lianna Farber, *An Anatomy of Trade in Medieval Writing: Value, Consent, and Community* (Ithaca, NY: Cornell University Press, 2006), pp. 148–49. Farber is here discussing the interpretation of "consent" in both marriage and exchange relations.
3. See Farber, *An Anatomy of Trade*; Joel Kaye, *Economy and Nature in the Fourteenth Century: Money, Market Exchange, and the Emergence of Scientific Thought* (Cambridge: Cambridge University Press, 1998); and Jacques LeGoff, *Your Money or Your Life: Economy and Religion in the Middle Ages*, trans. Patricia Ranum (New York: Zone, 1990). Older but influential studies include the works of Raymond de Roover, particularly "The Scholastic Attitude toward Trade and Enterpeneurship" rpt. in *Business, Banking, and Economic Thought (Selected Studies of Raymond de Roover)*, ed. Julius Kirshner (Chicago: University of Chicago Press, 1974), pp. 336–45;

Lester Little, *Religious Poverty and the Profit Economy* (Ithaca, NY: Cornell University Press, 1978); and John Baldwin, "The Medieval Theories of the Just Price," in *Pre-Capitalist Economic Thought* (New York: Arno, 1972). Diana Wood's recent survey, *Medieval Economic Thought* (Cambridge: Cambridge University Press, 2002) summarizes work in the field.

4. The definitive study of English anchoritism is still Ann Warren's *Anchorites and Their Patrons in Medieval England* (Berkeley and Los Angeles: University of California Press, 1985), but see also the earlier survey by Rotha Mary Clay, *The Hermits and Anchorites of England* (London: Methuen, 1914). Anchoritsm in northern France and the Low Countries has been discussed in Anneke Mulder-Bakker's *Lives of the Anchoresses*, which has been recently translated into English by Myra Heerspink Scholz (Philadelphia: University of Pennsylvania Press, 2005). Mulder-Bakker focuses in particular on the advisory and even "ministerial" roles taken on by anchoresses in urban communities.
5. See *The Book of Margery Kempe*, ed. Sanford Brown Meech (Early English Text Society o.s. 212. London: Oxford University Press, 1940), p. 42.
6. The "AB" dialect was first identified by J. R. R. Tolkien in "*Ancrene Wisse* and *Hali Meiðhad*," *Essays and Studies* 14 (1929): 104–26. For the AB texts' manuscript history, see Roger Dahood, "*Ancrene Wisse*, the Katherine Group, and the Wohunge Group," in *Middle English Prose: A Critical Guide to Major Authors and Genres*, ed. A. S. G. Edwards (New Brunswick, NJ: Rutgers University Press, 1984), pp. 1–5, and Bella Millet, George Jack, and Yoko Wada, *Ancrene Wisse, the Katherine Group, and the Wooing Group* (Woodbridge, UK: Brewer, 1996). The contents of one especially important collection of AB texts, BL Cotton MS Titus D. xviii (which includes the *Ancrene Wisse, Sawles Warde, Hali Meiðhad, þe Wohunge of Ure Lauerd,* and *Seinte Katerine*) have been translated into Modern English by Anne Savage and Nicholas Watson in their volume, *Anchoritic Spirituality: Ancrene Wisse and Associated Works* (New York: Paulist Press, 1991).
7. On anchoritic reading in the context of the AB texts, see Lara Farina, *Erotic Discourse and Early English Religious Writing* (New York: Palgrave Macmillan, 2006) and Elizabeth Robertson, "'This Living Hand': Thirteenth-Century Female Literacy, Materialist Immanence, and the Reader of the *Ancrene Wisse*," *Speculum* 78:1 (2003): 1–36.
8. All four prayers have been edited by W. Meredith Thompson in *Þe Wohunge of Ure Lauerd* (Early English Text Society o.s. 241. London: Oxford University Press, 1958).
9. Ll. 90-107 (Thompson, pp. 22–23). Translations mine.
10. Ll. 10-264 (Thompson, pp. 20–27).
11. *Wohunge*, ll. 71–2; *Ureisun* lines 31–34 (Thompson pp. 2, 22).
12. *Lofsong*, ll. 79–84 (Thompson p. 12).
13. *Ancrene Wisse: The English Text of the Ancrene Riwle*, ed. J. R. R. Tolkien (Early English Text Society, o.s. 249, London: Oxford University Press, 1962), pp. 43, 71.

14. Famously documented by Caroline Walker Bynum in *Holy Feast, Holy Fast: The Religious Significance of Food to Medieval Women* (Berkeley and Los Angeles: University of California Press, 1987) and in her *Fragmentation and Redemption: Essays on Gender and the Human Body in Medieval Religion* (New York: Zone, 1992).
15. *Seinte Katerine*, ed. S. R. T. O. D'Ardenne and E. J. Dobson, Early English Text Society, s.s. 7 (Oxford: Oxford University Press, 1981), pp. 80, 83. Translation mine. D'Ardenne and Dobson give the text of *Seinte Katerine* from both BL MS Royal 17 A. xxvii and BL Cotton MS Titus D. xviii. I quote from the Titus D. xviii version of the text since this manuscript also contains *þe Wohunge of Ure Lauerd*. However, the Royal MS 17 A. xxvii contains another member of the Wooing Group, the *Oreisun of Seinte Marie*, and is even more explicit about the sweet nature of reading using "swoteliche" where Titus D. xviii reads "softeliche."
16. The comparison of the persona to a whore is, however, brief and speculative: the *Wohunge* reads "mi fles to make me hore" (my flesh [fights] to make me a whore) (ll. 276–7, Thompson p. 27).
17. See the *OED* entries for "beget."
18. *Vices and Virtues*, ed. Ferd. Holthausen, Early English Text Society, o.s. 89 and 159 (Oxford University Press: London, 1888 and 1921), p. 17. The manuscript of *Vices and Virtues* is BL MS Stowe 34, which has been dated only as precisely as "c. 1200" by Holthausen. It is a small, thin manuscript, missing the first portion of the text and probably taken out of its original context and rebound. The hand, layout, and rubrication appear similar to early thirteenth-century manuscripts prepared in the West Midlands, particularly around Herefordshire, which is the originary location of the AB texts.
19. See the references in note 2 and also, on the English economy in particular: John Hatcher and Mark Bailey, *Modeling the Middle Ages: The History and Theory of England's Economic Development* (Oxford: Oxford University Press, 2001); and P. R. Schofield and N. J. Mayhew, eds., *Credit and Debt in Medieval England, c.1180–1350* (Oxford: Oxbow, 2002). Abelard's discussion of the Trinity is in his *Theologia* (PL 178: 97–102). Bonaventure's discussion is cited in Wood, *Medieval Economic Thought*, pp. 150–51.
20. *Vices and Virtues*, pp. 77, 79, 121.
21. See Warren, *Anchorites and Their Patrons*, for extensive discussion of financial support for anchors. See also *The Life of Christina of Markyate: A Twelfth-Century Recluse*, ed. and trans. C. H. Talbot (Toronto: University of Toronto Press, 2001) pp. 124–27, on the bids of rival monasteries for Christina's affiliation.
22. LeGoff, *Your Money or Your Life*, pp. 78–79. The exemplum is from Caesarius of Heisterbach's *Dialogus miraculorum,* Vol. 2, ed. J. Strange (Cologne, 1851), pp. 335–36, available in translation as *The Dialogue on Miracles*, Vol. 2, trans. H. von Scott and C. C. Swinton Bland (London, 1929), pp. 313–14.

23. Marc Shell, *Money, Language, and Thought* (Baltimore: Johns Hopkins University Press, 1993), pp. 34–36.
24. Ll. 645–58 (Thompson, *Þe Wohunge of Ure Lauerd*, pp. 37–38).
25. *Ancrene Wisse,* pp. 221–22. Translation mine.
26. L. 549 (Thompson, *Þe Wohunge of Ure Lauerd*, p. 35); *Ancrene Wisse*, p. 198.
27. Shell, *Money, Language and Thought*, pp. 34–35; Sarah Kay, *The Chansons de Geste in the Age of Romance* (Oxford: Clarendon Press, 1995). On the relation of literary genre, particularly romance, to economic history, see also R. Howard Bloch, *Etymologies and Genealogies: A Literary Anthropology of the French Middle Ages* (Chicago: University of Chicago Press, 1983) and Judith Kellogg, *Medieval Artistry and Exchange: Economic Institutions, Society, and Literary Form in Old French Narrative* (New York: Peter Lang, 1989).

CHAPTER 10

# WOMEN AND PROPERTY CONFLICTS IN LATE MEDIEVAL ENGLAND

*Anna Dronzek*

Historical analyses of women, wealth, and power in the Middle Ages frequently address the concrete realities of one or a few elite women's access to and use of wealth, focusing on how the power that wealth bestowed intersected with the other legal and cultural limitations that medieval women faced. Especially prominent in such discussions are queens and abbesses, women who possessed significant access to wealth and other bases of power, and who left behind the most detailed records for historians to mine. This volume includes a number of nuanced examples of this approach: Theresa Earenfight's examination of how María of Castile, Queen-Lieutenant of the Crown of Aragon, grappled with her husband's encroachments on the queen's traditional sources of income; Núria Silleras-Fernández's account of the rise and fall of another queen of Aragon, the former concubine Sibil·la de Fortià; Helen Gaudette's reconstruction of the building projects of Queen Melisende of Jerusalem; and Ana Maria S. A. Rodrigues and Manuela Santos Silva's scrutiny of how the medieval queens of Portugal used their income to extend royal power generally, rather than strengthen their own.

As all of the above authors make clear, however, wealth in the Middle Ages was not only a means, but also a symbol. Even in the absence of specific details about exactly what kind of wealth, how much, and how it was deployed, literary scholars can trace its cultural impact, often thereby gaining access to social ranks below queen and abbess. Lara Farina uses devotional literature for anchoresses to trace a vocabulary of trade and profit that elucidates how medieval people felt about economic practices.

Daniel M. Murtaugh finds in medieval *fabliau* new values resulting from the rise of the "rich peasant." And M. C. Bodden uses writings by Chaucer and Margery Kempe to explore how the exchange of money and wealth is central to the formation of women's identities.

This chapter bridges these two approaches by using the archival records beloved of historians to examine the kind of cultural meaning of wealth found in analyses by literary scholars, with the goal of seeing how that cultural meaning played out in the lives of real women. The form of wealth I address here is real property (or land), which remained throughout the Middle Ages arguably the most reliable and desirable basis for affluence, power, and authority.

The rich archival resources of late medieval England allow me to look beyond the very top of the social hierarchy, and to speak more broadly of groups rather than individuals.

While access to real property may have granted agency to medieval women, as many scholars have recently argued, women's relationship to land also integrally shaped their family identities.[1] Property conflicts brought before the court of Chancery in late medieval England show that the likelihood that a woman would face challenges to her property claims, and the nature of those challenges, varied according to a woman's identity as a wife, widow, mother, daughter, sister, or niece. The degree to which others were willing to challenge a woman's claim to land held by right of a particular family identity reveals the strength or weakness of that identity, at least in the context of land-holding, but potentially, given the importance of land ownership in medieval society, in other contexts as well.

Preliminary quantitative analysis of these cases suggests that late medieval English people understood access to and control over property to be an important part of the family identities of wife and widow, but a much weaker part of a woman's identity as sister, daughter, or niece. Qualitative analysis, in contrast, highlights the mutability and relativity of identity: one person's wife was another person's daughter and yet a third person's mother. The slipperiness of identity created tensions evident in the conflicts over property examined here. While these cases provide yet more evidence of the greater control over land that women enjoyed as wives and especially widows, they also raise questions about how easily we can equate the control of land with women's agency.

This chapter contends that the stronger a woman's family identity was, the less frequently such a woman would face legal challenges to land held by right of that family identity. Such a premise might seem to imply that all women in these cases, whether wives, widows, daughters, sisters, or nieces, had equally valid claims to the lands in question, something unlikely to be the case. Undoubtedly there were women who came before the chancellor to make illegitimate claims to property, but we can never know what proportion they contributed to the whole. Moreover, while collectively, some groups of women enjoyed stronger claims to property than others—for example, widows were guaranteed at least one-third of their husbands' lands to hold for life, whereas daughters might inherit only in the absence of brothers—it is unlikely that a greater number of challenges directed at one subgroup are random, or reflect that group's propensity to pursue illegitimate claims. Rather, such differences more likely result from social and cultural perceptions of that subgroup. Finally, as a court of equity or conscience, Chancery was an arena for cases unable to be sued at the common law. Therefore, any advantages that one group of women (e.g., widows) might have had over another (e.g., daughters) in common law were technically irrelevant in Chancery. In the absence of any evidence suggesting otherwise, to assume that one group of women—for example, women claiming land from their fathers—was inherently less law-abiding than any other group of women, seems a less reasonable assumption than that all kinds of women were equally likely to bring fraudulent cases—at a rate we cannot calculate and therefore cannot incorporate into the current study.

When I speak of identity in this context, I mean less the internal sense of self with which we associate the concept today, and more the "social self," defined by David Gary Shaw as "a bundle of perceptions held about an individual by a social world."[2] Shaw argues that an individual's identity or self derives from the conjunctions between that individual and the social, economic, and cultural structures in place in the world into which she or he is born. In the property conflicts detailed in Chancery petitions, women negotiated the social, economic, and cultural structures of both the family and the late medieval land-ownership in an attempt to defend their interests. While as individuals, women may have identified themselves in a variety of ways, the petitions demonstrate that late medieval England more readily recognized women's identities as wives and widows than as other family members. Therefore, wives and widows had what Shaw describes as larger social selves than daughters, sisters, or nieces.[3]

My analysis draws upon petitions brought before England's chancellor in the late fourteenth and fifteenth centuries.[4] By the reign of Richard II, Chancery had developed into a court of equity to which men and women could bring cases without remedy at the common law.[5] Such cases fell into two categories: those whose plaintiffs lacked the resources to sue at common law, due either to poverty or to overmighty opponents; and those whose injustices could not be remedied due to deficiencies or blind spots in the common law itself. As J. H. Baker explains the latter category:

> The stock example was that of the debtor who gave his creditor a sealed bond, but did not ensure that it was cancelled when he paid up. The law regarded the bond as incontrovertible evidence of the debt, and so payment was no defence. Here the debtor would suffer an obvious hardship if he was made to pay twice; but the mischief was a result of his own foolishness, and the law did not bend to protect fools.[6]

Chancery developed as the court to which such "fools" might take their cases and gain the Chancellor's aid in enforcing the dictates of conscience—moral concepts of right and wrong—rather than the strict rules of evidence found in common law.

As a court of conscience, Chancery dealt with a wide range of issues, and one of the most prominent was claims to land. Margaret Avery has suggested that by the mid-fifteenth century, Chancery had become primarily a venue for landowners wishing to circumvent the restrictions that common law placed on the disposition of property, with a corresponding decline in the number of cases brought due to inability to sue at the common law.[7] Later authors have revised Avery's conclusions, pointing out that the geographical scope of her sample skewed the results in favor of cases dealing with property, and drawing attention to the proportion of cases addressing commercial matters.[8] Nonetheless, while Avery may have overstated the degree to which such property cases dominated among those brought to Chancery, she clearly identified a significant purpose for which late medieval people turned to that court. The primary legal instruments to which late medieval landowners resorted to dispose of their land as they wished were the entail and the use. The entail determined that land could descend only to the lineal heirs of the original holder.[9] The use, also called feoffment to use, and which figures more prominently in Chancery petitions than the entail, has been clearly defined by K. B. McFarlane as

> a simple, but flexible, means of devising land by will . . . All that was necessary was that a man should grant his lands, or any part of them, to a number of his friends, usually called his feoffees, to hold to his *use* as long as he instructed them and to dispose of when he was dead in accordance with his *last* will.[10]

Because both the entail and the feoffment to use were designed to operate outside the common law rules of inheritance, any snags in their administration could not be settled by common law, but instead became a matter of conscience and came before the chancellor. Such snags arose frequently. In a sample of 6,850 cases, Timothy Haskett has identified 46.7 percent as dealing with real property—almost exactly twice as many as those in the next closest category, cases dealing with commercial instruments.[11]

What has received less attention, however, is the frequency with which women appeared in these property cases. This is despite the fact that as early as 1973 McFarlane recognized that the use and the entail affected men and women differently. McFarlane argued that the use and the entail reflected the English nobility's strong belief that all children should be provided for, in a way that usually did not disadvantage the common law heir; but he noted that "if, on the other hand, a common law heir was to be disinherited, it was likely to be a woman."[12] In a sample of 3,900 Chancery petitions, 663, or 17 percent, involved women bringing cases involving property conflicts, the overwhelming majority of which involved challenges to uses.[13] While 17 percent can hardly be said to dominate, these women's cases nonetheless provide historians with a significant body of material from which to draw.

In addition, Haskett calculates that while women's presence in Chancery increased over the fifteenth century, their representation as respondents grew significantly. He speculates that "[t]heir heightened liability may well reflect increased participation in matters of property and inheritance or a more vulnerable state as executors or heirs."[14] Haskett does not follow up this question, but the pattern he describes is consistent with both Avery's description of Chancery as a venue for dealing with land, and the increased employment of the use noted by MacFarlane.

The Chancery petitions do not represent all women equally, providing insight into only women above the rank of peasant. Being a peasant was not synonymous with being poor, and many late medieval peasants may well have been as wealthy as franklin or yeoman landowners, given the greater availability of land after the Black Death. Peasants did not, however, petition the Chancellor about land; petitioners were those who enjoyed rights of ownership, and overwhelmingly were at least yeoman, gentry, or rich merchants.[15] Petitioners therefore represented a narrow slice of English society, which, despite increasing urbanization, was still overwhelmingly populated by peasants. This narrow slice, however, extended well beyond royalty or the elite nobility, including landowners both great and small.

Unfortunately, the exigencies of record survival result in a unique set of difficulties in working with Chancery petitions. First, almost no late medieval resolutions survive, which makes it much more difficult to use these cases to uncover women's actual experiences of dealing with property.[16] We can trace the kinds of strategies presented in the petitions, but cannot know whether women's strategies in dealing with property conflicts actually worked, and correspondingly, whether their control over property granted them agency in society more broadly. Even without the resolutions to these cases, however, the Chancery petitions reveal a great deal about the assumptions and understandings that medieval people brought to the question of women and property, assumptions and understandings that were just as likely to shape women's family identities as the official outcomes of legal cases.

The other problem inherent to working with Chancery petitions is one uncommon for medievalists: the sheer volume of surviving bills. My own rough count of documents generated between the last quarter of the fourteenth century and 1515 totals over 38,000.[17] Sampling therefore becomes necessary, which in itself presents difficulties given that many sampling techniques rely on chronological distribution, and that the overwhelming majority of Chancery cases can be dated only approximately.[18] This chapter draws on a sample of 236 cases chosen from the reigns of Henry VI and Edward IV, and identified through the descriptions given in the catalogue of Early Chancery Proceedings (C1) in the National Archives.[19] While the tumult of the Wars of the Roses renders these reigns less representative of "ordinary" life, the conflict doubtless highlighted underlying tensions and conflicts, providing more fodder for this study. This sample allows us to examine the frequency with which women who believed they had a claim to property faced challenges to their claim, the source from which these women derived their claim to the land, and, where known, their relationship to the individual or individuals challenging them. The results suggest that women's claims to property acquired through marriage appeared more legitimate to contemporaries than their claims to property inherited from blood relatives—or more cynically, that the latter category of claims appeared more vulnerable to challenge. This sample also reveals the tensions that women's roles/identities created within families, whether generated or exacerbated by land.

Finally, Chancery petitions, like all legal records, are difficult to handle as historical evidence because, as many have pointed out, they privilege conflict and discord over peace and harmony. For every property conflict that appears in Chancery, innumerable claims passed unchallenged. Moreover, legal records draw on legal discourses, sources that some might consider overly specialized and irrelevant to people's "real" lives. I argue, however, that what happened in court was relevant not only in court, but outside of it, and had the potential to influence individuals' lives in significant and long-lasting ways. "What happened in court" does not mean simply the legal resolution, which obviously affected people's lives directly. Going to court was not just receiving a judgment or resolution, but a process. The process of going to court itself, the way that a plaintiff presented him or herself or the ways that the court system itself required people to present themselves, shaped people's sense of self.[20] And people of late medieval England—or certainly those who had any land to defend—were notoriously litigious, making prodigious and informed use of the varied English courts.[21] Therefore, the labels that were applied to people during legal proceedings mattered—whether referring to family roles like mother, father, wife, husband, daughter, son, or to other aspects of social identity.

Although these quantitative elements are suggestive, they need to be used in conjunction with the qualitative elements that these cases also provide. Natalie Zemon Davis was one of the first historians to comment on the narrative qualities of premodern legal records, examining the stories that sixteenth-century people told when they wrote to the king of France asking for letters of remission, or for pardon for crimes punishable by death.[22] Although many individual details varied, Davis's subjects followed particular narrative patterns rooted in sixteenth-century French culture, and Davis writes, "I marvel at the literary qualities of these texts, or I might say, their 'fictional' qualities, by which I mean the extent to which their authors shape the events of a crime into a story."[23] Davis's words apply equally well to the Chancery petitions. Petitioners too told stories, and in doing so, they were influenced both by lawyers and by the need to describe a crime that fit recognizable legal principles. Nonetheless, given that Chancery operated according to principles of equity—or as late medieval petitioners put it, "truth and conscience"—rather than the stricter principles of common law, Chancery petitions offered perhaps greater leeway for story-telling than other legal accounts, and success in Chancery may even have relied upon story-telling ability.[24] While some petitions show a direct debt to the standards of common law for their phrasing, there were no requirements that a Chancery petition state its claim in any specific way. Thus, when authors chose their words, they did so carefully, but with a degree of freedom not allowed in other legal venues, and guided not just by legal requirements but by their beliefs about what was right or wrong—or at least, what would be most convincing. Petitioners received help from lawyers in writing their petitions, although assessments of the degree of lawyerly influence vary, but this assistance does not mean that petitions contradicted petitioners' own sentiments.[25] Thus, the choices that petitioners made help us understand the mentalities of family identities that simultaneously derived from and shaped the family structures and marriage patterns underpinning the conflicts.

Turning to the quantitative elements, the 17 percent of cases of property conflict in which women appeared reveal with whom women brought cases to the court. As in other medieval English legal venues, most women did not plead alone. Of the 236 cases examined in detail here, the majority of women (53 percent) petitioned with their husbands, consistent with the legal principle that a married woman had no legal identity apart from her husband.[26] An additional 13 percent of women appeared as part of a larger group of men and women, usually but not always including their husbands. While a relatively large percentage of women—31 percent, or 74 cases—pleaded alone, the majority of these women (59, or 80 percent) were widows. Only in 5 cases, or 2 percent of the total, did women plead with a group of women, all of which were groups of sisters. The significance of these numbers for women's family identity lies in the fact that they suggest that women were much more likely to appear in court in the role of wife or widow than as a daughter, sister, or niece, although some women complicated the picture by identifying themselves as both wife or widow and daughter, or even in one case, granddaughter.[27] Again, the legal principles that underlay the English courts make this unsurprising, but it is clear that Chancery was little different from common law, and that women's legal experience in late medieval England was much more likely to strengthen their identity as a wife or widow rather than as a daughter, sister, or niece. Survival of the resolutions to these cases would have allowed us to determine whether wives and widows enjoyed more success in Chancery than daughters, sisters, or nieces. If women in the latter group were more successful than women in the former, despite appearing in smaller numbers, they may have actually enjoyed a stronger family identity than the other group. Without the resolutions, we can only speculate. Nonetheless, the predominance of wives and widows in cases brought suggests that the public at large perceived Chancery as a court to which wives and widows might bring cases successfully, or they would not have continued to do so in such numbers.

More interestingly, Chancery petitions allow us to see from whom or by what right women claimed the property in question. The patterns in these cases suggest that people in medieval England more readily accepted women's claims to property from marriage than from family inheritance, again demonstrating the strength of women's identities as wives and widows. 118, or 50 percent, of the cases examined here involved land claimed by inheritance, whether from a father, a more distant male relative, a female relative, or in the woman's own right. Only 76, or 32 percent of claims to property derived from marriage. In the remaining 18 percent of cases it was not possible to determine the origin of the property claim; while these women therefore may have derived their claims from someone to whom they were unrelated, the most we can presume is that in these cases, the source of the property claim was either unknown, or considered irrelevant. Conversely, this suggests that when petitioners did specify the source, it mattered to them. These numbers further demonstrate that people in late medieval England recognized women's identities as wives and widows more readily than those of daughter, sister, or niece.

Cases in which the plaintiff and respondent were related help to refine this conclusion further. In 16 percent of the 236 conflicts, women's property claims were challenged by a relative, whether connected through marriage or by blood. Clearly, the majority of property challenges that women faced did not involve kin, but this 16 percent merits attention nonetheless. It likely underrepresents the number of property challenges women faced from relatives, as such interfamilial conflicts may have taken place in the context of a kin network willing and able to help resolve the conflict without resorting to court. While the litigiousness of late medieval society suggests that people did not necessarily see activity in court as necessarily damaging to one's or one's family's reputations, the respect accorded to mediation and arbitration as means of solving conflicts suggests a preference for avoiding legal action when possible. Nonetheless, kin were more likely to challenge claims by family inheritance than were strangers. In the sample as a whole, as noted earlier, 50 percent of the cases involved land claimed by inheritance, but among challenges made by kin, this number rises to 60 percent; claims by marriage, which inspired 32 percent of the disputes in the general sample, inspired only 27 percent of disputes within families (in the remaining 13 percent of the cases it was not possible to determine from whom the property claim derived). To consider these proportions from another perspective, relatives challenged 13 percent of the cases in which women claimed property through marriage, compared to 19 percent of the cases in which property was claimed through inheritance. Breaking this down further, challenges from kin occurred in 20 percent of cases in which women claimed land from their fathers, 18 percent of cases in which they claimed land from other male relatives, and a whopping 44 percent of cases in which women claimed land from a female relative. This last number may suggest a significant hostility to women's right to bequeath land, but as in only nine cases do women claim land from a woman relative, the four that involved challenges by kin may only be a statistical anomaly.

Cases involving claims derived through marriage also include women who encountered conflicts over land that they administered as executors of their husbands' wills. Such cases do not, properly speaking, comment on women's own claims to property, although they highlight some of the obstacles women might face in trying to administer it. Haskett finds, however, that women were more likely to appear in Chancery to defend their own position as heirs rather than in their role as executors, and that in fact, over the course of the later Middle Ages the proportion of women as executors decreases compared to the proportion of women as heirs.[28] Given that women acting as executors for their deceased husbands are by definition claiming control over land by right of marriage, including these women in the general sample artificially inflates the number of cases in which kin challenged women's claims to land by marriage. This again demonstrates that a woman claiming land by blood right was more likely to face challenges than one claiming land by marriage.

The fewer challenges faced by women claiming property acquired through marriage are perhaps unsurprising given that such claims were usually only temporary. Many cases in which women made claims to land from their husbands, for instance, involved the woman's dower, lands that she could hold to her use during her life, but could not alienate. A woman's possession of the rights to such land might be a nuisance to other family members, but it was only a temporary one and, in theory at least, it did not result in the property in question leaving the family. A woman's claim to property through her family inheritance, however, generated greater tensions within the family at large, because it resulted in property leaving the patrilineal estate permanently. These legal realities helped contribute to the sense of family identity playing out in the petitions: a woman's identity as wife or widow was stronger, at least in terms of claims to property, than her identity as a daughter, sister, niece, or granddaughter.

Although suggestive, statistics are difficult to interpret in a vacuum. Examining the language used to discuss challenges to women's property claims helps to flesh out our picture of women's claims to property and nuances our understanding of their family identities. The qualitative evidence emphasizes women's identities as wives/widows by revealing the care people took to prove that they had not disadvantaged such women's claims to land in any way. But it also reveals the tensions inherent in the identity of a wife or widow, and the kind of family conflicts such identities could generate, tensions inherent in an identity more susceptible to change or erasure than an identity drawn from blood relationships: because a husband might die and a woman might remarry, wife and widow were identities contingent on circumstance and subject to change.

A concern that recurs throughout the sample petitions is their authors' desire, almost anxiety, to demonstrate that they took wives' and widows' claims to land seriously. Robert and Elizabeth Moton explained that Robert's brother, Aleyn Moton, was enfeoffed with others in the manor of Peckleton and other lands, "upon trust and to that entent that he said feoffees shulde make astate ageyn of the said manere londes and tenements...to the said Robert Moton and Elizabeth his wife to have and to hold to theyme and to the heirs and thassignes of the same Robert Moton" [upon trust and to that intent that the said feoffees should make estate again...to the said Robert Moton and Elizabeth his wife, to have and to hold to them and to the heirs and assigns of the same Robert Moton]. Although the feoffees had done so, Robert and Elizabeth claimed that "hit is a comon noyes and sclaundre yn the said shire of Leyc'" [it is a common rumor and slander in the said shire of Leicester] that Aleyn had made estate to Robert's son, Reynold, now deceased, before he made estate to Robert and Elizabeth—in effect, voiding the estate made to Robert and Elizabeth. According to this "common noise," Aleyn's purpose in making estate to Reynold was "to barre exclude and put oute the said Elizabeth of hir ioynture of the said manere londes and tenementes with thappurtenances after the decese of the said Robert Moton contrarie to thentent abovesaid" [to bar, exclude, and put out the said Elizabeth of her jointure of the said manor, lands, and tenements with the appurtenances after the decease of the said Robert Moton, contrary to the intent aforesaid]. The petitioners asked the chancellor to grant a writ of *dedimus potestatem* to a justice of the King's Bench to examine Aleyn and establish the truth of the matter.[29]

The Motons' case highlights the tensions raised by conflicting family interests: it opposes the interests of a wife to that of a son. The petition describes Reynold as the son of Robert, but not as the son of Robert and Elizabeth, suggesting that Elizabeth was Reynold's stepmother, not his biological mother. Common noise, or public opinion, saw these interests as opposed to such an extent that it held that Aleyn had acted in Reynold's interests (and it is worth noting that since Reynold was dead by this point, he could not have played a part in encouraging such rumor at the time of the bill). The Leicestershire community, presumably that in which Elizabeth and Robert lived as the lands in question were in Lincolnshire and Staffordshire, was quick to believe that a feoffee would uphold the rights of a son over the rights of a stepmother.

At the same time, however, the case also strongly supports the right of a wife to land—in this case, her jointure—by demonstrating how important it was to Aleyn that he be able to clear his name of such rumor. According to the bill, Aleyn—who was physically unable to travel to court himself—was "hevy and sory of the noyse and sclaundre surmytted upon hym" [mournful and sorry of the noise and slander imputed to him] and sought the services of the justice to register his testimony on the case, "for the suerte and sekernes of theastate of the said Robert and Elizabeth his wife" [for the safeguard and security of the estate of the said Robert and Elizabeth his wife].[30] He wished to clear himself of any suspicion that he had sought to defraud his sister-in-law, because this was a grave accusation to face.

A similar case appears in an answer to a petition presented by Alice, widow of William, Lord Lovell, against Robert Echard. Alice contended that Echard falsely claimed to be enfeoffed in a piece of land to which she herself had the legal claim. Echard responded that he had been enfeoffed legally, arguing that Robert Deyncourt, an ancestor in unspecified degree to Alice, had enfeoffed him in the lands in question, to the intent that he should make estate to Alice and her sister Margaret, wife of Rauff, Lord Cromwell.[31] According to Echard, after the enfeoffment, Rauff asked him to make estate of Cromwell's choosing (rather than according to Deyncourt's wishes). Echard agreed, on the condition that

> hys Lordeshyp wold feythfully promytte hym that the seid inheryters [Alice and Margaret] shuld not by that estat makyng be dysherited. And thanne the said Lord Cromwell takyng a dysplesur with the answer of the seid Robert Echard seid in this wise: "Suppose ye that I wolde be that person that wold dysheryte my wyfe and hyr suster; by Goddes crosses I late you verily undyrstond that the feoffement that I desyr to have mad, I do it rather for the suwerte of the inherytaunce of my seid wyfe and of her suster, thann for any othir thyng: and that I verily promytte you as ye shall knowe hereafter.
>
> [his Lordship would faithfully promise him that the said heirs should not by that estate-making be disinherited. And then the said Lord Cromwell, taking a displeasure with the answer of the said Robert Echard, said in this wise: "Do you suppose that I would be someone who would disinherit my wife and her sister? By God's crosses, I let you truly understand that the feoffment that I desire to have made, I do it for the safeguard of the inheritance of my said wife and her sister, rather than for any other thing: and that I truly promise you, as you shall know hereafter."][32]

In Echard's account, Cromwell took offense at the very notion that he might not appropriately provide for his wife (and her sister). The significance of this point is heightened by the petition's direct quotation of Cromwell, an uncommon practice. Petitioners were more interested in creating a narrative that suited their interests than providing comprehensive, objective details of the events in question and usually only summarized or paraphrased what they or others had said. Echard's care to repeat Cromwell's precise words, including the oath "by God's crosses," reveals the importance he placed on this sentiment. Echard's goal, of course, was to exonerate himself of Alice's charges, and thus we cannot take his report of Cromwell's words at face value. We can, however, note that Echard thought it a useful tactic to emphasize his own concern that Alice and Margaret might be disinherited, and Cromwell's strong sense that such an accusation amounted to a personal insult.

Finally, it is also striking—although, again, perhaps unsurprising—that the language used in cases in which the litigants were relatives is much more emotionally charged than in many of the cases in which they were unrelated. Such emotional weight demonstrates the greater tensions that women's claims to land generated within families than without. As a whole, emotional language is common enough in Chancery petitions that it takes on the quality of formula. Given that petitioners needed to justify their presence in Chancery by demonstrating their inability to sue at the common law, and that the premise on which such justification rested was often the petitioners' own weakness, poverty, or lack of resources, they tended to paint pitiful portraits of themselves as "poor" and "humble" creatures desperately in need of aid. Many cases involving people with no kin relationship employ quite pathetic language to elicit the chancellor's sympathy, and many cases involving relatives remain dispassionate and make little emotional appeal.

But some cases involving relatives employ emotional language distinct from the general pleas of helplessness in other cases, demonstrating the greater tensions in interfamilial conflicts. For instance, Thomas and Johanne Fitz Harry petitioned the chancellor for assistance against John Lyngen, Johanne's son with her first husband, Rauf. Rauf Lyngen had made Johanne and John the executors of his will and had also declared that after his death Johanne should have the manor of Sutton for the term of her life. Johanne contended that John, "not dredyng God the kyng nor his lawes" [not dreading God, the king, or his laws], had come

> with the nombre of xl. misrulid persones with hym, arraied in maner of were...into the maner of Sutton, where the seid Johanne his moder dwellid, and ther entrid and shette the yate of the place, and as *cruelle and eville disposid child, contrarie to Gods lawe and nature*, toke the seid Johanne his moder, and hur servantez, and kept them in warde; and when the seid Johanne wolde have departid for to have hadde socoure, her seid sonne *unkyndely* toke and huld hur faste, *in violente and ungoodely wise*, that she might nat depart. [my emphasis]
>
> [with the number of forty misruled persons with him, arrayed in manner of war...into the manor of Sutton, where the said Johanne his mother dwelled, and there entered and shut the gate of the place, and as a cruel and evil-disposed child, contrary to God's law and nature, took the said

> Johanne his mother and her servants and kept them under guard, and when the said Johanne would have departed to find help, her said son unkindly took her and held her fast, in violent and ungodly wise, that she might not depart].[33]

Johanne's characterization of John as a "cruel and evil-disposed child, contrary to God's law and nature" is exceptional in the mass of Chancery petitions, and it highlights the heightened tension inherent in cases in which relative opposed relative. Johanne's case is also notable because it is one of the only instances in which we see a woman relying on her identity as a mother to enforce her claim to a piece of property, and in so doing, it highlights the mutability and relativity of family identity. Johanne's legal claim to the manor in question came from her marriage to Rauf Lyngen, but the language of her petition relies upon cultural expectations of a son's proper behavior to his mother to make the charges against John. Her identity as a mother is both marital and familial, in that it derives from her marriage to Rauf Lyngen, but creates a blood relationship with her son. John's challenge to her claim fits the pattern of challenging women's claims to land through kin relationships, but Johanne's defense of her claim is consistent with the stronger identity of a wife/widow.

John's surviving response references this very mutability by pointing out the dangers to a family estate of a widow remarrying. John claimed that he had the right to his father's goods as administrator of his father's soul, and that Johanne had kept them from him "by the stirrynge and counsaile of the said Thomas Fitz Harry and othir" [by the urging and counsel of the said Thomas Fitz Harry and other]—or in other words, that his mother's new husband was trying to get his hands on goods to which he had no right.[34] The internal family conflict intensified with the introduction of another man, an outsider, and the consequent destabilizing of the woman's identity as her first husband's wife. What claim to a man's land did a wife really have once she was no longer that man's wife? Her role as that man's widow continued, but when she remarried she became another man's wife. The Lyngen/FitzHarry case clearly confirms the difficulty women faced balancing these two roles and their competing identities. As noted earlier in this chapter, women themselves recognized and possibly claimed their multiple family identities, with fifty-two women who petitioned the chancellor identifying themselves as both wife/widow and daughter.

The questions of how women's claims to property related to their family identities and to what degree their claims to land granted them agency remain vexed ones. Examining the combination of quantitative and qualitative evidence found in the Chancery petitions suggests a possible modification to McFarlane's view of the use and its impact on women. Although some landholders may have employed the use to disherit women heirs, others seem to have used it as a way to ensure and protect a wife's portion, given the degree to which women's claims to property as wives faced fewer challenges than those claims through kinship. The use's negative implications therefore may not be fully merited.

To what degree did these family identities and claims to property grant women agency? Certainly by pleading in Chancery, medieval women made use of the legal system to try to enforce their claims to property. Unfortunately, we cannot know on whose initiative they pursued these case—choosing to pursue a case on one's own initiative sheds a very different light on women's agency than lending a legal standing by one's presence in a case at the request of a husband or other male relative. Moreover, too few resolutions survive to determine whether these women were on the whole successful, and this, too, is an important part of the puzzle. If women brought claims to court, but were largely unsuccessful, we again see a different picture of agency than if their claims succeeded. Women clearly continued to believe that their cases could be successful, because they continued to bring such cases before the chancellor. Whether their belief was misplaced or not is impossible to determine. But if Chancery petitions offer the illusion of revealing women's agency, what they provide instead is the framework within which that agency (or lack thereof) might be exercised.

Finally, petitions describing challenges to women's property claims tell us just as much about how property shaped men's family identities as well as women's. If women faced fewer challenges to property claims acquired through marriage than through inheritance, the corollary is that husbands had an easier time providing for their wives than fathers did for their daughters, uncles for their nieces, brothers for their sisters, or grandfathers for their granddaughters. For all the emphasis on the patriarchal nature of medieval society, Chancery petitions suggest that in late medieval England at least, husband was a stronger identity than father, or at least, father of daughters. While England was less strictly patrilineal than Florence in the fifteenth century, where women severed ties with their natal homes on marriage and became fully absorbed into their husbands' lineage, in England as in Florence people expected daughters to marry and become wives, moving from the one identity to the other rather than retaining both. This anticipated transformation weakened the identity of daughter in a way that affected men as well as women.[35] The identity of husband, however, was not quite as contingent or slippery as the identity of wife, because widower was never as strong an identity as widow. While petitions frequently identify women as both the wife of one man and the widow of another, men are rarely identified by their marital status at all, and only rarely do any former wives appear (usually only if a right to property derived from them). Widowers frequently remarried, but retained no identity as "husband of first wife" to complicate their identity as "husband of second wife," because men's identities were much more strongly rooted than women's in class and occupation than in marital status.

Fully considering the way that property shaped men's family identities would require analyzing challenges to men's property claims as well as women's. For instance, the sample addressed here can reveal little about how late-medieval English society understood the relationship between fathers and sons, and expanding the sample is an endeavor outside the scope of this chapter. Further research is necessary to understand what access to property meant men *as men*, and put these meanings in a broader context of men's *and* women's property rights. Too often, it seems, these subjects have been discussed separately—men's property rights as a part of legal or administrative history, and women's as a part of social history. Only by bringing them together will we gain the clearest picture of women, wealth, and power in the Middle Ages.

## Notes

1. Significant discussions of women, property, and agency include Theodore Evergates, ed., *Aristocratic Women in Medieval France* (Philadelphia: University of Pennsylvania Press, 1999) (although Evergates's collection is not exclusively devoted to women and property per se, all of its articles discuss women and property at some length); Barbara Hanawalt, "The Dilemma of the Widow of Property for Late Medieval London," in *The Medieval Marriage Scene: Prudence, Passion, Policy*, ed. Sherry Roush and Cristelle L. Baskins (Tempe, AZ: Arizona Center for Medieval and Renaissance Studies, 2005), pp. 165–80; Barbara J. Harris, *English Aristocratic Women, 1450–1550: Marriage and Family, Property and Careers* (Oxford: Oxford University Press, 2002); Martha C. Howell, *The Marriage Exchange: Property, Social Place, and Gender in Cities of the Low Countries, 1300–1550* (Chicago: University of Chicago Press, 1998); Shennan Hutton, "'On herself and all her property': Women's Economic Activities in Late Medieval Ghent," *Continuity and Change* 20 (2005): 325–49; Anu Lahtinen, "'So the respectable widow sold her land to him': Gender, Marriage and Property Transactions in Fourteenth and Fifteenth Century Finland," in *Family, Marriage, and Property Devolution in the Middle Ages*, ed. Lars Ivar Hansen (Tromsø, Norway: Dept. of History, University of Tromsø, 2000); Lahtinen, "Gender and Continuity: Women, Men and Landed Property in Medieval Finland," in *History and Change*, ed. Anu Lahtinen and Kirsi Vainio-Korhonen (Helsinki: Finnish Literature Society, 2004);

Amy Livingstone, "Noblewomen's Control of Property in Early Twelfth-Century Blois-Chartres," *Medieval Prosopography* 18 (1995): 55–72; Linda McMillin, "The House on Saint Pere Street: Four Generations of Women's Land Holding in Thirteenth-Century Barcelona," *Medieval Encounters* 12:1 (2006): 62–73; Cynthia Neville, "Women, Charters, and Land Ownership in Scotland, 1150–1350," in *Journal of Legal History* 26:1 (2005): 25–54; Frederik Pederson, "'*Maritalis affectio*': Marital Affection and Property in Fourteenth-Century York Cause Papers," in *Women, Marriage, and Family in Medieval Christendom: Essays in Memory of Michael M. Sheehan, C.S.B.*, ed. Constance Rousseau and Joel Rosenthal (Kalamazoo, MI: Medieval Institute Publications, 1998), pp. 175–209; Jane Whittle, "Inheritance, Marriage, Widowhood and Remarriage: A Comparative Perspective on Landholding in North-east Norfolk, 1440–1580," *Continuity and Change* 13:1 (1998): 33–72. For an excellent exploration of the topic in a slightly later period, see Amy Louise Erickson, *Women and Property in Early Modern England* (London and New York: Routledge, 1995).

2. David Gary Shaw, *Necessary Conjunctions: The Social Self in Medieval England*, The New Middle Ages (New York: Palgrave Macmillan, 2005), p. 15. Shaw is explicit about his debt to Hume's definition of the self as "a bundle or collection of different perceptions, which succeed each other with an inconceivable rapidity." Davd Hume, *A Treatise of Human Nature* (Harmondsworth: Penguin, 1969), p. 300 (bk. I, sect. 6), cited in Shaw, *Necessary Conjunctions*, p. 12.
3. Shaw, *Necessary Conjunctions*, pp. 18, 121–44, 200. Drawing on different sources from this study, Shaw also argues for women's "larger" selves as wives than as other dependents.
4. The National Archives (TNA): Public Record Office (PRO) C 1 Early Chancery Proceedings.
5. The best introduction to the medieval court of Chancery is Timothy Haskett, "The Medieval English Court of Chancery," *Law and History Review* XIV:2 (Fall 1996): 245–313. See also J. H. Baker, *An Introduction to English Legal History*, 3rd ed. (London: Butterworths, 1990), pp. 113–15.
6. Baker, *An Introduction to English Legal History*, p. 118.
7. Margaret Avery, "The History of the Equitable Jurisdiction of Chancery before 1460," *The Bulletin of the Institute of Historical Research* 42 (1969): 129–44. Avery attributes this to the increasing employment of the use (to be discussed below), although Baker, *An Introduction to English Legal History*, p. 120, argues that the dominance of property cases in Chancery was not solely attributable to the rise of uses. J. L. Barton, "The Medieval Use," *Law Quarterly Review* 81 (1965): 562–77, suggests that the chancellor assumed jurisdiction over such cases by the reign of Richard II. R. H. Helmholz, "The Early Enforcement of Uses," *Columbia Law Review* 79 (1979): 1503–13, suggests that the enforcement of uses originally fell under ecclesiastical jurisdiction. See also Margaret Avery, "Evaluation of the Effectiveness of the Court of Chancery under the Lancastrian Kings," *Law and Quarterly Review* 86 (1970): 84–97.

8. Nicholas Pronay, "The Chancellor, the Chancery and the Council at the End of the Fifteenth Century," in *British Government and Administration: Studies Presented to H. B. Chrimes*, ed. H. Hearder and H. R. Loyn (Cardiff: University of Wales Press, 1974), pp. 87–103; Mark Beilby, "The Profits of Expertise: The Rise of the Civil Lawyers and Chancery Equity," in *Profit, Piety and the Professions in Later Medieval England*, ed. Michael Hicks (Gloucester: Sutton Publishing, 1990), pp. 72–90; Penny Tucker, "The Early History of the Court of Chancery: A Comparative Study," *The English Historical Review* 115: 463 (Sept. 2000): 791–811.
9. The most comprehensive examination of the entail is Joseph Biancalana, *The Fee Tail and the Common Recovery in Medieval England, 1176–1502* (Cambridge: Cambridge University Press, 2001).
10. K. B. McFarlane, *The Nobility of Later Medieval England: The Ford Lectures for 1953 and Related Studies* (1973; rpt., Oxford: The Clarendon Press, 1997), p. 69 (emphasis in the original).
11. Haskett, "The Medieval English Court of Chancery," p. 296.
12. McFarlane, *The Nobility of Later Medieval England*, pp. 71–72 (quote from p. 72). S. H. Rigby discusses this phenomenon briefly in his *English Society in the Later Middle Ages* (London: Macmillan Press, 1995), pp. 264–66, although he emphasizes more strongly than McFarlane the degree to which women were disinherited, and does not address the other elements of the entail and use that made them attractive to late medieval landowners (in particular, the fact that they rendered land immune to wardship and to forfeiture for treason).
13. For the purposes of this chapter I have set aside the cases in which women appeared only as respondents, as such cases were only 3 percent of the total.
14. Haskett, "The Medieval English Court of Chancery," 287. Emma Hawkes, " '[S]he will . . . protect and defend her rights boldly by law and reason . . . .': Women's Knowledge of Common Law and Equity Courts in Late-Medieval England," in *Medieval Women and the Law*, ed. Noël James Menuge (Woodbridge: Boydell and Brewer, 2000), pp. 145–62, argues for women's greater familiarity with late medieval English law and willingness to take cases to court than has been previously realized, but her conclusions are more informed by literary analysis than knowledge of the legal technicalities of Chancery, and it is difficult to integrate them with Haskett's and my own calculations.
15. Haskett, "The Medieval English Court of Chancery," pp. 290–91, calculates that 75 percent of the men in his sample who identified themselves by a lay rank named themselves as esquires, knights, and gentlemen, and 33 percent of those who identified themselves by a trade named themselves as merchants. This calculation is restricted to men because women largely self-identified (and were identified by others) according to marital status rather than to social rank or occupation.
16. The number of surviving resolutions for the Early Chancery Proceedings is extremely small, allowing for no generalization about women's successes

in court. Resolutions to Chancery cases only survive in significant number from the sixteenth century.

17. This total derives from the catalogue of Early Chancery Proceedings (C 1) in the National Archives. This catalogue is printed as *List of Early Chancery Proceedings Preserved in the Public Record Office,* Lists and Indexes v. 12, 16, 20 (London: H.M.S.O. etc., 1901–1936; rpt., Kraus Reprint Corp., 1964), and may be accessed electronically at <http://www.nationalarchives.gov.uk/catalogue/>, June 2007. The total is only a rough estimate as it is difficult to determine the exact number of documents associated with a case from the catalogue, as different cataloguers' practices for dealing with multidocument cases varied.
18. In most cases, the only evidence of the petition's date is found in the person of the chancellor to whom it was addressed. Some chancellors held office for only a few years, giving a relatively narrow date range, but when a chancellor stayed in office for roughly eighteen years, as was the case with John Stafford, Bishop of Bath and Wells and Archbishop of Canterbury, the chronological range broadens impossibly. Moreover, other petitions address only "my lord Chancellor," and therefore cannot be dated in any precise fashion. For one response to these issues in constructing a broader sample of Chancery petitions than those consulted here, see Haskett, "The Medieval English Court of Chancery," pp. 282–83.
19. Haskett, "The Medieval English Court of Chancery," pp. 283–84, correctly warns against relying too heavily on the catalog descriptions, which are not always accurate. Given the abundance of these records, however, the catalog is the most expedient way to identify relevant cases, and if anything, using the catalog is more likely to underrepresent than overrepresent cases of women in conflicts over property, as it is easy to discard a case for which the description misleadingly suggested its relevance, whereas it is impossible to tell how many cases might fit the category under study here, but for which the nineteenth-century cataloguers wrote a misleading description.
20. Shaw, *Necessary Conjunctions*, discusses arbitration in the borough court as a means of identity formation, pp. 72–91.
21. For an interesting consideration of the way that ordinary English people understood their legal system, see Anthony Musson, *Medieval Law in Context: The Growth of Legal Consciousness from Magna Carta to the Peasants' Revolt* (Manchester, Manchester University Press, 2001).
22. Natalie Zemon Davis, *Fiction in the Archives: Pardon Tales and Their Tellers in Sixteenth-Century France* (Stanford, CA: Stanford University Press, 1987).
23. Davis, *Fiction in the Archives*, p. 2.
24. For one example of the phrase "truth and conscience," see the closing of TNA: PRO C 1/9/143. The closings of petitions ring changes on the themes of truth, right, conscience, faith, charity, and occasionally law, usually ending with some variety of the phrase "for the love of God in the way of charity."

25. Timothy S. Haskett, "Country Lawyers? The Composers of English Chancery Bills," in *The Life of the Law, Proceedings of the Tenth British Legal History Conference*, ed. P. Birks (London: 1993), pp. 9–23, argues that Chancery petitions were composed almost wholly by lawyers. In contrast, Barbara A. Hanawalt, *Growing Up in Medieval London: The Experience of Childhood in History* (New York and Oxford: Oxford University Press, 1993), p. 15; Marjorie McIntosh, *Controlling Misbehavior in England: 1370–1600* (Cambridge: Cambridge University Press, 1998), p. 119; and Tucker, "The Early History of the Court of Chancery," p. 790, argue that plaintiffs played a significant role in the composition of petitions. Cordelia Beattie, "Meanings of Singleness: The Single Woman in Late Medieval England," Ph.D. thesis, University of York [UK], 2001, pp. 162–63, helpfully reviews these perspectives and concludes, reasonably, that "Thus, while a petition cannot be read simply as evidence of what a petitioner said, it should not be understood as merely a product of a lawyer. The writing of a petition would have involved both the telling of a story, not necessarily unprompted, by the petitioner, and the composition of the written bill by someone knowledgeable of the correct form and language." In support of Hanawalt, McIntosh, Tucker, and Beattie, it is worth noting that a number of petitions, when naming the respondents in the closing formulae (in which the petition asked the chancellor for a particular writ or action directed at a particular person), refer to the respondent as being at that time present in court (e.g., TNA: PRO C 1/27/135, which states, "Wherfor please your gracioux lordship in als meche as the seid John Asshefeld is at this day present in the Chauncerie by fore your lordship...to examyne the premysses and after your noble discrecion to rule & comaunde the John Asshefeld & Anne his wyff to make astat un to your seid besecher as lawe & concyence requyren"). It is possible, of course, that such language was added to a previously composed text at the time that the petition was presented, as a kind of rhetorical flourish, incorporated seamlessly by the scribe into the copy entered into the official record, and therefore does not counter the argument that these documents were shaped most influentially by lawyers. Such additions (if they are additions), however, do suggest the possibility for improvisation in the final presentation of the petition, and hence a degree of flexibility in their composition.
26. The sample of 236 cases consists of petitions I have transcribed completely from the originals in the National Archives; the larger sample draws only on the descriptions provided in the catalogue. As noted earlier, Haskett is correct that the early nineteenth-century cataloguers did not always accurately describe the contents of a case, but as a quick and dirty method of categorizing cases, sampling from the catalogue provides a larger context for the more detailed analysis drawn directly from the petitions themselves.
27. In TNA: PRO C 1/27/186, the petitioner identifies herself as "Anne, widow of William Chamberleyn knight, and granddaughter of Cecile daughter of Thomas Mortymer, knight."

28. Haskett, "The Medieval English Court of Chancery," pp. 288–89.
29. TNA: PRO C 1/15/124.
30. TNA: PRO C 1/15/124.
31. TNA: PRO C 1/1/77. Echard's response is to C 1/1/76, brought by Alice, widow of Lord Lovell. Alice and Margaret's relationship to Robert Deyncourt is not clear; they may have been his grand-nieces.
32. TNA: PRO C 1/1/77.
33. TNA: PRO C 1/1/70.
34. TNA: PRO C 1/1/71.
35. Christiane Klapisch-Zuber, *Women, Family, and Ritual in Renaissance Italy*, trans. Lydia G. Cochrane (Chicago: University of Chicago Press, 1987).

# CHAPTER 11

# PRIVATE PROPERTIES, SEIGNIORIAL TRIBUTES, AND JURISDICTIONAL RENTS: THE INCOME OF THE QUEENS OF PORTUGAL IN THE LATE MIDDLE AGES

*Ana Maria S. A. Rodrigues and Manuela Santos Silva*

The Kingdom of Portugal emerged in the twelfth century as a result of the territorial and political development of a previous county of the Kingdom of Leon. Since then and until the last decade of the fifteenth century, there were thirteen queens-consorts in this realm. Most of them came from other kingdoms of the Iberian Peninsula (table 11.1) and their marriages tended to be a result of war and peace negotiations between Portugal and a neighbor contender or ally. Some of the marriage contracts were settled in battlefields to avoid war; others were negotiated to assure an alliance against a mutual enemy. Even the union between Philippa of Lancaster (queen, 1387–1415) and João I of Portugal (king, 1383–1433), which might seem a singular case at first sight, fits entirely in this scenario. Philippa was the daughter of a famous character of the fourteenth-century history of England, John of Gaunt, who called himself "King of Castile and Leon,"[1] and claimed the Castilian throne for himself and his wife, Constance of Castile. With this marriage, he wanted to grant the support of his Portuguese son-in-law to his pretensions while João I expected to enlarge the boundaries of his kingdom and to secure its autonomy.[2]

Marriage contracts made in such circumstances, and particularly if they intended to put an end to a period of war between two kingdoms, could include some exchange of lands and goods. For instance, when

Fernando I (king, 1367–83) decided not to marry the very young daughter of the Castilian king Enrique of Trastámara because he had fallen in love with the Portuguese noblewoman Leonor Teles (queen, 1372–83), his kingdom lost several boundary towns that had been promised by the bride's father.[3] This fact would never be forgiven by his contemporary Portuguese subjects and contributed to the hostility they always showed to the queen.[4]

Marriage between the Portuguese kings and their brides, most of them daughters of other sovereigns or of very important members of allied kingdoms' royal courts (figure 11.1), did not imply only political or territorial advantages, though. Many of the future queens were already proprietors in their own countries and kept being so. The Roman matrimonial law had imposed that the bride's family should pay a dowry to the groom, but at least in the western Iberian peninsula it took some time until this old custom was completely restored after the Visigothic and Islamic periods. The evidence seems to indicate that, during the first reigns, it was not expected that the brides would bring anything else than a few personal objects.[5] Isabel (queen, 1282–1336), the Aragonese princess who was to marry Dinis (king, 1279–1325), is known to have been the first royal bride who brought with her a dowry given by her father as the Roman legal tradition had established.[6] But apart from jewels, clothes, or money, some of the queens received lands from their parents at the time of their marriages.[7] And the ties that united them to their original families could be so tightly sustained that even as queens of a foreign country they would still inherit some of their parents' personal belongings, as it happened to Philippa of Lancaster after the death of her father.[8]

The maintenance of such bonds with motherland was helped by the fact that the components of the new queen's retinue were people to whom she was connected by emotional ties. Some of her relatives, as well as a certain number of female friends who would become her ladies-in-waiting in her new country, and also a few servants and officials would leave their country of origin some time before the wedding to form her nuptial escort.[9] Some of them were to return shortly after the ceremony, others were to stay in Portugal for good. In their new kingdom they would be composing the queen's entourage, relying on their Lady to provide them with some essential emoluments, if not full economic support.

The fact that the queens were entitled to maintain their own household (*Casa da Rainha*) may have been one of the factors that contributed to guarantee their financial autonomy from the very beginning of their married life. As early as their betrothals they were normally presented with the promise of receiving several Portuguese towns and lands. And when they arrived in Portugal, it was certain that the ruling king, the bridegroom or his father, would fulfill that promise. Accordingly, these royal concessions were made either *propter nuptias* or as *arras* (dower). The latter was an ancient use of Semitic origin,[10] very popular in the Iberian Peninsula once it had been brought to the legal royal tradition through the Visigothic law code; it seems to have been created in order to assure the wife's maintenance as a widow.[11] However, in Portugal the queens were able to profit from their dowers as soon as they got married.[12] In fact, the *arras*, according to the German tradition, was considered a kind of a purchase of the bride's body and seen as a validation of the marriage contract.[13]

The dower should correspond to a portion of the husband's possessions at the time of the wedding. Therefore, it is not surprising that its composition could differ from queen to queen. It was not hereditary. It was personal and not transmissible. With the death of the queen, whatever she had received as dower was to return unchanged to the Crown and the king was free to decide upon its destiny. This method had its own virtues: it ensured the dowager-queen a lifetime support, even when a new queen was already playing her previous role. At the same time, it did not prevent the queen-consort from receiving other properties or rents in donation from her husband nor from increasing her private patrimony by purchase and inheritance.[14]

There is not much evidence left concerning the first five queens' properties. Therefore, we cannot pretend to have drawn up a complete map of their domain (figure 11.2). According to the fragmentary information gathered, there was a great dispersion of the conceded lands, villages, and towns, scattered all over the north and the center of the kingdom, especially in areas where the Crown had managed to monopolize the territory recovered from the Moors. An early insistence in the donation of the towns of Torres Vedras and Alenquer can be noticed though.[15]

With later queens, however, the situation becomes clearer. Isabel of Aragón received her domain through four different concessions. The first corresponded to the main occasion that generally marked the beginning of a queen's patrimony, her marriage to Dinis of Portugal. The other donations were made later and reveal a new policy launched by her husband, who wanted to enlarge the Crown's domain and powers. Consequently, the saint queen got hold of several towns—Abrantes, Óbidos, Porto de Mós, Leiria, Arruda, Torres Novas, Atouguia—a few castles—Vila Viçosa, Monforte, Sintra, Ourém, Feira, Gaia, Larnoso, Nóbrega, Chaves, Portel, Montalegre—and some tenements—Reguengos de Gondomar, Rebordãos e Codões, Quinta da Fanga da Fé, Lezíria da Atalaia.[16]

Her successor, Beatriz of Castile (queen, 1309–59), gained her numerous sources of income both from her husband Afonso IV (king, 1325–57) and from her son Pedro I (king, 1357–67), who was already a widower at the time of his enthronement. She received the urban centers of Viana do Alentejo, Évora, Vila Viçosa, Vila Real, Gaia, Vila Nova (the last two exchanged for Sintra in 1334), Torres Novas, Óbidos, Atouguia, Ourém, Porto de Mós and Cheleiros, some tenements in Santarém and the Lezíria da Atalaia.[17]

Constança Manuel (married, 1340, died 1348/9), wife of Pedro I and mother of the last king of the first Portuguese dynasty, did not get anything else other than the properties that were given to her as *arras*: Montemor-o-Novo, Alenquer, and Viseu.[18] The fact that she died young and never became a queen may have been one of the reasons for the scarcity of her domain. The preference that her husband showed for his lover Inés de Castro may also have played a role.[19]

Leonor Teles, the beloved wife of Fernando I was the owner not only of a much larger geographical area of jurisdiction—including Vila Viçosa, Almada, Sintra, Alenquer, Abrantes, Sacavém, Torres Vedras, Óbidos, Atouguia, Aveiro, Pinhel, apart from a few estates—but also of very extensive prerogatives. It is really hard to find, in the document that secures her the ownership of her domain, any restriction as to a complete exercise of power, even in what judicial matters are concerned.[20] Nevertheless, we must be aware that she had no patrimony of her own.[21]

The new dynasty started with new procedures toward the queens' domain. Indeed Philippa of Lancaster only received six towns, all of them situated in the Portuguese Estremadura, a region where the king was the main landowner. But this small group of towns—Óbidos, Sintra, Alenquer, Torres Vedras, Torres Novas, Alvaiázere—will constitute, from then on, the fixed part of the queens' domain. Therefore, even in the absence of a queen, they will be kept together under the administration of an official known as the purveyor of the queens' lands (*Provedor das Terras das Rainhas*).[22] These six urban centers or some of their rents could still be alienated by the king in favor of someone else but only for a short time, a conditional period that would end with the arrival of a new queen.[23] And, in case the Crown prince took a wife during the lifetime of his mother, there was a rule to be followed: the queen was asked to give up half of this domain on behalf of the princess, who was expected to profit only from that part until the death of her mother-in-law.[24]

The fact that there was henceforth a fixed group of towns composing the queens' domain did not prevent the reigning kings from increasing the patrimony of their wives or enlarging their areas of jurisdiction if they wished to do so. This is what happened to Leonor of Lancaster (queen, 1471–1525), wife of João II (king, 1472–95), sister of Manuel I (king, 1495–1521) and no doubt the architect of this unexpected succession. Having suffered the pain of seeing her only male child, Afonso, die in his youth, she managed to provide her brother, the next in the line of succession, with a large household, and gave the decisive impulse that raised him to the throne by preventing her husband from legitimizing a bastard.[25] Her contribution was also essential to the new king's marriage to her deceased son's widow, Isabel of Castile (queen, 1497–98). In return for Leonor's continuous support, Manuel I increased the domain she had received from her father-in-law and her husband with new donations, and extended her jurisdiction, thus securing her influence and affluence during the whole of his reign, notwithstanding the existence of three other queens, his own three successive wives.[26]

The queens enjoyed of considerable wealth and very extensive powers in their domain, granted by the donation charters. To start with, they received all the monarchs' possessions in each of the six towns and the surrounding countryside, consisting not only of public facilities (such as markets, ports, rivers, and so on) but also of buildings and lands ascribed to the king's service. In addition, they were entrusted with the royal rights and the royal rents perceived locally. By the words used to describe these concessions—they were invested with "toda jurdiçom baixa E alta . . . mero misto Jnperio"[27] [whole jurisdiction high and low . . . absolute mixed Empire]—we could be driven to believe that, as far as jurisdiction was concerned, there were no limits imposed on the queens by their husbands. Nonetheless, several authors have already pointed out that the donation charters' statements should not be taken literally.[28] Some rights remained inseparable from the king's royal person, the most important of which was *correição maior*, a last resort appeal that included the possibility of proclaiming death sentences.[29] Consequently, from the sentences of the queens or their judges (*ouvidores* or *meirinhos*), appeals could still be made to the royal court of justice, where the king himself or his *corregedor* would have the last word.[30] To fully estimate the extent and the value of the property, rights and rents transferred by the kings to their wives in the queens' domains, it would be necessary to analyze the case of each of the donated towns. As it is impossible to do so in this chapter, we will present one case as an example.

There are three main documents that allow us to know what kind of prerogatives and revenue the queens enjoyed in Torres Vedras: the town's two charters of privileges (*forais*) and the inquiry that preceded the reformation of the old *foral*.[31] The first charter of privileges was conceded to Torres Vedras by Afonso III (king, 1245–79) in 1250. The town existed long before that, though, as it was a Moorish citadel that surrendered to the first king of Portugal after the conquest of Lisbon in 1147, probably without any fighting.[32] The reasons for this concession at a late date might be the scarce population and the incipient economic development of the urban center and its rural district that only started to show signs of being reverted in the second quarter of the thirteenth century.[33] Nevertheless, the king chose as model for the local charter of privileges the *foral* of Santarém-Coimbra-Lisboa of 1179 that was especially adequate for great cities with buoyant crafts and abundant commercial transactions. This contributed to the swift and intense growth of the town in the following decades.

Two and a half centuries later, however, many things had changed. Royal law had replaced local customs and rules, thus rendering useless a considerable part of the old *forais*. Currency had been devaluated several times and new coin had been minted, making the taxes fixed in cash in the charters of privileges obsolete. A reformation of the *forais* was asked for by the population and desired by the king, who was then restructuring the administration and centralizing the power. A commission was therefore nominated by him to prepare the reformation. It started to work shortly before 1496, making inquiries all over the country about the contents of the local *forais* and the royal charters that had granted more rights and privileges at later stages, and took twenty-five years to finish the task.[34] In the case of Torres Vedras, the remaining evidence of the inquiry is not dated but the new *foral* was issued in 1515.

Concerning the Crown's possessions that were transferred to the queens by the charters of donation, the inquiry reveals that the king owned the local market place and four shops nearby in Torres Vedras; the town's royal granary, wine press, and wine cellar; and, scattered in the countryside, four more wine-cellars, a few tenements [*casais*[35]], and the so-called *Reguengos*, vast royal estates that had been divided into lots handed over to peasant families for them to cultivate under contract. It was an important mass of landed and urban property that allowed the storage and processing of the crops, and generated a considerable income in cash and in kind.

From the lands of the *Reguengos*, the farmers had to deliver every year a fourth of the total production, twenty more *alqueires*[36] of mixed cereal—wheat and barley—as payment to the royal official (*mordomo*) who came to measure the grain, and a third of the output as repayment for the use of the royal mills. In contrast, the whole of the tenements only paid a sum in cash that did not exceed 800 *reais*.[37] For the use of the market place, the traders had to pay 2 *reais* for the selling of an ox or a cow; one *real* for each pack of dried fish, sardine, vegetables, or fruit brought to the stall, and a whiting for each pack of fresh fish; one small loin for the selling of a pig, and one *ceitil*[38] for the selling of a goat, an ewe or shellfish.[39]

Other sources let us know that the king also possessed locally the castle and the royal palace with its private chapel. Originally, the monarchs and the court took up quarters at the castle when they visited Torres Vedras. Beatriz of Guillén (queen, 1253–1303), the first recipient of the town,[40] bought several houses and pieces of ground outside the castle walls and had a palace built where she spent part of her widowhood. This palace was enlarged by her son, King Dinis, and became the usual dwelling place for the queens and their household during their stays in town.[41] By spending large periods there, they could keep their local officials under close scrutiny, listen to the complaints of their subjects, give responses to them, and therefore reinforce their fidelity. They could also consume the foodstuffs that were produced in their lands and wine-presses or received as rents, and sell the remainder at the market or have it stored until the prices were more rewarding. In addition to these buildings and lands, all the royal rights and rents the kings enjoyed in Torres Vedras were also transferred to the queens by the donation charters. As they are extremely varied, we have gathered them in three units to facilitate the analysis: monopolies and fiscal rights, jurisdictional rights, and patronage of the local churches.

Some of the monopolies concerned the means of production the townsmen needed to carry out their economic activities. By the old *foral*, they were free to build and to exploit baker's ovens, pottery furnaces, and all kinds of shops. But brick and roof-tile kilns were retained by the king, who imposed a tax of 10 percent of the output for their use.[42] However, the most important monopoly in this region was *relego*, concerning the selling of wine. As medieval wines were of bad quality and became deteriorated very easily, it was crucial to be able to sell them quickly.[43] In Torres Vedras, the king could sell his wine during the first three months of the year with no competition; only after this period, or after the exhaustion of his cellars, the wine of the other local producers could be sold as well. At first, this monopoly only concerned the sales in town: the boundaries within which it was enforced in 1250 by a royal charter included the urban center and the surrounding fields but not the entire rural area submitted to urban rule (*termo*).[44] Nevertheless, king Manuel I, in the new *foral*, extended the monopoly to the whole *termo* and fixed new instructions to prevent abuse: the wine delivered to the king as payment for taxes or as rent for tenements should be inspected and registered in a special book by the king's officials, so that no strange wine would be added to it and sold during the closed season. The wine that came from outside the region could be sold during that season but should be submitted to an additional tax (*relegagem*) of one *almude*[45] for each pack sold.[46]

As to other fiscal rights, all the economic agents involved in productive activities in town and in the countryside were expected to pay taxes to the Crown. Those who drew their support from agriculture paid specific taxes according to the means of production they had at their disposal. The more burdened were those who had at least one plough and two oxen, as they had to pay both the *jugada* and the *oitavo*. The latter consisted of one-eighth of the output of flax and wine; the former was at first a payment of one *moio*[47] of grain for each plough used in tilling the land.[48] Isabel of Lancaster (queen, 1447–55), in a period of economic crisis granted the local farmers the privilege to pay just 20 *alqueires* for as many ploughs as they wanted to use.[49] This privilege was renewed several times during the reign of Afonso V (king, 1438–81) until it was finally integrated in the new *foral* by Manuel I.[50]

Some of these rich farmers were exempt from the tax: those who were enrolled as knights and cross-bowmen in the local army,[51] the tenants of the church and the nobility who only tilled land belonging to their lords,[52] and a few other men who had managed to obtain fiscal privileges from the kings.[53] Nevertheless, most of them had to pay, and it was a heavy burden indeed. The peasants who did not possess a plough with the corresponding animals and had to rent or to borrow one to till their land only paid a fourth of the tribute. And those who could only use their hands and a hoe, the so-called diggers (*cavões*), paid a fourth of the fourth. Finally, the poorer who did not possess tools or lands and had to work for wages were totally exempt.[54] Associated to agriculture, cattle-breeding was also submitted at least to two impositions: the owners of animals that caused damage to the crops had to pay fines[55] and the escaped cattle (*gado do vento*) would revert on behalf of the king if the owners did not vindicate it and pay for the wrongs caused.[56] Where hunting is concerned, the old charter of privileges reports exclusively that rabbit-hunters should deliver a rabbit with its fur if they were locals or a tenth of the captured animals if they were outsiders.[57] Fishing was submitted to the old royal tax of 10 percent (*dízima do pescado*), which applied throughout the country,[58] and the new tax of 10 percent (*dízima nova*) that Afonso V imposed in 1458. Both were incorporated into the new *foral*.[59]

Crafts were not excessively burdened by taxation. We saw earlier that anyone could open a shop or a workshop and use it to manufacture and sell goods without being exposed to tributes; only those who hired the king's shops because they did not possess enough capital to invest in such business had to pay rents. But trade and transports were submitted to many different charges. A toll (*portagem*) was collected from all the goods that entered or left the town, excepted if they were foodstuffs brought by the residents for their own consumption, in which case no tax was due; locals could also be exempt of this tribute by paying once a year a small sum known as *soldada*. Therefore, the toll concerned almost exclusively foreigners who had to pay the king a small amount of money for each item sold in the marketplace (such as rough materials, animals, manufactured goods) or the tenth (*dízima*) of the whole pack.[60] The new *foral* maintained the *dízima* but fixed the other payments in new currency and rose them according to the inflation that had occurred since 1250.[61] As for transports, muleteers had to pay an annual sum known as *foro* that amounted to 20 *reais* in 1515, no matter how many donkeys or mules they had at their service. Knights and other privileged men who possessed good horses and used them to transport and sell goods were exempt of this tax.[62]

The last of the king's fiscal rights to be transmitted to the queens was taxation of ethnic and religious minorities. Free Muslims and Jews lived in Portugal under the immediate dependence upon the sovereigns, who protected them in exchange for a great number of taxes, tributes, and services.[63] In Torres Vedras, the presence of Jews has been documented only after the mid-thirteenth century but there are signs that they might have settled there even before the town fell in Christian hands, in 1147, or shortly after it.[64] The Jewish community with its separate quarter in the city (*Judiaria*) dates from the reign of Afonso IV.[65] According to local documents, the members of this community paid to the Crown the so-called old service (*serviço velho*), a sum of money in sign of submission and a percentage of each commercialized good, the "new service" (*serviço novo*) imposed by King João I (another amount of money), and also a tax for the right to have a religious education (*genesim*).[66] To manage the royal estates, collect all these taxes, chase the debtors, and try the causes concerning these matters, a great number of officials were necessary—counters, tax collectors, inquirers, judges, notaries—whose nomination or confirmation was also transferred from the kings to the queens.[67]

How much were all these rights and rents worth? Unfortunately, there are no consistent series of account books allowing us to answer that question satisfactorily. However, a few royal charters from the fifteenth century provide us with data that can be used in comparative terms. In 1450, queen Isabel of Lancaster gave an acquittance of 156,143 *reais* for the rents of Torres Vedras.[68] Eleven years later, when Afonso V decided to concede an annuity to his sister-in-law Filipa after the death of his wife, he fixed it in the rents of the same town that were worth then 180,000 *reais*. But he was careful to explain that this amount did not include the rent from the *reguengo* of Randide, which he had previously donated to Afonso de

Miranda, nor the rent of flax, equally donated but to Filipa Coutinho.[69] This sum was therefore inferior to the actual revenue offered by the town. Even if we take this into consideration, as we compare it to the revenue afforded in 1473 by other royal towns belonging to the queens, such as Óbidos (650,000 *reais*), Abrantes (457,000 *reais*), Sintra (380,500 *reais*), or Alenquer (355,000 *reais*),[70] we can clearly see that Torres Vedras was far from being in the first rank of urban wealth and had even lost ground to other towns that were originally its equals.

When we move our attention from the global amounts to specific sums we reach the same conclusion. After the banishment of the Jews from the kingdom in 1496,[71] Manuel I had to compensate several noblemen of his court for the loss of the taxes these Jews had to pay to the Crown, which he had donated to them. In 1499, because of the loss of the taxes on the Jewish communities of a few agglomerations, Martinho de Castelo Branco received 40,000 *reais* in royal rents from Torres Vedras, which were specified as follows: 26,034 *reais* from the *reguengo* of Coutada; 6,663 *reais* from the toll of Saint Peter's fair and 250 *reais* from the toll of Saint Sebastian's fair; 6,960 *reais* in rents from the tenements of Condado.[72] The rents from the Jews of Torres Vedras were then worth 12,640 *reais*.[73] It was not a considerable amount: in the same period, the rents from the Jewish community of the village of Arronches were worth 8,000 *reais* and those from a town like Tomar 31,777 *reais*.[74]

The administration of justice by the queens also generated income because certain crimes were punished with fines. In Torres Vedras, in 1250, breaking into the home of a town dweller in arms represented an expenditure of 200 *soldos*. The same amount should be paid for homicide and rape whereas insults and dirty words were punished with 60 *soldos* and theft with 540 *soldos*.[75] In 1515, these fines were extended to a new set of situations and converted to new currency.[76] They constituted a part of the remuneration of the *alcaide* who was simultaneously a justice official and the governor of the local castle. Another justice official, the *mordomo*, was also partially remunerated with another judicial royal right with economic consequences, the so-called tenth of the execution of sentences.[77]

The nomination of the justice officials—judges, enquirers, porters, jailers, and others besides the two already mentioned—belonged to the king and was transferred to the queens as well. The case of the *alcaide* is particular, though, and needs further attention. The military command, as the supreme justice, was considered *regalia* that should never be alienated from the person of the king. However, we know that the right to appoint the military governor of the castle of Torres Vedras, among others, was specifically conceded at least to queen Beatriz of Guillén.

The eventual appointee would have to swear allegiance to the king and be confirmed by him in the office.[78] Isabel of Aragón also received from her husband the right to choose the *alcaides* of her castles under the same conditions.[79] But there is no evidence that any queen ever actually used this prerogative: all the nomination charters that we have found in Torres Vedras proceed from the monarchs.[80] The governors defended the castle and commanded the local contingent of troops in case of war. They had under their orders the captains who were responsible for the recruitment, inspection, and training of the crossbowmen who served afoot or on horseback, according to their fortune; again, we have no evidence that any of these officials were ever nominated by the queens.[81] It was the governors' duty to keep the castle and the city walls in good condition and to undertake repairs if necessary, for which they could use compelled work from the inhabitants of the town and the surrounding countryside. The *alcaides* were also responsible for maintaining peace and order, namely by serving warrants and watching prisoners, which they did through minor officials chosen by them. This gave them an extensive power of coercion. Together with the city council, they elected the municipal officials who were in charge of inspecting the local market and judging minor economic crimes, the *almotacés*, who were remunerated by the produce of a tax that was collected on foodstuffs sold at the market (*almotaçaria*). The queens also appointed the writing officials who wrote all the necessary documents: not only the clerks (*escrivãos*) adjoined to the court of justice and the seigniorial administration but also the public notaries (*tabeliães*) that drew up all the deeds; each of the latter paid the queens a tax for the use of their office. In the reign of King Dinis, there were five *tabeliães* in Torres Vedras and they paid 150 *libras*.[82] Less than a century later, they were already nine[83] and the amount paid had certainly increased accordingly. In 1515, it had reached 1,212 *reais*.[84]

The last of the rights that the queens generally received from their husbands were the rights of patronage on the four local collegiate churches. They consisted of the presentation of the dean and of some of the canons to the bishop for him to confirm their nomination to the benefice. The queen and her retinue could also take up lodgings in the premises, be fed when visiting the church, and receive subsidies in special cases.[85] We found no evidence that either the queens or the kings ever exerted the latter, as they had a palace in town, but several kings used the presentation to local church benefices to reward clerics who had served them loyally and to place their own churchmen as heads of these important clerical institutions to control them thereafter.[86] Apparently, only one queen, Beatriz of Guillén, did the same.[87]

In conclusion, we may say that the queens received a very wide set of property, rights, and revenues in Torres Vedras as in their other estates, but they did not always make the most of it. We do know that they used these estates as a source of income, for there are many complaints from the local inhabitants to the king about their excessive fiscal exigency.[88] It was this income that allowed them to maintain their retinue, be generous to the poor, and act as patrons of the church and the arts.[89] We also know that the queens were effective in their intervention in local affairs because, on one hand, they often protested against the obstacles the king's officials put in their way. On the other hand, they overflowed their prerogatives by submitting the king's charters to their approval before letting them be proclaimed locally and by appointing their own officials to charges whose nomination belonged to the city council.[90] Yet when they did nominate their officials, the men they chose did not always belong to their household. Among the queens' officials in Torres Vedras, we have found more vassals, esquires, and servants of the king, the princes, other local lords, and the castle governors than those of the queens.[91]

Even when the queens had the right to appoint very influential magistrates and ecclesiastics such as the castle governors and the deans of the collegiate churches, they did not always use it to reward noblemen of their court and clerics of their chapel: they often benefited the king's or other lords' men.[92] Consequently, the queens' household and domain do not appear to have constituted a parallel power, a potential source of conflict and opposition to the king, as it sometimes happened with other seigniorial households, but rather an extension of the royal court and the Crown estates that the king could rely on in case of need.[93]

**Table 11.1** Portuguese royal marriages

| *Queens of Portugal* | *Date of Wedding* | *Origin* |
|---|---|---|
| Mafalda (Mahaut) | 1146 | Savoy |
| Dulce of Aragón | 1174 | Aragon |
| Urraca of Castile | 1208/9 | Castile |
| Mécia Lopez of Haro | 1245 | Biscaia/León |
| Beatriz of Guillén | 1246 | Castile |
| Isabel of Aragón | 1281 | Aragón |
| Beatriz of Castile | 1309 | Castile |
| Constança Manuel | 1340 | Castile |
| Leonor Teles de Meneses | 1372 | Portugal |
| Filipa of Lancaster | 1387 | England |
| Leonor of Aragón | 1428 | Aragón |
| Isabel of Lancaster | 1447 | Portugal |
| Leonor of Lancaster | 1471 | Portugal |

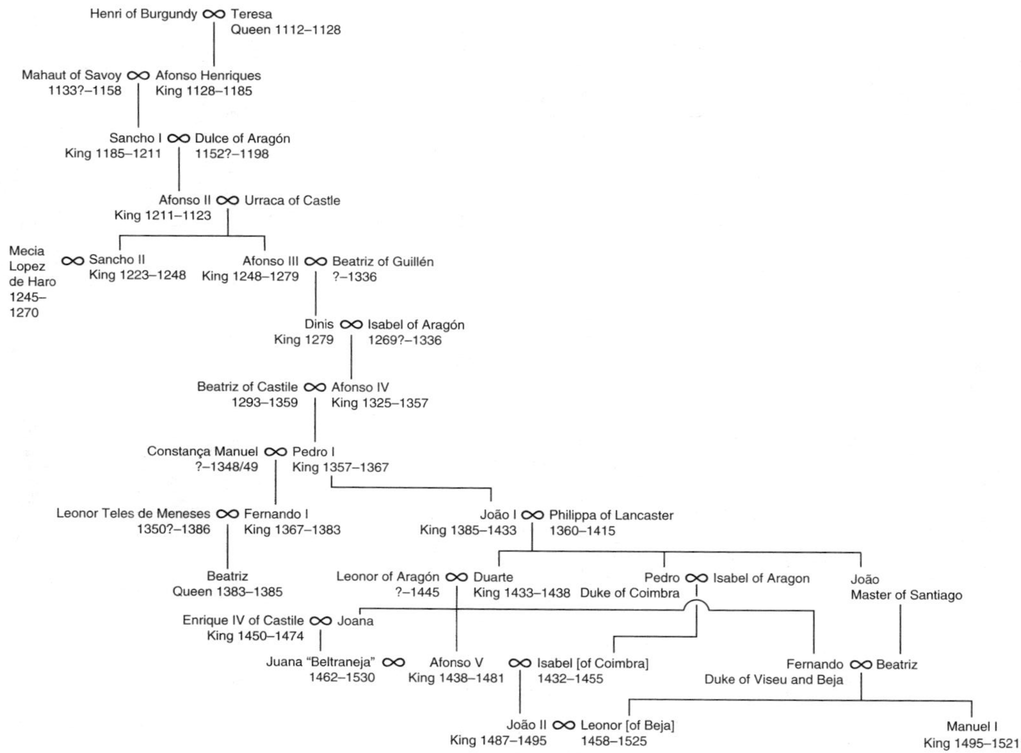


**Figure 11.1** Portuguese royal family

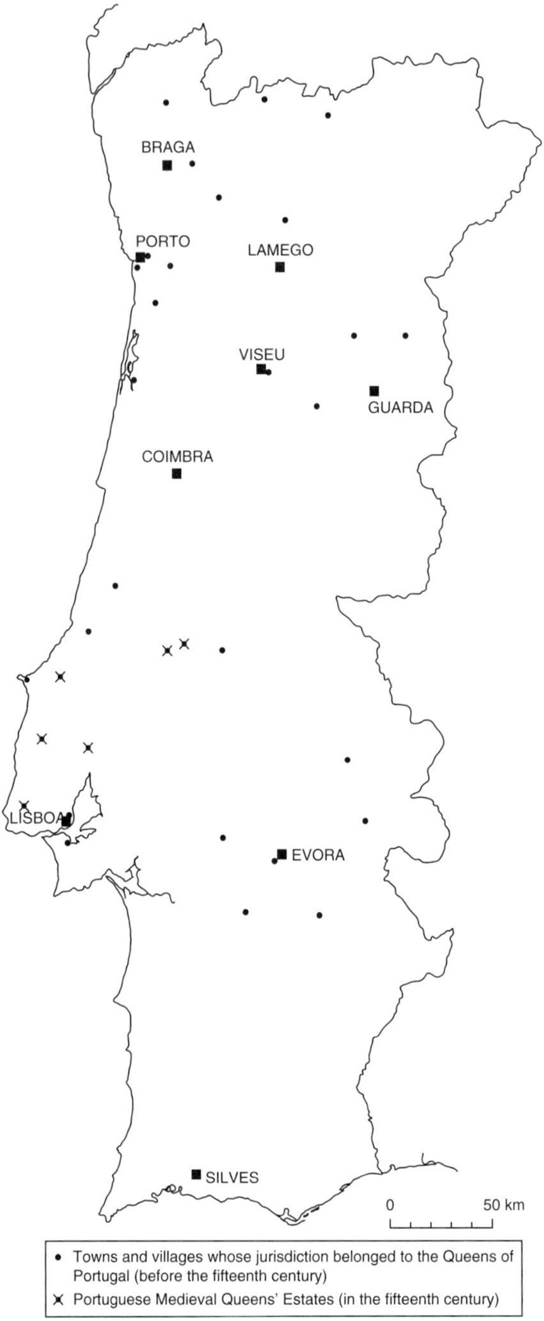


**Figure 11.2** The Queens' patrimony

## Notes

1. "Johan par la grace de Dieu Roy de Castille et Leon de Tolide etc.," *John of Gaunt's Register*, ed. Sydney Armitage-Smith, 2 vols., Camden Third Series, vol. 20 (London: Offices of the Society, 1911), vol. I, doc. 322, p. 138. "...Duque d Alancrasto, que era casado com dona Costança filha que ffora del Rey dom Pero, por cujo azo se o dito Duque chamava Rey de Castela...." See also the Portuguese chronicler Fernão Lopes, *Crónica de D. João I*, ed. Anselmo Braamcamp Freire, 2 vols. (Oporto: Livraria Civilização, 1979), vol. II, p. 112.
2. A. H. de Oliveira Marques, *Portugal na crise dos séculos XIV e XV* (Lisbon: Presença, 1987), p. 532.
3. Fernão Lopes, *Crónica de D. Fernando*, ed. Salvador Dias Arnaut (Oporto: Livraria Civilização, 1979), pp. 159–60.
4. A similar case of mismatch in the crown of Aragon is presented in this volume by Núria Silleras-Fernández, "Money Isn't Everything: Concubinage, Class and the Rise and Fall of Sibil.la de Fortià, Queen of Aragon (1377–87)."
5. Maria Paula Marçal Lourenço, "O Domínio Senhorial da Casa das Rainhas (1642–1781): Património, Estado e Poder," in *Amar, Sentir e Viver a História. Estudos de Homenagem a Joaquim Veríssimo Serrão*, 2 vols. (Lisbon: Colibri, 1995), II: 985–1004, esp. p. 988.
6. Francisco da Fonseca Benevides, *Rainhas de Portugal. Estudo Histórico com muitos documentos*, 2 vols. (Lisbon: Typographia Castro Irmão, 1878), vol. I, pp. 161–62.
7. D. António Caetano de Sousa, *Provas da História Genealógica da Casa Real Portuguesa*, 2nd edn., 12 vols. (Coimbra: Atlântida, 1947), vol. II, no. 42, p. 275.
8. "Testament of John, Duke of Lancaster": "xxiii. Item. I leave to my very dear daughter, Philippa, Queen of Portugal, my second best circlet of gold and covered gold chalice." Anil de Silva-Vigier, *The Moste Highe Prince...John of Gaunt, 1340–1399* (Edinburgh-Cambridge-Durham: Pentland Press, 1992), p. 371.
9. Philippa of Lancaster took with her a very high figure of the English diplomacy as her chancellor, apart from the customary ladies-in-waiting. William J. Entwistle and Peter E. Russel, "A Rainha D. Felipa e a sua corte," in *Memórias e Comunicações—Congresso do Mundo Português*, 19 vols. (Lisbon: Comissão Executiva dos Centenários, 1940), vol. II: 317–46, esp. p. 336.
10. Paulo Merêa, "Um problema filológico-jurídico: a palavra 'arras,'" *Novos Estudos de História do Direito* (Barcelos: Ed. do Minho, 1937), pp. 139–49, esp. p. 139.
11. Frederico Francisco de la Figanière, *Memorias das Rainhas de Portugal (D. Theresa—Santa Isabel)* (Lisbon: Typographia Universal, 1859), p. xiii.
12. Benevides, *Rainhas de Portugal*, vol. I, p. 4.
13. Figanière, *Memorias das Rainhas de Portugal*, p. xviii. Ana Maria S. A. Rodrigues noticed that in the marriage contracts of the fifteenth century,

these crude expressions had been replaced by "for the honor of her lineage and body," and "for the honor of her lineage and person." "For the honor of her lineage and body: The dowers and dowries of some late medieval queens of Portugal," *e-Journal of Portuguese History* 5:1 (2007) 3: 1–13.

14. Isabel Beceiro Pita, "Los dominios de la familia real castellana (1250–1350)," *Génesis medieval del Estado Moderno: Castilla y Navarra (1250–1370)* (Valladolid: Ambito Editores, 1987), pp. 79–106, esp. p. 99.
15. J. P. Franco Monteiro, *As Donatarias de Alenquer: História das Rainhas de Portugal e da sua casa e estado* (Lisbon: M. Gomes Editor, 1893), pp. 1–3; Ruy d'Abreu Torres, "Rainhas, Casa das," in *Dicionário de História de Portugal*, ed. Joel Serrão, 6 vols. (Oporto: Livraria Figueirinhas, 1981), vol. V: 230–32, esp. p. 230.
16. Lisbon, Instituto dos Arquivos Nacionais/ Torre do Tombo (IAN/TT), Chancelaria de D. Dinis, L. 1, fols. 41, 201–201v.
17. IAN/TT, Chancelaria de D. Pedro I, L. 1, fol. 1. Benevides, *Rainhas de Portugal*, I: 187–88.
18. Benevides, *Rainhas de Portugal*, I: 199–200.
19. On this, see Maria Cristina Pimenta, *D. Pedro I* (Lisbon: Círculo de Leitores, 2003).
20. IAN/TT, Chancelaria de D. Fernando, L. 2, fol. 60B.
21. As Ana Maria Rodrigues puts it: "Leonor Teles [queen, 1372–83] was already married to João Lourenço da Cunha when Fernando I fell in love with her and the annulment of this matrimony was requested in haste for them to be able to sanctify their union. As a result, the king himself had to make a donation *propter nuptias* to his wife 'as dowry and dower' [. . .] because her family had not yet recovered economically from the loss of her first dowry" as "the law determined that the adulterous wife lost her dowry to the deceived husband." Rodrigues, "For the honor of her lineage and body," p. 4.
22. IAN/TT, *Estremadura*, L.5, fols. 5v-6v; L.7, fol. 167v.
23. Manuela Santos Silva, "Óbidos *Terra que foi da Rainha D. Filipa.* O Senhorio de Óbidos de 1415 a 1428," *A Região de Óbidos na Época Medieval. Estudos* (Caldas da Rainha: Património Histórico, 1994), pp. 85–110, esp. pp. 92–93.
24. Manuela Santos Silva, "Notícia sobre a segunda doação régia de Alenquer, Óbidos e Sintra à Rainha D. Leonor de Lencastre (Évora, 15 de Abril de 1491)," in *A Região de Óbidos na Época Medieval*, pp. 111–20, esp. p. 113.
25. Manuela Mendonça, *D. João II. Um percurso humano e político nas origens da modernidade* (Lisbon: Estampa, 1991) pp. 454–66.
26. Ivo Carneiro de Sousa, *A Rainha D. Leonor (1458–1525). Poder, misericórdia, religiosidade e espiritualidade no Portugal do Renascimento* (Lisbon: FCG/ FCT, 2002), pp. 148–58.
27. Óbidos, Arquivo Histórico da Câmara Municipal de Óbidos, Livro do Tombo do Concelho, fols. 11–13.
28. J. L. Bermejo Cabrero, "Mayoría de Justicia del Rey y Jurisdicciones Señoriales en la Baja Edad Media Castellana," *Actas de las I Jornadas de*

*Metodología Aplicada de las Ciencias Históricas. Vol. 2: Historia Medieval* (Santiago de Compostela: Universidad de Santiago de Compostela, 1975), pp. 207–215, esp. p. 207.

29. Eduardo Borges Nunes, ed., *Ordenaçoens do Senhor Rey D. Afonso V,* 5 vols. (Lisbon: Fundação Calouste Gulbenkian, 1984), II: 294–95.
30. Marcelo Caetano, *História do Direito Português (1140–1495)* (Lisbon: Verbo, 1981), pp. 330–31.
31. Alexandre Herculano, ed., *Portugaliae Monumenta Historica. Leges et consuetudines,* 2 vols. (Lisbon: Academia das Ciências de Lisboa, 1856), 1: 634–36; Luís Fernando de Carvalho Dias, ed., *Forais Manuelinos do Reino de Portugal e do Algarve conforme o exemplar do Arquivo Nacional da Torre do Tombo de Lisboa,* 5 vols. (Beja: Soc. Editora Ala Esquerda, 1962), 3: 45–47. IAN/TT, Gaveta XX–12–41.
32. Manuela Santos Silva, "Alguns passos da acção do Conquistador na Estremadura litoral: o caso específico da região envolvente de Óbidos," *2º Congresso Histórico de Guimarães "D. Afonso Henriques e a sua Época,"* 6 vols. (Guimarães: Câmara Municipal de Guimarães/Universidade do Minho, 1997), 2: 109–16, esp. p. 113.
33. António Balcão Vicente, Carlos Guardado da Silva, Pedro Gomes Barbosa, and Pedro Marujo do Canto, *O Foral Medieval da Vila de Torres Vedras 15 de Agosto de 1250* (Torres Vedras: Câmara Municipal de Torres Vedras-Cultura, 2001), pp. 10–11.
34. João José Alves Dias, Isabel M. R. Mendes Drumond Braga, and Paulo Drumond Braga, "A Conjuntura," *Portugal do Renascimento à crise dinástica,* ed. João José Alves Dias (Lisbon: Presença, 1998), 689–760, esp. p. 714.
35. The word *casal* has two meanings: it means a couple but also the productive unit that can provide for a couple and his children.
36. The *alqueire* was a measure of capacity that varied from 14 kg to 18 kg, according to the region.
37. IAN/TT, Gav. XX–12–41. The *real* was an account currency (*moeda de conta*); at this date, there were 25,840 *reais* in a golden mark and 2,400 *reais* in a silver mark.
38. The *ceitil* was a copper coin worth 1/6 of the *real* at this date.
39. Dias, *Forais Manuelinos,* 3: 47.
40. Ana Maria Seabra de Almeida Rodrigues, *Torres Vedras. A vila e o termo nos finais da Idade Média* (Lisbon: FCG/JNICT, 1995), p. 466.
41. Rodrigues, *Torres Vedras,* pp. 172–74.
42. Herculano, *Portugaliae Monumenta Historica, Leges,* 1: 634, and Dias, *Forais Manuelinos,* 3: 47.
43. Mário Viana, *Os vinhedos medievais de Santarém* (Cascais: Patrimonia, 1998), pp. 150–58.
44. IAN/TT, Corporações Religiosas, Alcobaça, m. 8, no. 3.
45. The *almude* was a measure of capacity that varied from 14 to 18 liters, according to the region.
46. Dias, *Forais Manuelinos,* 3: 46.
47. The *moio* was a measure of capacity worth 56 *alqueires.*

48. Herculano, *Portugaliae Monumenta Historica, Leges*, 1: 634–35.
49. J. M. Cordeiro de Sousa, ed., *Fontes Medievais de História Torreana* (Torres Vedras: Câmara Municipal, 1958), vol. 68, p. 78.
50. Sousa, *Fontes Medievais*, LXXII, pp. 84–85 and Dias, *Forais Manuelinos*, 3: 46.
51. Herculano, *Portugaliae Monumenta Historica, Leges*, 1: 635.
52. Nunes, *Ordenaçoens do Senhor Rey D. Afonso V*, L. II, pp. 243–69.
53. Ana Maria S. A. Rodrigues, "A sociedade urbana torriense e os privilegiados da coroa," *Espaço, gente e sociedade no Oeste: Estudos sobre Torres Vedras medieval* (Cascais: Patrimonia, 1996), pp. 291–316, esp. p. 302.
54. Herculano, *Portugaliae Monumenta Historica, Leges*, 1: 635.
55. The whole of these fines was called *renda do verde* and is reported among the royal rights and rents of Torres Vedras donated by Isabel of Castile, in 1492, to Rodrigo de Meneses and confirmed by Manuel I to the donee's daughter, Joana, in 1500. See Sousa, *Fontes Medievais*, 95: 131–32 and 102: 144–47.
56. Dias, *Forais Manuelinos*, 3: 47.
57. Herculano, *Portugaliae Monumenta Historica, Leges*, 1: 635.
58. Henrique da Gama Barros, *História da administração pública em Portugal nos séculos XIII a XV*, Torquato de Sousa Soares, ed., 11 vols. (Lisbon: Sá da Costa, 1945-54), 9: 285–89.
59. Dias, *Forais Manuelinos*, 3: 47.
60. Herculano, *Portugaliae Monumenta Historica, Leges*, 1: 635.
61. Dias, *Forais Manuelinos*, 3: 47.
62. Herculano, *Portugaliae Monumenta Historica, Leges*, 1: 635 and Dias, *Forais Manuelinos*, 3: 46.
63. On them see Maria José Pimenta Ferro Tavares, *Os Judeus em Portugal no século XV*, 2 vols. (Lisbon: Universidade Nova–FCSH, 1982), 1: 159–98; and Maria Filomena Barros, *A Comuna muçulmana de Lisboa: sécs. XIV e XV* (Lisbon: Hugin, 1998), pp. 6–70.
64. Pedro Ferreira Gomes Barbosa, *Grupos marginais nos documentos de Santa Maria de Alcobaça (séculos XII e XIII)* (Lisbon: Faculdade de Letras, 1988), p. 11; and Rodrigues, *Torres Vedras*, p. 578.
65. Rodrigues, *Torres Vedras*, pp. 130–33 and 579.
66. Sousa, *Fontes Medievais*, 45: 50–51; 95: 131–32; and 102: 144–47.
67. IAN/TT, Ch. D. Afonso V, L. 13, fols. 128, 138v, 143-143v, 144v, 155v; Gav. XIV–8–8, XV–24–8, XV–5–9, XV–9–31. Corpo Cronológico, P. I, m. 1, no. 49.
68. IAN/TT, Chancelaria de D. Afonso V, L. 3, fol. 29.
69. IAN/TT, Místicos, L. 3, fols. 230v–3.
70. Jorge Faro, *Receitas e despesas da fazenda real de 1384 a 1481 (Subsídios documentais)* (Lisbon: Instituto Nacional de Estatística, 1965), pp. 83–84.
71. On this dramatic event, see Francisco Bethencourt, "A Expulsão dos Judeus," *O Tempo de Vasco da Gama*, Diogo Ramada Curto, ed. (Lisbon: CNCDP/Difel, 1998), pp. 271–80.
72. IAN/TT, Místicos, L. 4, fols. 94–5 (as it often happens in medieval documents, the addition of the parts do not correspond to the total amount).

73. IAN/TT, Místicos, L. 4, fols. 64–65.
74. Tavares, *Os Judeus*, pp. 166–67.
75. Herculano, *Portugaliae Monumenta Historica, Leges*, 1: 634.
76. Dias, *Forais Manuelinos*, 3: 46.
77. Dias, *Forais Manuelinos*, 3: 46–47.
78. IAN/TT, Ch. D. Afonso III, L. 1, fol. 159v.
79. Manuela Santos Silva, *Estruturas Urbanas e Administração concelhia: Óbidos Medieval* (Cascais: Patrimonia, 1997), pp. 131–32.
80. IAN/TT, Ch. D. Fernando, L. 2, fol. 78, L. 3, fol. 38v. Ch. D. João I, L. 2, fol. 26. Ch. D. Afonso V, L. 33, fol. 38. Ch. D. João II, L. 11, fol. 13v. Estremadura, L. 10, fol. 293 v. A. H. de Oliveira Marques, ed., *Chancelarias Portuguesas. D. Pedro I (1357–1367)* (Lisbon: INIC/CEH, 1984), no. 13, p. 7. The same seems to have happened in two other towns belonging to the queen, Óbidos and Alenquer. Silva, *Estruturas urbanas*, pp. 132–34; João Pedro Ferro, *Alenquer Medieval (Séculos XII-XV). Subsídios para o seu estudo* (Cascais: Patrimonia, 1996), p. 258.
81. IAN/TT, Ch. D. Afonso V, L. 2, fol. 41v, L. 3, fol. 88, L. 11, fol. 66, L. 13, fols. 179v, 181, L. 25, fol. 89, among others.
82. A. H. de Oliveira Marques, "A população portuguesa nos fins do século XIII," *Ensaios de História Medieval*, 2nd ed. (Lisbon: Vega, 1980), pp. 195–220, esp. p. 6.
83. Ana Maria S. A. Rodrigues, "A população de Torres Vedras em 1381," *Espaços, gente e sociedade*, pp. 45–84, esp. p. 68.
84. Dias, *Forais Manuelinos*, 3: 47.
85. Ana Maria S. A. Rodrigues, "As colegiadas de Torres Vedras nos séculos XIV e XV," *Espaços, gente e sociedade*, pp. 195–274, esp. 197–200.
86. IAN/TT, Gav. XIX–6–31, XIX–14–3, fols. 54, 55v, 58, 58v. Padroados, L. 1, fols. 6, 12, 103v–104, L. 2, fols. 4, 9v, 30v. Marques, *Chancelarias Portuguesas. D. Pedro I*, no. 517, p. 209; no. 690, p. 320; no. 843, p. 386; no. 918, p. 423; no. 992, p. 465.
87. IAN/TT, Gav. XIX–15–36.
88. Silva, "Óbidos," pp. 96–7; Silva, *Estruturas urbanas*, p. 135; Rodrigues, *Torres Vedras*, pp. 493–94.
89. The patronage of queens and other powerful women is discussed in this book by Erin L. Jordan, "Exploring the Limits of Female Largesse: The Power of Female Patrons in Thirteenth-century Flanders and Hainaut" and Helen A. Gaudette, "The Spending Power of a Crusader Queen: Melisende of Jerusalem."
90. Silva, "Óbidos," p. 91; Silva, *Estruturas urbanas*, pp. 136–37; Maria Helena da Cruz Coelho, "Relações de domínio no Portugal concelhio de meados de Quatrocentos," *Revista Portuguesa de História* 35 (1990): 235–89, esp. p. 256; Rodrigues, *Torres Vedras*, p. 481.
91. Ana Maria S. A. Rodrigues, "Poderes concorrentes e seus agentes na Torres Vedras quatrocentista," in *Amar, Sentir e Viver a História. Estudos de Homenagem a Joaquim Veríssimo Serrão*, 2 vols. (Lisbon: Colibri, 1995), 1: 49–73, esp. pp. 63–64. The same seems to have happened in

Alenquer, as is shown in the tables published by Ferro, *Alenquer Medieval*, pp. 58–67.

92. It has been shown that even some of the highest posts of the queens' household were held by the king's vassals. Rita Gomes, *The Making of a Court Society. Kings and Nobles in Late Medieval Portugal* (Cambridge: Cambridge University Press, 2003), pp. 59–60.
93. The same seems to have happened in the Crown of Aragon, as shown in this book by Theresa Earenfight, "Royal Finances in the Reign of María of Castile, Queen-Lieutenant of the Crown of Aragon, 1432–53."

CHAPTER 12

# ROYAL FINANCES IN THE REIGN OF MARÍA OF CASTILE, QUEEN-LIEUTENANT OF THE CROWN OF ARAGON, 1432–53

*Theresa Earenfight*

Medieval royal finances reflected the complex amalgam of the commingling of institutional, personal, legal, and spiritual so neatly captured in Ernst Kantorowicz's famous formulation of the king's two bodies.[1] But there is more than one twinned body in a monarchy, and it belongs to the queen. This is, of course, self-evident, yet until recently the queen was rarely, if ever, included in scholarly considerations of the royal fisc.[2] Scholarly interest in queens has surged since the 1970s and two studies, both concerned with England, led the way for the study of queens and money—Margaret Howell's work on the Queen's Gold in the reign of Eleanor of Provence and John Carmi Parsons's analysis of the fiscal accounts of Eleanor of Castile.[3] This chapter is not, however, a quantitative study of a queen's household accounts, personal wealth, and income and expenditures. I am interested in the power relations between the queen and king and how getting and spending of money is both the driving force in this relationship and a precise indicator of other, more subtle, forms of power and influence mediated by gender and the wider political culture. As Helen Gaudette, Ana Maria Rodrigues, and Manuela Santos Silva point out in their studies of queens and royal finances in this volume, queens may be loftier than other women and most men, but they are subordinate to a king. The household economy ruled even at this level of society. They operated within a unique monetary zone that was simultaneously private and public.

In the medieval Crown of Aragon, reginal finances are more complex than elsewhere because since the early fourteenth century Aragonese queens were also governmental lieutenants with broad authority. This distinctive job description meant that an Aragonese queen-lieutenant's finances had not two, but three separate components. Like other queens, she had a private account for her personal wealth, which derived from her natal family, was under her control alone, and could be bequeathed as she chose. Also like her counterparts elsewhere in Europe, as queen she had a household account and cadre of officials to tend to her personal needs and that of her immediate family. This account, similar to that for the Portuguese queens described by Rodrigues and Santos Silva, is known in the Crown of Aragon as the *Cambra de la Reyna*. It was not the queen's per se but was earmarked specifically for her as queen to support the costs of sustaining her household, her donations, her building campaigns, and her patronage. But as queen-lieutenant, an Aragonese queen had an additional financial account that was also part of the royal treasury and supervised by a bureaucracy and a staff of officials who handled the fiscal administration of the peninsular realm(s) she governed. This account was designated for the expenses incurred by her through her office of queen-lieutenant to pay her administrative expenses and the salaries of her staff of lawyers, secretaries, and assistants. But, because both the reginal and the lieutenant's account were funded by the royal treasury, there was the potential for considerable confusion and wiggle room for inventive fiscal officers in the fifteenth century trying to balance the royal budget. This distinctive institutional situation raises a number of questions: How much control did Aragonese queens-lieutenants have over their various accounts—personal, reginal, or that of the queen-lieutenant? How clear was the separation between her personal finances and those of the realm? What does this mean in terms of the legal and fiscal relationship between the queen's own finances and the royal treasury? What does this suggest about the financial limits of a queen's political power, authority, and influence?

To explore these questions, I take as an example Queen María of Castile,[4] wife of Alfonso V "the Magnanimous," king of the Crown of Aragon (1416–58).[5] She governed Catalunya from 1420 to 1423 and again from 1432 to 1453 while her husband was occupied with the conquest and governance of the kingdom of Naples.[6] For an unprecedented twenty-six years she had control over the provincial governors, prelates and religious orders, the nobility, the army, the municipal government, and all other subjects regardless of legal status. She could grant constitutions and make laws in accordance with royal authority and could sign letters in her own hand according to her own conscience. She was empowered to carry out justice, both civil and criminal, and to name judges and delegates. Assisted by a royal council separate from the king's, she had full royal authority in Catalunya.[7] Her decades-long tenure as queen-lieutenant has left behind an impressive number of extant archival material that permits a unique opportunity to study financing the queen as queen-lieutenant over time yet within a single reign.

As Lieutenant General, she had the authority to receive all royal income; to make and sign orders for subsidies; and could freely spend any money not earmarked specifically for Naples. The ultimate fiscal decision-making power lied in Alfonso's hands, not hers, but her considerable *de jure* authority grew in proportion to the length of the king's absence.[8] With Alfonso, she shared responsibility for the chief officials of the justice, chancery, and, most important for the issue at hand, the finance departments. Thus, both bureaucratic overlap and time and long distances made for a cumbersome arrangement. In the *privilegio* of 1420, and all its subsequent emendations, Alfonso gave María leeway in financial administration. Although he delegated fiscal authority to María, Alfonso still preferred to supervise his finances from a central treasury.[9] This worked well up to a point. Transfers of money, goods, and letters of credit were handled efficiently enough when the realm was relatively small and compact, but the addition of the kingdom of Naples strained the system. Even the most efficient treasurer could not be everywhere at once, and financial administration in Catalunya, the wealthiest of the realms of the Crown of Aragon and home of most of the royal demesne lands, was problematic. Because Catalunya was more populous than the kingdoms of Valencia and Aragón, and its commerce more extensive, it took more time and effort to collect subsidies, taxes, tolls, and rents. As the seat of María's court, it required a larger staff than in Valencia, and the management of the royal patrimony was more complicated than in Aragón.[10] Although both the *Mestre Racional*— a chief auditor, the financial equivalent of the chancellor who supervised the accounts of officials of both the royal patrimony and the treasury, both the king's and the queen's—and the treasurer of Catalunya technically were subordinate to the treasurer general in Naples, they possessed a formidable array of judicial and executive powers and substantial discretionary authority.[11] The Mestre Racional of each constituent realm was responsible for the collection and disbursal of all royal funds; he controlled allowances in money and in kind given to members of the royal household; and he directed judicial inquiries into allegations of misconduct by officials employed in any financial office.[12] In concert with the queen-lieutenant's chamberlain (*camarlench*) who managed the household finances, on paper at least, María had considerable flexibility and control over expenditures.

Disputes over money, particularly fiscal shortfalls in the Catalan treasury, arose between Alfonso and María. There was more at stake than just a struggle for control of money. It was indicative of a wider problem that afflicted the Crown of Aragon during Alfonso's reign. Improved accounting practices and centralized control could not solve the persistent problem of insufficient income. The economy of most of the Crown realms prospered in general during Alfonso's reign, but the prosperity was by no means uniform. The Catalan economy had been in a slump since the mid-1420s, and it was showing only feeble signs of recovery. This sluggishness, due to structural defects in the economy and expensive Italian wars, limited its competitive strength, resulted in a decrease in the volume of trade, which in turn led to a decline of the taxable wealth.[13] Alfonso engaged in many wars, which ordinarily direct the flow of "monetary current" toward the capital city, but when Naples displaced Barcelona, a negative cash flow in Barcelona resulted. As the costs of business rose and currency was devalued, ordinary revenues did not yield a substantial surplus over the sums necessary for ordinary government.[14]

Routine subsidies and forced loans from the Iberian realms were not enough to support the cost of routine trans-Mediterranean government plus the burden of protracted warfare in Italy, the Mediterranean, and Castile. In a state of war, which was common throughout the 1440s and early 1450s, Alfonso's revenues fell short of his needs by between 200,000 and 300,000 ducats a year. This sum had to be raised in Spain and Italy by customary aids, grants from the parliamentary assembly (*Corts*), clerical subsidies, indirect taxation, sale of offices and privileges, fines, and loans.[15] Alfonso's initial response was to appeal to his subjects for more money, more often. He had little difficulty with the parliamentary assemblies of Aragón and Valencia whose economies were stable, even prosperous at times, but the Catalans felt they had borne the brunt of taxation and military expenditures and they made demands that he was unwilling to grant. In return for their money, they wanted more power. They insisted that the king's council be chosen with the consent of the Corts, that the *Audiència* should render judgments independently of the king, and that royal orders that violated the constitutions or *Usatges* of Catalunya were to be nullified.[16]

Enormous debts from wars in Italy, peasant unrest in Catalunya and Majorca, commercial stagnation in Barcelona, and the high cost of long-distance government put great strain on the treasury. Alfonso's testy relationship with ruling elites in Barcelona over taxation, which the Catalans considered excessive for what they felt they should be getting in return, and the king's two-decades-long absence added to the problem. With María governing the peninsular realms, Alfonso studiously avoided confronting the Catalans over taxes and sought alternative sources to finance his government. One of these alternatives was the systematic recovery of properties alienated from the royal patrimony.

On the face of it, recovering lands alienated from the royal patrimony and streamlining fiscal accounting are good things. Medieval monarchs were careful to protect their patrimony and all lands acquired during their reign, and the legal concept of inalienability of sovereignty, and since the reign of Jaume II there had been a clear tendency to treat Crown lands as a single entity, especially when it came to endowing sons with lands.[17] In this, the kings were only occasionally successful. Problems arose in Majorca and Sicily over the status of cadet princes. Second and third wives wanted to provide land and money for their children. And there were always allies to compensate for loyal service. So, by 1400, enough of the Crown lands had slipped out of the royal treasury that kings, starting with Martí in 1399, began a conscientious effort to recover the alienated lands.

From the king's perspective, this is all to the good. Steady, reliable income from royal lands guaranteed smooth and reasonably predictable revenue streams that gave some hope of prudent fiscal management. A royal treasury that lives mostly off the income from its own properties was less likely to overtax its subjects. Of course, convincing a lord—secular or clerical—to relinquish very desirable—and even some not so desirable—properties called for tremendous persuasive talents. And yet, with enough bait—legal action, usually accompanied by a military threat, coupled with lifetime grants of the revenue from a property in exchange for certain privileges usually did the trick—they did indeed relinquish those lands, especially during Alfonso's reign. Seeing royal finances only from the king's point of view shows a rosy picture. Seen from the queen's point of view, however, a much less appealing scene comes into view. My purpose here is to describe Aragonese royal finances form the queen's perspective.

At issue are two related developments that on the surface seem harmless, and in fact, are fiscally sound, but which proved harmful to María's ability to manage her financial affairs. First, to maximize income with a minimum of entailments, Alfonso tightened up administrative control from Naples. He wanted to control all fiscal decisions from Naples, which is not a bad thing per se. In fact, it was a good idea given the ever-present problem of corruption among fiscal officers who are far removed from the king himself. But he also cast his eye on María's own treasury and her financial officials, which traditionally were under the exclusive purview of the queen and her treasurer. Second, in his pursuit of both money and control over it, he left no resources untouched, even those of his wife. As he cast his eye around for revenue, he spied the Cambra de la Reyna, properties, lands and revenues, at least some of which had been the queen's since the reign of Jaume I in the 1300s, and began to bring them under direct management of the royal patrimony. In so doing, he began to undo a precedent and a practice nearly 200 years old, with important implications for women and money.

Alfonso's fiscal reforms early in his reign centered on the office of the Mestre Racional. In 1419 Alfonso instituted a separate Mestre Racional for Valencia and did the same for Aragón and Catalunya later.[18] Having a separate Mestre Racional who controlled the accounts of both the treasury and the royal patrimony, coupled with a chamberlain (*camarlench*) who managed the household finances, gave each lieutenant greater flexibility and control over expenditures than before. But after the conquest of Naples in 1436, when it became clear that he was not planning to return to Barcelona anytime soon, and in fact, never would, Alfonso decided to centralize Crown finances. In 1439 he created the office of the treasurer general in Naples to whom he granted authority over all other treasurers. His reforms attempted to eliminate, or at least minimize, the overlap of central and regional authority. But the distinctions between the treasurer general in Naples and each Mestre Racional, particularly with respect to tax collection, were not clearly delineated and were complicated by antiquated accounting and auditing methods. Such an arrangement left plenty of room for ingenuity and fraud. For instance, an audit conducted in 1448 after the death of the Treasurer General Mateu Pujades revealed not only that he had never rendered any proper account, but also that he owed very large sums of money to the Crown. Pujades's estate was seized and his family ordered to pay the debt. To Alfonso, the lesson was clear. He stipulated that all officials who handled royal funds would be subject to a periodic audit by the Mestre Racional and personally held accountable for all sums.[19] The Pujades scandal increased Alfonso's discomfort with granting María rather wide discretionary powers in the financial department. But his reforms were too restrictive. In 1449, María pleaded poverty and complained to him that she needed more control over her finances because her officials were not getting paid regularly. She sent her official Berenguer de Montpalau to Naples to argue her case directly to Alfonso, who claimed to need more money to pay the costs of war in Italy. It took almost a year of pleading with "sweet and gracious words" ("paraules molt dolses e gracioces") for her to once again receive funds from Alfonso and retain local control over expenditures in Catalunya.[20]

Even the most efficient treasurer could not be everywhere at once. It took more time and effort just to collect revenues in Catalunya—a populous, prosperous, commercial powerhouse and the home of most of the lands in the royal patrimony. María's court, located in Barcelona, Valencia, and Perpinyan, required a large staff, and the management of the royal patrimony was complicated.[21] In 1440, he bowed to reality and extended María's local control over financial matters, noting that because María was part of his body—a striking use of the royal body metaphor discussed at length by Kantorowicz—and his lieutenant, he would entrust her with money collected in Catalunya that pertained to the royal fisc. She could receive, recover, and hold ("recepere recuperare et habere") all receipts, fines, and redemptions ("apochas fines quitancias"); make and sign orders for subsidies, including death taxes and criminal fines ("remissiones mortis et altius cuiuscumque criminis"); and she could collect any moneys collected by the administration of justice ("tribunus omnimodem et comiteribus plenarie"). Above all, she was free to spend any money not earmarked for Naples ("cum libera et generali administratio").[22]

These were important reforms that, on the face of it, augmented María's authority as queen-lieutenant. But after the 1448 audit of the treasurer general of Catalunya, Alfonso held María responsible and insisted that only he could control who served on her council, what they were to do, and for how long. No matter how well intentioned, Alfonso's actions undermined María's authority. Her court required a large well-educated staff and staffing it from Naples was nearly impossible, not to mention funding it. At the same time, the contentious debate over the manumission of the remença peasants was heating up and María needed to be able to make quick decisions and not be hamstrung by Alfonso, who continued to refuse all requests to return to Catalunya to deal with his peninsular realms.

The issue for María was not just money, it was the power to appoint her own officials. During the late 1440s and early 1450s, María worked closely with Berenguer de Montpalau, the governor of the Cambra de la Reyna, theoretically in charge of her personal court but distinct from her chamberlain. His title does not tell the whole story of his importance to her, however. Montpalau functioned as her eyes and ears in the Corts and in her dealings with local officials.[23] He was invaluable to her, going where she could not go and doing what she could not do, either because she was a woman or because she was often ill.[24] He handled her personal finances, often traveling to Naples to justify certain expenses or requests for additional funds for the queen's court.[25] One of her first actions after the restoration of her authority over the Cambra was to personally appoint the officials of her Cambra.

Still, Alfonso kept the treasuries of Catalunya, Valencia, and Aragón perpetually under funded. A nearly constant state of war in Italy throughout the 1440s and early 1450s left Alfonso with a shortfall of between 200,000 and 300,000 ducats a year. When his frequent appeals to his subjects for more money were met with icy refusals, he turned to other sources: he raised forced loans; he borrowed from courtiers, nobles, and merchants; he pawned his jewels.[26] In 1446 he intensified the recuperation of alienated lands and lordships alienated, but this contributed to María's fiscal crisis.[27] As she argued in her letters to Alfonso, it cost money to recover the alienated properties, and she could not depend on the trickle of money from Naples to persuade the municipal and comital lords to subsidize the cost of the repatriation. Landholders had to present relevant documents, obtain the king's assent, take a new oath of fealty, and, of course, pay a fee for the privilege of holding these lands. If relevant documents could not be produced, the landholder risked forfeiture to the Crown.[28] His actions stirred up hostilities and the outcry was loud, articulate, and widespread.[29] The lords flooded María's law courts with litigation concerning disputed property titles.[30] Even the powerful Count of Pallars, the bishop of Lleida, and the Count of Cardona were not spared.[31] And neither was the queen.

What was most at risk were Crown lands, often those newly conquered or acquired from legal action, that had been earmarked to support the queen's household. Jaume I was perhaps the earliest Aragonese king to do so, when he gave Teresa Gil Vidaure half of the tithes for the castles of Jérica and Toro. This was a lease, but a permanent one, and a custom that would solidify into a right over the next 300 years.[32] In the fourteenth century, however, the Cambra de la Reyna became an important institution. Pere IV had been obliged by his marriage contract to provide Elionor of Sicily with a minimum source of revenues, and in 1359 he began granting her various *aljamas*. The most important are Tortosa, in Catalunya; in Aragón, Huesca, Calatayud, Borja, Magallón, and Tarazona; and in Valencia, Játiva, Alcira, Elche, Crevillente, and Murviedro; and estates in Sicily.[33] The lands in the Cambra de la Reyna were governed as direct lordships, comparable to similar arrangements in England and France.[34] The lands themselves and the revenues were not held by an individual, as a personal holding or possession, but rather were the property of the queen as part of the institution of monarchy, and thus were not permitted to be included in any bequests or endowments.[35]

In addition to the revenue from these sources, María also had personal wealth some of which she controlled exclusively, including dowry and dower properties, inherited property from her natal family, and any gifts outright from the king. María's dowry consisted of the marquisate of

Villena, the revenues of Andújar and Medellín (in the Extremadura), the lordship of the castles of Aranda and Portillo (in Castile) worth 30,000 *doblas*. Her father, King Enrique III of Castile, stipulated that her lordship of Villena should not be alienated from his patrimony and he and Fernando I of Aragon agreed to a cash payment of 200,000 *doblas*. She was also to receive 560,000 *maravedís* in rents from Seville, plus smaller, token sums from various Castilian towns.

None of this seems terribly striking at first glance, but let us look closer at what really happened. Matrimonial strategies, especially dowries, were essential to kingdom building throughout Europe in the twelfth, thirteenth, and fourteenth centuries. Property set aside for a royal dowry generally fell into three categories: forfeited lands (often from dispossessed Jews or Muslims, the *aljamas*), newly acquired lands (as in the case of Valencia, Majorca, and Sicily[36]), and lifetime rents from properties, which forms the core of the Cambra de la Reyna. This last category resembles an apanage but it is attached to the office of the queen, not her person, and thus cannot be bequeathed personally.

Dowries were key components of the fisc, but over time, kings like Enrique III chose increasingly to pay the dowry in cash. There are several reasons for this strategic shift. First, whereas revenue from estates trickled in, cash was preferred as a way to quickly infuse a sorry treasury. Second, since the thirteenth century, preservation of royal patrimony was an important consideration, especially in light of laws strictly regulating nonpartible inheritance, primogeniture, and the creation of royal apanages.[37] Third, the general outcry that ensued when Alfonso IV granted lands in Tortosa and Valencia to his second wife, Leonor of Castile and their sons Fernando and Juan made subsequent kings think twice before they gave a gift of land to a loved one. Therefore, converting landed endowments into a cash payment, which is legally a temporal, not a perpetual grant, left the Crown patrimony intact.

It is noteworthy that whereas many kings were guilty of excessively endowing their wives—Alfonso IV, Joan I, and Martí in Aragon come quickly to mind—Alfonso V was completely the opposite. He was parsimonious to a fault, long before his estrangement from María. Most remarkably, there is no mention of his granting a dower for María. Her dowry was substantial and her own family was generous in providing for her, but her husband's family was not.

One final point concerns the status of the queen's lands within the royal patrimony. Alfonso seemed to think that queen's lands were not part of the royal patrimony, that it was the Cambra de la Reyna, the queen's personal account, under her jurisdiction with her own officials, as opposed to an account for the office of the queen. But because it was never the personal possession of an individual queen, the queen's Cambra was not ever fully detached from the Crown. The revenues were used to support her, and from them she not only maintained her court but also endowed convents, hospitals, and fed the poor. No matter who the accountant was, no matter which ledger books recorded the transactions, the property by law could not be disposed of as a bequest, grant, donation, or gift to anyone, individual or corporation, without the express grant of the king.

But as Alfonso converted alienated properties into Crown property, he incorporated lands that had been granted to a particular queen, which had entered into the Cambra de la Reyna. A few examples from Aragón illustrate my point. Alfonso incorporated into the patrimonio real three towns—Aínsa and Fraga, in Huesca, and Borja and Magallón in Zaragoza—from the Cambra. I briefly outline the transactions themselves because of the insight they provide into the machinations of royal finance. In 1386 Pere IV had granted Aínsa to Violante, wife of then-prince Joan; in 1428, Alfonso brought the property into the patrimonio. Fraga's history is more complicated. It became a royal town during the reign of Jaume II; it was granted to Guillem de Montcada in 1320 when he married Margarita de Luna, who sold it ten years later to Leonor of Castile for 20,000 sueldos. In 1374, Fraga was ceded to María of Portugal, widow of Fernando, the son of Alfonso IV and Leonor of Castile, as part of the disposition of her dowry (in 1368 the property was ceded to her and her son Pere, Count of Urgel). In 1398, Maria de Luna, wife of King Martí, received the town, and it remained part of the Cambra de la Reyna until 1420, when Alfonso incorporated Fraga into the patrimonio real.

Borja and Magallón are more complicated, so I will sketch out only the major transactions. In 1366 Pere IV granted the towns to Bertran du Guesclin, stipulating that they revert to the Crown at his death. Twelve years later Guesclin sold them to Lope de Luna, who in turn paid the king 27,000 florins; in 1438, it passed from the Luna family to the Crown. But then Alfonso sold the revenues only from the towns to Bernat de Requesens; the lands themselves remained inalienable. In 1444, when Alfonso confirmed the transaction, he noted—and this is the interesting part, the part that needs further research—that in 1431 he bought these lands from the executors of Violant's will, and that this action was prejudicial to Queen María, because she lost these properties from her Cambra. María, in her capacity as lieutenant general, paid the executors of Violant's estate 27,000 florins for Borja and Magallón and the barony of Cocentaina in Valencia. Finally, in 1458, at María's death, the two towns reverted permanently to the patrimonio real.

The problem with all of these transactions—when a dowry is commuted to a cash payment and when the properties that were part of the Cambra de la Reyna are incorporated into the royal patrimony—is that in all instances, the Crown's gain is the queen's loss. She loses her rights to lordship that come with the possession of land. The money, especially in the case of María's dowry, simply disappeared into a very needy treasury. Even though the law very specifically limits a husband's rights to dispose of his wife's dowry, to Alfonso, once it entered the treasury he regarded it as Crown property and promptly spent it. The law is ambiguous as to the disposition of the cash from her dowry into the treasury, but once it was there, because control of the treasury was so jealously guarded by Alfonso, María lost any jurisdiction over the rents, leases, and lordship she might have had a right to. Just as she lost the land and lordship, she lost and had to fight to regain control over her Cambra. This seriously limited her status and authority as the lieutenant general. Unlike queens who retain some measure of financial power through their own lands, María lost an important source of political leverage that cost her dearly in the difficult negotiations over the question of peasant manumission.

Alfonso's actions suggest that he considered a dower in royal financial terms and thus not governed by long-standing laws and customs. To him, it was an inter-vivos gift, stipulated in antenuptial contracts, that provided for a queen's livelihood after a king's death, but his status as king did not prevent him from using it for the good of the realm rather than the good of his wife. It was, in other words, alienable from her person to the treasury. Because of the ambiguity of the office of the queen-lieutenant in terms of private personal wealth and public monarchical funds, the legal stipulations regulating its use were unclear. This left open questions concerning a queen's "patrimony" properties: Were they legally comparable to an apanage? Could they legally be considered alienations, treated as inter-vivo gifts? There is, to my present knowledge, no medieval political theory or legal statement on these questions. Most theory on alienation of patrimony is concerned with sons, not wives. The *patrimonio real* documents for the kingdom of Aragón show clearly how Alfonso took back properties that had once been part of the royal patrimony, some of which were originally granted to queens suggesting that he considered the Cambra de la Reyna and household accounts part of his patrimony.[38] He could do so, I suspect, because the legal ambiguity of the queen's finances made the lands tempting sources of revenue for a king like Alfonso who play fast and loose with money. His actions, however prudent in broad fiscal terms, had a very real impact on María's immediate fiscal needs.

On paper, María of Castile possessed a wide range and scope of authority, but the poverty of her own finances was a recurrent theme. In practice, however, the actual extent of her power as queen-lieutenant was at least undercut and undermined, if not seriously curtailed, by her deficient finances. Her prestige was diminished by her inability to pay her own staff and the nobles, clerics, and ruling elites surely realized that the king controlled the purse strings. It is no wonder that the members of the town councils took her less seriously and decided it was worth the time and effort to shuttle back and forth to Naples to gain access to the king's ear. María may have been Alfonso's political partner in governance of the realm, but by curtailing her fiscal resources, her own Cambra, and her ability to manage them, he made sure that she was never a serious threat to him.

## Notes

1. Ernst Kantorowicz, *The King's Two Bodies: A Study in Mediaeval Political Theology* (Princeton, NJ: Princeton University Press, 1967).
2. See John W. Baldwin, *The Government of Philip Augustus: Foundations of French Royal Power in the Middle Ages* (Berkeley and Los Angeles: University of California Press, 1986).
3. Margaret Howell, *Eleanor of Provence: Queenship in Thirteenth-Century England* (Oxford: Blackwell, 1998); Howell, "The Resources of Eleanor of Provence as Queen Consort," *English Historical Review* 102 (1987): 372–93; John Carmi Parsons, *Eleanor of Castile: Queen and Society in Thirteenth-Century England* (New York: St. Martin's Press, 1995); Parsons, ed., *The Court and Household of Eleanor of Castile, 1290* (Toronto: Pontifical Institute of Medieaval Studies, 1977).
4. María's designation, "of Castile," refers to the place of her birth, not the kingdom she ruled. Francisca Hernández-León de Sánchez, *Doña María de Castilla, Esposa de Alfonso el Magnánimo* (Valencia: Universidad de Valencia, 1959), pp. 59–61.
5. The medieval Crown of Aragon consisted of several distinct political entities gathered together under a single ruler. The crown originated in 1137 with the marriage of Petronila of Aragón and Ramón Berenguer IV, count of Barcelona. The rest of the crown realms were added by conquest: the kingdom of Mallorca and the Balearic islands between 1229 and 1235; Valencia, 1238; Sicily, 1282; and Sardinia, 1322. At various other times and with varying degrees of success, the Aragonese kings controlled Corsica and the duchy of Athens. To keep matters simple when referring to this federative polity, I will refer to the Crown of Aragon when discussing it as a whole and, when otherwise necessary, specify individual regional kingdoms or counties. Thomas N. Bisson, *The Medieval Crown of Aragon* (Oxford: Clarendon Press, 1986), pp, 27–31, 64–67, 87–89, 93, 95–96, 111.

6. On Alfonso's reign, see Alan Ryder, *The Kingdom of Naples under Alfonso the Magnanimous* (Oxford: Clarendon Press, 1976); Ryder, *Alfonso the Magnanimous: King of Aragon, Naples, and Sicily, 1396–1458* (Oxford: Clarendon Press, 1990); Bisson, *Medieval Crown of Aragon*, 140–47; Ferran Soldevila, *Història de Catalunya*, 3 vols. (Barcelona: Editorial Alpha, 1934), vol. 2, pp. 41–80.
7. Arxiu de la Corona d'Aragó (Barcelona), Cancilleria registers (henceforth, ACA: C), registers 2948–3280.
8. Ryder, *Kingdom of Naples*, pp. 1–26.
9. Angeles Masia de Ros, "El maestre racional en la Corona de Aragón. Una pragmatica de Juan II sobre dicho cargo," *Hispania* 10 (1950), pp. 25–60, esp. 35–36.
10. Ryder, *Kingdom of Naples*, p. 191.
11. Masia de Ros, "El maestre racional," pp. 25–60; Alan Ryder, "The Evolution of Imperial Government in Naples under Alfonso V of Aragon," in *Europe in the Late Middle Ages*, ed. John Rigby Hale, John Roger Loxdale Highfield, and Beryl Smalley (Evanston, IL: Northwestern University Press, 1965), pp. 332–57, esp. pp. 351–54; Bisson, *Medieval Crown of Aragon*, p. 156.
12. Ryder, *Kingdom of Naples*, pp. 18–20, 57, 170, 191; José María Font i Rius, "Las instituciones de la corona de Aragón en la primera mitad del siglo XV," *Ponencias del IV Congreso de la Histório de la Corona de Aragón* (Barcelona: Comisión Permanente de los Congresos de la Corona de Aragón, 1976), pp. 209–23, esp. pp. 209–11.
13. Claude Carrère attributes the downturn to structural defects such as the inflexibility of maritime enterprise and the high cost of money relative to that of the Catalun merchants' trading partners, but Mario del Treppo argues that there was a political component to the sluggish economy because the Catalan economy was closely connected to Alfonso's military and political maneuvers in Italy. Claude Carrère, *Barcelone: centre èconomique à l'époque des difficultés, 1380–1462*, 2 vols. (Paris and The Hague: Mouton, 1967), pp. 656–63, 691–718; Mario del Treppo, *Els mercaders catalans i l'expansió de la corona catalano-aragonesa al segle XV*, trans. Jaume Riera i Sans (Barcelona: Curial, 1976; originally published as *I mercanti catalani e l'expansione della Corona d'Aragona nel secolo XV*, Naples: L'Arte Tipografica Napoli, 1972), pp. 160–240, 255–77, 535–53.
14. Alan Ryder agrees with del Treppo's argument for the role of politics in economics: Alfonso tried to use economic links among the various realms as a way of creating an artificial bond to hold together the Crown. As Alfonso's political fortunes surged, so did the economy, and vice versa. Business with the Crown, especially in the traffic of the products of war, could be especially lucrative but depended on continued skirmishing, which was unpredictable, unstable, and, in the end, counterproductive. Alfonso tried to support local commerce by buying Catalan cloth and Sicilian grain to support his army, a scheme that worked for a few years but quickly fell apart when his opponents signed the Peace of Lodi in

1453. The bottom fell out of the artificially high cloth and grain markets, and the economy as a whole suffered. Ryder, *Alfonso the Magnanimous*, 370–74; Ryder, "Cloth and Credit: Aragonese War Finance in the Mid-Fifteenth Century," *War and Society* 2:1 (May 1984): 1–21.

15. A six-month campaign in Ancona cost Alfonso 80,000 ducats; entertaining the Emperor Frederick III for ten days cost more than 100,000 ducats. Alfonso fought ceaseless skirmishes with Castile and battled pirates along the Catalan, Valencian, and Mallorcan coastlines. Ryder, *Kingdom of Naples*, 174.
16. Bisson, *Medieval Crown of Aragon*, 141, 143, 145.
17. See, for example, Atanasio Sinués Ruiz and Antonio Ubieto Arteta, eds., *El Patrimonio Real en Aragón durante la edad media* (Zaragoza: Anubar, 1986); Peter Linehan, "Frontier Kingship: Castile, 1250–1350," in *La Royaute sacrée dans le monde chrétien*, ed. Alain Boureau and Claudio Sergio Ingerflom (Paris: École des Hautes Études en Sciences Sociales, 1992), pp. 71–79; Charles T. Wood, *The French Apanages and the Capetian Monarchy, 1124–1328* (Cambridge, MA: Harvard University Press, 1966).
18. Masia de Ros, "El maestre racional en la Corona de Aragón," pp. 35–6.
19. Ryder, *Kingdom of Naples*, pp. 170–7; Ryder, "Evolution of Imperial Government," pp. 350–51.
20. ACA: C Secretorum 3227: 43v–44v, 22 April 1449; 75r–76r, 24 July 1449; 93r–v, 21 October 1449; 95r, 29 October 1449; 99v–100v, 6 December 1449; 104r–105r, 24 January 1450; 121r–123v, 6 February 1450; and 134v–136v, 3 September 1450.
21. Ryder, *Kingdom of Naples*, p. 191.
22. Arxiu Reial de Valencia, Maestre Racional (hereafter, ARV MR) register 9050, 14v–15r, 3 October 1440; Hernández-León de Sánchez, *Doña María de Castilla*, 94. On the symbolism of the royal body, see Kantorowicz, *The King's Two Bodies*, pp. 207–32.
23. ACA:C Secretorum 3227, 42r–43v, 22 April 1449.
24. She placed him in charge of collecting the unpopular *maridatge* subsidy Alfonso requested to pay for the marriage of his illegitimate children in Italy. ACA:C, Secretorum 3227, 53r–55v, 9 June 1449; 57r–58v, 30 June 1449; 75r–76r, 24 July 1449.
25. ACA:C Secretorum 3227, 43v–44v, 22 April 1449; 75r–76r, 24 July 1449; 93r–v, 21 October 1449; 99v–100v, 6 December 1449; 104r–105r, 24 January 1450; 121r–123v, 6 May 1450; 134v–136v, 3 September 1450.
26. He had little difficulty with the parliamentary assemblies of Aragón and Valencia, but the Catalans felt they had borne the brunt of taxation and military expenditures and they made demands that he was unwilling to grant. In return for their money, they insisted that the king's council be chosen with the consent of the Corts, that the *Audiència* should render judgments independently of the king, and that royal orders that violated the Constitutions or *Usatges* of Catalunya were to be nullified. For a brief summary, see Bisson, *Medieval Crown of Aragon*, pp. 141, 143, 145; Ryder, *Kingdom of Naples*, p. 174.

27. Similar attempts date to the end of the fourteenth century. For a careful analysis of the nature and extent of the problem, see María Teresa Ferrer i Mallol, "El patrimoni reial i la recuperació dels senyorius jurisdiccionals en les estats catalano-aragoneses a la fi del segle XIV," *Anuario de Estudios Medievales* 7 (1970–71), pp. 351–491.
28. Anyone caught forging documents to circumvent the process was threatened with the same fate. Ryder, *Alfonso the Magnanimous*, pp. 43, 49–51, 65.
29. And they were not the only ones to complain. Besalú faced similar opposition in Mallorca in 1450. ACA:C Secretorum 3227, 107r–108r, 4 February 1450.
30. These suits (*pro luïcione*) were especially numerous in the Ampurdà, in the locales of Verges, La Tallada, Bellcaire, Albons, Monells, Ullastret, La Pera, Palau Sator, Sant Pere Pescador, Les Olives, and Pelacals. The documents are numerous and contained in several registers. Among the most important are ACA:C Secretorum 2699, 155r–157v, 25 January 1449; Curiae 2656, 165r–v, 26 February 1449; Curiae 2655, 54r–55v, 1 March 1449. See also María's orders to her royal officials: ACA:C Curiae 3203, 11v–12v, 14 October 1448); 18v, 26 October 1448; 30r, 23 December 1448; and 60r, 5 April 1449. Santiago Sobrequés i Vidal, "Política remensa de Alfonso el Magnánimo en los últimos años de su reinado (1447–1458)," *Anales del instituo de estudios gerundenses* (1960): 117–54; esp. p. 122; Santiago Sobrequés i Vidal and Jaume Sobrequés i Callicó, *La guerra civil catalana del segle XV,* 2 vols. (Barcelona: Edicions 62, 1973), vol. 1, pp. 15–16.
31. ACA Generalitat, N-657, 56v–57v, 27 April 1448; 67v–68r, 22 April 1448; 68v–69v, 24 May 1448.
32. Robert I. Burns, *The Crusader Kingdom of Valencia: Reconstruction on a Thirteenth-Century Frontier*, 2 vols. (Cambridge, MA: Harvard University Press, 1967), vol. 1, p. 165.
33. In Huesca, Calatayud, Murviedro, Alcira, Morella (1359), Montblanc, Tarrega, Villagrassa (1360), Tarazona (1361), Tortosa, Torella, Borja, Burriana (1364), Eslida (1365), and the Jewish *aljamas* of Barcelona and Valencia. ACA:C 1534: 137 (5 October 1359); 1536: 45 (20 February 1360); 1536: 62 (20 February 1360); 1537: 48 (15 June 1361). The Muslims of Eslida asked to be given to the queen. ACA:C 1205: 60 (31 March 1365). Cited in John Boswell, *The Royal Treasure: Muslim Communities under the Crown of Aragon in the Fourteenth Century* (New Haven, CT and London: Yale University Press, 1977), pp. 205–7.
34. When Elionor took over the major Aragonese aljamas, she regulated their finances minutely. She prohibited the taking of loans that were not in the best interests of the aljamas. ACA:C 1570, fol. 87, 6 March 1361; In Boswell, *The Royal Treasure*, pp. 205–7. The queen's zeal prompted Pere to tighten up his procedures, but the Aragonese aljamas' financial state worsened and in 1413–14 Leonor of Albuquerque had to point out to the creditors of her hard-pressed aljama in Zaragoza that "all of the

goods of the aljama are not sufficient to pay its debts." ACA:C 2422: 60 (1413); ACA:C 2423: 273 (1414); published in Francisco Macho y Ortega, "Documentos relativos a la condición social y jurídica de los mudéjars Aragonese," *Revista de ciencias jurídicas y sociales* 5 (1922), pp. 143–60, 444–64, esp. pp. 158–59.

35. In Valencia the queen had income from some of the sheep flocks. Burns, *The Crusader Kingdom of Valencia*, vol. 1, p. 167.
36. On the estates in Sicily, see Ryder, *Alfonso the Magnanimous*, p. 89.
37. Henry III of England, whose wife Eleanor of Provence was one of the most shrewd estate managers in the Middle Ages, noted in 1247 that there is no surer proof of the king's intention to retain property in the royal hand than to assign it to the queen, presumably because laws governing women's inheritance rights would limit her ability to dispose freely any rents, income, or fixed property.
38. Núria Silleras Fernández, *Power, Piety, and Patronage in Late Medieval Queenship: Maria de Luna* (New York: Palgrave Macmillan, 2008), 32.

# BIBLIOGRAPHY

## Medieval Texts


Abelard, Peter. *Opera theologica. Corpus Christianorum Continuato Mediaevalis XIII.* Turnholt: Brepols, 1987.

*Ancrene Wisse: The English Text of the Ancrene Riwle.* Ed. J. R. R. Tolkien. Early English Text Society, o.s. 249, London: Oxford University Press, 1962.

Aristotle. *Politics.* Trans. Benjamin Jowett. New York: The Modern Library, 1943.

Augustine of Hippo. *De bono coniugali, De sancta virginitate.* Ed. and trans. P. G. Walsh. Oxford: Clarendon Press, 2001.

Barros, Henrique da Gama. *História da administração pública em Portugal nos séculos XIII a XV.* Ed. Torquato de Sousa Soares, 11 vols. Lisbon: Sá da Costa, 1945–54.

Bautier, Robert-Henri and Janine Sornay. *Les Sources de l'histoire économique et sociale du moyan âge, Les états de la Maison de Bourgogne.* Paris: Éditions du CNRS, 1984.

Boccaccio, Giovanni. *Concerning Famous Women* [*De claris mulieribus*]. Trans. Guido A. Guarino. New Brunswick, NJ: Rutgers University Press, 1963.

*The Book of Margery Kempe.* Translated by B. A. Windeatt. Harmondsworth, UK: Penguin Books, 1994.

———. Ed. Sanford Brown Meech. Early English Text Society, o.s. 212. London: Oxford University Press, 1940.

Caesarius of Heisterbach. *Dialogus miraculorum.* Ed. J. Strange. Cologne: 1851.

*Chronique Rimée de Philippe Mouskes.* Ed. Baron de Reiffenberg. Brussels: M. Hayez, 1836.

*Le compte general du receveur d'Artois pour 1303–4.* Edited by Bernard Delmaire. Brussels: J. Duculot, 1977.

Coussemaker, Édouard de, ed. *Inventaire Analytique et Chronologique des Archives de la Chambre des Comptes à Lille.* Lille: M. Quarré, 1865.

Dante, *La commedia secondo l'antica volgata.* Ed. Giorgio Petrocchi. 4 vols. Milan: A. Mondadori, 1966–1967.

Delaborde, H. F., Elie Berger, C. F. Brunel, and Charles Samaran, eds. *Recueil des Actes de Philippe Auguste.* Paris, 1916.

Devillers, Léopold, ed. *Cartulaire de l'Abbaye de Épinlieu.* Mons: 1867.

*The Dialogue on Miracles.* Trans. H. von Scott and C. C. Swinton Bland. London: 1929.

Dias, Luís Fernando de Carvalho, ed. *Forais Manuelinos do Reino de Portugal e do Algarve conforme o exemplar do Arquivo Nacional da Torre do Tombo de Lisboa*. 5 vols. Beja: Soc. Editora Ala Esquerda, 1962.

Douët-d'Arcq, L. *Comptes de l'argenterie des rois de France au xiv*[e] *siècle*. Paris: Jules Renouard et Cie, 1851; rpt., New York, London: Johnson Reprint Corporation, 1966.

———. *Nouvelle recueil de comptes de l'argenterie des rois de France*. Paris: Librairie Renouard, 1874.

Faro, Jorge. *Receitas e despesas da fazenda real de 1384 a 1481 (Subsídios documentais)*. Lisbon: Instituto Nacional de Estatística, 1965.

Fawtier, Robert and François Maillard, eds. *Comptes royaux (1285–1314)*. Paris: Imprimerie Nationale, 1954.

Foppens, Jean Francois, ed. *Diplomatum Belgicorum Nova Collectio sive Supplementum ad Opera Diplomatica Auberti Miraei*. Brussels: 1734.

Furnivall, F., ed. *The Fifty Earliest English Wills in the Court of Probate, London. A. D. 1387–1439*. Oxford: Oxford University Press, 1964.

Garcés de Cariñena, Pedro. *Nobiliario de Aragón, anotado por Zurita, Blancas y otros autores*. Edited by M. I. Ubieto Artur. Zaragoza: Anubar, 1983.

Herculano, Alexandre, ed. *Portugaliae Monumenta Historica. Leges et consuetudines*. 2 vols. Lisbon: Academia das Ciências de Lisboa, 1856.

*John of Gaunt's Register*. Ed. Sydney Armitage-Smith, 2 vols. Camden Third Series, vol. 20. London: Offices of the Society, 1911.

Langland, William. *Piers Plowman: The C Version*. Ed. George Russell and George Kane. London: Athlone Press, 1997.

*The Life of Christina of Markyate: A Twelfth-Century Recluse*. Ed. and trans. C. H. Talbot. Toronto: University of Toronto Press, 2001.

*List of Early Chancery Proceedings Preserved in the Public Record Office*, Lists and Indexes v. 12, 16, 20. London: H.M.S.O. etc., 1901–1936; rpt., Kraus Reprint Corp., 1964.

Littlehales, H., ed. *The Medieval Records of a London City Church 1420–1559 (St. Mary at Hill)*. London: Early English Text Society, 1905.

Lopes, Fernão. *Crónica de D. Fernando*. Ed. Salvador Dias Arnaut. Oporto: Livraria Civilização, 1979.

———. *Crónica de D. João I*. Ed. Anselmo Braamcamp Freire. 2 vols. Oporto: Livraria Civilização, 1979.

Luykx, Theo. *Johanna van Constantinopel, Gravin van Vlaanderen en Henegouwen, haar Leven (1199/1200–1244), haar Revgeering (1205–1244), vooral in Vlaanderen*. Antwerp: N.V. Standaard, 1946.

Marques, A. H. de Oliveira, ed. *Chancelarias Portuguesas. D. Pedro I (1357–1367)*. Lisbon: INIC, CEH, 1984.

Marx, Karl, and Friedrich Engels. *The Communist Manifesto*. With an introduction by A. J. P. Taylor. Hammondsworth, UK: Penguin, 1967.

Michaëlsson, Karl. *Le livre de la taille de Paris, l'an 1296*. Göteberg: Elanders Boktryckeri Aktiebolag, 1958.

———. *Le livre de la taille de Paris, l'an 1297*. Göteberg: Elanders Boktryckeri Aktiebolag 1962.

———. *Le livre de la taille de Paris, l'an de grace 1313*. Göteberg: Wettergren & Kerbers Förlag, 1951.

Muckle, J. T. "The Letter of Heloise on Religious Life and Abelard's First Reply." *Mediaeval Studies* 17 (1955): 240–81.

———. "The Personal Letters between Abelard and Heloise." *Mediaeval Studies* 15 (1953): 47–94.

Mussely, Charles and Émile Molitor, eds. *Cartulaire de l'ancienne église collégiale de Notre Dame de Courtrai*. Gand: 1880.

*Nouveau receuil complet des fabliaux*. Ed. Willem Noomen and Nico van den Boogaard. Assen, Netherlands: VanGorcum, 1983.

*Noveau receuil de contes, dits, fabliaux et autre pieces*. Ed. Achille Jubinal. Paris: Chez Callamel, 1842.

Nunes, Eduardo Borges, ed. *Ordenaçoens do Senhor Rey D. Afonso V.* 5 vols. Lisbon: Fundação Calouste Gulbenkian, 1984.

Parsons, John C., ed. *The Court and Household of Eleanor of Castile, 1290.* Toronto: Pontifical Institute of Mediaeval Studies, 1977.

Pere III el Cerimoniós. *Crònica*. Ed. A. Cortadellas. Barcelona: Edicions 62, 1995.

Piot, Charles, ed. *Cartulaire de l'Abbaye Eename*. Bruges: De Zuttere-van Kersschaver, 1881.

de Pisan, Christine. *The Book of the City of Ladies* [*Le livre de la cité des dames*]. Trans. Earl Jeffrey Richards. New York: Persea Books, 1982.

Prost, Bernard. *Inventaires mobiliers et extraits des comptes des ducs de Bourgogne de la Maison de Valois (1363–1477)*. 2 vols. Paris: E. Leroux, 1902–1904.

Radice, Betty. *The Letters of Abelard and Heloise*. London: Penguin, 1974.

*De Rekeningen der graven en gravinnen uit het Henegouwsche huis*. Ed. J. Smit. 3 vols. Amsterdam and Utrecht: J. Müller, 1924–39.

Richard, Jean. *Saint Louis: Crusader King of France*. Trans. Jean Birrell. Cambridge: Cambridge University Press, 1992.

Richard, Jules-Marie. "Documents des xiiie et xive siècles relatifs à l'hôtel de Bourgogne (ancien hôtel d'Artois) tirés du trésor des chartes d'Artois." *Bulletin de la société de l'histoire de Paris et de l'Île-de-France* 17 (1890).

———. *Inventaire-Sommaire des Archives departementales antérieures à 1790, Pas-de-Calais, Archives Civiles—Série A*. 2 vols. Arras: Imp. de la Société du Pas-de-Calais, 1878, 1887.

*The Riverside Chaucer*. Ed. Larry D. Benson. Third edition. Boston: Houghton Mifflin, 1987.

Röhricht, Reinhold, ed. *Regesta Regni Hierosolymitani* 1097–1291. 2 vols. New York: Burt Franklin, 1960.

Silva-Vigier, Anil de. *The Moste Highe Prince... John of Gaunt, 1340–1399.* Edinburgh-Cambridge-Durham: The Pentland Press, 1992.

*Seinte Katerine,* ed. S. R. T. O. D'Ardenne and E. J. Dobson. Early English Text Society, s.s. 7. Oxford: Oxford University Press, 1981.

*Las siete partidas del rey Don Alfonso el Sabio*. 3 vols. Madrid: Real Academia de la Historia, 1972.

Smith, Adam. *The Wealth of Nations*. Oxford: Clarendon Press, 1979.

Sousa, J. M. Cordeiro de, ed. *Fontes Medievais de História Torreana.* Torres Vedras: Câmara Municipal, 1958.

Teulet, Alexandre, Joseph de Laborde, Elie Berger, and Henri-Francois Delaborde, eds. *Layettes du Trésor des Chartes.* Paris: 1863–1909.

Thomas, A. H. *Calendar of Plea and Memoranda Rolls Preserved among the Archives of the Corporation of the City of London at the Guildhall, 1413–1437.* Cambridge: Cambridge University Press, 1843.

Thompson, W. Meredith. *Þe Wohunge of Ure Lauerd.* Early English Text Society, o.s. 241. London: Oxford University Press, 1958.

Udina Abello, Antoni, ed. *Els testaments dels comtes de Barcelona i dels reis de la Corona d'Aragó.* Barcelona: Fundació Noguera, 2001.

Vanhaeck, Maurice, ed. *Cartulaire de l'Abbaye de Marquette.* Lille: S.I.L.I.C., 1937.

Van Hollebeke, Léopold. *L'Abbaye de Nonnenbossche de l'ordre de St. Benoit, pres d'Ypres (1101–1796).* Bruges: Vandecasteele-Werbrouck, 1865.

*Vices and Virtues.* Ed. Ferd. Holthausen. Early English Text Society, o.s. 89 and 159. Oxford University Press: London, 1888 and 1921.

Vives, Juan Luis. *The Education of a Christian Woman: A Sixteenth-Century Manual.* Ed. and trans. Charles Fantazzi. Chicago: University of Chicago Press, 2000.

Wauters, Alphonse, ed. *Table Chronologique des Chartes et Diplômes Imprimés concernant l'histoire de la Belgique.* Brussels: Kiessling et Cie., 1903–12.

Wilkinson, John, Joyce Hill, and W. F. Ryan, eds. and trans. *Jerusalem Pilgrimage, 1099–1185.* London: Hakluyt Society, 1988.

William of Tyre. *Chronicle.* In *Corpus Christianorum, continuatio mediaevalis.* Vols. 63–63A. Ed. R. B. C. Huygens, H. E. Mayer, and G. Rösch. Turnhout: Brepols, 1986.

———. *A History of the Deeds Done Beyond the Sea.* Translated by E. A. Babcock and A. C. Krey. New York: Columbia University Press, 1943.

Zurita, Jerónimo. *Anales de la Corona de Aragón.* Zaragoza: Consejo Superior de Investigaciones Científicas, 1978.

## Modern Studies

Abram, A. "Women Traders in Medieval London." *Economic Journal* 26 (1916): 276–85.

Adair, Penelope. "Countess Clemence: Her Power and Its Foundation." In *Queens, Regents and Potentates.* Ed. Theresa M. Vann. Dallas, TX: Academia Press, 1993. 63–72.

Adams, Henry. *Mont Saint Michel and Chartres.* Boston: Houghton Mifflin, 1933.

Adler, Judith. "Travel as Performed Art." *American Journal of Sociology* 94:6 (1989): 1366–91.

Alford, John A. *Piers Plowman: A Glossary of the Legal Diction.* Cambridge: Brewer, 1988.

Amariglio, Jack L. "The Body, Economic Discourse, and Power: An Economist's Introduction to Foucault." *History of Political Economy* 20:4 (Winter 1988): 583–613.

Amsler, Mark. "The Wife of Bath and Women's Power." *Assays* 4 (1987): 67–83.

Angold, Michael. *The Fourth Crusade: Event and Context*. New York: Pearson Longman, 2003.

"An Interview with Henri Lefebvre (interviewers G. Burgel, M. G. Dezes, and translated by E. Kofman)." *Environment and Planning D: Society and Space* 5:1 (1987): 30.

Appadurai, Arjun, ed. *The Social Life of Things: Commodities in Cultural Perspective*. Cambridge: Cambridge University Press, 1986.

Archer, Janice. "Working Women in Thirteenth-Century Paris." PhD Dissertation, University of Arizona, 1995.

Asch, Ronald G. "Court and Household from the Fifteenth to the Seventeenth Centuries." In *Princes, Patronage, and the Nobility: The Court at the Beginning of the Modern Age, c.1450–1650*. Ed. Ronald G. Asch and A. M. Birke. Oxford: Oxford University Press, 1991. 1–38.

Astell, Ann W. *The Song of Songs in the Middle Ages*. Ithaca, NY: Cornell University Press, 1990.

Avery, Margaret. "Evaluation of the Effectiveness of the Court of Chancery under the Lancastrian Kings." *Law and Quarterly Review* 86 (1970): 84–97.

———. "The History of the Equitable Jurisdiction of Chancery before 1460." *The Bulletin of the Institute of Historical Research* 42 (1969): 129–44.

Baker, Donald C. "A Crux in Chaucer's Franklin's Tale: Dorigen's Complaint," *Journal of English and Germanic Philology* 60 (1960): 56–64.

Baker, J. H. *An Introduction to English Legal History*. 3rd ed. London: Butterworths, 1990.

Baldwin, John W. "Consent and the Marital Debt: Five Discourses in Northern France around 1200." In *Consent and Coercion to Sex and Marriage in Ancient and Medieval Societies*. Ed. Angeliki E. Laiou. Washington: Dunbarton Oaks Research Library and Collection, 1993.

———. "La décennie décisive: les années 1190–1203 dans le règne de Philippe Auguste." *Révue Historique* 266 (1981): 311–37.

———. *The Government of Philip Augustus: Foundations of French Royal Power in the Middle Ages*. Berkeley and Los Angeles: University of California Press, 1986.

———. "The Medieval Theories of the Just Price." *Transactions of the American Philosophical Society* 49:4 (1959): 1–94 (Rpt. in *Pre-Capitalist Economic Thought*. New York: Arno, 1972).

Barber, Malcolm. *The Two Cities: Medieval Europe 1050–1320*. London: Routledge, 1992.

Barbosa, Pedro Ferreira Gomes. *Grupos marginais nos documentos de Santa Maria de Alcobaça (séculos XII e XIII)*. Lisbon: Faculdade de Letras, 1988.

Barros, Maria Filomena. *A Comuna muçulmana de Lisboa: sécs. XIV e XV*. Lisbon: Hugin, 1998.

Barton, J. L. "The Medieval Use." *Law Quarterly Review* 81 (1965): 562–77.

Bates, Ulku U. "Women as Patrons of Architecture in Turkey." In *Women in the Muslim World*. Ed. Luis Beck and Nilda Keddie. Cambridge, MA: Harvard University Press, 1978. 245–60.

Baudoux-Jung, Nathalie. "La construction de tours de la ville d'Amiens d'après les 'marchés à tasque' (fin XIVe–début XVe siècle)." In *La ville au Moyen-Âge. I: Ville et espace*. Ed. Noël Coulet and Olivier Guyotjeannin. Paris: Éditions du CTHS, 1998.

Bautier, Robert Henri, ed. *La France de Philippe Auguste: le temps des mutations: actes du colloque international*. Paris: Editions du Centre national de la recherce scientifique, 1982.

Beattie, Cordelia. "Meanings of Singleness: The Single Woman in Late Medieval England." PhD thesis, University of York (UK), 2001.

Bédier, Joseph. *Les fabliaux: Etudes de littérature populaire et d'histoire littéraire du moyen age*. 6th ed. 1893; repr. Paris: Champion, 1964.

Beilby, Mark. "The Profits of Expertise: The Rise of the Civil Lawyers and Chancery Equity." In *Profit, Piety and the Professions in Later Medieval England*. Ed. Michael Hicks. Gloucester: Sutton, 1990. 72–90.

Benevides, Francisco da Fonseca. *Rainhas de Portugal. Estudo Histórico com muitos documentos*. 2 vols. Lisbon: Typographia Castro Irmão, 1878.

Benito, Ricardo Izquierdo. "La vivienda en Toledo a fines de la Edad Media: Elementos constructivos." In *La ciudad medieval: De la casa al tejido urbano*. Ed. Jean Passini. Cuenca: Ediciones de la Universidad de Castilla-La Mancha, 2001. 281–301.

Berman, Constance. "Women as Donors and Patrons to Southern French Monasteries in the Twelfth and Thirteenth Centuries." In *The Worlds of Medieval Women: Creativity, Influence, and Imagination*. Ed. Constance H. Berman, Charles W. Connell, and Judith Rice Rothschild. Morgantown: West Virginia University Press, 1985.

Berman, Constance and Mariam Shadis. "A Taste of the Feast: Reconsidering Eleanor of Aquitaine's Female Descendants." In *Eleanor of Aquitaine: Lord and Lady*. Ed. Bonnie Wheeler and John Carmi Parsons. New York: Palgrave Macmillan, 2003. 177–211.

Bethencourt, Francisco. "A Expulsão dos Judeus." *O Tempo de Vasco da Gama*. Ed. Diogo Ramada Curto. Lisbon: CNCDP/Difel, 1998. 271–80.

Biancalana, Joseph. *The Fee Tail and the Common Recovery in Medieval England, 1176–1502*. Cambridge: Cambridge University Press, 2001.

Bianciotto, Gabriel. "De *Constant du Hamel*." *Renardus* 6 (1993): 15–30.

Bienvenu, Jean-Marc. "Aliénor d'Aquitaine et Fontevraud." *Cahiers de civilization medievale* 29 (1986): 15–27.

Bird, Rebecca Bliege and Eric Alden Smith. "Signaling Theory, Strategic Interaction, and Symbolic Capital." *Current Anthropology* 46:2 (April 2005): 221–48.

Bisson, Lillian. *Chaucer and the Late Medieval World*. New York: St. Martin's Press, 1998.

Bisson, Thomas N. *The Medieval Crown of Aragon: A Short History*. Oxford: Clarendon Press, 1986.

———, ed. *Cultures of Power: Lordship, Status, and Process in Twelfth-Century Europe*. Philadelphia: University of Pennsylvania Press, 1995.

Bitel, Lisa M. *Women in Early Medieval Europe 400–1100.* Cambridge: Cambridge University Press, 2002.

Bloch, Marc. *Esquisse d'un histoire monétaire de l'Europe.* Paris: Librairie Armand Colin, 1954.

Bloch, R. Howard. *Etymologies and Genealogies: A Literary Anthropology of the French Middle Ages.* Chicago: University of Chicago Press, 1983.

Boas, Adrian J. *Archaeology of the Military Orders: A Survey of the Urban Centres, Rural Settlements and Castles of the Military Orders in the Latin East (c.1120–1291).* New York: Routledge, 2006.

———. *Jerusalem in the Time of the Crusades: Society, Landscape, and Art in the Holy City under Frankish Rule.* London and New York: Routledge, 2001.

Bolton, J. L. *The Medieval English Economy, 1150–1550.* London: J. M. Dent and Sons, 1987.

Boscolo, Alberto. *La Reina Sibil·la de Fortià.* Barcelona: Rafael Dalmau, 1971.

Boswell, John. *The Royal Treasure: Muslim Communities under the Crown of Aragon in the Fourteenth Century.* New Haven, CT and London: Yale University Press, 1977.

Bouchard, Constance. "The Structure of a Twelfth-Century French Family: The Lords of Seignelay." *Viator* 10 (1979): 36–59.

Bourdieu, Pierre. *The Logic of Practice.* Cambridge, MA: Polity Press, 1990.

Bourlet, Caroline. "L'anthroponymie à Paris à la fin du xiiie siècle d'après les rôles de la taille du règne de Philippe le Bel." In *Genèse médiévale de l'anthroponymie moderne.* Ed. Monique Bourin and Pascal Chareille. Tours: Publications de l'Université de Tours, 1992.

Bove, Boris. *Dominer la ville: prévôts des marchands et échevins parisiens de 1260 à 1350.* Paris: Editions CTHS, 2004.

———. "Vie et mort d'un couple de marchands-drapiers parisiens, d'après les testaments de Jeanne et Étienne Haudry (1309, 1313)." *Paris et Île-de-France, Mémoires* 52 (2001): 71.

Bowers, Terence N. "Margery Kempe as Traveler." *Studies in Philology* 97:1 (2000): 1–28.

Bradbury, Jim. *Philip Augustus: King of France, 1180–1223.* New York: Longman, 1998.

Braddick, Michael J. and John Walter. *Negotiating Power in Early Modern Society: Order, Hierarchy and Subordination in Britain and Ireland.* Cambridge: Cambridge University Press, 2001.

Braudel, Fernand. *Capitalism and Material Life, 1400–1800.* Trans. Miriam Kochan. New York: Harper and Row, 1973.

Briggs, Robin. *Witches and Neighbors: The Social and Cultural Context of European Witchcraft.* New York: Penguin, 1998.

Brooke, Christopher. *The Medieval Idea of Marriage.* Oxford: Oxford University Press, 1989.

Brown, Catherine, "*Muliebriter*: Doing Gender in the Letters of Heloise." In *Gender and Text in the Later Middle Ages.* Ed. Jane Chance. Gainesville: University Press of Florida, 1996. 25–51.

Brown, Elizabeth. "Eleanor of Aquitaine Reconsidered: The Woman and Her Seasons." In *Eleanor of Aquitaine: Lord and Lady.* Ed. Bonnie Wheeler and John C. Parsons. New York: Palgrave Macmillan, 2003. 1–54.

Brundage, James. "Concubinage and Marriage in Medieval Canon Law." In *Sexual Practices and the Medieval Church*. Ed. Vern L. Bullough and James Brundage. Buffalo: Prometheus Books, 1982. 118–28.

———. "The Merry Widow's Serious Sister: Remarriage in Classical Canon Law." In *Matrons and Marginal Women in Medieval Society*. Ed. Robert R. Edwards and Vickie Ziegler. Woodbridge, UK: Boydell, 1995. 33–48.

———. "Sexual Equality in Medieval Canon Law." In *Medieval Women and the Sources of Medieval History*. Ed. Joel T. Rosenthal. Athens: University of Georgia Press, 1990.

———. "Widows and Remarriage: Moral Conflicts and Their Resolution in Classical Canon Law." In *Wife and Widow in Medieval England*. Ed. Sue Sheridan Walker. Ann Arbor: University of Michigan Press, 1993. 17–31.

Burns, Robert I. *The Crusader Kingdom of Valencia: Reconstruction on a Thirteenth-Century Frontier*. 2 vols. Cambridge, MA: Harvard University Press, 1967.

Bynum, Caroline Walker. *Fragmentation and Redemption: Essays on Gender and the Human Body in Medieval Religion*. New York: Zone, 1992.

———. *Holy Feast, Holy Fast: The Religious Significance of Food to Medieval Women*. Berkeley and Los Angeles: University of California Press, 1987.

Cabrero, J. L. Bermejo. "Mayoría de Justicia del Rey y Jurisdicciones Señoriales en la Baja Edad Media Castellana." *Actas de las I Jornadas de Metodología Aplicada de las Ciencias Históricas. Vol. II: Historia Medieval*. Santiago de Compostela: Universidad de Santiago de Compostela, 1975. 207–15.

Caetano, Marcelo. *História do Direito Português (1140–1495*). Lisbon: Verbo, 1981.

Caetano de Sousa, D. António. *Provas da História Genealógica da Casa Real Portuguesa*. 2nd ed. 12 vols. Coimbra: Atlântida, 1947.

Campbell, Marian. "Paris, miroir ou lumière pour l'orfèvrerie anglaise vers 1300?" In *1300: L'art au temps de Philippe le Bel*. Ed. Danielle Gaborit-Chopin and François Avril. Paris: Ecole du Louvre, 2001. 203–18.

Carande, Ramón. "Sevilla, fortaleza y mercado: Algunas instituciones de la ciudad, en el siglo XIV especialmente, estudiadas en sus privilegios, ordenamientos y cuentas." In *Anuario de Historia del Derecho Español*. Vol. 2. Madrid: Centro de Estudios Históricos, 1925.

Carrére, Claude. *Barcelone: centre économique a lépoque des difficultés, 1380–1462*. 2 vols. Paris and The Hague: Mouton, 1967.

Carruthers, Mary. "The Wife of Bath and the Painting of Lions." *Proceedings of the Modern Language Association* 94:2 (1979): 209–22.

Casagrande, Carla. "The Protected Women." In *A History of Women in the West. Vol. 2: Silences of the Middle Ages*. Ed. Christiane Klapish-Zuber. Cambridge: Cambridge University Press, 1992. 70–104.

Caspi-Reisfeld, Keren. "Women Warriors during the Crusades, 1095–1254." In *Gendering the Crusades*. Ed. Susan B. Edgington and Sarah Lambert. New York: Columbia University Press, 2002. 94–107.

Caviness, Madeline H. "Anchoress, Abbess, and Queen: Donors and Patrons or Intercessors and Matrons?" In *The Cultural Patronage of Medieval Women*. Ed. June Hall McCash. Athens: University of Georgia Press, 1996.

Chance, Jane. "Classical Myth and Gender in the Letters of 'Abelard' and 'Heloise': Gloss, Glossed, Glossator." In *Listening to Heloise: The Voice of a Twelfth-Century Woman*. Ed. Bonnie Wheeler. New York: St. Martin's Press, 2000. 161–85.

Charles, Lindsey and Lorna Duffin, eds. *Women and Work in Pre-Industrial England*. London: Croom Helm, 1985.

Cheal, David. *The Gift Economy*. London and New York: Routledge, 1988.

Cheyette, Frederic. *Ermengard of Narbonne and the World of the Troubadours*. Ithaca, NY: Cornell University Press, 2001.

Chibnall, Marjorie. "The Empress Matilda and Bec-Hellouin." *Anglo-Norman Studies* 10 (1988): 35–48.

———. *The Empress Matilda: Queen Consort, Queen Mother, and Lady of the English*. Oxford: Oxford University Press, 1993.

Chown, John F. *A History of Money: From AD 800*. London: Routledge, 1994.

Christelow Moers, Stephanie. "The Division of Inheritance and Provision of Non-Inheriting Offspring among the Anglo-Norman Elite." *Medieval Prosopography* 17 (1996): 3–44.

Cipolla, Carlo. *Before the Industrial Revolution: European Society and Economy, 1000–1700*. Third edition. New York: Norton, 1994.

Clanchy, M. T. *Abelard: A Medieval Life*. Oxford: Blackwell, 1997.

———. *From Memory to Written Record: England 1066–1307*. Second edition. Oxford: Blackwell, 1993.

Clark, Alice. *The Working Life of Women in the Seventeenth-Century*. New York: Dutton, 1919.

Clay, Rotha Mary. *The Hermits and Anchorites of England*. London: Methuen, 1914.

Coelho, Maria Helena da Cruz. "Relações de domínio no Portugal concelhio de meados de Quatrocentos." *Revista Portuguesa de História* 35 (1990): 235–89.

Coulton, G. G. *Five Centuries of Religion*. 4 vols. Cambridge: Cambridge University Press, 1923–50.

Cowell, Andrew. *At Play in the Tavern, Signs, Coins, and Bodies in the Middle Ages*. Ann Arbor: University of Michigan Press, 1999.

Dahood, Roger. "*Ancrene Wisse*, the Katherine Group, and the Wohunge Group." In *Middle English Prose: A Critical Guide to Major Authors and Genres*. Ed. A. S. G. Edwards. New Brunswick, NJ: Rutgers University Press, 1984. 1–5.

Dalarun, Jacques. "The Clerical Gaze." In *A History of Women in the West. Vol. 2: Silences of the Middle Ages*. Ed. Christiane Klapish-Zuber. Cambridge: Cambridge University Press, 1992. 15–42.

Dale, Marian. "The London Silkwomen of the Fifteenth Century." *Economic History Review* 4:3 (October 1933): 324–35.

Davis, Natalie Zemon. *Fiction in the Archives: Pardon Tales and Their Tellers in Sixteenth-Century France*. Stanford, CA: Stanford University Press, 1987.

Davis, Natalie Zemon. "Women in the Crafts in Sixteenth-Century Lyon." In *Women and Work in Pre-industrial Europe*. Ed. Barbara Hanawalt. Bloomington: Indiana University Press, 1986. 167–97.

D'Avray, D. L. *Medieval Marriage: Symbolism and Society.* Oxford: Oxford University Press, 2005.

Day, John. *The Medieval Market Economy.* Oxford: Blackwell, 1987.

De Grazia, Victoria and Ellen Furlough. *The Sex of Things: Gender and Consumption in Historical Perspective.* Berkeley and Los Angeles: University of California Press, 1996.

Delaney, John J. *Dictionary of Saints.* New York: Doubleday, 1980.

Delany, Sheila. "Sexual Economics, Chaucer's Wife of Bath and *The Book of Margery Kempe.*" In *Feminist Readings in Middle English Literature: The Wife of Bath and All Her sect.* Ed. Ruth Evans and Lesley Johnson. London: Routledge, 1994. 71–87.

Dias, João José Alves, Isabel M. R. Mendes Drumond Braga, and Paulo Drumond Braga. "A Conjuntura." *Portugal do Renascimento à crise dinástica.* Ed. João José Alves Dias. Lisbon: Presença, 1998. 689–760.

*Diccionari Biogràfic.* 4 vols. Barcelona: Alberti, 1969.

Dronke, Peter. *Women Writers of the Middle Ages: A Critical Study of Texts from Perpetua (†203) to Marguerite Porete (†1310).* Cambridge: Cambridge University Press, 1984.

Duby, Georges. *The Chivalrous Society.* Trans. Cynthia Postan. Berkeley and Los Angeles: University of California Press, 1977.

———. *The Knight, the Lady and the Priest: The Making of Modern Marriage in Medieval France.* Trans. Barbara Bray. Chicago: University of Chicago Press, 1994.

———. *The Legend of Bouvines: War, Religion and Culture in the Middle Ages.* Berkeley and Los Angeles: University of California Press, 1990.

———. *Rural Economy and Country Life in the Medieval West.* Trans. Cynthia Postan. Columbia: University of South Carolina Press, 1968.

———. "Women and Power." In *Cultures of Power: Lordship, Status and Process in Twelfth-Century Europe.* Ed. Thomas Bisson. Philadelphia: University of Pennsylvania Press, 1995. 69–85.

Dyer, Christopher. *Standards of Living in the Later Middle Ages: Social Change in England, 1200–1320.* Cambridge: Cambridge University Press, 1989.

———. "Were There Any Capitalists in Fifteenth-Century England?" In *Enterprise and Individuals in Fifteenth-Century England.* Ed. Jenny Kermode. Stroud: Sutton, 1991. 1–24.

Earenfight, Theresa. "Absent Kings: Queens as Political Partners in the Medieval Crown of Aragon." In *Queenship and Political Power in Medieval and Early Modern Spain.* Ed. Theresa Earenfight. Aldershot, UK: Ashgate, 2005. 33–51.

———. "Partners in Politics." In *Queenship and Political Power in Medieval and Early Modern Spain.* Ed. Theresa Earenfight. Aldershot, UK: Ashgate, 2005. xiii–xxviii.

Edwards, Robert R. *The Flight from Desire: Augustine and Ovid to Chaucer.* New York: Palgrave Macmillan, 2006.

Elliott, Dyan. *Spiritual Marriage: Sexual Abstinence in Medieval Wedlock.* Princeton, NJ: Princeton University Press, 1993.

Entwistle, William J. and Peter E. Russel. "A Rainha D. Felipa e a sua corte." In *Memórias e Comunicações—Congresso do Mundo Português*. 19 vols. Lisbon: Comissão Executiva dos Centenários, 1940. II: 317–46.

Erickson, Amy Louise. *Women and Property in Early Modern England*. London and New York: Routledge, 1995.

Evergates, Theodore. *The Aristocracy in the County of Champagne, 1100–1300*. Philadelphia: University of Pennsylvania Press, 2007.

———, ed. *Aristocratic Women in Medieval France*. Philadelphia: University of Pennsylvania Press, 1999.

Facinger, Marian F. "A Study of Medieval Queenship: Capetian France, 987–1237." *Studies in Medieval and Renaissance History* 5 (1968): 3–47.

Fagniez, G. *Etudes sur l'industrie et la classe industrielle au XIIIe et au XIVe siècle*. Paris: 1877.

Farber, Lianna. *An Anatomy of Trade in Medieval Writing: Value, Consent, and Community*. Ithaca, NY: Cornell University Press, 2006.

Farina, Lara. *Erotic Discourse and Early English Religious Writing*. New York: Palgrave Macmillan, 2006.

Farmer, Sharon. "*Biffes, Tiretaines* and *Aumonières*: The Role of Paris in the International Textile Markets of the Thirteenth and Fourteenth Centuries." In *Medieval Clothing and Textiles*, vol. 2. Ed. Robin Netherton and Gale R. Owen-Crocker. Woodbridge, UK: Boydell, 2006. 75–89.

———. *Surviving Poverty in Medieval Paris: Gender, Ideology and the Daily Lives of the Poor*. Ithaca, NY: Cornell University Press, 2001.

Ferrante, Joan. *To the Glory of Her Sex: Women's Roles in the Composition of Medieval Texts*. Bloomington: Indiana University Press, 1997.

Ferrer i Mallol, María Teresa. "El patrimoni reial i la recuperació dels senyorius jurisdiccionals en les estats catalano-aragoneses a la fi del segle XIV." *Anuario de Estudios Medievales* 7 (1970–71): 351–491.

Ferro, João Pedro. *Alenquer Medieval (Séculos XII-XV). Subsídios para o seu estudo*. Cascais: Patrimonia, 1996.

Figanière, Frederico Francisco de la. *Memorias das Rainhas de Portugal (D. Theresa—Santa Isabel*. Lisbon: Typographia Universal, 1859.

Fitchen, John. *Building Construction before Mechanization*. Cambridge, MA: MIT Press, 1990.

Folda, Jaroslav. *The Art of the Crusaders in the Holy Land, 1098–1187*. Cambridge: Cambridge University Press, 1995.

Font i Rius, José María. "Las instituciones de la corona de Aragón en la primera mitad del siglo XV." *Ponencias del IV Congreso de la História de la Corona de Aragón*. Barcelona: Comisión Permanente de los Congresos de la Corona de Aragón, 1976. 209–23.

Forey, Alan. *The Military Orders from the Twelfth to the Early Fourteenth Centuries*. Toronto: University of Toronto Press, 1992.

Fossier, Robert. *Peasant Life in the Medieval West*. Trans. Juliet Vale. Oxford: Blackwell, 1988.

Foucault, Michel. *History of Sexuality*. 2 vols. New York: Pantheon, 1978.

Frakes, Jerold C. *Brides of Doom: Gender, Property, and Power in Medieval German Women's Epic*. Philadelphia: University of Pennsylvania Press, 1994.

Fredell, Joel. "Margery Kempe: Spectacle and Spiritual Governance." *Philological Quarterly* 75:2 (Spring 1996): 137–66.

Freedman, Paul. *Images of the Medieval Peasant*. Stanford, CA: Stanford University Press, 1999.

French, Katherine L. "Maidens' Lights and Wives' Stores: Women's Parish Guilds in Late Medieval England." *Sixteenth Century Journal: The Journal of Early Modern Studies* 29:2 (Summer 1998): 399–425.

Fuente, María Jesús. *Reinas medievales en los reinos hispánicos*. Madrid: La esfera de los libros, 2003.

Galloway, Andrew. *The Penn Commentary on Piers Plowman*. Vol. 1. Philadelphia: University of Pennsylvania Press, 2006.

Gastle, Brian. "Breaking the Stained Glass Ceiling: Mercantile Authority, Margaret Paston, and Margery Kempe." *Studies in the Literary Imagination* 36:1 (Spring 2003): 123–46.

———. "Chaucer's 'Shaply' Guildsmen and Mercantile Pretensions." *Neuphilologische Mitteilungen* 99:2 (1998): 211–6.

Gaudette, Helen A. "The Piety, Power, and Patronage of the Latin Kingdom of Jerusalem's Queen Melisende." Unpublished PhD Dissertation, Graduate Center, City University of New York, 2005.

Georgianna, Linda. "Any Corner of Heaven: Heloise's Critique of Monasticism." *Mediaeval Studies* 49 (1987): 221–53.

Géraud, Hercule. *Paris sous Philippe-le-Bel d'après des documents originaux et notamment d'après un manuscrit contenant 'Le Rôle de la Taille' imposée sur les habitants de Paris en 1292*. Repr. ed. Tübingen, Max Niemeyer Verlag, 1991.

Gerish, Deborah. "Ancestors and Predecessors: Royal Continuity and Identity in the First Kingdom of Jerusalem." *Anglo-Norman Studies* 20 (1997): 127–50.

Girona Llagostera, Daniel. *Itinerari del Rei en Joan I (1387–1396)*. Barcelona: Extret de la Revista d'Estudis Universitaris Catalans, 1931.

Godding, Philippe. "Le droit au service du patrimoine familial: les Pays-Bas Méridionaux (12e–18e siècles)." In *Marriage, Property and Succession*. Ed. Lloyd Banfield. Berlin: Duncker and Humboldt, 1992. 15–35.

Gomes, Rita. *The Making of a Court Society: Kings and Nobles in Late Medieval Portugal*. Cambridge: Cambridge University Press, 2003.

Green, Richard Firth. *A Crisis of Truth: Literature and Law in Ricardian England*. Philadelphia: University of Pennsylvania Press, 1999.

Greenhill, Eleanor. "Eleanor, Abbot Suger and Saint-Denis." In *Eleanor of Aquitaine: Patron and Politician*. Ed. William Kibler. Austin: University of Texas Press, 1976. 81–113.

Hafter, Daryl M., ed. *European Women and Preindustrial Craft*. Bloomington: Indiana University Press, 1995.

Hallam, Elizabeth M. and Judith Everard. *Capetian France, 987–1328*. 2nd ed. New York: Longman, 2001.

Hamilton, Bernard. "Women in the Crusader States: The Queens of Jerusalem (1100–1190)." In *Medieval Women*. Ed. Derek Baker. Oxford: Oxford University Press, 1978. 143–74.

Hanawalt, Barbara. "The Dilemma of the Widow of Property for Late Medieval London." In *The Medieval Marriage Scene: Prudence, Passion, Policy*. Ed. Sherry Roush and Cristelle L. Baskins. Tempe: Arizona Center for Medieval and Renaissance Studies, 2005. 165–80.

———. *Growing Up in Medieval London: The Experience of Childhood in History*. Oxford: Oxford University Press, 1993.

———. "Remarriage as an Option for Urban and Rural Widows in Late Medieval England." In *Wife and Widow in Medieval England*. Ed. Sue Sheridan Walker. Ann Arbor: University of Michigan Press, 1993. 141–64.

———, ed. *Women and Work in Preindustrial Europe*. Bloomington: Indiana University Press, 1986.

Harris, Barbara J. *English Aristocratic Women, 1450–1550: Marriage and Family, Property and Careers*. Oxford: Oxford University Press, 2002.

Harvey, David. *The Condition of Postmodernity*. Oxford: Blackwell, 1990.

Harvey, Paul D. A. *The Peasant Land Market in Medieval England*. Oxford: Clarendon Press, 1984.

Haskett, Timothy. "Country Lawyers? The Composers of English Chancery Bills." In *The Life of the Law, Proceedings of the Tenth British Legal History Conference*. Ed. P. Birks. London: 1993. 9–23.

———. "The Medieval English Court of Chancery." *Law and History Review* XIV:2 (Fall 1996): 245–313.

Hatcher, John and Mark Bailey. *Modeling the Middle Ages: The History and Theory of England's Economic Development*. Oxford: Oxford University Press, 2001.

Hawkes, Emma. "'[S]he will . . . protect and defend her rights boldly by law and reason . . .': Women's Knowledge of Common Law and Equity Courts in Late-Medieval England." In *Medieval Women and the Law*. Ed. Noël James Menuge. Woodbridge: Boydell and Brewer, 2000. 145–62.

Heller, Sarah-Grace. "Anxiety, Hierarchy, and Appearance in Thirteenth-Century Sumptuary Laws and the *Roman de la rose*." *French Historical Studies* 27:2 (2004): 311–48.

Helmholz, R. H. "The Early Enforcement of Uses." *Columbia Law Review* 79 (1979): 1503–13.

Hemptinne, Thérèse de. "Vlaanderen en Henegouwen onder de erfgenamen van de Boudewyns, 1070–1244." *Algemene geschiedenis der Nederlanden*. Haarlem: 1982.

Herlihy, David. *Opera Muliebra: Women and Work in Medieval Europe*. New York: McGraw-Hill, 1989; Philadelphia, PA: Temple University Press, 1990.

———. *Women, Family and Society in Medieval Europe: Historical Essays, 1978–1991*. Providence, RI: Berghahn Books, 1995.

Hernández-León de Sánchez, Francisca. *Doña María de Castilla, Esposa de Alfonso el Magnánimo*. Valencia: Universidad de Valencia, 1959.

Heyd, W. *Histoire du commerce du levant au moyan âge*. Translated into French by Furcy Raynaud. 2 vols. Leipzig: Otto Harrassowitz, 1923, 1936.

Higounet, Arlette. "La femme du Moyen Âge en France dans la vie politique, économique et sociale." In *Histoire mondiale de la femme*. Ed. by Pierre Grimal. Paris: Nouvelle librairie de France, 1974. Vol. 2, pp. 135–70.

———. *Les comptes de la taille et les sources de l'histoire démographique de Perigeux au XIVe siècle*. Paris: S.E.V.P.E.N., 1965.

Hillgarth, J. N. *The Spanish Kingdoms, 1250–1516*. 2 vols. Oxford: Clarendon Press, 1976–78.

Hillion, Yannick. "La Bretagne et le Rivalité Capétians-Plantagenets. Un Exemple: La duchesse Constance (1186–1202)." *Annales de Bretagne et du pays de l'Ouest* 92 (1985): 111–44.

Hilton, R. H. *English and French Towns in Feudal Society: A Comparative Study*. Cambridge: Cambridge University Press, 1992.

Hinton, David. "'Closing' and the Later Middle Ages." *Medieval Archaeology* 43 (1999): 172–82.

Hirsch, Eric and Michael O'Hanlon, eds. *The Anthropology of Landscape: Perspectives on Place and Space*. Oxford: Clarendon Press, 1995.

Hivergneaux, Marie. "Queen Eleanor and Aquitaine, 1137–1189." In *Eleanor of Aquitaine: Lord and Lady*. Ed. Bonnie Wheeler and John Carmi Parsons. New York: Palgrave Macmillan, 2003. 55–76.

Hoch, Martin. "The Crusaders' Strategy against Fatimid Ascalon and the 'Ascalon Project' of the Second Crusade." In *The Second Crusade and the Cistercians*. Ed. Michael Gervers. New York: St. Martin's Press, 1992.

Holt, J. C. "Feudal Society and the Family in Early Medieval England: The Heiress and the Alien." *Transactions of the Royal Historical Society* 35 (1985): 1–28.

Hörisch, Jochen. *Heads or Tails: The Poetics of Money*. Trans. Amy Horning Marschall. Detroit: Wayne State University Press, 2000.

Howell, Margaret. *Eleanor of Provence: Queenship in Thirteenth-Century England*. Oxford: Blackwell, 1998.

———. "The Resources of Eleanor of Provence as Queen Consort." *English Historical Review* 102 (1987): 372–93.

Howell, Martha C. "The Gender of Europe's Commercial Economy, 1200–1700." *Gender and History* 20:3 (November 2008): 519–38.

———. *The Marriage Exchange: Property, Social Place, and Gender in Cities of the Low Countries, 1300–1550*. Chicago: University of Chicago Press, 1998.

———. *Women, Production and Patriarchy in Late Medieval Cities*. Chicago: University of Chicago Press, 1986.

Hughes, Diane Owen. "From Brideprice to Dowry in Mediterranean Europe." In *The Marriage Bargain: Women and Dowries in European History*. Ed. Marion A. Kaplan. New York: Haworth Press, 1985. 13–58.

Hume, E. E. *Medical Work of the Knights Hospitallers of St. John of Jerusalem*. Baltimore: Johns Hopkins University Press, 1940.

Huneycutt, Lois L. "*Alianora regina anglorum*: Eleanor of Aquitaine and Her Anglo-Norman Predecessors as Queens of England." In *Eleanor of Aquitaine: Lord and Lady*. Ed. Bonnie Wheeler and John Carmi Parsons. New York: Palgrave Macmillan, 2003. 115–32.

———. "Female Succession and the Language of Power in the Writings of the Twelfth-Century Churchmen." In *Medieval Queenship*. Ed. John Carmi Parsons. New York: St. Martin's Press, 1993. 189–201.

———. "Intercession and the High-Medieval Queen: The Esther Topos." In *Power of the Weak*. Ed. Jennifer Carpenter and Sally-Beth MacLean. Urbana: University of Illinois Press, 1995. 126–46.

———. *Matilda of Scotland: A Study in Medieval Queenship*. Rochester, NY: Boydell, 2003.

Hutton, Diane. "Women in Fourteenth-Century Shrewsbury." In *Women and Work in Pre-Industrial England*. Ed. Lindsey Charles and Lorna Duffin. Dover, NH: Croom Helm, 1985. 83–99.

Hutton, Shennan. "'On herself and all her property': Women's Economic Activities in Late Medieval Ghent." *Continuity and Change* 20 (2005): 325–49.

Hyde, Lewis. *The Gift: Imagination and the Erotic Life of Property*. New York: Random House, 1979.

Irvine, Martin. "Heloise and the Gendering of the Literate Subject." In *Criticism and Dissent in the Middle Ages*. Ed. Rita Copeland. Cambridge: Cambridge University Press, 1996.

Ivars, Andrés. "La 'indiferencia' de Pedro IV de Aragón en el Gran Cisma de Occidente (1378–1382)." *Archivo Ibero Americano* 29 (1921): 21–97.

Johns, Susan M. *Noblewomen, Aristocracy and Power in the Twelfth-Century Anglo-Norman Realm*. Manchester: Manchester University Press, 2003.

Johnson, Penelope D. "Agnes of Burgundy: An Eleventh-Century Woman as Monastic Patron," *Journal of Medieval History* 15 (1989): 93–104.

———. *Prayer, Patronage, and Power: The Abbey of la Trinité, Vendôme, 1032–1187*. New York: New York University Press, 1981.

Jones, Jennifer. *Sexing La Mode: Gender, Fashion, and Commercial Culture in Old Regime France*. Oxford: Oxford University Press, 2004.

Jones, Nancy A. "By Woman's Tears Redeemed: Female Lament in St. Augustine's *Confessions* and the Correspondence of Abelard and Heloise." In *Sex and Gender in Medieval and Renaissance Texts: The Latin Tradition*. Ed. Barbara K. Gold, Paul Allen Miller, and Charles Platter. Albany: State University of New York Press, 1977. 15–40.

Jordan, Erin. "The 'Abduction' of Ida of Boulogne: Assessing Female Agency in Thirteenth-Century France." *French Historical Studies* 30 (2007): 1–20.

———. *Women, Power, and Religious Patronage in the Middle Ages*. New York: Palgrave Macmillan, 2006.

Jordan, William Chester. *From Servitude to Freedom: Manumission in the Sénonais in the Thirteenth Century*. Philadelphia: University of Pennsylvania Press, 1986.

———. *Women and Credit in Pre-Industrial and Developing Societies*. Philadelphia: University of Pennsylvania Press, 1993.

Kamuf, Peggy. *Fictions of Feminine Desire: Disclosures of Heloise*. Lincoln: University of Nebraska Press, 1982.

Kantorowicz, Ernst. *The King's Two Bodies: A Study in Medieval Political Theology*. Princeton, NJ: Princeton University Press, 1967.

Kaplan, Marion A. "Introduction." In *The Marriage Bargain: Women and Dowries in European History*. Ed. Marion A. Kaplan. New York: Haworth Press, 1985. 1–11.

Karras, Ruth Mazo. *Common Women: Prostitution and Sexuality in Medieval England*. Oxford: Oxford University Press, 1996.

———. *Sexuality in Medieval Europe: Doing Unto Others*. New York: Routledge, 2005.

Kay, Sarah. *The Chansons de Geste in the Age of Romance*. Oxford: Clarendon Press, 1995.

Kaye, Joel. *Economy and Nature in the Fourteenth Century: Money, Market Exchange, and the Emergence of Scientific Thought*. Cambridge: Cambridge University Press, 1998.

Kellogg, Judith. *Medieval Artistry and Exchange: Economic Institutions, Society, and Literary Form in Old French Narrative*. New York: Peter Lang, 1989.

Kibler, William W., ed. *Eleanor of Aquitaine: Patron and Politician*. Austin: University of Texas Press, 1976.

Klapisch-Zuber, Christiane. *Women, Family, and Ritual in Renaissance Italy*. Trans. Lydia G. Cochrane. Chicago: University of Chicago Press, 1987.

Komter, Aafke E. "Women, Gifts, and Power." In *The Gift: An Interdisciplinary Perspective*. Ed. Aafke E. Komter. Amsterdam: Amsterdam University Press, 1996.

Kostov, Spiro. *The Architect: Chapters in the History of the Profession*. New York: Oxford University Press, 1977.

Kowaleski, Maryanne and Judith Bennett. "Crafts, Gilds, and Women in the Middle Ages: Fifty Years after Marian K. Dale." *Signs: Journal of Women in Culture and Society* 14:2 (Winter 1989): 474–88.

Kuehn, Thomas. *Illegitimacy in Renaissance Florence*. Ann Arbor: University of Michigan Press, 2005.

Labarge, Margaret Wade. *Women in Medieval Life: A Small Sound of the Trumpet*. London: Hamilton, 1986.

Lachaud, Frédérique. "Textiles, Furs and Liveries: A Study of the Material Culture of the Court of Edward I (1272–1307). DPhil: Oxford, 1992.

Lahtinen, Anu. "Gender and Continuity: Women, Men and Landed Property in Medieval Finland." In *History and Change*. Ed. Anu Lahtinen and Kirsi Vainio-Korhonen. Helsinki: Finnish Literature Society, 2004.

———. "'So the respectable widow sold her land to him': Gender, Marriage and Property Transactions in Fourteenth and Fifteenth Century Finland." In *Family, Marriage, and Property Devolution in the Middle Ages*. Ed. Lars Ivar Hansen. Tromsø, Norway: Dept. of History, University of Tromsø, 2000.

Lalinde, Jesús. "Virreyes y lugartenientes medievales en la Corona de Aragón." *Cuadernos de Historia de España* 31–32 (1960): 98–172.

Lamb, H. H. *Climate, History and the Modern World*. Second edition. London: Routledge, 1995.

———. *Weather, Climate & Human Affairs*. London: Routledge, 1988.

Lambert, Sarah. "Queen or Consort: Rulership and Politics in the Latin East, 1118–1228." In *Queens and Queenship in Medieval Europe*. Ed. Anne Duggan. Suffolk: Boydell, 1997. 153–69.

La Monte, John L. *Feudal Monarchy in the Latin Kingdom of Jerusalem, 1100–1291.* Cambridge, MA: The Medieval Academy of America, 1932.

Lazard, Madeleine. "Jacquette de Montbron, une bâtisseuse humaniste." In *Royaume de Fémynie: Pouvoirs, contraintes, espaces de liberté de femmes, de la Renaissance à la Fronde.* Ed. Kathleen Wilson-Chevalier and Éliane Viennot. Paris: Champion, 1999. 17–26.

Lefebvre, Henri. *La production de l'espace.* Paris: Anthropos, 1974. Published in English as *The Production of Space.* Oxford: Blackwell, 1991.

LeGoff, Jacques. *Your Money or Your Life: Economy and Religion in the Middle Ages.* Trans. Patricia Ranum. New York: Zone, 1990.

Lehmann, Andrée. *Le Rôle de la femme dans l'histoire de France au Moyen-âge.* Paris: Berger-Levrault, 1952.

Lincy, Le Roux de. *Histoire de l'Hotel de Ville de Paris.* Paris: J. B. Dumoulin, 1846.

Linehan, Peter. "Frontier Kingship: Castile, 1250–1350." In *La Royaute sacrée dans le monde chrétien.* Ed. Alain Boureau and Claudio Sergio Ingerflom. Paris: École des Hautes Études en Sciences Sociales, 1992. 71–79.

Little, Lester K. *Religious Poverty and the Profit Economy in Medieval Europe.* Ithaca, NY: Cornell University Press, 1978.

Livingstone, Amy. "Diversity and Continuity: Family Structure and Inheritance in the Chartrain, 1000–1200." In *Mondes de l'Ouest et villes du monde. Regards sur les sociétés médiévales.* Ed. Catherine Laurent, Bernard Merdrignac, and Daniel Pichot. Rennes: Presses universitaires de Rennes, 1998. 415–29.

———. "Noblewomen's Control of Property in Early Twelfth-Century Blois-Chartres." *Medieval Prosopography* 18 (1995): 55–72.

Loats, Carol L. "Gender, Guilds, and Work Identity: Perspectives from Sixteenth-Century Paris." *French Historical Studies* 20:1 (Winter 1997): 15–30.

Loengard, Janet Senderowitz. "*Rationabilis Dos*: Magna Carta and the Widow's 'Fair Share' in the Earlier Thirteenth Century." In *Wife and Widow in Medieval England.* Ed. Sue Sheridan Walker. Ann Arbor: University of Michigan Press, 1993. 59–80.

Loisne, M. Le Comte de. "Itineraire de Robert II, Comte d'Artois." *Bulletin philologique et historique (jusqu'à 1715) du Comité des travaux historiques et scientiques* (1913): 362–83.

Lopez, Robert S. *The Commercial Revolution of the Middle Ages, 950–1350.* Cambridge, U.K.: Cambridge University Press, 1976 [1971].

———. *Medieval Trade in the Mediterranean World.* London: Oxford University Press, 1955.

LoPrete, Kimberly A. "Gendering Viragos: Medieval Perceptions of Powerful Women." In *Victims or Viragos?* Ed. Christine Meek and Catherine Lawless. Dublin: Four Courts Press, 2005. 17–38.

———. "The Gender of Lordly Women: The Case of Adela of Blois." In *Pawns or Players? Studies on Medieval and Early Modern Women.* Ed. Christine Meek and Catherine Lawless. Dublin: Four Courts Press, 2003. 90–110.

Lorcin, Marie-Thérèse. "Les Revenants dans les Fabliaux." *Reinardus* 2 (1989): 91–101.

Lundberg, Shelly and Robert A. Pollak. "Bargaining and Distribution in Marriage." *Journal of Economic Perspectives* 10:4 (1996): 139–58.

Lysons, Samuel. "Copy of a Roll of Purchases Made for the Tournament in Windsor Park, in the Sixth Year of Edward the First." *Archaeologia* 17 (1814): 297–310.

Macho y Ortega, Francisco. "Documentos relativos a la condición social y jurídica de los mudéjars Aragonese." *Revista de ciencias jurídicas y sociales* 5 (1922): 143–60, 444–64.

Marçal Lourenço, Maria Paula. "O Domínio Senhorial da Casa das Rainhas (1642–1781): Património, Estado e Poder." In *Amar, Sentir e Viver a História. Estudos de Homenagem a Joaquim Veríssimo Serrão.* 2 vols. Lisbon: Colibri, 1995. II: 985–1004.

Marques, A. H. de Oliveira. "A população portuguesa nos fins do século XIII." *Ensaios de História Medieval.* Second edition. Lisbon: Vega, 1980. 195–220.

———. *Portugal na crise dos séculos XIV e XV.* Lisbon: Presença, 1987.

Martin, Therese. "The Art of a Reigning Queen as Dynastic Propaganda in Twelfth-Century Spain." *Speculum* 80:4 (October 2005): 1134–71.

Martindale, Jane. "Eleanor of Aquitaine." In *Richard Coeur de Lion in History and Myth.* Ed. Janet L. Nelson. London: King's College London and the Centre for Late Antique and Medieval Studies, 1992. 17–50.

———. *Status, Authority and Power: Aquitaine and France, 9th to 12th Centuries.* Aldershot, UK: Ashgate, 1997.

Maria de Ros, Angeles. " El maestre racional en la Corona de Aragón. Una pragmatica de Juan II sobre dicho cargo." *Hispania* 10 (1950): 25–60.

Massey, Doreen. *Space, Place and Gender.* Cambridge: Polity Press, 1994.

Maurer, Helen. *Margaret of Anjou: Queenship and Power in Late Medieval England.* Woodbridge, UK: Boydell, 2005.

Mauss, Marcel. *The Gift: The Form and Reason for Exchange in Archaic Societies.* Trans. W. D. Halls. New York and London: Norton, 1990.

Mayer, Hans Eberhard. "Studies in the History of Queen Melisende of Jerusalem." *Dumbarton Oaks Papers* 26 (1972): 95–182.

McCash, June Hall, ed. *The Cultural Patronage of Medieval Women.* Athens: University of Georgia Press, 1996.

McCormick, Michael. *Origins of the European Economy: Communications and Commerce, A.D. 300–900.* Cambridge: Cambridge University Press, 2001.

McCracken, Peggy. "The Curse of Eve: Female Bodies and Christian Bodies in Heloise's Third Letter." In *Listening to Heloise: The Voice of a Twelfth-Century Woman.* Ed. Bonnie Wheeler. New York: St. Martin's Press, 2000. 217–30.

McFarlane, K. B. *The Nobility of Later Medieval England: The Ford Lectures for 1953 and Related Studies.* 1973; rpt., Oxford: Clarendon Press, 1997.

McIntosh, Marjorie. *Controlling Misbehavior in England: 1370–1600.* Cambridge: Cambridge University Press, 1998.

McKee, Sally. "Women under Venetian Colonial Rule in the Early Renaissance: Observations in Their Economic Activities." *Renaissance Quarterly* 51:1 (Spring 1998): 34–67.

McKitterick, R. "Women in the Ottonian Church: An Iconographic Perspective." In *Women in the Church: Studies in Church History*. Ed. W. J. Scheils and D. Wood. Oxford: Blackwell, 1990. 79–100.

McLaughlin, Megan. "The Woman Warrior: Gender, Warfare and Society in Medieval Europe," *Women's Studies* 17 (1990): 193–209.

McLeod, Glenda. "'Wholly Guilty, Wholly Innocent": Self-Definition in Héloïse's Letters to Abélard." In *Dear Sister; Mediveal Women and the Epistolary Genre*. Ed. Karen Cherewatuk and Ulrike Wiethaus. Philadelphia: University of Pennsylvania Press, 1993.

McMillin, Linda. "The House on Saint Pere Street: Four Generations of Women's Land Holding in Thirteenth-Century Barcelona." *Medieval Encounters* 12:1 (2006): 62–73.

McNamara, Jo Ann. "Women and Power through the Family Revisited." In *Gendering the Master Narrative*. Ed. Mary C. Erler and Maryanne Kowaleski. Ithaca, NY: Cornell University Press, 2003. 17–30.

McNamara, Jo Ann and Suzanne Wemple. "The Power of Women through the Family in Medieval Europe, 500–1100." In *Women and Power in the Middle Ages*. Ed. Mary Erler and Maryanne Kowaleski. Athens: University of Georgia Press, 1988. 83–102.

Mendonça, Manuela. *D. João II. Um percurso humano e político nas origens da modernidade*. Lisbon: Estampa, 1991.

Ménard, Philippe. *Les Fabliaux: Contes à rire du Moyen Age*. Paris: Presse Universitaires de France, 1983.

Menéndez Pidal, Ramón, et al., *Historia de España*. 42 vols. Madrid: Espasa-Calpe, 2005.

Merêa, Paulo. "Um problema filológico-jurídico: a palavra 'arras.'" *Novos Estudos de História do Direito*. Barcelos: Ed. do Minho, 1937. 139–49.

Metzger, Therese and Mendel. *Jewish Life in the Middle Ages: Illuminated Hebrew Manuscripts of the Thirteenth to the Sixteenth Centuries*. New York: Alpine Fine Arts Collection, 1982.

Millet, Bella, George Jack, and Yoko Wada. *Ancrene Wisse, the Katherine Group, and the Wooing Group*. Woodbridge, UK: Brewer, 1996.

Miskimin, Harry A. *Cash, Credit and Crisis in Europe, 1300–1600*. London: Variorum Reprints, 1989.

Mitchell, Linda. *Portraits of Medieval Women: Family, Marriage and Politics in England, 1225–1350*. New York: Palgrave Macmillan, 2003.

Mollat, Michel. *The Poor in the Middle Ages: An Essay in Social History*. New Haven, CT: Yale University Press, 1986.

Monteiro, J. P. Franco. *As Donatarias de Alenquer: História das Rainhas de Portugal e da sua casa e estado*. Lisbon: M. Gomes Editor, 1893.

Mulder-Bakker, Anneke. *Lives of the Anchoresses*. Trans. Myra Heerspink Scholz. Philadelphia: University of Pennsylvania Press, 2005.

Musson, Anthony. *Medieval Law in Context: The Growth of Legal Consciousness from Magna Carta to the Peasants' Revolt*. Manchester, Manchester University Press, 2001.

Nederman, Cary and Martin Morris. "Rhetoric, Violence, and Gender in Machiavelli." In *Feminist Interpretations of Niccolò Machiavelli*. Ed. Maria J. Falco. University Park: Pennsylvania State University Press, 2004. 267–86.

Nelson, Janet. "Medieval Queenship." In *Women in Medieval Western European Culture*. Ed. Linda E. Mitchell. New York: Garland, 1999. 179–207.

Neville, Cynthia. "Women, Charters, and Land Ownership in Scotland, 1150–1350." *Journal of Legal History* 26:1 (2005): 25–54.

Newman, Barbara. *From Virile Woman to Woman Christ: Studies in Medieval Religion and Literature*. Philadelphia: University of Pennsylvania Press, 1995.

Nicholas, David. *Medieval Flanders*. New York: Longman, 1986.

Nicholas, Karen. "Countesses as Rulers in Flanders." In *Aristocratic Women in Medieval France*. Ed. Theodore Evergates. Philadelphia: University of Pennsylvania Press, 1999. 111–37.

———. "Women as Rulers: Countesses Jeanne and Marguerite of Flanders (1212–78). In *Queens, Regents and Potentates*. Ed. Theresa M. Vann. Dallas: Academia Press, 1993. 73–89.

Nicholson, Helen. *The Knights Hospitallers*. New York: Boydell, 2001.

Nouvet, Claire. "The Discourse of the 'Whore': An Economy of Sacrifice." *Modern Language Notes* 105 (1990): 750–73.

Ogilvie, Sheilagh. *A Bitter Living: Women, Markets, and Social Capital in Early Modern Germany*. Oxford: Oxford University Press, 2003.

Otis, Leah Lydia. *Prostitution in Medieval Society: The History of an Urban Institution in Languedoc*. Chicago: University of Chicago Press, 1985.

Ousterhout, Robert. "Architecture as Relic and the Construction of Sanctity: The Stones of the Holy Sepulchre." *Journal of the Society of Architectural Historians* 62:1 (2003): 4–23.

Parisse, Michel, ed. *Veuves et veuvage dans le haut moyen age*. Paris: Picard, 1993.

Parsons, John C. *Eleanor of Castile: Queen and Society in Thirteenth-Century England*. New York: St. Martin's Press, 1995.

———. "Family, Sex, and Power: The Rhythms of Medieval Queenship." In *Medieval Queenship*. Ed. John C. Parsons. New York: St. Martin's Press, 1993. 1–12.

Peck, Linda Levy. *Consuming Splendor: Society and Culture in Seventeenth-Century England*. Cambridge: Cambridge University Press, 2005.

Pederson, Frederik. "'*Maritalis affectio*': Marital Affection and Property in Fourteenth-Century York Cause Papers." In *Women, Marriage, and Family in Medieval Christendom: Essays in Memory of Michael M. Sheehan, C. S. B.* Ed. Constance Rousseau and Joel Rosenthal. Kalamazoo, MI: Medieval Institute Publications, 1998. 175–209.

Pelner Cosman, Madeleine. *Women at Work in Medieval Europe*. New York: Facts on File, 2000.

Phelps-Brown, E. R. and Sheila Hopkins. "Seven Centuries of Building Wage." *Economica* 22 (1955): 195–206. Repr. in *A Perspective on Wages and Prices*. London: Methuen, 1981. 1–12.

Pimenta, Maria Cristina. *D. Pedro I*. Lisbon: Círculo de Leitores, 2003.

Pipponier, Françoise. *Costume et vie sociale: La cour d'Anjou xiv^e–xv^e siècle*. Paris: Mouton, 1970.

Pirenne, Henri. *Economic and Social History of Medieval Europe*. Trans. I. E. Clegg. New York: Harcourt Brace Jovanvich, 1956; first French edition 1933.

Pita, Isabel Beceiro. "Los dominios de la familia real castellana (1250–1350)." In *Génesis medieval del Estado Moderno: Castilla y Navarra (1250–1370)*. Valladolid: Ambito Editores, 1987. 79–106.

Postan, M. M., ed. *The Cambridge Economic History of Europe*. Second edition. Cambridge: Cambridge University Press, 1966.

Pounds, Norman John Greville. *An Economic History of Medieval Europe*. Second edition. London: Longman, 1994.

Power, Eileen. *Medieval English Nunneries*. London: Cambridge University Press, 1922.

Pronay, Nicholas. "The Chancellor, the Chancery and the Council at the End of the Fifteenth Century." In *British Government and Administration: Studies Presented to H. B. Chrimes*. Ed. H. Hearder and H. R. Loyn. Cardiff: University of Wales Press, 1974. 87–103.

Raftis, J. Ambrose. *Peasant Economic Development within the English Manorial System*. Stroud: Sutton, 1996.

Reilly, Bernard F. *The Kingdom of León-Castilla under Queen Urraca, 1109–1126*. Princeton, NJ: Princeton University Press, 1982.

Reyerson, Kathryn L. *The Art of the Deal: Intermediaries of Trade in Medieval Montpellier*. Leiden: Brill, 2002.

———. *Business, Banking and Finance in Medieval Montpellier*. Toronto: The Pontifical Institute of Mediaeval Studies. 1985.

———. "Women in Business in Medieval Montpellier." In *Women and Work in Preindustrial Europe*. Ed. Barbara A. Hanawalt. Bloomington: Indiana University Press, 1986. 117–44.

Reynolds, Philip Lyndon. *Marriage in the Western Church: The Christianization of Marriage during the Patristic and Early Medieval Periods*. Leiden: E. J. Brill, 1994.

Richard, Jean. *Saint Louis: Crusader King of France*. Trans. Jean Birrell. Cambridge: Cambridge University Press, 1992.

Riera Sans, Jaume. "La coronació de la reina Elionor (1352)." *Acta Mediaevalia* 26 (2005): 485–92.

Rigby, S. H. *English Society in the Later Middle Ages*. London: Macmillan Press, 1995.

Riley-Smith, Jonathan. *The Knights of St. John in Jerusalem and Cyprus, c. 1050–1310*. London: MacMillan, 1967.

Robertson, Elizabeth. "'This Living Hand': Thirteenth-Century Female Literacy, Materialist Immanence, and the Reader of the *Ancrene Wisse*." *Speculum* 78:1 (2003): 1–36.

Roca, Josep Maria. "Johan I d'Aragó." *Memorias de la Real Academia de Buenas Letras de Barcelona*. 11 vols. Barcelona: Institució Patxot, 1929.

———. "La Reyna empordanesa." *Memorias de la Real Academia de Buenas Letras de Barcelona* 10 (1928): 9–212.

Rodgers, Edith. *Discussion of Holidays in the Later Middle Ages*. New York: Columbia University Press, 1940.

Rodrigues, Ana Maria Seabra de Almeida. "For the honor of her lineage and body: The dowers and dowries of some late medieval queens of Portugal." *e-Journal of Portuguese History* 5:1 (2007) 3: 1–13.

———. *Espaço, gente e sociedade no Oeste. Estudos sobre Torres Vedras medieval.* Cascais: Patrimonia, 1996.

———. "Poderes concorrentes e seus agentes na Torres Vedras quatrocentista." In *Amar, Sentir e Viver a História. Estudos de Homenagem a Joaquim Veríssimo Serrão*. 2 vols. Lisbon: Colibri, 1995. 1: 49–73.

———. "A sociedade urbana torriense e os privilegiados da coroa." In *Espaço, gente e sociedade no Oeste. Estudos sobre Torres Vedras medieval.* Cascais: Patrimonia, 1996. 291–316.

———. *Torres Vedras. A vila e o termo nos finais da Idade Média* (Lisbon: FCG/ JNICT, 1995.

Rollo-Koster, Joëlle. "From Prostitutes to Brides of Christ: The Avignonese Repenties in the Late Middle Ages," *Journal of Medieval and Early Modern Studies* 32:1 (2002):109–44.

Roover, Raymond de. "The Scholastic Attitude toward Trade and Enterpeneurship." Rpt. in *Business, Banking, and Economic Thought (Selected Studies of Raymond de Roover)*. Ed. Julius Kirshner. Chicago: University of Chicago Press, 1974. 336–45.

Rose, G. and M. Ogborn. "Feminism and Historical Geography." *Journal of Historical Geography* 14 (1988): 405–9.

Rosen-Ayalon, Myriam. "Three Perspectives on Jerusalem: Jewish, Christian, and Muslim Pilgrims in the Twelfth Century." In *Jerusalem: Its Sanctity and Centrality to Judaism, Christianity, and Islam*. Ed. Lee I. Levine. New York: Continuum, 1999. 326–46.

Rösener, Werner. *The Peasantry of Europe*. Trans. Thomas M. Barker. Oxford: Blackwell, 1994.

Rosenthal, Joel T. "Fifteenth-Century Widows and Widowhood." In *Wife and Widow in Medieval England*. Ed. Sue Sheridan Walker. Ann Arbor: University of Michigan Press, 1993. 33–58.

Ryder, Alan. *Alfonso the Magnanimous: King of Aragon, Naples, and Sicily, 1396–1458*. Oxford: Clarendon Press, 1990.

———. "Cloth and Credit: Aragonese War Finance in the Mid-Fifteenth Century." *War and Society* 2:1 (May 1984): 1–21.

———. "The Evolution of Imperial Government in Naples under Alfonso V of Aragon." In *Europe in the Late Middle Ages*. Ed. John Rigby Hale, John Roger Loxdale Highfield, and Beryl Smalley. Evanston: Northwestern University Press, 1965. 332–57.

———. *The Kingdom of Naples under Alfonso the Magnanimous*. Oxford: Clarendon Press, 1976.

Sack, Robert D. *Conceptions of Space in Social Thought*. London: Macmillan, 1980.

Sahlins, Marshall. *Stone Age Economics*. Chicago: Aldine-Atherton, 1972.

Saller, Sylvester John. *Excavations at Bethany (1949–1953).* Publications of the Studium Biblicum Franciscanum 12. Jerusalem: 1957.

Sanpere Miquel, Salvador. *Las damas d'Aragó.* Barcelona: Impresa de la Renaixensa, 1879.

Santinelli, Emmanuelle. *Des femmes éplorées? Les veuves dans la société aristocratique du haut Moyen Age.* Villeneuve d'Ascq: Presses Universitaires de Septentrion, 2003.

Sarasa Sánchez, Esteban. "Mitos y ritos feudales en Aragón. El caso de doña Brianda de Luna," *I Congreso de Aragón de Etnología y Antropología.* Zaragoza: Consejo Superior de Investigaciones Científicas, 1979. 127–32.

———. *Sociedad y conflictos sociales en Aragón, siglos XIII–X: Estructuras de poder y conflictos de clase.* Madrid: Siglo XXI, 1981.

Sargentson, Carolyn. *Merchants and Luxury Markets: The Marchands Merciers of Eighteenth-Century Paris.* London: Victoria and Albert Museum, 1996.

Savage, Anne and Nicholas Watson, eds. *Anchoritic Spirituality: Ancrene Wisse and Associated Works.* New York: Paulist Press, 1991.

Sawyer, Birgit. "Women as Bridge-Builders: The Role of Women in Viking-Age Scandinavia." In *People and Places in Northern Europe, 500–1600: Essays in Honour of Peter Hayes Sawyer.* Ed. Ian Wood and Niels Lund. Woodbridge, UK: Boydell, 1991. 211–24.

Schein, Sylvia. *Gateway to the Heavenly City: Crusader Jerusalem and the Catholic West (1099–1187).* Aldershot, UK: Ashgate, 2005.

Schofield, P. R. and N. J. Mayhew, eds. *Credit and Debt in Medieval England, c.1180–1350.* Oxford: Oxbow, 2002.

Schulenberg, Jane Tibbetts. "The Heroics of Virginity: Brides of Christ and Sacrificial Mutilation." In *Women in the Middle Ages and the Renaissance.* Ed. Mary Beth Rose. Syracuse, NY: Syracuse University Press, 1986. 29–72.

Semmler, Josef. "Die Residenzen der Fürsten und Prälaten im mittelalterlichen Paris (12.-14. Jahrhundert)." *Mélanges offerts à René Crozet,* ed. Pierre Gallais and Yves-Jean Riou. 2 vols. Poitiers: Société d'études médiévales, 1966. 2:1217–36.

Seidel, Linda. *Legends in Limestone: Lazarus, Gislebertus, and the Cathedral of Autun.* Chicago: University of Chicago Press, 1999.

Shadis, Miriam. "Piety, Politics and Power: The Patronage of Leonor of England and Her Daughters Berneguela of Léon and Blanche of Castile." In *The Cultural Patronage of Medieval Women.* Ed. June Hall McCash. Athens: University of Georgia Press, 1996. 202–27.

Shaw, David Gary. *Necessary Conjunctions: The Social Self in Medieval England.* New York: Palgrave Macmillan, 2005.

Shell, Marc. *Money, Language, and Thought.* Baltimore: Johns Hopkins University Press, 1993.

Silleras-Fernandez, Nuria. *Power, Piety and Patronage in Late Medieval Queenship: Maria de Luna.* New York: Palgrave McMillan, 2008.

———. "Queenship en la Corona de Aragón en la Baja Edad Media: estudio y, propuesta terminólogica," *La Corónica: A Journal of Medieval Spanish Language and Literature* 32:1 (2003): 120–25.

Silleras-Fernandez, Nuria. "Spirit and Force: Politics, Public and Private in the Reign of Maria de Luna (1369–1406)." In *Queenship and Political Power in Medieval and Early Modern Spain.* Ed. Theresa Earenfight. Aldershot, UK: Ashgate, 2005. 78–80.

———. Widowhood and Deception: Ambiguities of Queenship in Late Medieval Crown of Aragon." In *Shell Games: Studies in Scams, Frauds, and Deceits* (1300–1650). Ed. M. Crane, R. Raiswell, and M. Reeves. Toronto: Centre for Reformation and Renaissance Studies, 2004.

Silva, Manuela Santos. "Alguns passos da acção do Conquistador na Estremadura litoral: o caso específico da região envolvente de Óbidos." In *2º Congresso Histórico de Guimarães "D. Afonso Henriques e a sua Época."* 6 vols. Guimarães: Câmara Municipal de Guimarães, Universidade do Minho, 1997. 2: 109–16.

———. *Estruturas Urbanas e Administração concelhia. Óbidos Medieval.* Cascais: Patrimonia, 1997.

———. "Notícia sobre a segunda doação régia de Alenquer, Óbidos e Sintra à Rainha D. Leonor de Lencastre (Évora, 15 de Abril de 1491)." In *A Região de Óbidos na Época Medieval. Estudos.* Caldas da Rainha: Património Histórico, 1994. 111–20.

———. "Óbidos *Terra que foi da Rainha D. Filipa.* O Senhorio de Óbidos de 1415 a 1428." In *A Região de Óbidos na Época Medieval. Estudos.* Caldas da Rainha: Património Histórico, 1994. 85–110.

Sinués Ruiz, Atanasio and Antonio Ubieto Arteta, eds. *El Patrimonio Real en Aragón durante la edad media.* Zaragoza: Anubar, 1986.

Sivery, Gerard. *Structures agraires et vie rurale dans le hainaut à la fin du Moyen Age.* Lille: 1977.

Sledd, James. "Dorigen's Complaint." *Modern Philology* 45:1 (1947): 36–45.

Smith, D. Vance. *Arts of Possession: The Medieval Household Imaginary.* Minneapolis: University of Minnesota Press, 2003.

Sobrequés i Vidal, Santiago. *Els barons de Catalunya.* Barcelona: Editorial Teide, 1957.

———. "Política remensa de Alfonso el Magnánimo en los últimos años de su reinado (1447–1458)." *Anales del instituo de estudios gerundenses* (1960): 117–54.

Sobrequés i Vidal, Santiago and Jaume Sobrequés i Callicó. *La guerra civil catalana del segle XV.* 2 vols. Barcelona: Edicions 62, 1973.

Soja, Edward W. *Thirdspace: Journey to Los Angeles and Other Real-and-imagined Places.* Oxford: Blackwell, 1996.

Soldevila, Ferran. *Història de Catalunya.* 3 vols. Barcelona: Editorial Alpha, 1934.

Sommerville, Margaret R. *Sex and Subjection: Attitudes to Women in Early Modern Society.* New York: E. Arnold, 1995.

Sousa, Ivo Carneiro de. *A Rainha D. Leonor (1458–1525). Poder, misericórdia, religiosidade e espiritualidade no Portugal do Renascimento.* Lisbon: FCG/FCT, 2002.

Southern, R. W. *The Making of the Middle Ages.* New Haven, CT: Yale University Press, 1953.

Spiegel, Gabrielle. *Romancing the Past: The Rise of Vernacular Prose Historiography in Thirteenth-Century France.* Berkeley and Los Angeles: University of California Press, 1993.

Spufford, Peter. *Money and Its Use in Medieval Europe.* Cambridge: Cambridge University Press, 1988.

———. *Power and Profit: The Merchant in Medieval Europe.* New York: Thames and Hudson, 2003.

Stafford, Pauline. *Queens, Concubines and Dowagers: The King's Wife in the Early Middle Ages.* London: Leicester University Press, 1998.

Stock, Brian. *The Implications of Literacy: Written Language and Models of Interpretation in the Eleventh and Twelfth Centuries.* Princeton, NJ: Princeton University Press, 1983.

Stone, Gregory B. "The Insistence of the Body in the Old French Fabliau Estormi." *Exemplaria* (1990): 449–73.

Stretton, Tim. *Women Waging Law in Elizabethan England.* Cambridge: Cambridge University Press, 1998.

Stuard, Susan Mosher. "Marriage Gifts and Fashion Mischief." In *The Medieval Marriage Scene: Prudence, Passion, Policy.* Ed. Sherry Roush and Cristelle L. Baskins. Tempe: Arizona Center for Medieval and Renaissance Studies, 2005. 169–85.

Swanson, Heather. *Medieval Artisans: An Urban Class in Late Medieval England.* Oxford: Blackwell, 1989.

Tasis, Rafael. *Joan I, el rei caçador i músic.* Barcelona: 1959.

Tavares, Maria José Pimenta Ferro. *Os Judeus em Portugal no século XV.* 2 vols. Lisbon: Universidade Nova–FCSH, 1982.

Thrupp, Sylvia I. *The Merchant Class of Medieval London 1300–1500.* Ann Arbor: University of Michigan Press, 1989.

Tibble, Steven. *Monarchy and Lordship in the Latin Kingdom of Jerusalem, 1099–1291.* New York: Oxford University Press, 1989.

Todd, Barbara J. "The Remarrying Widow: A Stereotype Reconsidered." In *Women in English Society 1500–1800.* Ed. Mary Prior. London: Methuen, 1985. 54–92.

Tolhurst, Fiona. "The Great Divide?: History and Literary History as Partners in Medieval Mythography." *Historical Reflections/Réflexions historique* 30 (2004): 7–27.

Tolkien, J. R. R. "*Ancrene Wisse* and *Hali Meiðhad.*" *Essays and Studies* 14 (1929): 104–26.

Torres, Ruy d'Abreu. "Rainhas, Casa das." In *Dicionário de História de Portugal.* Ed. Joel Serrão. 6 vols. Oporto: Livraria Figueirinhas, 1981. 5: 230–32.

Treppo, Mario del. *Els mercaders catalans i l'expansió de la corona catalano-aragonesa al segle XV.* Trans. Jaume Riera i Sans. Barcelona: Curial, 1976. (Originally published as *I mercanti catalani e l'expansione della Corona d'Aragona nel secolo XV.* Naples: L'Arte Tipografica Napoli, 1972).

Tucker, Penny. "The Early History of the Court of Chancery: A Comparative Study." *The English Historical Review* 115:463 (Sept. 2000): 791–811.

Uitz, Erica. *The Legend of Good Women: Medieval Women in Towns and Cities.* Mt. Kisco, NY: Moyer Bell, 1990.

Unwin, Tim. "A Waste of Space? Towards a Critique of the Social Production of Space. . . ." *Transactions of the Institute of British Geographers.* New Series 25:1 (2000): 11–29.

Vale, Malcolm. *The Princely Court: Medieval Courts and Culture in North-West Europe.* Oxford: Oxford University Press, 2001.

Valone, Carolyn. "Architecture as a Public Voice for Women in Sixteenth-Century Rome." *Renaissance Studies* 15:3 (2001): 301–27.

———. "Roman Matrons: Various Views of the Cloister Wall." In *The Crannied Wall: Women, Religion, and the Arts in Early Modern Europe.* Ed. Mondon Craig. Ann Arbor: University of Michigan Press 1992. 49–72.

Verdon, Jean. "La vie quotidienne de la femme en France au bas moyen âge." In *Frau im spatmittelalterlichen Alltag.* Vienna: Veroffentlichungen des Instituts fur Mittelalterliche realienkunde Osterreichs, 1986.

Viana, Mário. *Os vinhedos medievais de Santarém.* Cascais: Patrimonia, 1998.

Vicens Vives, Jaume. *Els Trastàmares.* Barcelona: Editorial Teide, 1956.

Vicente, António Balcão, Carlos Guardado da Silva, Pedro Gomes Barbosa, and Pedro Marujo do Canto. *O Foral Medieval da Vila de Torres Vedras 15 de Agosto de 1250.* Torres Vedras: Câmara Municipal de Torres Vedras-Cultura, 2001.

Walpole, Ronald N. *Philip Mouskés and the Pseudo-Turpin Chronicle.* Berkeley and Los Angeles: University of California Press, 1947.

Ward, Jennifer. *Women in Medieval Europe, 1200–1500.* New York: Longman, 2003.

Warren, Ann. *Anchorites and Their Patrons in Medieval England.* Berkeley and Los Angeles: University of California Press, 1985.

Waugh, Scott L. *The Lordship of England: Royal Wardships and Marriages in English Society and Politics. 1217–1237.* Princeton, NJ: Princeton University Press, 1988.

Webb, Diana. "Queen and Patron." In *Queens and Queenship in Medieval Europe.* Ed. Anne J. Duggan. Suffolk: Boydell, 1997. 205–22.

Whittle, Jane. "Individualism and the Family Land Bond: A Reassessment of Land Transfer Patterns among the English Peasantry, c.1270–1580." *Past and Present* 160 (1998): 25–63.

———. "Inheritance, Marriage, Widowhood and Remarriage: A Comparative Perspective on Landholding in North-east Norfolk, 1440–1580." *Continuity and Change* 13:1 (1998): 33–72.

Wiesner, Merry. *Women and Gender in Early Modern Europe.* Cambridge: Cambridge University Press, 2000.

———. *Working Women in Renaissance Germany.* New Brunswick, NJ: Rutgers University Press, 1986.

Wijngaarden, Hilde van. "The Role of Women in the Survival of Poor Families in the Seventeenth Century." In *Women in Towns: The Social Position of Urban Women in a Historical Context.* Ed. Marjatta Hietala and Lars Nilsson. Stockholm: Stads- och kommunhistoriska institutet, 1999.

Wilson, Katharine and Glenda McLeod. "Textual Strategies I the Abelard/Heloise Correspondence." In *Listening to Heloise: The Voice of a Twelfth-Century Woman*. Ed. Bonnie Wheeler. New York: St. Martin's Press, 2000. 121–42.

Wolff, Phillipe. *Commerce et marchands de Toulouse (vers 1350–vers 1450).* Paris: Librairie Plon, 1954.

Wolff, R. L. "Baldwin of Flanders and Hainaut, First Latin Emperor of Constantinople: His Life, Death and Resurrection, 1171–1225." *Speculum* 27 (1952): 281–322.

Wood, Charles T. *The French Apanages and the Capetian Monarchy, 1124–1328.* Cambridge, MA: Harvard University Press, 1966.

Wood, Diana. *Medieval Economic Thought.* Cambridge: Cambridge University Press, 2002.

Wood, M. *The English Medieval House.* London: Phoenix House, 1965.

Woodward, Donald. *Men at Work: Labourers and Building Craftsmen in the Towns of Northern England, 1450–1750.* Cambridge: Cambridge University Press, 1995.

*World Tables: Third Edition.* Baltimore, MD: Johns Hopkins University Press, 1983.

Wrigley, T. M., M. J. Ingram, and G. Farmer, eds. *Climate and History: Studies in Past Climates and Their Impact on Man.* Cambridge: Cambridge University Press, 1981.

Yunck, John A. *The Lineage of Lady Meed.* South Bend, IN: University of Notre Dame Press, 1963.

Zalegui, J. Zabalo. *El Registro de Comptos del Reino de Navarra de 1280.* Pamplona: Diputación Foral de Navarra, 1972.

Ziolkowski, Jan M. *Letters of Peter Abelard, Beyond the Personal.* Washington, DC: The Catholic University of America Press, 2006.

# CONTRIBUTORS

**M. C. Bodden**, associate professor of English at Marquette University, works on medieval literature, with a leaning toward Early Modern English literature. "Evidence for Knowledge of Greek in Anglo-Saxon England," (1988), and "Anglo-Saxon Self-Consciousness in Language" (1987). She is the author of *The Old English Finding of the True Cross* (1987), and she has two books forthcoming, *Speaking as a Woman: Language as the Site of Revolt*, a discussion of gendered practices and identity, and *Religious Language: Privileging Violence towards Women.*

**Anna Dronzek** is the author of "Gender Roles and the Marriage Market in Fifteenth-Century England: Ideals and Practices," in Davis, Müller, and Jones (editors), *Love, Marriage and Family Ties in the Middle Ages* (2003); "Gendered Theories of Education in Fifteenth-Century Conduct Books," in Ashley and Clark (editors), *Medieval Conduct* (2001); and "What We Talk About When We Talk About Feminism," *Medieval Feminist Newsletter* (2000). She has taught medieval history at the University of Minnesota, Morris, Rhodes College, and the University of Denver, and is currently attending law school at the University of Colorado, Boulder.

**Theresa Earenfight** is associate professor of History and chair of the Medieval Studies Program at Seattle University. Her edited collection, *Queenship and Political Power in Medieval and Early Modern Spain* (2005), included her essay, "Absent Kings: Queens as Political Partners in the Crown of Aragon." She is the author of "Political Culture and Political Discourse in the Letters of Queen María of Castile," (2003); "Doing without the Persona of the Prince? Kings, Queens, and the Idea of Monarchy in Medieval Europe" (2007); and *The King's Other Body: María of Castile and the Crown of Aragon* (2009).

**Lara Farina**, associate professor of English at West Virginia University, focuses her research on medieval women's devotional literature and on medieval readers in their communities. She is the author of *Reading for*

*Pleasure: Erotic Discourse and Early English Religious Writing* (2006) and "Before Affection: Christ I and the Social Erotic" (2001).

**Sharon Farmer** is professor of History at the University of California, Santa Barbara. She is the author of *Surviving Poverty in Medieval Paris: Gender Ideology and the Daily Lives of the Poor* and *Communities of Saint Martin: Legend and Ritual in Medieval Tours*. She is currently working on a collection of essays on women and work in medieval Paris, as well as a monograph on the impact of the cultures of the Mediterranean on northern French material cultural in the late thirteenth and early fourteenth centuries.

**Helen A. Gaudette** is director of the College Preparatory Programs and an Adjunct Professor of History at Queens College, City University of New York. Her research focuses on the power, piety, and patronage of Queen Melisende in the Latin Kingdom of Jerusalem.

**Erin L. Jordan** is assistant professor in the Department of History at the University of Northern Colorado. She has written several articles on the social and economic aspects of monasticism in the southern Low Countries in the thirteenth century. Her book *Women, Power and Religious Patronage* (2006) investigates questions pertaining to inheritance, female rulers, and the feudal system in late twelfth- and early thirteenth-century France.

**Sally Livingston** is lecturer on History and Literature at Harvard University. A comparative medievalist, her research focuses on the relationship between women's ability to own property and marriage narratives. She is the co-author of "Outrunning Atalanta: Feminine Destiny in Alchemical Transmutation" (1980) and is currently at work on a literary history of medieval ideas of money.

**Daniel M. Murtaugh** is associate professor of English at Florida Atlantic University. He is the author of *Piers Plowman and the Image of God* (1978) and has published widely on Chaucer, Henryson, Spenser, Chretien de Troyes, and Dante.

**Ana Maria S. A. Rodrigues** is associate professor (*Profesora Associada*) in the Faculty of Letters at the University of Lisbon. The author of *Torres Vedres: A vila e o termo nos finais de Idade Média* (1995) and *Os Capitulares Bracarenses (1245–1374): Notícias biográficas* (2005), her research interests include rural and urban history, religious history, and gender history, with particular focus on the queen's household.

**Shelley E. Roff** is associate professor in the College of Architecture at the University of Texas at San Antonio. As an architectural historian, her research centers on the civic architecture and economy of the medieval city, especially the structures of maritime trade. She is at work on a monograph investigating the design, funding, and construction of the Llotja de Mar of medieval Barcelona, the commercial exchange building in the port of this city.

**Núria Silleras-Fernández** is assistant professor at the Department of Spanish and Portuguese of the University of Colorado at Boulder. She has published a monograph, *Power, Piety, and Patronage in Late Medieval Queenship: Maria de Luna* (2008) and numerous articles in English, Spanish, and Catalan. She is a historian and literary scholar whose research focuses on gender, politics, and religion in the Iberian Peninsula, Europe, and the Western Mediterranean in the Late Middle Ages and Early Modern periods.

**Manuela Santos Silva**, associate professor (*Profesora Auxiliar*) in the Faculty of Letters at the University of Lisbon, has published extensively on medieval Portugal, including *Óbidos Medieval: Estruturas Urbanas e Adminsitração Concelhia* (Cascais, 1997) and *A região de Óbidos na época medieval* (1994). Her research interests focus on regional and local history, with special focus on queens and the royal patrimony.

# INDEX

**Note**: Page numbers in **bold** denote illustrations or tables.